FLESH A⌐

The Lives, Death⌐
Of British M

TREVOR HAYWOOD

Published By
El Corvo Publishing
34 Lea Street, Kidderminster,
Worcs, DY10 1SW

ISBN 978-0-9555592-0-4

Printed and bound by
Biddles, 24 Rollesby Road, King's Lynn,
Norfolk, PE30 4LS

For my darling wife Susan

Also by Trevor Haywood

The Withering of Public Access
Walking With a Camera in Herries Lakeland
Changing Faculty Environments
Info Rich Info Poor: Access and Exchange in the Global Information Society
Only Connect: Shaping Networks and Knowledge for the New Millennium
Praise the Net and Pass the Modem: Revolutionaries and Captives in the Information
Society

Sales Information
Flesh and Bone is available from www.deathofkings.co.uk
Also from El Corvo Publishing, 34 Lea St, Kidderminster,
Worcs, DY10 1SW.
Contact haywood@clix.pt or tracy.haywood@tiscali.co.uk
Price £9.99 (€15)plus £1.50 P&P GB, £2.50 (€3.70) Continental Europe, £4 (€6.00)
outside Europe.

Acknowledgements

Many people have helped me along the way in producing this book but
two people in particular have made a sterling contribution.
They are my very good friends **Ingrid Ryder** and **Perce Muscutt**
who took on the unenviable task of acting as my editors.
They fixed my spelling, my punctuation and my grammar
and made many suggestions that proved invaluable in helping
me to sort out my ideas. I owe them a huge debt of thanks.
My thanks also to my wife, **Susan Haywood,** for
her fastidious work on the printer's proofs, truly a labour of love.
Needless to say any errors that remain are mine and mine alone.

Picture Acknowledgements

The cover picture of Edward II's effigy in Gloucester Cathedral
and the inside picture of Edward II's effigy is published
by kind permission of the **Dean and Chapter of Gloucester**
The picture of Henry IV's effigy in Canterbury Cathedral is published
by kind permission of the **Dean and Chapter of Canterbury**
The pictures of the effigies of Henry VII, Elizabeth I and Henry III are
published by kind permission of the **Dean and Chapter of Westminster**

Cover design by Andy Wright at
www.i4media.co.uk

CONTENTS LIST

Thee glories of our blood and state,
Are shadows, not substantial things,
There is no armour against fate,
Death lays his icy hands on Kings,
Sceptre and Crown,
Must tumble down,
And in the dust be equal made,
With poor crooked sithe and spade.

James Shirley 1596-1666

INTRODUCTION

'Death comes for us all, even for Kings he comes'.

Thomas More in A Man for All Seasons (Robert Bolt)

Flesh and Bone is a collection of short biographies on English and British monarchs. Each chapter includes a note on their lives, how they died, the kind of funeral they had and where they were buried. What makes this collection different from other collections of 'brief lives' is its emphasis on the last days and funerals of the forty-two monarchs included. Most of them assumed, some even planned, that their last journey would be one of solemn pomp and royal ceremony. Surprisingly, for many of them, it didn't turn out like that. Wishes declared with royal authority in life were often ignored after death and the capricious circumstances of their final hours, rather than an earlier royal decree, often dictated what happened next.

Westminster Abbey in London is the last resting place of 17 kings and queens of England. It was also where even Oliver Cromwell chose to be buried. But the number of monarchs who, although buried there, don't have any kind of monument is surprising. Elizabeth I was the last English monarch to have, what we would call, a royal monument, complete with effigy, until Queen Victoria had effigies made for Albert and her at Frogmore in 1864. Another 10 monarchs are buried in St George's Chapel, Windsor but that leaves 14 others. Most are scattered around cathedrals and abbeys in England but some had the bad taste to be buried abroad, and some have no certain grave or monument.

I have arranged the chapters chronologically starting with Edward the Confessor, who was the first monarch to be buried in Westminster Abbey. The Saxon kings seem to be scattered all over the place, although there are quite a few jumbled up in boxes in Winchester Cathedral. Perhaps someone more energetic than me might do a similar book for them. If they do I guarantee to buy a copy. In certain cases, where I think it might be of interest, I have included a note on the burial of other members of the royal family e.g. Henry II's eldest son Henry the 'Young King', George duke of Clarence, brother of Edward IV and the wives of Henry VIII. I have also included the occasional non-royal, e.g. Geoffrey Chaucer, where there is a link with the royal household or some other interesting funerary circumstance as in the case of Ben Johnson. I have included Oliver Cromwell as he created something of a unique, almost monarchical position, for himself as Lord Protector and I have covered William III and Mary II together as he was clearly the executive authority of the duo, while she, while she reigned, did not really rule.

A.J.P. Taylor, historian and great communicator, often said that when he wanted to find out about something he wrote a book about it. *'Writing books is a way of teaching myself and discovering ideas that I never thought of before'*. It is in that spirit that I offer this small work. I have done my best to get the facts right. Anyone recognising mistakes or having additional material to add to any of the chapters should contact me at the e-mail address noted below. I will be pleased to remedy any errors before publishing a new edition. Now that's real wishful thinking!

Conceived as a popular guide to the lives, terminal sicknesses, deaths and burials of British kings and queens I have foresworn the use of cluttering footnotes but have provided a list of my main sources after the final chapter.

A book of 'bite-size' biographies, by one author, is a major challenge and the end result must disappoint some who find their own favourite stories and issues rejected as the rough scissor of selection and compression weeds them out. It is a great risk but in the end it is those stories that I believe will interest readers and grab their attention that have survived the delete key. It has been fun working on this little fancy. I hope you enjoy reading it as much as I have enjoyed putting it together.

Trevor Haywood, August 2007
e-mail: haywood@clix.pt

Burial location, date of death and age of each monarch

Buried in Westminster Abbey

Edward The Confessor
Died 5th January 1066 aged 61
Henry III
Died 16th November 1272 aged 65
Edward I
Died 7th July 1307 aged 68
Edward III
Died 21st June 1377 aged 64
Richard II
Probably murdered, early February 1400 aged 33
Henry V
Died 31st August 1422 aged 35
Edward V
Probably murdered August 1483 aged 12. His remains with those of his brother, Richard duke of York possibly lie in an urn in Westminster Abbey
Henry VII
Died 21st April 1509 aged 52
Edward VI
Died 6th July 1553 aged 15
Mary I
Died 17th November 1558 aged 42
Elizabeth I
Died 24th March 1603 aged 69.
The last British monarch to have a tomb erected in Westminster Abbey
James I
Died 27th March 1625 aged 58
Oliver Cromwell
Died 3rd September 1658 aged 59.
His body was later dug up and lost
Charles II
Died 6th February 1685 aged 54
William III
Died 8th March 1702 aged 51
Mary II
Died 28th December 1694 aged 32
Anne
Died 1st August 1714 aged 49

George II
Died 25th October 1760 aged 76
The last British monarch to be buried in Westminster Abbey

Buried in St George's Chapel Windsor

Henry VI
Murdered 21st May 1471 aged 49
Edward IV
Died 9th April 1483 aged 40
Henry VIII
Died 28th January 1547 aged 55
Charles I
Executed 30th January 1649 aged 48
George III
Died 29th January 1820 aged 81
George IV
Died 26th June 1830 aged 67
William IV
Died 20th June 1837 aged 71
Edward VII
Died 6th May 1910 aged 68
George V
Died 20th January 1936 aged 70
George VI
Died 6th February 1952 aged 56

Waltham Abbey

Harold II
Killed at the Battle of Hastings 14th October 1066 aged c44

Abbey of St Stephen, Caen, Normandy

William I (the Conqueror)
Died 9th September 1087 aged c60

Winchester Cathedral

William II (Rufus)
Died, possibly murdered, in the New Forest on 2nd August 1100 aged c40

Reading Abbey, Berkshire

Henry I.
Died 1st December 1135 aged 67.
Grave now lost

Faversham Abbey, Kent

Stephen
Died 25th October 1154 aged 57.
Grave now lost

Rouen Cathedral

Empress Matilda
Died 1167. The only daughter of
Henry I and mother of Henry II

Fontevrault Abbey, Loire, France

Henry II
Died 6th July 1189 aged 56

Richard I (the Lionheart)
Died 6th April 1199 aged 41

Worcester Cathedral

John
Died 19th October 1216 aged 48

Gloucester Cathedral

Edward II
Murdered 21st September 1327 aged 43

Canterbury Cathedral

Henry IV
Died 20th March 1413 aged 46

Grey Friars' Abbey, Leicester

Richard III
Died 22nd August 1485 aged 32.
Killed in battle, grave now lost.

Hursley Parish Church, Hampshire

Richard Cromwell
Briefly Lord Protector of the
Commonwealth. Died 1712 aged 86

St Germain-en-Laye, France

James II
Died 5th September 1701 aged 67

The Palace of Herrenhausen, Hanover, Germany

George I
Died 22nd June 1727 aged 67

Royal Mausoleum, Frogmore, Windsor

Victoria
Died 22nd January 1901 aged 81

Edward VIII
Died 28th May 1972 aged 77.
Buried in the private cemetery near
Victoria's mausoleum

Explanation of some terms

Abbeys and Cathedrals: Most of the older cathedrals we visit in England today were originally abbeys where a community of monks and nuns lived, worked and worshipped. This meant that as well as the abbey church (often today's cathedral) the site would have been covered with a variety of other buildings: refectories, washrooms, kitchens, dormitories and workrooms of various sizes. At the dissolution of the monasteries in 1543 some abbey churches had the lead stripped off their roofs and quickly fell into ruin, others were designated as Cathedrals. Many abbeys were just sold off to raise cash and the lucky purchaser could turn the abbot's lodgings and associated buildings into a grand house while the abbey church itself fell into ruin, as at Much Wenlock in Shropshire.

Censing: This was the act of anointing a coffin with incense by a leading cleric when it paused on a long journey or when it was met at the door of an abbey or cathedral.

Cerecloth: A cloth smeared or impregnated with wax or some other glutinous material and used as a winding sheet. After embalming early royal corpses were usually wrapped in such material often so manipulated as to be close to the contours of the body.

Chantry Chapel: To ensure that prayers were said for them after their death wealthy people would often endow a chantry. Pre-Reformation monarchs and aristocrats often bequeathed the income from a specific piece of land or estate to support a Chantry Priest who would say masses for their souls in perpetuity. These masses would often (but not always) be said at a chantry altar enclosed in a special chapel built, inside the church or abbey. These could be simple or very ornate structures built over or near to their actual tomb. The suppression of the chantries in 1547 by the Anglican reformers had two great impacts. Firstly visitors to a church would no longer hear the daily round of chantry masses that in the past would have been going on in many churches. Secondly the 'chantry money' once held in trust by churches, guilds and corporations was confiscated thus accruing great wealth to the crown. The brutal sequestering of chantry funds may well have encouraged parishes to abandon the old religion and embrace state protestantism.

The Covenant and the Covenanters: The Covenanters were supporters of a document or 'National Covenant' signed in 1638 by a number of Scottish lords and commoners. It asserted their right to their own presbyterian church in the face of King Charles I's 1637 demand that the Church of Scotland accept a new liturgy and the Book of Common Prayer. The Covenanters soon became the leading political force in Scotland and they succeeded in abolishing bishops in the Scottish Kirk. The signing of the 'Solemn League and Covenant' during the English Civil war brought about an alliance between the Covenanters and English Parliamentarians with whom, in religious matters at least, the Covenanters had much in common.

Hearse (old spelling Herse): A temporary monument raised over a grave and/or the carriage in which a body is carried to a grave. Those erected over graves were usually temporary and could be simple – just wooden structures to support a variety of candles round a covered coffin or elaborate confections that might stay for weeks or months over a grave. If a body had to be taken long distances for burial workmen were often commissioned to build a 'herse' at each overnight stopping point with the final one usually being the most elaborate and the most expensive.

Jacobite: From the Latin 'Jacobus' for James, Jacobite was the name given to anyone supporting the Stuart claim to the throne of England (after James II fled to France in 1678) against the protestant monarchs William and Mary. Many Scottish lords and commons remained Jacobite sympathisers until the rout of Bonny Prince Charlie in 1746. After that Jacobinism was a declining force in both Scotland and England as the Hanoverian kings consolidated their position. Some Tories (see below) during Queen Anne's reign, were often accused of being Jacobite sympathisers, most particularly by Sarah Churchill, the wife of the first duke of Marlborough.

Ledger: As well as describing an account book from around 1510 it was also used to describe a flat stone covering a grave as in 'a ledger stone'.

The Short Parliament: By 1640, Charles I had reigned for 11 years without a Parliament. He called one because his armies had been defeated by the Scottish Covenanter Army and he needed money to continue the war. The English country gentry in Parliament were angry at the king's behaviour in raising taxes via his royal prerogative and they presented Charles with a catalogue of complaints. Charles was horrified at the concessions that they demanded and he dissolved the Parliament. It had sat from 13th April 1640 until 5th May, 1640, hence its name, the 'Short Parliament'.

The Long Parliament: After the collapse of the Short Parliament Charles was forced to call another Parliament in 1640. The Scots army were still ensconced in northern England. They were costing Charles £850 a day and the crown was facing bankruptcy. This Parliament met for the first time on 3rd November 1640 and its members were now determined to achieve constitutional reform before agreeing to supply any money. This Parliament was no more malleable than the first, and again Charles became exasperated by their demands. This time he responded by taking troops into the chamber to arrest five men who he regarded as leaders of the faction against him. He failed to find them and on 22nd August 1642 the English Civil War began. The 'Long Parliament' sat for 13 years until Oliver Cromwell suppressed it in 1653. As far as Royalists were concerned however, this Parliament remained in session throughout the Commonwealth, until the restoration of Charles II in 1660.

Whigs and Tories: The name Whig was originally derived from a Scottish term of derision, a whiggamore, a Gaelic word for a cattle drover, while Tory, was an Irish word for outlaw. The terms entered English political discourse during the exclusion crisis of 1678-1681 when a group, known as the Whigs in the Parliament, opposed King Charles II's desire to name his Catholic brother James duke of York (later James II) as his heir. The Tories, on the other hand, supported James' claim to the throne, and the continuance of the Stuart line. Hence their association with the term Jacobite (see above). At this time both Whigs and Tories were more like loose groupings of like-minded individuals, often related by blood and marriage, than political parties, as we would know them today. It would be difficult, for instance, to differentiate between the views of moderate Whigs and moderate Tories.

In May 1711 Jonathan Swift attempted to define the two groups. He found that the Whigs supported the Glorious Revolution that brought William III to the throne, they opposed the 'Old Pretender' (the son of James II), they justified the succession of the House of Hanover, they believed that the British monarchy was not absolute *'but limited by Laws, which the Executive Power could not dispense with'* and they were tolerant of non Anglican protestants. The Tories on the other hand asserted a king or queen's hereditary right; *'that the Persons of Princes were Sacred: their lawful authority not to be resisted on any pretence; nor even their usurpations without the most extream Necessity'*. They also believed that breeches in the succession were highly dangerous, that the ruin of the Anglican Church would be attended by the ruin of the state and that no power should be given to those not of the established Anglican Religion.

EDWARD the CONFESSOR (born c1005, reigned 1042-1066)

Edward, later known as the Confessor, was the eldest son of the Saxon King, Ethelred II, by his second wife Emma, sister of Richard II duke of Normandy. When Edward was eight years old the Danish king, Swein Forkbeard, and his son Cnut, invaded England and drove Ethelred and his family into exile in Normandy. Ethelred returned on 'Forkbeard's death in 1014 and, in a rare act of military leadership, successfully drove Cnut out of England. His victory was short-lived. Differences soon arose between Ethelred and his warrior son by his first marriage, Edmund Ironside. Edmund felt himself to be a man worthier to be king than his father and he now sensed that his claim to the throne was likely to be usurped by Ethelred's sons by the Norman Emma and he rebelled.

After Ethelred died in 1016 Edmund Ironside fought the persevering Cnut bravely, but at the Battle of Ashingdon in Essex he was betrayed by a large force of his own men and suffered a major defeat. However, Edmund did not give up and Cnut decided that it was in his interest to negotiate with this formidable warrior. At Aldney in Gloucestershire they agreed to partition England between them, Wessex to Edmund the rest to Cnut. Edmund was not to enjoy his part for long as he died soon after this treaty and it was not difficult for Cnut to seize his half of the Kingdom. Edmund Ironside's grandson, Edgar the Atheling (Atheling meaning of the Saxon royal blood) would be briefly proclaimed King of England after Harold II's death at Hastings in 1066, but his followers soon abandoned him and he was forced to submit to William I.

In a surprising 'sleeping with the enemy move' Edward's mother, Emma, married King Cnut creating something of a complex dynastic situation that seemed to remove any chance of Edward returning to England let alone inheriting his father's kingdom. For the next twenty-nine years he lived in, and developed strong personal ties with, the ducal house of Normandy, including young William of Normandy (later William I of England) who was more than twenty years his junior. Edward would have witnessed the supporters of the eight year old 'bastard', William, struggling to save his birthright during the turmoil that followed duke Robert of Normandy's death in 1035. He couldn't help but be impressed by, and probably wished to emulate, young William's limpet-like tenacity for survival.

The sickly and childless Harthacnut, Emma's son by King Cnut, inherited his father's crown of England in 1040 and in 1041 invited Edward there in the hope that Edward's presence in England would secure the support of the Saxon earls against the Norwegian King, Magnus I of Norway, who looked on England with envious eyes. By a stroke of luck Harthacnut dropped dead at a wedding feast in 1042 and, by another stroke of luck, he had named his half-brother Edward as his successor. Whatever Magnus I of Norway thought about this Edward, by a strange twist of fate, was now in possession of the crown and succeeded his half-brother without any opposition or disturbance in 1042. With the support of the Saxon earls, including the powerful earl Godwine, eight years of uneasy peace followed. At this time England's politics were dominated by three great earls; Godwine, earl of Wessex; Leofric, earl of Mercia; and Siward, earl of Northumbria, all of whom now wanted a piece of the king's bounty.

But it was earl Godwine, by far the most powerful of the Saxon lords, who got closest to the king and in 1044 Edward made two of his sons, Swein and Harold, earls. The alliance was sealed even tighter when Edward married Godwine's daughter Edith in 1045. This peaceful alliance did not last long. In 1051, in a bid to shake off Godwine influence, Edward successfully moved against them, put Queen Edith in a nunnery and drove the male members of the family into exile. Around this time he also elevated more Normans to offices of state, including the appointment of a Norman as Archbishop of Canterbury. The Godwines successfully invaded England in 1052 and soon got things back to where they were before. After Godwine senior died in 1053 Harold inherited his title of earl of Wessex and began the journey that would make him the most powerful man in the realm after the king. He and his brothers Tosti, Gyrth and Leofwine became the props on which Edward's throne rested.

Reluctantly or not, Edward left much of the detailed governance of England to Harold while he concentrated on building his new abbey church at Westminster. Many legends surround the choosing of the site for the original church that was later to become Westminster Abbey including one that St Peter appeared as a bright light near modern day Lambeth in London, crossed over the river and consecrated an early church on the site. Another tells of a hermit of Worcester who, amid ghastly dreams of heaven and hell, was told by St Peter to take a message to king Edward to establish a Benedictine monastery at Thorney, two leagues from the city of London. The truth is more prosaic. Edward had a passionate devotion to St Peter in unison with a desire to have a place of burial on this ground. Whatever the inspiration Edward began building his great abbey to St Peter in 1045. He also embarked on enlarging the small residence built by King Cnut into the Palace of Westminster (in large part so that he could superintend the building of the abbey).

Although the son of a Saxon king, Edward's spiritual bond with Normandy was now to be manifest in stone. He was brought up a Norman and it was Norman bishops and Norman Romanesque architecture that would dominate his new conception. Edward spent one tenth of his income on this building and as its great lantern tower rose above the nascent capital this, the first cruciform church in England, would have seemed a fantastic marvel to the mid 11th century onlooker. King and Abbey were to be united sooner than anyone might have imagined. Edward's health began to fail during November 1065 possibly as a result of a series of strokes and later on Christmas Eve that year he became sick with a fever while celebrating Christmas at Westminster. He may haves suffered from a number of strokes but the chronicles report that the king concealed his illness so as not to disrupt the festivities, but he was sinking fast. On December 27th he retreated to his sick bed. Mindful that time was running out and of his long held desire to be buried in his new abbey, he ordered that the abbey be consecrated the next day, the 28th December (Holy Innocents Day). The formidable list of relics displayed at the consecration (Edward was a fervent collector) included the Virgin Mary's milk, hair, shoes and bed, some hairs from St Peter's beard, part of the body of St Buttulph and part of the jaw and some teeth of St Anastasia.

As he was dying Edward is supposed to have experienced visions, which bystanders interpreted as a prophecy of catastrophes to come. As usual everyone was waiting to hear who he would name as his heir. Before he died he declared that Harold Godwine should be King of The English. Though a pragmatic move based on the reality of the here and now this was a serious dynastic change as up until this time no one outside King Alfred's line, other than the family of the conquering Danes Swein and Cnut, had ever held the English kingship. Edgar the Atheling who was packed full of Saxon royal blood didn't even get a mention. The sincerity of Edward's deathbed declaration would fuel future scholars with a treasure trove of argument for and against Saxon Harold and the Norman duke William.

The king died on 5th January 1066 and was buried the next day in the newly consecrated abbey, in a stone sarcophagus below the pavement in front of the high altar. Starting a fashion that was to continue for many generations of English kings, Edward's body was dressed in his royal robes, a crown upon his head, a golden crucifix on a golden chain around his neck and St John's 'pilgrim's ring' on his finger. Little is known of his funeral ceremony but the queen, archbishops, eight bishops, eight abbots, all five earls and the usual nobles of the court were present for the Christmas festivities, so it is reasonable to assume that the funeral would have been conducted with some processional pomp.

The omens for sanctifying Edward started immediately after his last breath. Onlookers noted that in death his face was seen to blush like a rose, his beard to gleam like a lily and his hands to lie straight and white. But it was the last Saxon bishop, Wulfstan of Worcester, who initiated the supposed miracle-making properties of Edward's tomb. When threatened with dismissal due to his continued use of the Saxon language in Norman-occupied England Wulfstan cast his staff into the tomb slab calling on dead Edward to keep it if he should not remain a bishop. The staff remained fixed and unmoveable in the stone until King William I confirmed Wulfstan in his office whereupon the bishop alone was able to remove it. Later cures of a blind bell ringer and a hunchback at the tomb helped accelerate the movement that eventually led to Edward officially being declared a saint by Pope Alexander III in 1161.

The first king to build the biggest abbey in England, the first to be buried in it, Edward the Confessor also became the first English monarch to defy the reasonable assumption that an English king once laid to rest stayed still. As the list of miracles mounted, King Henry I, in order to resolve a dispute about whether the saintly king's body remained uncorrupted, allowed the tomb to be opened in 1102. The clerics involved found the '*whole body to be sound and flexible.... they next examined the flesh which was firm and pure as crystal, whiter than snow...*'. On this occasion Gundolp Bishop of Rochester tried to pull a hair from the still white beard until rebuked by Abbot Crispin. Sixty-one years later, at midnight on 13th October 1163, in recognition of Edward's recent canonisation, King Henry II and Thomas Becket transferred Edward's body to a new tomb enriched with statues of St John and St Edward in ivory and gold. Again everyone involved took the opportunity to have a peep at the corpse and study its state, and again it was reported to be in a wonderful condition. This time Abbot Lawrence, who had sought and gained Edward's canonisation, removed the ring of St John from the dead king's finger and placed it in the abbey's treasures. He also removed the vestments that covered the king and had three grand copes made from them.

'Saint' Edward's tomb was a 'feretory' i.e. a chest with openings for seeing and touching the lead coffin within. These openings allowed pilgrims seeking to be healed (some of whom stayed overnight with their limbs jammed in the niches) to actually make contact with the coffin. For reasons that are unclear at this distance in time Thomas Becket claimed the original Wulfstan's tomb slab for himself. In 1269 Edward's body was transferred yet again to a new shrine at the behest of Henry III who was in the middle of demolishing Edward's abbey to make way for an even more splendid one. This is more or less the abbey that we see today. This time Edward was reburied above ground in a grand pedestal covered in the most costly gold and jewels. Various bits of this great shrine were pillaged and pilfered over time and during the reign of Henry VIII, the pedestal was pulled down and the king reburied beneath it. In 1554 Queen Mary, in the process of returning England to the Catholic Church, had the pedestal re-erected and the king's body moved back into its upper part. She may have had the same trouble with builders that we often have today as some of the slabs that made up the shrine were clearly not put back properly.

If all this was not disturbance enough the men taking down the scaffolding after the coronation of King James II, in 1685, allowed part of it to collapse on the shrine breaking the coffin so that the head of the king could be seen '*sound and firm, the upper and lower jaws full of teeth, a golden band round the temple and all his bones and much dust in his coffin*'. One of the 'singing men' a Mr Charles Taylour riffled about inside the coffin and pulled out the gold crucifix and golden chain that was put on the body in January 1066. He proudly presented it to the Dean of Westminster who then presented it to James II who was happy to have it and sent the 'singing man' £50 for his trouble. Before fleeing England in 1688 and losing the gold crucifix in the process, James II did have the decency to seal up the Confessor's coffin with heavy metal plates and to bind it with iron bars. It has not been opened since but, as we will see later, the fashion for opening the tombs of English monarchs was to become a common occurrence in England.

Towards the end of 2005 archaeologists using high frequency radar to research the Cosmati pavement near Edward's shrine behind the current High Altar discovered what is believed to be the original, 1066, burial vault of Edward the Confessor. This was his first resting place and its discovery confirms that the saint, though moved and buffeted about over the centuries, didn't stray far from his original grave. It was his tomb that drew other kings and queens to be buried here, so it is appropriate that the morbid curiosity of his descendents has now thankfully come to an end. The abbey Edward the Confessor built, marvellous as it was to his generation, is now almost entirely gone, replaced by an even grander design by a King (Henry III) who was to venerate St Edward as much as Edward had venerated St Peter.

Edward's claim to sainthood is mainly based on the miracles reported at his tomb. Very little in his life, apart from building his great abbey, marked him out as being exceptionally pious. But in preparing the 'CV' that would promote him as a candidate for sainthood it was necessary to provide a few examples of saintly behaviour during his life. One early chronicle, sponsored by his Queen, Edith, declared that, although long married Edward, had always abstained from sexual relations in order to live a chaste, pious and unworldly life. Of course the childless Queen Edith may have wanted to use this text to explain, on her own behalf, that the lack of a direct heir was entirely due to Edward's saintly lifestyle. For this part of the 'CV' there is actually no proof at all.

HAROLD II (born c1022, reigned January 1066–October 1066)

Harold II was the son of Godwine earl of Wessex, one of the most powerful of the three great earldoms of Saxon England, and his wife Gytha of Denmark. Harold had no direct claim to the throne of England. He did have the blood of the Danes in his veins, being a cousin of Swein Estrithsson, King of Denmark and a nephew of King Cnut. Edward the Confessor made him earl of East Anglia in 1045, a key geopolitical role as a bastion against any further threat from Denmark, then held by the warlike Magnus I of Norway.

Around 1045 Harold was married, Danish fashion, without a Church blessing, to Edith 'Swan Neck', a wealthy East Anglian heiress, and had at least six children by her. This marriage is generally believed to have been a love match but lacking the sanction of the church the monks who wrote the history of these times inevitably referred to Edith as Harold's mistress rather than his wife. This 'Danish' marriage may have been for love but Harold also needed allies in England among the other powerful Saxon earls. As his marriage to Edith was not recognised by the church he was also able to marry the lady Alditha (the sister of Morcar of Northumbria and Edwin of Mercia) according to church rites. This alliance proved vital when Harold needed the support of both brothers in early 1066.

Up until Edward's dismissal of the Godwines in 1051, Harold was fully involved in the duties of his earldom, the royal court and the wider realm, at the request of the king. While his father was alive Harold also toiled with him in gaining the expansion of Godwine power and influence over the king. This influence was put in jeopardy in 1046 when Harold's elder brother Swein abducted the abbess of Leominster and kept her for a year. This outrage led to Swein being exiled and cast a stain on the Godwine clan. Later, back on English soil and intent on compounding his family's problems, Swein murdered his cousin earl Beorn. Again he was exiled but amazingly was allowed back into England in 1050 escorted home by the Bishop of Worcester.

By this time it was becoming clear that King Edward's wife Edith was probably barren and as such Edward might have seen her as little more than an unproductive symbol of Godwine domination. Yet divorcing her to secure an heir would precipitate a serious Godwine backlash. Swein's behaviour, his barren queen, the attack on his kinsman Eustace of Boulogne by the citizens of Dover and no doubt other issues of self-esteem prompted Edward to want rid of the Godwines and so he forced them into exile in October 1051. Godwine senior and most of the family went to Flanders, Harold and his brother Leofwine went to Ireland. The family 'bad boy' and eldest son of earl Godwine, Swein, was later sent from Flanders on pilgrimage to Jerusalem to expiate his many sins. Luckily for all concerned he died on the return journey.

With the Godwines away, Edward moved quickly to have Queen Edith put away into the keeping of the Abbess of Wilton, and began making arrangements for his divorce. This 'chaste and pious' king wanted an heir that was neither a grandson of a Godwine nor a son of Normandy. Such dynastic aims need a lot more time than Edward was to get. In 1052 Harold and his father's forces met up near the Isle of Wight and then sailed up the Thames to London where Edward was forced to accept terms, and reinstate Edith to his bed, and the earls to their lands and titles. But Godwine family matters soon took a turn for the worse. Swein's death near Constantinople in September 1052 was followed by that of Godwine senior in April 1053. Edward must have been pleased to see the back of them both. Harold now took centre stage. Perhaps there was a silver lining for everyone? Less tainted by the old feuds Harold soon established himself as Edward's first and foremost lieutenant. He was a fine warrior, an able administrator and a striking leader. Between 1053 and 1066 Harold ruled while Edward built. He defeated Gruffydd of Wales in 1063 and in 1065 he showed his loyalty to Edward by counselling that his own brother, Tosti, should be turned out of his earldom of Northumbria in order to avoid a bloody civil war in the north.

The Norman chroniclers have Harold visiting William of Normandy around 1064, although there are no English sources confirming this. The reasons for such a visit have never been clearly established. Was it to carry a message from Edward the Confessor naming William as his successor? Was it to secure a bride for Harold or to marry his sister off in a Norman Alliance? Was Harold just blown off course during a trip to another part of France? Was it to secure the release of his brother and nephew held hostage by William since 1052? Whatever the real reason for Harold's journey, that great work of Norman propaganda, the Bayeux Tapestry, begins with Harold's arrival in Normandy and goes on to develop its justification for William's eventual invasion by putting an oath-taking by Harold at the centre of its story. William, keeping Harold part prisoner, part guest, contrived to have Harold swear a solemn oath, on holy relics, to support his claim to the throne of England.

News of such an oath, a binding cornerstone of agreements between aristocrats in northern Europe at that time, would travel fast and contemporary observers would be convinced that no good would come to Harold if he broke it. An oathbreaker could expect retribution on earth as well as in heaven, so if the oath taking was true it gave William real power over Harold. Harold's discomfort might have been all the more intense if, as one theory has it, he had been tricked into swearing on holy relics, discreetly covered by a cloth, that were hidden from him. Released by William, Harold returned home with only his nephew Hakon. His brother Wulfnoth remained as William's prisoner. Although probably surprised by William's behaviour Harold was now under no illusion about William's intentions. The death of Edward the Confessor in January 1066 would soon put all the claimants, Harald Hardradi of Norway, William of Normandy and Harold of England on a war footing.

Despite the deathbed endorsement of Harold by the king, Edward's known love for all things Norman still left a question mark over who he would really have preferred to follow him. A further complication lay in the fact that the clear heir to the throne was Edgar the Atheling, the Saxon great nephew of Edward the Confessor. However this boy was only fourteen years old, and although he should have been considered as first in line to succeed no one seems to have taken up his cause or opposed Harold's 'usurpation' of his birthright. Pragmatism was alive and well in 1066. Why chose a weak boy over Harold, with all his military and administrative experience? If duke William and Harald Hardradi of Norway were indeed preparing to invade England a boy king would not be strong enough to defeat them.

The tradition among the Saxons was that a king was elected by a great council of nobles known as the Witan. As soon as Edward was dead Harold hastened to the Witan to seek their endorsement for his claim. Although keen to support Harold the Witan required that the late king should be buried before any new election could take place. Harold immediately arranged for Edward to be buried in his new abbey. The Witan elected Harold as king soon after and he was crowned later on the same day. This may look like indecent haste and indeed it was. Harold's policy would be to wrong foot William of Normandy and to close off any support there might be for Edgar the Atheling. Although there are no records to confirm it Harold was probably crowned in Westminster Abbey. Those archbishops, bishops and other notables assembled for Edward's funeral would be on hand later in the day to officiate at his coronation and it would be politic for Harold to start his kingship in the new temple and burial place of his predecessor. If so, he was the first of many English monarchs to be crowned there initiating the abbey as the place where kings and queens were (and still are) confirmed by solemn ceremonies at the start of their office and, for the next four hundred years at least, laid to rest amid solemn obsequies at the end of it. In April 1066 the long tail of Haley's comet was seen above the skies of England and old and young alike looked up and saw in it an omen of serious trouble to come. Interestingly such visitations were never read as good omens! Of course they were right. Fierce armies were soon on the move, leaving

Normandy to invade England, leaving Norway to invade England, and, led by King Harold, leaving London to defend England!

Harold's bold foray to the north of England to defeat his brother Tosti and King Harald Hardradi of Norway at Stamford Bridge, and his dash back to southern England to face William at Hastings, are well documented. At Hastings Harold would fight on foot, Danish fashion, he allowed no escape route for himself, and he stayed on the battlefield long enough to get killed. This outcome had all the hallmarks of Scandinavian leadership, honour and heroism. The Scandinavians loved a dead hero. They could make up long songs about the bloody battle and the feats of arms accomplished by the glorious dead. But the English needed more than a song and a dead hero. Harold, having confidently taken Edward's crown, owed it to them to stay alive to rally new forces and lead them against the Norman invader, as Edmund Ironside had done against Cnut. William only just succeeded at Hastings and what he held after the battle was just a sliver of land near the sea in southern England. Had Harold lived to fight another day that's all William might have kept and the story of England might have been very different.

But there was no escape route and there were to be no long songs. As dusk fell on that October day after the battle of Hastings in 1066 the corpse of King Harold II of England lay mangled and mauled among the bodies of his two younger brothers and his loyal *huscarls*. Ivo of Ponthieu, arriving in the Saxon lines after Harold had been killed, maliciously took the trouble to slash into his thigh almost severing it. This kind of post-mortem cruelty suggests that duke William and his knights had faced a more difficult task than they had anticipated. Harold had lost, but it was (as a later English general was to say in 1815) *'the nearest run thing you ever saw in your life'* for the bastard of Normandy', and the defiling of the body of his enemy was perhaps both an act of revenge and frustration.

Harold's face was barely recognisable. He was identified, with some difficulty perhaps by his armour or some distinguishing marks on his body. Tradition has it that his great love Edith 'Swan Neck' moved among the steaming bodies that day and picked him out perhaps recognising a mark or tattoo on the mangled remains. If Edith had indeed found her lover, William was in no mood to grant concessions to Harold's family with regard to the body's future resting place. He refused the request of the countess Gytha, Harold's mother, to take her son's body for burial even in return for the equivalent of its weight in gold. Instead William is said to have turned the body over to one William Malet, ordering him to bury Harold somewhere on the nearby seashore. After this we move into the realms of conjecture. The most likely outcome is that the women of Harold's family or the secular canons of Harold's own foundation, the Church of Holy Cross at Waltham in Essex, removed the body from its seashore grave and buried it under the old high altar there.

This church, enlarged by Harold when he was cured of an illness after a visit to its famous 'Holy Rood' (a large flint cross excavated near Glastonbury), later became rich from the pilgrims who flocked to its famous shrine. During the Conqueror's time the canons of Waltham needed to be careful. Williams's reticence in handing over the body may have been due to his poor claim to the English throne as well as a desire to prevent the dead Harold becoming a future focus as a martyr for the English. In this latter concern he seems to have been right. A cult did develop around Harold's grave which was not what the canons wanted as they settled into the reality of the Norman occupation.

The author of the Waltham Chronicle claimed to remember as a boy seeing the canons move Harold's body from the old church into the new Norman one in 1120. At this time they transferred Harold's body to a less distinctive location. Later, as part of his penance for the murder of Thomas Becket, Henry II founded the priory of Augustine cannons here in 1177, which was granted the status of an abbey shortly after. The Augustinian canons who took over the church, concerned not to draw attention to themselves as hosts of the last Saxon King of England, began fostering stories of Harold's miraculous escape from Hastings. In these stories he is supposed to have travelled to Denmark and Germany soliciting help to restore his kingdom. Other forms of the tale have him taking up a pilgrimage to expunge the guilt of his broken oath to William, and then living as a hermit in Chester or Canterbury.

How these stories gained any credence with Harold's grey marble tomb (however plain) still occupying a spot in the abbey church at Waltham is not explained. But it was clear that successive canons, regarding discretion as the better part of valour, decided that it was best that people forgot about him as a local hero and just got on with living the reality of the Norman dynasty. Later both King Edward I, and his wife Eleanor of Castile, lay in state in this abbey for several weeks while their funerals were being prepared in London.

Waltham Abbey was the very last abbey to be destroyed (1540) during the dissolution of the monasteries. So what William the Conqueror either forgot or ignored was easily torn up by the agents of a later king, and no sign of Harold's grave can now be seen. Waltham's famous Holy Rood also disappeared around the same time. A more recent claim for Harold's last resting place has been made for Holy Trinity Church in Bosham, near Chichester on the West Sussex coast. This tenth century Saxon church is depicted at the beginning of the Bayeux Tapestry just before Harold takes his boat trip across the channel. An eight year old daughter of King Cnut, (who supposedly died in a nearby millstream), is buried at this church under a stone decorated by the Black Raven of the Danes.

Harold II, the 'nine-month king' and defeated hero of Hastings is thus one of several English monarchs who have no certain grave or monument. The odds are that he lies somewhere under the ground within the ruins of Waltham Abbey but the 'Conqueror' would no doubt be pleased to know that there is still no certain spot where we might congregate to remember him.

WILLIAM I (the Conqueror) (born c1027 reigned 1066-1087)

William I was the son of Robert II, duke of Normandy and Herleva who has been variously identified as the daughter of an undertaker, a tanner or just a woman who lived in the ducal household. William was thus illegitimate at a time when 'bastards' were common among north European nobility and his early name 'William the Bastard of Normandy' would carry little stigma and be really no more than an extension of his Christian name. Within a year or two of William's birth his mother was married off to one of Robert's followers with whom she had two more sons, Robert later count of Mortain and Odo, later Bishop of Bayeux. As adults these two half-brothers would be among Williams's most important supporters. Duke Robert was the lord of a territory that needed constant vigilance to keep and protect. Apart from his own quarrelsome relatives, his neighbours in Brittany, Bêlleme, and of course France were always looking to weaken his position. During his time as duke Robert also gave support and shelter to King Ethelred of England and his sons, Edward the Confessor and Alfred, when they all sought exile, from the Danes.

Around 1035 duke Robert set off on a pilgrimage to Jerusalem. Bastard William was his only son and before he left he took the trouble to persuade his barons, and the King of France, to agree that William should succeed him. This was a prescient move as duke Robert died on his way home. William was only eight years old when he inherited Normandy from his father. As a child duke getting his inheritance was easier than keeping it and William spent much of his youth hiding from those who would try to take it from him. The duchy was beset with feuds and William's guardians often had to resort to disguising the boy to prevent his being murdered. As he grew to manhood William became personally involved in the constant struggle to keep predators from eating away at his duchy. In this rough, violent school he grew to be a strong, confident warrior, who made the most of his Norman cavalry's mobility in war. He also became a cynical observer of men and only trusted those who were very close to him.

William came of age around 1042 and at around the same time he married Matilda, daughter of count Baldwin of Flanders. The pope had forbidden the marriage on the grounds of consanguinity but William went ahead anyway; Flanders was too useful, and powerful, an ally to lose on a technicality. Unlike many of his contemporaries, William was never recorded as having taken a mistress. Matilda bore him at least nine children, four sons and five daughters, and husband and wife seemed to have been very happy together, both living to see all their sons survive to adulthood. The oldest was Robert Curthose, later duke of Normandy, followed by Richard who was killed in a hunting accident in the New Forest, William Rufus, later King William II, and Henry, later King Henry I of England and duke of Normandy. Their great struggles with each other would come later, for now, William concentrated on keeping and extending his father's patrimony. His early capacity for cruelty was highlighted during the battle for the castle of Alençon. The story goes that the defenders mocked William from the battlements by waving and beating furs and pelts in an allusion to Williams's origins as the son of a tanner's daughter. They paid for their mockery by having their hands and feet cut off after William captured the town. William used cruelty, and the threat of cruelty, as an instrument of terror throughout his life.

In 1062 after a series of successful campaigns against the French King Henry I and his allies William added the County of Maine to his dominions, interestingly using the pretext of an oath, made to him in private, as an excuse to take it. William was known as a brave and resourceful leader, a wily negotiator, ambitious, determined and ruthless in dealing with the coalitions that tried to take any part of Normandy from him. A master in the art of war he would bring all these qualities to bear as he landed on the beaches of Sussex in 1066.

William's contacts with Edward the Confessor during 1051-52 when the Godwine family were sent into exile remain the subject of fierce debate. Some chronicles claim that, perhaps in remembrance of the family who had sheltered him in Normandy as a young man, Edward promised William the throne in 1051, while the Godwines were in exile, and when the eighteen year-old William is thought to have visited England. No such visit is recorded anywhere but in 1052 the Norman Archbishop of Canterbury Robert of Jumièrges, visited William after fleeing from the Godwines. Seeking to ingratiate himself with his host it may have been he who left William with the impression that Edward had designated him as his heir. This is, of course, supposition but William, hazarding so much on a risky invasion, must have believed that he had been so designated and it may have been Archbishop Robert (with or without any royal sanction) who sowed the seed. That Edward the Confessor had Godwine's youngest son and nephew sent as hostages to William at around the same time does suggest that Edward retained more than just a casual link with William.

In the absence of any recorded evidence William's claims to the English throne rested on two shaky foundations. One was that his grandfather, Richard II duke of Normandy, was the brother of Emma, mother of Edward the Confessor by Ethelred. Lacking any English royal bloodline this link is more of a dotted line than a full black one on any genealogical chart. Two that William had once had Harold Godwine in his power in Normandy and made him swear on some holy relics that he would support William's claim to the crown of England. Well an almost- prisoner might well say that wouldn't he? Neither of these would carry much weight if it weren't for 'The Confessor's' known love of all things Norman.

On Edward the Confessor's death and Harold's assumption of the crown of England William moved fast. His first move was to get the support of the pope for a lawful invasion of England. Pope Alexander II seemed happy to sanction the project and even provided a papal banner to be carried during the invasion. William then began the process of convincing his somewhat shaky supporters that an invasion of England was not as risky as they all thought. He began assembling a great army, a cosmopolitan mixture of Normans, Bretons, Flemings and other French soldiers, and the huge fleet he needed to carry it across the channel. Promises of booty, lands and William's reputation as a military leader, must have overcome whatever doubts remained as, after some delays, William's fleet arrived at Pevensey just before dawn on 28th September 1066. William then waited on the south coast where, with his army ravaging the land with impunity, he was able to display his strength and Harold's weakness. The battle at Senlac hill, known to us as the Battle of Hastings, lasted all day suggesting that both armies were evenly matched so far as numbers were concerned. In the end William's generalship, his ability to use archers to inflict casualties at a distance and the mobility of his cavalry won the day. Whatever the theories and justifications for William's invasion, in the end it was force of arms that gave William the crown and it was by force of arms that he would keep it.

Immediately after Hastings William spent some time ravaging the lands west of London. This was a classic Norman tactic, a morale-sapping display of calculated cruelty in a wide sweep through Kent and Surrey leaving a belt of burning towns and villages in its wake. Londoners would have no illusions about what would happen if they tried to oppose him. After accepting the submission of the Witan at Berkhamstead, William entered the capital in December 1066. He immediately visited Westminster Abbey where he gave 50 marks in silver and rich palls (coverings) for the altar and Edward's tomb. He was crowned on Christmas day 1066 at the crossing beneath the central tower directly over the Edward the Confessor's grave. Altogether a piece of symbolism, spin and public relations that would not disgrace the media machine of a modern prime minister. This coronation would be imitated in one form or another in this place by another thirty-eight kings and queens of England. Some of those assembled to witness the coronation indicated their acceptance of the new king by shouting out their support in English. William had surrounded the Abbey with some heavy security and, confused by these strange sounds, the Norman guards posted outside panicked and set fire to some houses nearby. Many of those inside the church ran out to quench the blaze or to do a bit of looting during the confusion. William's reign had started with fire and, ironically, a fire would also accompany the end of it.

William set about making his new kingdom Norman with ruthless vigour. He and his greedy companions gradually consolidated their position through the weight of their heavy armour (the equivalent of a number of active tank regiments today) and the rapid building of mote and bailey castles to pacify local populations. William's occupation did face some opposition in the north and west of the country but it was mostly all over by 1071. William was never a man to take half measures. The 'harrying' of the north that he carried out in early 1070 involved devastating Northumbria to such an extent that the land would be incapable of sustaining a future rebellion. It remained incapable of sustaining any form of life for several years. Around 10,000 Normans subjugated a nation of between one and two million people. William was on a mission. Within a decade of 1066 less than one percent of the population held virtually all the land, and almost all of that one percent was Norman. Almost four thousand Anglo Saxon nobles lost their land to a group of less than two hundred Norman barons, each one building a castle to control the area they had been given. William was changing not only the structure of landholding in England but also the very nature of the landscape. His other great initiative was that the power of a king in England was radically altered. Before William, a Saxon king was a leader among a powerful group of nobles who each wielded independent control over their own lands. After the Saxon nobility was wiped out William claimed sovereignty over all the land and it was he alone who parcelled it out among his followers.

From King William I onwards kings of England became the fountainhead from which all vacated land was redistributed. This was a major change from the power held by the Saxon kings before him. Yet another change was just as important. After the death of a Saxon lord his whole family, brothers, cousins and uncles all arrived at the funeral expecting to get a slice of the dead man's holdings. This way the greater family stayed united and trouble free but the extent of the original holding was much diminished. This was not the Norman way. For Normans the key issue was keeping the inheritance in tact and thus arose the primacy of primogeniture in England where, usually, the eldest son got the lot and then did his best to expand and extend it via marriage, war or subterfuge.

William appointed no Englishmen as bishops or archbishops. The last English earl, Waltheof of Northumbria was executed in 1076 and the Domesday Book of 1086 shows only four major landholders of English birth left. Many of the barons to whom all this land was transferred also had important landholdings in France or Normandy, and so where once the political and dynastic links of England had been with Scandinavia they now shifted sharply to northern France. The rapid transformation of the aristocracy of England from Saxon to Norman French under William was to have profound consequences for the development of English language, art and culture. Edward the Confessor's 'Norman' abbey would soon be just one among many. But William also had to keep Normandy and Maine and this meant regular forays across the channel to defend these domains. After 1072 he made only four visits back to England and, like his descendent Richard I, treated England more as a source of revenue than a sovereign kingdom to be nurtured and developed. Even the Domesday Book had its gestation, in part, in William's need to quarter and provision a large army to meet a threatened invasion from King Swein of Denmark. Nonetheless this efficient piece of information management provided William with the most comprehensive list of who owned what in his new realm, giving him all the information he needed to tax, coerce and bribe his subjects in the future.

On 2nd November 1083 William's much loved wife Matilda died and the tough old soldier is said to have been inconsolable, crying for many days afterwards and vowing to abstain from sex from this time on. The last ten years of William's life were spent in conflict with Philip I of France and his own eldest son, Robert. He had designated Robert as his heir in Normandy but he made no move to give him any responsibility or power over it while he lived. The disgruntled Robert, easily seduced by William's enemies, became involved in their intrigues and at the siege of Gerberoi actually inflicted a wound on his father. Father and son settled their differences for a time but it did not last and by 1087 Robert was plotting with the King of France again.

William had spent much of his life in the saddle and it was the saddle that helped end it. Sometime in May 1087 he became ill enough to postpone an attack on Robert and Philip I until the summer. Whether this unknown illness contributed to his eventual death we shall never know for he rose from his sick bed, took charge of his army and crossed the channel to defeat the French. The war, as would often be the case for William's descendants, centred on the Vexin, a disputed territory between Rouen and Paris. In July William launched a surprise attack on the town of Mantes which he captured and put to the sword. The great warrior was now around sixty years old, had put on a lot of weight and probably suffered from a distension of his abdomen that made him look excessively corpulent. He may also have been suffering from some form of intestinal obstruction. William of Malmsbury describes William as riding through Mantes, which his troops were burning and pillaging, when his horse in leaping across a wide trench caused the high Norman pommel of his saddle to push hard into his distended belly and burst his bowels.

This injury, to the area between his legs and buttocks, caused the king to collapse in violent pain and the army to stall in its carnage. Damage of this kind could rupture the urethra. The surgeons attending the king quickly examined him and declared that his death was inevitable. The speed of their diagnosis suggests that they saw blood in his urine and, possibly, that it had also leaked outside the urethra visibly staining the abdomen. In great pain William was taken from Mantes to the Priory of St Gervaise near Rouen where physicians could attend him. They could do little to help. Reportedly enduring great pain William took a number of weeks to die. Uncharacteristically the tardy onset of death seems to have given him time to reflect on his violent and often barbarous life particularly his persecution of the Saxon English after Hastings. *'I have persecuted its [England's] native inhabitants beyond all reason. Whether noble or commons I have cruelly oppressed them; many I have unjustly disinherited'*. William had endowed many monasteries in preparation for this day hoping that they would help *'combat demons and sins of the flesh'*. As further insurance he directed that all his treasure in Rouen should be distributed to various churches and the poor, and that there should be an amnesty to all prisoners. Like the Confessor, William had a favourite abbey that he had built at Caen in the name of St Stephen and where he had earlier ordered that he should be buried. This foundation was part of a penance forced on him by the pope for ignoring his edict and marrying Matilda. The pope also insisted that Matilda should build an abbey and this she had also done in Caen, the Abbaye aux Dames, where she still lies buried.

William died 9th September 1087 and if his final days were tortured by memories of his past sins his funeral would have elements of a ghoulish burlesque. Firstly those around him as he died, fearing a break down of law and order on the publication of his death, took to their heels to protect their own property leaving unsupervised servants to plunder the bedchamber. They took everything that wasn't hammered or nailed down; his clothes, household linen, furniture, arms, silver and vestments all disappeared leaving William naked on the bare floor. Scenes like this would be repeated in the death chambers of other kings e.g. Henry II and Edward III and suggests that the circumstances surrounding the death of a medieval king could be as undignified and capricious as for any common man.

The Archbishop of Rouen gave an order that the king's body should be taken to the Monastery of St Stephen at Caen but no one was there to carry it out. Eventually an obscure Norman named Herluin arranged for William's body to be taken down the river Seine to Caen. From this boat a group of mourners lifted the corpse and set off in some semblance of a procession to the monastery but William was not to process smoothly. A severe fire on the route interrupted the mourners and the corpse had to be left while they scattered to help put it out. Further indignities were in store. As the king was carried towards the abbey altar a knight stepped forward and forbade the burial. He declared that the land on which the monastery was built had been taken from his family by force and without payment therefore the ground could not be regarded as legally consecrated.

William's youngest son Henry (later Henry I) chaired a quick meeting of those present and all agreed that the family had indeed been deprived of the land by force. The knight was given 60 shillings on the spot to cover the site of the grave together with a promise of a full restitution of his father's estate later. The knight agreed and William was ready to be consigned. However the stone coffin produced to take the king was now found to be too small for him. The swollen state of his body meant that it had to be squashed and forced into it but this undignified 'stuffing' caused the raddled corpse to burst and fill the church with such a horrible stench that the last rites had to be cut short to stop the congregation from fainting.

As he gloated over the mangled corpse of King Harold at Hastings William could never have imagined the macabre farce that would accompany his own end. The great warrior duke of Normandy and King of England, left alone, stripped of his possessions, dropped while a fire was extinguished, squashed into an absurd coffin, and only buried after some unseemly haggling over a slice of ground. Thereafter William rested in peace, for a time at least. Eventually that ill-fitting stone coffin was enclosed in a fine shrine built by William Rufus, his third son and successor as King of England. This remained undisturbed until 1532 when an inquisitive pope instructed that the tomb be opened and the body examined. Despite the 'bursting' the body was found to be in a fair state of preservation. Thirty years later some Calvinists invaded the church and tore up the tomb scattering the remains. One thighbone was all that could be found and in 1642 this was reburied under a monument that was itself replaced a century later. In 1783 in the midst of French revolutionary fervour this monument was also demolished and the thighbone mislaid. More recently the French government declared that a thighbone discovered in the old tomb did indeed belong to William and reburied it under a new tomb on 9th September 1987. A thighbone! All that remains of great William the only man to invade and successfully conquer England. No wonder the French were so keen to make his thighbone their own.

WILLIAM II (known as William Rufus) (born c1060 reigned 1087-1100)

William II known as William Rufus was born around 1060, the third son of William I and his wife Matilda of Flanders. His two elder brothers were Robert, known as Curthose, duke of Normandy and Richard, who died sometime before 1074. He had one younger brother Henry, who would succeed him as King Henry I, and five sisters. Tradition has it that as a youth Rufus was put into the household of the famous scholar and monk, Lanfranc who was Abbot of Caen. Later historians gave William the nickname Rufus, from his fair hair and ruddy complexion, and this name is used here to prevent confusion with his father.

As he lay dying near Rouen in 1087 William I faced the challenge of what to do with his great conquests. He had been in dispute with his eldest son Robert Curthose for some years before he died but at the time of William's death Robert had disappeared and no one knew where he was. During the five weeks of painful illness that preceded William's death he seems to have toyed with the idea of disinheriting Robert entirely in favour of Rufus. But in the end his Norman supporters persuaded him to at least confirm Robert as duke of Normandy. Williams's second son, Richard, had been killed in a hunting accident some thirteen years earlier, and so William left his crown of England to his third son, Rufus. He left his fourth son, Henry, the not inconsiderable fortune of £5,000 in silver, to be taken from the king's treasury.

Rufus had been deeply attached to his father, never wavering in his loyalty during the rebellions of his elder brother Robert and, as William lay dying, he gave Rufus leave to go to England to claim the crown and secure his inheritance before Robert had any chance to oppose him. The young Henry followed him, travelling speedily to Winchester, where the royal cash was held, to supervise the weighing out of his treasure. From there Henry returned to Normandy for his father's funeral and was able to pay the 60 shillings needed to secure his father's grave. On 26th September 1087 Rufus was crowned King William II of England by Archbishop Lanfranc in Westminster Abbey. He was twenty-seven years old and although an experienced soldier he had little knowledge of government. He was certainly helped in his audacious dash for the crown by Lanfranc's experienced hand, by the absence of many of the great lords in Normandy, and duke Robert's disappearance. When Robert eventually turned up in Normandy Odo, bishop of Bayeux, a half-brother of William the Conqueror, began organising a rebellion, in England, against Rufus and, with some other barons, secured a number of castles. Duke Robert, attended by his youngest brother Henry, prepared to invade England to join the rebels. He was too slow and too late. Rufus' speedy response soon had the rebellion in tatters and all the rebels in his hands.

Rufus, like his father was short, thickset and inclined to stoutness. He was a voluble companion with his friends in private but he was not an eloquent speaker in public and had a tendency to stutter when excited. He often covered this up by beginning a sentence with a blasphemy or by swearing. He could summon up a ferocious and intimidating temper when he wanted to but he had the bluff honour of a soldier when faced with a fellow soldier's defiance. He was renowned for his bravery and was famed for rarely losing a battle although he never fought a big pitched battle in his life. He declared that his men loved him so much that they would follow him through raging seas. Perhaps they were just hoping to survive long enough to benefit from his well known generosity. Brought up in the coarse world of his father's knights and soldiers, the military life in all its facets fascinated Rufus and he felt a brotherly bond with those who donned harness and armour whether they were with him or against him.

When Rufus became king in 1087 the Norman settlement of England was only 21 years old and, no great innovator or lawmaker, Rufus just worked on the template that his father had forged. He spent his first six years as king in England moving around the country, at some cost to his subjects, fighting the Welsh and protecting his northern borders against the Scots. His passion for hunting led him to extend the royal hunting preserves, particularly the forest sites, including his father's recent creation, the New Forest. These preserves were always unpopular with those who lived on or near them. They were subject to deadly penalties for the removal of any of the king's game and Rufus earned even more resentment by tightening up penalties and seeing that they were enforced with vigour. Rufus, like his father, was fortunate in the servants who guided him through the tedious work of administration. Despite his cynicism of church mystery and symbolism he could not help but use educated clerics as councillors and advisors, including Archbishop Lanfranc, and the Saxon, Wulfstan, bishop of Worcester. The recently completed Domesday Book, kept safely in the royal treasury at Winchester, was also a great aid to Rufus in administering England. To levy taxes a king required information and in the Domesday Book Rufus had all the information his tax-collectors needed, and Rufus was an energetic and ruthless tax collector.

A big spender needed big revenue and Rufus' efficient collectors made him a very rich king. Rufus also squeezed extra cash by raising the thresholds of taxes that the nobility had to pay to make family alliances or secure the continuity of their family estates. The death of a baron had always prompted payment of a 'relief' by his heir to secure his patrimony. Rufus amended this to his confiscating the land and the heir having to buy it back from him. He also required a payment before a baron could give any female member of his family away in marriage, he forced heiresses to remarry and charged them for the privilige, and he took into custody land left by a baron, who had died with under age children. When his brother Henry became king in 1100 the resentment against Rufus' oppressive taxes had built up to such an extent that Henry thought it best to quickly declare that he would renounce the late kings 'unjust exactions'.

In February 1091, having made peace with Robert, Rufus crossed over to Normandy to help him secure his duchy and their relationship seemed to improve. But by Christmas of the same year they had quarrelled again. These quarrels put a strain on the normally straightforward lines of feudal duty and obligation. Many of the Norman nobility held estates on both sides of the channel and the disputes between Robert and Rufus put them on the horns of a huge dilemma. Rufus' half-uncle, the one-time rebel, Odo, Bishop of Bayeux, put his finger on it: 'how can we give proper service to two mutually hostile and distant lords? If we serve Duke Robert well we shall offend his brother William, and he will deprive us of our revenues and honours in England. On the other hand if we obey King William, Duke Robert will deprive us of our patrimonies in Normandy'. A classic medieval 'no win' situation!

A solution, of sorts, arose in 1096 when Robert took the cross to join the first crusade. Robert crossed over to England and a papal legate brokered a deal between the brothers whereby Rufus paid Robert 10,000 marks in silver for the custody and revenues of Normandy for the next three years. For Rufus this was cheap at the price. Young Henry was mollified by being given two counties in Normandy and duke Robert left them both in September 1095 with everyone expecting that he would never return. Rufus now had all of his father's land but, like his father, he had to fight others to keep it. This meant Rufus had to spend much more time in Normandy to restore all the borders secured by his father. William I had died after fighting at Mante, in the Vexin, in the Seine valley. This border territory would always remain a matter of dispute between the future kings of England and France. Rufus couldn't dislodge the French heir Louis (later Louis VI) from the Vexin, but he did build the great castle of Gisors which remained a key Norman stronghold there, against the French, until it was lost by King John in 1203.

Both in England and in Normandy William's mixture of sly diplomacy, military skill and bribery proved effective in maintaining his domains. Despite these qualities the history of these times was being written by monks who didn't like him and he, in turn, had little respect for them. Rufus believed that his father had been too generous in giving land and treasure to the church (William's bad conscience again!) leaving him insufficient revenues to fund the military operations that were still necessary to define and hold the borders of England and Normandy. One way he resolved this was to keep vacant church offices empty so that he could siphon off the income. In this he was always selective. As abbeys bought in more cash than bishoprics he concentrated on not replacing abbots. At the time of his death he was enjoying the revenues from three bishoprics and twelve abbeys.

In 1093 when he was taken ill and thought he might die and need a reference to keep him out of purgatory Rufus appointed Anselm, a devoted scholar monk, as Archbishop of Canterbury. Given their respective personalities it was inevitable that as soon as Rufus got better they would quarrel. Rufus wanted more cash from the Church while Anselm was busy reforming the Church, ordering his clergy to put away their wives and prohibiting their sons from inheriting their father's benefices, all along the lines of the reforms started by Pope Gregory VII. These reforms also proclaimed that churchmen should be appointed by churchmen rather than by kings or other nobles.

This was not a reform that Rufus wanted. The Domesday Book showed that the Church owned about one quarter of the entire wealth of England and Rufus and his lords were not going to give up the slice they took, via their appointment of abbots and priests, easily. Anselm strongly supported Pope Urban II who had taken up Gregory VII's 'free the church' anthem but, like Thomas Becket years later, the rest of Anselm's bishops advocated compromise. They were not prepared to oppose or confront the king outright. The English Church and state were starting that journey into controversy that would surface many times later between kings, archbishops and popes. Not known for his interest in religious affairs Rufus really preferred more of a fuzzy ambivalence in these matters and he found Anselm's stubborn 'radicalism' annoying. This dispute rumbled on, eventually resulting in Anselm choosing to go into exile in November 1097 and Rufus happily seizing all the property of the See of Canterbury. Outliving Rufus, Anselm would return to quarrel with the next king!

Rufus' acquisitive habits were accompanied by a passion for personal pleasure and adornment. He enjoyed wearing his blonde hair long and parted in the middle, shamelessly showing a bare forehead! He loved garish jewellery, dancing and hunting. He was a bit of a dandy and wore short tunics and shoes with impossible curled up points. The gaiety, licentiousness and effeminate behaviour of his court, appalled contemporary churchmen. They were quick to discern that, ever wilfully unconventional, and never being linked with a queen or a mistress, or fathering any children, Rufus' libertine behaviour might be finding outlets in darker, more forbidden ways. These monkish scribes were probably fascinated by the stories they heard about Rufus: a possible homosexual, an atheist, a blasphemer, a conspicuous consumer of trifles, he had all the ingredients of modern celebrity and they were writing it all down.

Seemingly at the height of his success Rufus was killed on 2nd August 1100 by a stray arrow while hunting in the New Forest. A controversial life was capped by an equally controversial death. It seems that there were two parties hunting in the New Forest on that day. One made up of the king with just one attendant (unusual in itself) and a larger party that was hunting with the king's younger brother Henry. The story that gained most currency by chroniclers was that the king, contrary to his usual custom, went hunting in the afternoon attended by one Walter Tirel, count of Poix, near Amiens. They had both dismounted to wait for the beaters to drive the deer across their path when the Frenchman, keen to show off his prowess with the crossbow, let fly an arrow at a passing stag. The arrow missed the stag but glanced off a tree and struck Rufus in his breast killing him outright. Tirel ran from the scene without informing anyone of the incident and promptly took ship for France.

When it was realised that the king was missing a search was made and a charcoal burner named Purkiss is supposed to have found the body with the arrow still in place. It has fascinated historians ever since that the unpopular Rufus was killed while his younger brother Henry was in the vicinity. Henry had long coveted the crown of England and seems to have responded to the news of his brother's death with alacrity, anticipation even? Yet again Henry sped off to Winchester, this time to seize all the royal treasure and have himself proclaimed king. His brother's body followed slowly behind, on the charcoal burner's cart.

The monks at the abbey of St Swithin in Winchester were horrified to have to deal with the body of the blaspheming enemy of the Church and buried it quickly with few holy rites and no ceremony. Henry was not there, having moved on to London to be crowned in Westminster Abbey on Sunday 5th August. Proclaimed and crowned within three days? Perhaps Henry was prepared? His elder brother, Robert, was still away, jouneying home from the first crusade, and so any claim he might make would have to face the reality of Henry's possession. Rufus was supposed to have been buried under one of the great towers at Winchester and there is a plain purbeck and limestone tomb there long thought to be his grave. However modern scholarship has confirmed this as the tomb of Henry of Blois (brother of King Stephen) Bishop of Winchester 1129-71.

Winchester Cathedral is home to six mortuary chests resting on top of the presbytery screens, one chest between each bay on each side. These chests are supposed to have been put there in 1525 on the orders of Bishop Fox and contain (or contained) the bones of some pre-conquest kings and bishops. One of these chests bears an inscription declaring that it holds the bones of William Rufus along with those of the Danish King Cnut, adding a nice little question mark over the exact site of Rufus' remains. These chests were opened at the time of Oliver Cromwell and all the bones shifted and chucked around as the playthings of parliamentary soldiers. The contents of each chest is now pure conjecture and Rufus' bones (if there) may well be scattered between two or even three of them. The burial of Rufus was unexpected and unwanted. So it is not surprising that when the central tower of Winchester collapsed and fell into the church one year after his burial in 1101 many godly people saw it as retribution for giving a Christian grave to a monstrous agent of the ungodly. But even the chroniclers who recorded the collapse note that *'it would have fallen down in any case because it was so badly built'*.

Rufus only reigned for 13 years and perhaps his real memorial stands not in Winchester but in two great monuments still visible in London. He took the trouble to complete and improve the tower fortress that his father had started in London and that we call the Tower of London. And he was personally responsible for commissioning, and building the magnificent Westminster Hall that was completed in 1099. At almost 240 feet long and 68 feet wide (covering an area of about half an acre) it has been the scene of many important events in English history including the trials of Thomas More, Charles I, the Gunpowder Plot conspirators and Warren Hastings. It was also often the venue for the post-coronation banquets held by many future kings. More pertinent to the present work it has also been the place where many monarchs, and some distinguished statesmen, were later to lie in state. The first of such was a statesman, William Gladstone (1898), followed by Edward VII (1910), George V (1936), George VI (1952), Queen Mary (1953), Sir Winston Churchill (1965) and Queen Elizabeth the Queen Mother (2002). The magnificent hammer-beam roof structure was designed and installed during the reign of Richard II. Rufus was said to have boasted that this hall was just a *'mere bed chamber'* compared to the royal palace he intended to put beside it. An accidental or purposeful crossbow bolt put paid to that dream.

HENRY I (born 1068 reigned 1100-1135)

The fourth and youngest son of William the Conqueror and Matilda of Flanders, Henry was the great opportunist of the family. He was born after his father had sired a succession of five daughters and two years after he had conquered England (*'born in the purple'* they said). This latter endowment seems to have given Henry a life-long belief that he had a much stronger claim to the English throne than either of his older brothers. Henry was the first English king since Alfred the Great to be literate, and to be educated, to some extent, in the liberal arts. His literacy marked him out from his father and brothers and, from the 14th century onwards, he came to be styled as 'Henry Beauclerc'.

Henry was present at his father's death. William I, having left Normandy to Robert and England to Rufus, left Henry £5,000, a serious treasure for the time. Henry had also been left his mother's lands in England but Rufus granted these to one of his own councillors and there is no evidence that Henry ever enjoyed their revenues. However Henry's liquidity came in handy during the spring of 1088, when his brother, Robert Curthose, needed cash to organise an invasion of England to defeat Rufus. For £3,000 Robert sold, or pawned, a whole chunk of western Normandy to Henry, including the abbey of Mont San Michel after which Henry, no longer landless, assumed the title of count of the Cotentin.

Henry spent the next eleven years fighting first for Robert and then for Rufus as their tug-of-war for supremacy zigzagged across Normandy. In 1090 he helped Robert defeat the rich merchants of Rouen who, encouraged by Rufus, rebelled against their duke. This conflict ended in a bloody fight through the streets of the city. While duke Robert sought refuge in a church Henry and his men emerged triumphant and one of the leading rebels fell into Henry's hands. Henry took him to the top of a tower in Rouen castle and pushed him off to his death below; declaring that it was no more than a reasonable punishment for a rebel. The poor man's body was then tied to a horse's tail and dragged through the streets of the city as an example.

Robert's gratitude to Henry was short-lived. In 1091 Rufus brought his army to north-eastern Normandy ready to challenge Robert who, with no church to hide in, soon capitulated. They agreed to make peace and to divide Normandy between them, to the exclusion of Henry, who they besieged at Mont San Michel. Cut off from help and short of water Henry was forced to leave the abbey with only his baggage and a few companions. For a year Henry became a homeless, wanderer until the citizens of the hilltop castle of Domfront invited him to rule them. All they asked was that they could keep their traditional customs and that Henry would agree never to abandon them. Henry, in need of a home, agreed and this citadel was all Henry had to his name until Rufus again made overtures to Henry to help him fight Robert.

Henry's two brothers, once so joined together at Mont San Michel, were now in disagreement again and, supported by Rufus, Henry led raids across Normandy until he had reclaimed most of his old lands in the western side of the duchy. In 1096 something of a breakthrough in brotherly quarrels emerged when Robert mortgaged Normandy to Rufus before leaving to go on crusade. After this Henry stayed close to Rufus, remaining on good terms with him until his death. Henry's seizure of the throne in August 1100 has to be seen in the context of the ever-swinging pendulum that characterised relations between him and his brothers after their father's death in 1087. Henry never forgot that agreement between Rufus and Robert in 1091 that sent him into poverty, and excluded him from inheriting either England or Normandy. Henry was clever and he soon surrounded himself with clever advisors. After Rufus' death he was accompanied by two brothers Henry and Robert Beaumont. Both intelligent men, with vast holdings in England and France who, between them, probably helped Henry put together his all important coronation charter.

Aware of the damage Rufus had done to the crown's reputation Henry's own coronation charter explicitly disavowed the misconduct of his predecessor and promised justice, good government and the upholding of the laws of Edward the Confessor. The Anglo Saxon Chronicle noted: '*in his days, no man dared to wrong another. He made peace for man and beasts*'. This, the first coronation charter to be written down and published widely, immediately put distance between Henry and Rufus and advertised his intention to return to the laws of a king revered both by the church and the nobility. Away would go those excessive payments to retain a family's land, there would be no charges for heiresses or widows to marry, and the revenues of the church during vacancies would not be touched. This was music to the ears of both church and barons. Although Henry broke parts of this oath later, the sale of heiresses in particular became a handy source of cash, for now it advertised a sea change in the exercise of royal management that all parties welcomed. It was a masterstroke of public relations and papered over the audacity of Henry's move in pre-empting his elder brother.

Robert Curthose returned from his crusade in the autumn of 1100 to resume the lordship of Normandy that he had mortgaged to Rufus. As he had done in 1088 Robert also wanted England and he invaded with an army to take on Henry in July 1101. Henry always preferred negotiation to war and the brothers came to an accord that satisfied both parties. It was a fragile peace and Henry spent his time after 1101 building up support among the Norman barons ready for the next confrontation. Henry and Robert engaged in two more, inconclusive struggles before, in September 1106, Henry won a decisive victory over Robert at the battle of Tinchebrai about 40 miles east of Avranches. Henry took his brother prisoner and he was not going to let him go! Henry, like his father, was now King of England and duke of Normandy. He had re-forged his father's Anglo-Norman state under one rule and his policy now would be to put in place mechanisms to keep it.

The unfortunate Robert Curthose, who might have been England's first King Robert if the dice had fallen another way, showed precious little sign of martial accomplishment during his wars with Rufus or Henry. But he seems to have found his form against the Muslims during the first crusade. In fact he acquitted himself so well that he was offered the honour (or was it the poison chalice?) of becoming King of Jerusalem. After being captured at Tinchebrai he was held a prisoner for the rest of his life (28 years) in various English castles. He died in Cardiff Castle in 1134 aged eighty, just a few months before Henry I also died. Robert is buried beneath the Chapter House in Gloucester Cathedral. He has a fine bright red effigy, carved from Irish bog oak, with legs crossed and in crusader's armour, made a century after his death. This is one of the finest wooden effigies in England and is possibly a tribute from some warriors of the third crusade to the memory of a hero of the first. It rests on a 15th century tomb chest in the South Ambulatory.

Soon after his accession Henry made one of his sharpest moves by marrying Princess Matilda, daughter of King Malcolm III of Scotland. As well as securing his northern border, this strengthened his claim to the throne. Matilda's mother was a sister of Edgar the Atheling and a granddaughter of Edmund Ironside; their children would thus have a direct line back to Alfred the Great and the old Wessex line of kings, as well as to Norman William. Matilda, though not taking any vows, had been raised in a convent and some contemporaries alleged that by wearing a nun's habit she had given up her right to marriage. When Stephen was looking around for reasons to discredit Henry and Matilda's daughter, the Empress Matilda, in 1135 his supporters rooted out this old chestnut as evidence of her bastardy. Henry's union with Matilda was fruitful but not lucky. They had three children but one of their sons died young and their remaining son, William, died in the 'white ship' that capsized amid drunken partying as they left harbour for England on 25th November 1120. His only remaining legitimate child was his daughter Matilda, but Henry was both fruitful and lucky with his children born out of wedlock.

After Rufus' questionable sexuality the history-writing monks now had an overtly heterosexual king to scribble about. Henry acknowledged over twenty illegitimate children (still a record for an English king) one of them by Nesta, the daughter of Rhys ap Tewdr (pronounced 'Tudor'), ruling prince of South Wales. The by-product of such an extensive family meant that Henry had a batch of natural sons who, when older, could don armour and sword for their father, and a brood of daughters to marry off to important men who would then be linked to him by strong family ties. Henry managed to marry his natural daughters off in an almost geo-political configuration around the edges of his Anglo-Norman domains. He did build great castles on his frontiers but the princes his daughter's married, in Brittany, Montmirail, the French Vexin and Scotland were a far stronger wall against the predations of Louis of France.

Henry made another clever move when, shortly after his coronation, he recalled the troublesome Archbishop Anselm from exile in 1100. Anslem was one of the most respected churchmen of his time but he had not changed: he still wanted church supremacy over church appointments. Like Rufus, Henry would not agree and in 1103 Anselm volunteered for exile again and stayed in the city of Lyons. He returned to Henry in 1106 and accepted the compromise that abbots and bishops should do homage to the king for their lands but they would be appointed from and by the church. In practice, at least for the time being, this meant that Henry preserved the reality of royal control. Anselm is important for initiating a debate that would later see the edicts of popes as a much more powerful force in English church affairs than had been the case before. Sixty years after Anselm's death another Archbishop, Thomas Becket, (who, ironically, petitioned for Anselm's sainthood) would make a similar stand against royal authority but he would not die in his bed.

The rift with Anselm had left a number of major ecclesiastical appointments vacant. Henry's new accord with Anselm meant that he could get on with appointing intelligent men to bishoprics who could help him manage his state. One of these was Roger, Bishop of Salisbury, a man of extraordinary energy and ability. He directed royal administration throughout Henry's reign and even served as Regent in England after 1123. Roger helped Henry redesign the royal accounting system which became known as the exchequer and began the records of its annual audits known as the pipe rolls. This department now became the main financial department of an increasingly bureaucratic government.

The department of the exchequer comprised a department of receipt, the Lower Exchequer, and an office of audit known as the Upper Exchequer. It gained its name from the chequered table-cloth which served as a counting board on which calculations were made in the sight of both sheriffs and exchequer officials. Henry also busied himself with other major reforms including one, very important one, as far as his subjects were concerned, relating to the provisioning of his court as it moved about the country. Rufus had often passed through his kingdom like a marauding wind, pillaging the countryside to feed his entourage. Henry put a stop to this setting out strict rules regarding the requisition of supplies and laying down fixed prices for their purchase. He also arranged that key officers of his household should receive a fixed daily allowance for their bread, wine, candles and other consumables obviating their need to live off the land. The minting of coinage, with so many mints scattered about the country, was always a problem and Henry clamped down on false coining and 'clipping' with severe penalties for those who broke his rules. Henry drew most of the great magnates of England into his government by the systematic and calculated use of patronage. Gone were the days of indiscriminate gifts, awards, offices and appointments, now reason and order would govern how the king disposed of his patronage.

The peace of Tinchebrai made in 1106 was no guarantee of peace in troublesome Normandy and from 1111 onwards Henry was enmeshed in an almost constant struggle against the fluctuating alliance of Anjou, Flanders and King Louis VI of France. The fulcrum on which this anti-Henry movement rested was Robert Curthose's son, William Clito.

Always a skilled negotiator Henry looked to his family to bring in new allies. In 1110 Henry arranged for his daughter, Matilda, to marry Henry V, emperor and King of Germany, and in June 1119 he persuaded Foulke V of Anjou to break with Louis VI and to marry his daughter (also named Matilda) to Henry's son, William. All seemed to be going Henry's way until young William died in the 'white ship' in 1120. This put both his dreams of a male succession in England, and peace with Anjou, in jeopardy. Henry's queen, Matilda, had died in 1118 but having proved himself to be a fertile partner, and wasting no time after the death of young William, Henry married Alice of Louvan. Surprisingly, despite Henry's previous fecundity, their fifteen year marriage would prove to be childless. This lack of a second family seems to have been something to do with Henry as, after his death, Alice remarried and bore several children.

Yet another death, this time of the emperor Henry V in 1125, left Henry's daughter, Matilda, a young widow. With his own marriage barren and his daughter widowed Henry needed some sign that his dynasty was going to continue. In January 1127 he gathered all his nobles together in a big set-piece occasion for them to swear fealty to Matilda as the rightful heir to England and Normandy. His illegitimate son Robert earl of Gloucester and his nephew Stephen of Blois vied with each other to be first to show their loyalty and swear the oath. Stephen was the son of Henry's sister, Adela of Blois, and Henry was very fond of him. After all this oath-taking, and in order to salvage his alliance with Anjou against William Clito, Henry arranged for the twenty-five year old Matilda to marry the fourteen-year-old Geoffrey of Anjou and the wedding took place in June 1128. The death of William Clito, six weeks after this marriage, ended the crisis that had prompted it and brought an end to most of the opposition to Henry in Normandy.

For the last seven years of Henry's life he was able to rule his Norman domains in peace. However, peace in marriage was something that Matilda and Geoffrey of Anjou were finding hard to achieve. They disliked each other, their domestic life was turbulent and Matilda went home to father. It was beginning to look as if Henry would not live to see his dynasty continue after all. A great council of king and barons agreed that Matilda should go back to Geoffrey, and Matilda complied. Although not the most romantic of reconciliations it did have the desired effect. Matilda gave birth to a son, the future Henry II on 5th March 1133. Although the Anglo-Norman succession now looked secure the 'happy' parents turned their anger on Henry, demanding that he hand over all the castles that they claimed he had promised them at the time of their wedding. Henry refused and all parties left each other nursing grievances. Matilda would never see her father again.

During December 1135 King Henry I returned from hunting and sat down to a dinner of lampreys, an ugly eel like fish with a sucker on its head, by which it sucks the life out of its prey. According to the chronicler, Henry of Huntingdon, Henry was exceedingly fond of this dish, though his physicians had forbidden him to eat them. After this dinner he became very ill. Henry had always had a great fear of assassination and so his doctors would have taken great pains to prove that they had advised him to avoid this particular food. The speed of the illness points to some form of acute gastrointestinal condition such as a duodenal perforation. This would cause peritonitis, fever, vomiting, rapid collapse and a speedy death. Many writers describe Henry as dying from Ptomaine poisoning. This is a generic name for certain alkaloid bodies found in putrefying animal and vegetable matter that can be very poisonous. This would suggest that the lampreys were possibly not fit for consumption – perhaps bought a few days earlier and stored, prepared or cooked badly (they have poisonous filaments on their back which must be removed before cooking) – but nothing about the condition of the fish was ever noted. Henry died on the night of the 1st December 1135 aged 67. Before dying he was asked who should succeed him and he *'assigned all lands on both sides of the sea to his daughter in lasting and lawful succession'*, but did not mention Matilda's husband, Geoffrey count of Anjou, because of *'his threats and insults'*.

Henry was at his castle of Lyons-la-Foret in Normandy at the time of his death but his last wish was that he should be buried at the Cluniac (later Benedictine) abbey, he had started to build in 1121, at Reading in England. The building was not yet completed but despite fierce competition from a number of Norman monasteries, including Rouen, (it was always a big pull to have a king's tomb in a church) his wishes were complied with. This would entail a long journey by land and sea and so some preservation of the corpse would be necessary.

The day after his death the body was taken to the Church of our Lady in Rouen attended by a huge escort of 20,000 men. There, at night (according to William of Malmsbury), in certain recesses of the church the body was disembowelled and roughly embalmed, and the entrails taken for burial at the church of St Mary de Pratis near Rouen. According to Oderic *'the gross body of the king was opened by a skilful butcher and preserved with fragrant balsam'* and then completely covered in bulls' hides to be carried on an uncoffined bier perhaps covered by a pall of herseloth. In an incident reminiscent of his 'bursting' father one chronicler reported that the king's body gave off a foul and offensive stench after death (those lampreys must have been bad!) and that the man who extracted the brain through the king's nose during its embalming suffered so much from the smell that he died in great pain a few days later. From Rouen, the king's body was taken to Caen, and the abbey Church of St Stephen where his father, William the Conqueror, was buried. Here it lay for most of December, *'until winter should grow a little milder and bring gentler breezes'*. Such a 'breeze' came soon after Christmas 1135 and the king's body was taken by ship to England and then to the abbey Church at Reading in Berkshire. This was now far enough advanced in its construction for Henry to be buried in a grave before the high altar.

His funeral, on 5th January 1136, was attended by his queen (his second wife) Adelaide of Louvan, the new king, Stephen of Blois, the two archbishops and most of the bishops and nobles of England. The queen gave a hundred shillings for the maintenance of a lamp to burn constantly over his grave and a fine effigy, possibly not unlike those of his Plantagenet descendents at Fontevrault, was erected over the spot. The church was not finally consecrated until 1164, a ceremony overseen by Archbishop Thomas Becket in the presence of Henry II and many nobles. The abbey was suppressed at the dissolution and part of the building was made a royal lodging that was used occasionally by Henry VIII, Edward VI and Queen Mary Tudor. The last abbot, who like Sir Thomas More would not acknowledge Henry VIII's supremacy of the Church in England, was executed as a traitor in 1539 outside the abbey's inner gateway. A story gained currency in the sixteenth century that Henry was buried in a silver coffin and it is thought that this inspired workmen demolishing the choir (to help with the rebuilding of St Mary's in Reading) to break into his tomb. Frustrated at finding only a stone sarcophagus they are supposed to have scattered the royal remains. Today Reading Abbey is a poor ruin and all that reminds us of Henry the great administrator and opportunist is a small plaque in the south transept close to his last resting place and a large memorial cross in the Forbury Gardens.

Henry I was ruthless, energetic, opportunistic, cruel, efficient and clever. Perhaps the cleverest of all the Conqueror's children he ruled England with firmness, skill and cunning for thirty-five years. Unlike his father and brothers Henry was also careful, sober and methodical. His cruel punishments, mutilations and the incarceration of his brother Robert for so long, often offended his contemporaries and some later historians have characterised his reign as oppressive and savage. But he worked within the standards of the time, standards which at 800 years distance we can hardly begin to comprehend. The silly quarrel with Matilda and Geoffrey in 1135, though none of them could have known it at the time, would prove to be a catalyst for a most horrendous and tragic civil war. By not having being in contact with her father for several months and by not being at his bedside when he died, Matilda was not on the spot to claim her inheritance. If she had been it is highly likely that her claim to both England and Normandy would have been supported without hesitation by the barons and churchmen assembled there. Stephen of Blois, count of Boulogne, would not have been able to race to England to steal the crown and England would have been spared one of its most bloody and miserable civil wars.

Henry I, Archbishop Anselm and Roger of Salisbury may seem dull and dreary after the colour and controversy of the two Williams, but from 1106 until his death in 1135, despite his problems in Normandy, there was no revolt against Henry in England. A king who could keep the peace, in England, for over 30 years deserved to have had his bones rest in peace.

STEPHEN (born c1097 reigned 1135-1154)
MATILDA (born1102 reigned as uncrowned Queen of England for five months between 1141 and 1142)

King Stephen (often styled Stephen of Blois) was born around 1097 the son of Adela, daughter of William the Conqueror and her husband Stephen count of Blois. King Henry I liked Stephen and treated him extremely well, granting him estates on both sides of the channel. By 1130 Stephen was the richest man in Henry's domains, while his brother Henry of Blois, Abbot of Glastonbury and Bishop of Winchester, was the richest churchman in England. The Blois family were thus very well set up and Henry's generosity to such a close male relative could have sent out mixed messages to the very male baronial caste of the time. It was widely known that Stephen was Henry's favourite nephew and Stephen was considered by his contemporaries to be an honourable and popular man. William of Malmsbury noted that, *'he had by his good nature and the way he jested, sat and ate in the company of even the humblest,, earned an affection that can hardly be imagined'.*

At the time of Henry I's death his daughter, and heir, Matilda was married to, and had two sons by, Geoffrey of Anjou. Despite a generally miserable marriage to Matilda it was this count Geoffrey who, by the token of wearing a sprig of broom in his helmet ('planta genesta'), would father the first of that line of kings we call the Plantagenets. Matilda had quarrelled with her father some months before he died and was not present at his deathbed. As soon as he heard of Henry I's death, and, despite having been the first to swear the oath to support Matilda in 1127, Stephen, took advantage of the split between Matilda and her father, and seized the initiative. He hastened to London from his base in Boulogne where he was quickly accepted as king by the leading Londoners. From London he moved on to Winchester to seize the royal treasure and secure the support of his younger brother, Bishop Henry.

Matilda, based in Normandy, was outmanoeuvred by this fast and fancy footwork. All the chroniclers report disorder and confusion after Henry I's death particularly in Normandy. Once the Normans heard of the king's death they, *'rushed out hungrily like ravening wolves to plunder and ravage mercilessly'.* Normandy was *'set on fire by the treacheries of the Normans'.* England was not immune to the opportunists who saw justice and peace buried with King Henry and *'...every man, seized by a strange passion for violence, raged cruelly against his neighbour and reckoned himself the more glorious the more guiltily he attacked the innocent'.*

Stephen was quick to gather support from all those who opposed the oath in support of Matilda, as Henry's heir in 1127, and he produced a variety of justifications that they could be happy with. One was that Henry had imposed it on his lords and that an oath not freely taken was invalid, and thus by breaking it no one committed perjury. Another justification was the welcome given to him by London and the ancient right of its leading citizens to choose their king. At a time of such uncertainty the preference of London's citizens would be for the immediate recognition of a king in order to forestall damage to business and further dangers to the realm. Whatever the justifications Stephen conjured up for his action the result was going to be the usual struggle for supremacy by the two contenders. But in this case the wars just went on and on for nineteen years until in the end both sides were worn out by it.

That was all in the future. For now Stephen got on with ruling his new kingdom, making peace with David, King of the Scots, and holding a fabulous Easter court in London. Stephen crossed into Normandy in March 1137 and was there in May when Geoffrey of Anjou began his invasion of the duchy. After making a speedy truce with Geoffrey, Stephen returned to England in December where he had to go north to deal with the Scots who had broken the terms of the recent treaty and were harrying Northumberland. During 1138 a series of armed risings against Stephen, by barons in the west country, led by Matilda's half-brother, Robert earl of Gloucester, fuelled rumours that Matilda was coming to England to claim the crown by force. Matilda had decided to invade England and she arrived in the autumn of 1139 staying initially with Adelaide of Louvan, the widow of her father, Henry I, at her castle at Arundel. Incredibly Stephen allowed Matilda to leave Arundel and move on to Bristol a courtesy that no one other than Stephen could understand. The generous and lenient Stephen was yet to learn how to make war. During the first half of 1140 Stephen ran about his kingdom without a plan, without a strategy, just 'fire-fighting' challenges by rebellious subjects as and when they arose.

In February 1141 Stephen's journeying came to an end after he was captured by Robert of Gloucester's forces while he was besieging Lincoln castle. Stephen fought bravely, on foot, swinging a great Norse axe during the battle but many of his forces, who had not expected to have to fight a pitch battle, drifted away. The king was taken by Matilda to Bristol Castle where he was kept in close confinement and as Matilda rejected all the terms offered for his release many of his supporters never expected to see him again. By June 1141 Matilda was acclaimed queen and began negotiating with Londoners for her coronation. Unfortunately her 'imperial' arrogance, financial demands, and poor judgement set the city against her and they chased her away tucking into her 'coronation' feast as she went. But for her haughty temper she might have kept the kingdom there and then. It was not to be and the wars went on.

Stephen's wife, also named Matilda, kept his campaigns going while her husband was a prisoner and Empress Matilda lost all the advantage she had when her most important ally Robert of Gloucester was captured and she had to return Stephen in exchange for him. The liberated Stephen celebrated being 'king' again by wearing his crown at the traditional Christmas feast at Westminster, but news of his capture at Lincoln had disturbed the fragile peace in Normandy. Duke Geoffrey, seizing his chance, invaded the duchy once again in 1141. In this war of capture and be captured Matilda had her own 'miraculous' escape. In 1142 while besieged in Oxford Castle she was reportedly lowered from the walls of the castle in a basket at night. Then wearing a white cloak she escaped in the snow across the frozen Thames to join her followers. Matilda's great ally Robert of Gloucester died in October 1147 and although she stayed in the West country, as a thorn in Stephen's side for a time, she had begun to lose heart. She was not really achieving anything and in early 1148 she returned to join her husband Geoffrey in Normandy. Geoffrey had been busy taking Normandy bit by bit, piece by piece until his complete victory, with the fall of Rouen, in 1144. His victory was followed by his investiture as duke of Normandy. Geoffrey died in August 1151 and Matilda now transferred all her hopes for gaining her birthright in England to her son, duke Henry of Normandy, (later Henry II). Stephen seems to have underestimated the importance of Normandy in the cross channel mix of lands owned by his own supporters having visited it only once, during 1137.

By the early 1150's the barons on both sides of the civil war were becoming war-weary. More and more barons and church leaders began to believe that although Stephen, as an anointed king, should keep the crown, young duke Henry of Normandy, rather than Stephen's son Eustace, should be named as his rightful heir. Once this idea gained ground among Stephen's supporters the question of 'what are we fighting for' was bound to arise. Stephen must have been aware of this. Unlike Henry I he never asked his barons to swear allegiance to Eustace. After all it was he who had proved how useless that big public oath-taking event had been. Instead Stephen sought to get the blessing of his bishops by having Eustace anointed (as was the French Capitian custom) king while Stephen was still alive. But the bishops would not play ball falling back on the old line that his son could not succeed him as Stephen had acquired the crown illegally, by perjury. Stephen locked the bishops up for a time but soon released them on seeing the futility of a battle with a united church.

With Matilda in Normandy urging on her son Henry and Stephen trying to get Eustace accepted as his heir the balance of activity was shifting from the older to the younger generation. Of the two sons fate seemed to be on the side of young Henry. In early 1150 Geoffrey had invested his son as duke of Normandy and, after Geoffrey's death, Henry also became count of Anjou. Henry's star was definitely in the ascendant. Building on his good fortune Henry surprised Stephen by sailing to England in January 1153, a perilous voyage to make in midwinter. He would meet a king in mourning. Stephen's beloved wife Matilda of Boulogne had died in 1152. She had been a constant source of strength to Stephen, loyal and steadfast she had mustered armies and taken them about England to wherever they were needed and he was devastated by her loss.

On a cold January morning duke Henry's and King Stephen's armies faced each other across a flooded River Avon near Malmsbury. The two opponents sat in their tents as heavy rain drenched their armies, the weather almost a metaphor for how everyone felt about this endless war. The two opponents did not clash here by the river instead they agreed a truce. Stephen retired to London while Henry stayed in the west giving out grants to the church and to his own followers, and a few bribes to his opponents. This was a time when some key supporters deserted Stephen and those that stayed by him were only playing a game of 'wait and see'. None of them had the stomach for a full blown confrontation with duke Henry. Peace negotiations were already going on behind the scenes before yet another stand off between the armies occurred at Wallingford in August 1152. Again no one wanted to fight.

Stephen, exhausted by grief, had lost the will to go on campaigning and the two armies at Wallingford rested while negotiations for a perpetual peace were begun. The negotiations produced, more or less what everyone expected. Stephen would rule England for his lifetime but duke Henry would be recognised as his heir and succeed him after his death. This was not what Stephen's son Eustace wanted to hear and he left his father's court in a rage. Fate joined Henry's side yet again when Eustace died suddenly on 17th August. This added grief brought the curtain down on any fight that Stephen had left and he ratified the terms of the Wallingford accord at Winchester on 6th November 1152. Duke Henry left England for Normandy in April 1153 after fears that he might be assassinated by Flemish mercenaries. Despite all the trouble taken to put the treaty of 1152 together it still depended on Stephen's cooperation and goodwill. Though tired and worn out no one would have predicted his death, at Dover, at the age of fifty-seven, less than two years after that negotiated peace.

Gervaise of Canterbury says that *'the king was suddenly seized with pain in the iliac region (the area just above the groin) along with a discharge from haemorrhoids'*. The sudden onset, the pain just above the groin and the passage of blood from the anus suggests that the king died of a ruptured abscess of the appendix (leading to peritonitis) accompanied by bleeding from piles. About eight hundred and fifty years later King Edward VII was the victim of a similar attack but was saved thanks to advances in medical science. The following year, the delay is not accounted for in any written record, Stephen's body was taken for burial to the abbey at Faversham in Kent where his wife Matilda of Boulogne and his son Eustace were also buried. His tomb is yet another casualty of the dissolution of the monasteries, with his monument being destroyed and his body thrown into a nearby river. One story has it that he was buried (or re-buried) in the church of St Mary of Charity in Faversham but there are no records available to prove this.

For virtually the whole nineteen years of his reign Stephen had to struggle with the Empress Matilda to keep his crown. Some later chroniclers declared that *'Christ and his saints slept'* while these two combatants captured, escaped and re-captured each other in a violent game of martial chess across the land. It would have been no consolation to Stephen to know that his successor would also die tired and worn out by the ravages of war and family betrayal. Stephen's great adversary Empress Matilda died in Rouen in 1167 aged sixty-four. Whatever her failings she had been a formidable woman. She had been married to an Emperor and to a count of Anjou who conquered Normandy. She had fought in many battles.

She had been a Queen of England for five months and she gave birth to a future King of England whose domains would stretch from Scotland to the Pyrenees. She mellowed in old age, retired to Rouen and lived for thirteen years after her son Henry II became King of England. She also became his trusted advisor; he valued her council and she helped mediate for him during various quarrels. She was buried first at the abbey of Bec in Normandy and then later reburied in the Cathedral at Rouen. Her epitaph reads *'Here lies the daughter, wife and mother of Henry'*.

HENRY II (born 1133 reigned 1154-1189)

Henry II, King of England, duke of Anjou, duke of Normandy, duke of Aquitaine, count of Maine and Tours was born on 5th March 1133 at Le Mans in Normandy. He was the eldest of three sons born to Geoffrey Plantagenet, count of Anjou and the Empress Matilda, only heir to King Henry I of England. Henry is regarded as the first of the Angevin (taken from Anjou) kings of England and the first 'Plantagenet'. The latter name was not used by any contemporary of either Henry II, his sons or their heirs. In fact it only turns up as a royal surname in the 1460s when Richard duke of York, during his quarrels with Henry VI, calls himself 'Richard Plantagenet'. During his own lifetime Henry II was often referred to as Henry Fitzempress out of regard for his mother the widow of Emperor Henry V. Not withstanding that Plantagenet may be a modern descriptor, it will be used in this work as a convenient 'family' name for Henry's descendents.

Henry was six-years-old when his mother began her long wars with King Stephen in England and his father, Geoffrey, began his steady conquest of Normandy. While his father lived Henry was invested as duke of Normandy and at his death became count of Anjou. In May 1152 Henry married the beautiful and intelligent ex-wife of Louis VII of France, Eleanor of Aquitaine, and at one bound became lord of nearly all of western France. Louis responded by forming a grand alliance against Henry with the aim of destroying this over-mighty vassal before he could consolidate his gains. Henry's success in defending his borders and defeating Louis brought his martial prowess to the notice of all Europe and was the start of a reputation for military skill that he retained almost until his death.

In January 1153, Henry, braving winter seas, sailed for England to confront his mother's old adversary, King Stephen. His expedition would have the most extraordinary outcome and he would return to Normandy in 1153 as the accepted heir to the English throne. So firm was the agreement reached in England in 1152 that, just eight weeks after King Stephen's death, in December 1154, Henry was crowned, King Henry II in Westminster Abbey. The Plantagenet era beginning that day would last, in England, for three hundred and thirty one years, long after the family had lost the great continental domains from which they sprang. But for now England was firmly a part of the great circle of lands that Henry ruled on the continent. It was from there that the Plantagenets drew their culture, language and heritage, and it was a largely French ruling class that would administer and organise their Kingdom of England.

Holding on to those continental domains would dominate the lives of Henry and his descendants. They would move in and out of that large orbit, itinerant lords of a diverse and bellicose domain, making laws, waging war, collecting taxes, punishing subjects, settling disputes and nearly always having to handle disputes with the King of France. Henry was the fittest of them all to meet this challenge. A bundle of boundless energy he traversed the vast distances of his domains for thirty-five years, in what today would be described as a possessed and frenzied fashion, sometimes leaving one place before his baggage had arrived. He confounded his enemies by the speed with which he travelled often surprising them into submission. No other characteristic so defines him as this limitless energy.

Henry, though not fat, was a barrel of a man. He had a strong square chest and bow legs from all his hours in the saddle and he had red hair which he kept closely shaved. Contemporaries particularly noted his blue-grey eyes so soft and kind when he was relaxed but *'gleaming like fire when his temper was aroused'*. Henry's ferocious temper would regularly get him into trouble. Once during a conversation when someone praised the King of Scots Henry *'fell out of bed screaming, tore up his coverlet, and threshed around the floor, cramming his mouth with the stuffing of his mattress'*. For leisure Henry enjoyed hunting, hawking, reading, and discussions with any learned men who crossed his path. He loved the outdoors and he often sought the solace of forests when the intrigues of court and government were wearing him down. He was always unpredictable with his family, often generous, but at other times mean spirited and he was always careful not to give them too much power. His challenge was that with four adult boys all seeking more power than he was ever willing to give them the scene was always set for furious family quarrels.

Henry's first quarrel was with his brother Geoffrey who believed that his father's will ordained that after Henry had gained England Geoffrey was to have Touraine, Anjou and Maine in addition to the castles he already held. Henry crossed the channel in January 1156 and forced Geoffrey to renounce his claims and Geoffrey's convenient death in 1158 ensured that they would not be raised again. Henry's need to attend to so many matters outside England provided the wellspring for his great legacy: a self-sustaining system of the king's justice that could function effectively during his long absences. Building on the work of his grandfather Henry I, he laid the foundation of a permanent system of justice with regular courts, professional judges, established procedures and written records. The Assize of Northampton in 1176 divided the country into six circuits and three itinerant justices were allocated for each circuit for revenue and judicial purposes. The writ system, a letter authenticated by a seal, commanding local Sheriffs to execute 'proper' justice on the king's behalf also developed considerably under Henry.

It was through the law that Henry first attempted to deal with his most unruly subject Thomas Becket, his one time chancellor and later Archbishop of Canterbury. Becket's adoption of mother church as a heartfelt cause, after his elevation to the see of Canterbury, came as a surprise to all who had known him. The rumblings began in 1163. In that year Becket insisted on a variety of protections for the church including the acceptance by Henry that clergy could only be tried and punished in ecclesiastical courts. His adamant stand on these issues, without engaging in the usual trimming and compromise that kept church and state in some kind of equilibrium, surprised even his bishops. Becket had been lobbying for Archbishop Anselm, he who had so thwarted William Rufus and Henry I, to be made a saint and he now looked as if he was donning the mantle of Anselm as a deifier of kings!

After Becket forbade the marriage of Henry's brother William to a wealthy heiress on the grounds of consanguinity the battle lines were drawn. At the Council of Clarendon in 1164 the leaders of the English church had agreed 16 articles that would in future govern the relations between church and state. They included no appeals to Rome without the king's approval and that clerks found guilty of crimes should be defrocked and then sentenced by a secular court. With up to one sixth of the adult population in clerical orders this article could fill Henry's courts with thousands of errant clerks. Henry certainly intended it to embrace his aberrant archbishop.

Henry brought Becket to trial at the Council of Northampton in October 1164. The principal charge, one that future kings would regularly use against royal servants who had fallen out of favour, was that Becket had misappropriated revenues. Charged with losing around £30,000, which had supposedly passed through his hands when he was Chancellor, Becket smelt the coffee and fled in disguise to France. There he stayed in exile, a distant, but noisy thorn in the ing's side until 1170. After six years and many months of fragile negotiation Henry agreed peace terms with Becket at Fréteval in July 1170. After making peace with Henry, Becket returned to Canterbury, arrogant as ever, and foolishly unmoveable he promptly excommunicated his old enemies the Archbishop of York and the Bishops of London and Salisbury. Not surprisingly they all fled to Normandy to complain to Henry about their over mighty brother, and Henry, plagued once again by Becket's stubbornness, broke into a fierce rage. But in among this farrago of deceit and double-dealing Henry too was not without blame. He had promised the restitution of various confiscated lands and revenues which he had not delivered. Of equal importance, because symbolic acts, executed in public, mattered in medieval Europe, Henry had failed to give Becket the 'kiss of peace' at Fréteval. He would refuse to do this again in 1189 when he would not exchange 'the kiss' with his perfidious son Richard at their last meeting. Clearly this was one medieval symbol that meant a lot to Henry and his failure to exchange it with Becket signalled that he was not happy with the terms of the peace. He had also promised to join Becket in England and travel with him to Canterbury. He didn't turn up. Had he kept his promise he might have forestalled the archbishops rush to excommunication and prevented the disaster that was soon to overtake both of them.

All Henry's work on the better government of England couldn't save him from the plague of his own violent temper and this time it would lead him into the murky origins of the murder of an archbishop. During that fit of temper in Normandy, after the bishops had reported, he screamed within earshot of his followers: '*What miserable drones and traitors have I nourished and promoted in my household, who let their Lord be treated with such shameful contempt by a low born cleric*'. As ill luck would have it four knights heard his cry and they had no doubt what it was their king wanted. They rode to Calais and then on to Canterbury where they cleft open Becket's skull in his own church. Founding a legend and putting the soul of their king in mortal danger, they rode off again into obscurity. Though Becket's murder could not be attributed to him directly the world knew that Becket was a thorn that Henry wanted removed. Thus the 'Canterbury Four' were never seen as anything else but agents of that wish, whatever the truth of the king's wishes leading up to it.

On hearing of Becket's murder Henry disappeared into seclusion for three days before employing his fertile mind to work out how he was going to deal with the inevitable papal storm. In the end he held up his hands and declared that though he never desired the Becket's murder, his incautious temper and his words may have encouraged the murderers. He knelt at the door of the cathedral of Avranches in a highly public display of penance and revoked all the contentious edicts against the church that had prompted the rift with Becket, and the Church was satisfied. Less easily sorted was Henry's equally bad tempered and quarrelsome family. Henry spent much of his life dealing with the rivalry and ambition of his sons and, on their behalf, the intrigues of his wife, Eleanor of Aquitaine. Despite spending nearly 16 years under close arrest she devoted many of her waking hours to ensuring her sons' inheritance. She was particularly concerned to see that her eldest son Richard inherited her own duchy of Aquitaine. Struggle followed struggle, betrayal followed betrayal and as Henry moved into his fifties his seemingly inexhaustible energy began to desert him.

He died at his castle of Chinon in the Loire Valley on 6th July 1189, probably as a result of a cerebral haemorrhage, with only his bastard son Geoffrey, by his mistress the 'Fair Rosamund', at his side. He was tired and corpulent, worn out by a year of almost constant marching and warring around his territories in France and broken in spirit by the treachery of his eldest son Richard who (like the conqueror's son Robert years before him) had joined a King of France in a war against his father. Only two days before his death Henry had suffered an ignominious defeat by an alliance of Philippe (II) Augustus of France and Richard and had had to accept humiliating peace terms at a meeting at Colombiers (now Villandry). He was so weak from a badly abscessed anal fistula (a long narrow pipe-like ulcer) that his men had to hold him upright on his horse during the meeting. Without demure he meekly accepted the French king's terms and the once great warrior king was then carried back to Chinon on a litter.

All he had worked for, the independence of his territories on the continent covering over half of what we call modern day France, was now in the hands of his enemies. On his sick bed he called for a list of those who had joined with King Philippe. Part of his treaty with the French king was that he would pardon all those who had made war against him. The first name on the list was count John, Henry's youngest and favourite son. '*Is it true that John, my heart, John whom I loved more than all my sons, and for whose gain I have suffered these evils, has forsaken me*'? This revelation pushed him further into despair and after lapsing into delirium and then a coma he died. Despair and depression may not have killed Henry but it certainly hastened his death.

His body is supposed to have been ravaged by his household retainers who stole all his personal effects leaving him naked on his deathbed. Later a young knight covered the dead king with a cloak and later still his bastard son Geoffrey and William the Marshal (the king's most loyal and devoted subject) found enough royal insignia, rings, gloves, sceptre, shoes, spurs, sword etc., to give the king a more regal appearance in death. Henry was then taken to the abbey of Fontevrault in the Loire Valley rather than to Grandmont as he had once requested. King Richard I arrived at Fontevrault to see his father's corpse and kneeled to make some peremptory prayers over his father's body. As the new king rose to his feet blood reportedly flowed from the nostrils of the dead one and kept on flowing until his son left. The onlookers nodded! It was surely a sign of a spirit much angered by the proximity of the one who had betrayed him. On 10th July 1189 Henry was buried in the nuns' choir. A tomb with a fine effigy was raised soon afterwards and one Ralph of Diceto transcribed the epitaph that was engraved on it.

'I am Henry the King. To me divers realms were subject.
I was duke and count of many provinces.
Eight feet of ground is now enough for me,
whom many kingdoms have failed to satisfy.
Who reads these lines, let him reflect
upon the narrowness of death, and in my case behold
the image of our mortal lot. This scanty tomb doth now suffice
for whom the earth was not enough'.

Henry's monument, painted in pastel blue can still be seen at Fontevrault, alongside that of his wife the famed Eleanor of Aquitaine. The six kings before Henry were clean-shaven but Henry began a fashion for wearing beards that English kings were to follow for the next two hundred years. Eleanor survived both her husband Henry and her son Richard. She died at Fontevrault aged eighty-two on 1st April 1204 as her youngest son, King John, was losing nearly all his father's domains in France. After a brilliant, colourful and sometimes tragic life, Eleanor had been consecrated as a nun, in her favourite abbey of Fontevrault, in 1202. She only survived for two years at the abbey, and was then buried, by the nuns, in a tomb near that of her husband and her second son Richard I.

The eldest son of Henry II and Eleanor was called Henry the 'Young King' as his father (foolishly) had him crowned king while he still lived giving rise to all kinds of rebellions, plots and counterplots by this 'king without a kingdom'. However, this troublesome eldest son did not live long. He died aged twenty-eight in 1183 after falling ill with dysentery. His eyes, brain and entrails were buried beside the gravesite chosen by Henry II for himself in the monastery of Grandmont. His body was to be buried in Rouen Cathedral, but as his funeral cortège passed through Le Mans the citizens (sensible of the cash a royal tomb could bring to the town) seized the body, still covered in the young man's coronation gown, and buried it in their own cathedral. Cheated of a key attraction to their own church the people of Rouen threatened to burn Le Mans to the ground if the corpse was not returned to them. Eventually Henry II intervened and insisted that his son must be buried in the place he had chosen. His tomb can still be seen today on the north side of the high alter in Rouen Cathedral.

It is a testament to the extent that France was the natural home of the early Plantagenets that all Henry's close family, bar one, were buried in France. Henry the 'Young King' at Rouen, Geoffrey, Henry's fourth son, at Notre-Dame in Paris and Henry himself, his wife Eleanor of Aquitaine, Richard I, and John's widow, Isabelle of Angouleme, were all were buried at Fontevrault. The effigy's of these last four Plantagenets now lie in the centre of a grand and empty abbey whose stone walls, clean and devoid of all ornament, look as if they have just been washed and scrubbed down for the visitor. Joanna, Henry II's daughter who was once Queen of Sicily, was also buried at Fontevrault but there is no effigy of her there. During the French revolution all the Plantagenet tombs at Fontevrault were disturbed and vandalised and the bones exhumed and scattered never to be recovered. The abbey itself was converted into a prison. Later the desecrated tombs were collected together and set up in the crypt. The prison was closed in 1963 and the abbey was restored. The four royal effigies were moved back to the church and together with the fantastically ornate nuns' kitchen are all that remain of the great abbey that Eleanor knew.

The tempestuous Henry and Eleanor were both celebrated as larger than life figures when they were alive. Their painted effigies, still side by side today, though hardly accurate portraits, still exhibit some of the pose and presence of medieval power. Queen Victoria, who often involved herself in the repair and maintenance of royal monuments, once made a formal request to the French government for the bodies of the two kings and two queens of England buried at Fontevrault (then still a prison) to be returned home to England. The local Prefect, to whom the matter was referred declined her invitation, no doubt satisfied that the Plantagenets laid there were French citizens who were already at home.

RICHARD I (born 1157 reigned 1189-1199)

Richard I, later to be known as 'Coeur de Lion', was born on 8th September 1157 at Oxford, the third son of Henry II and Eleanor of Aquitaine. Little is known of his education but as well as excelling in the marshal arts, he spoke good Latin and enjoyed writing music and singing songs. Later, as duke of Aquitaine, he was a noted patron of the troubadours and Muslim sources suggest that he had an interest in Arabic culture.

By the late 1160s Richard's father was planning to divide his dominions between his sons. This King Lear-like behaviour, wanting to give his sons power, but really wanting to hold on to it, would bedevil relations between Henry and his sons until his death in 1189. In January 1169 the treaty of Montmirail allowed for Richard to do homage for Aquitaine to King Louis VII of France and to marry Alice, Louis's daughter. Four years later, encouraged by King Louis, Richard joined his mother and his brothers, Henry the 'Young King' and Geoffrey, in rebellion against their father but Henry outwitted them and they had to come to terms with him in September 1174. Richard's mother, Eleanor had been captured by Henry in November 1173 and would be kept confined under guard for most of the next 16 years until Henry died. In 1175 Henry II gave Richard command of the armies in Aquitaine with the challenge of punishing all rebels and bringing the duchy to heel. This task would occupy Richard for the next 13 years and his reputation as a skilled but ruthless commander would grow from his tireless campaigning in Aquitaine.

In 1182 Henry II sought to have his sons Richard and Geoffrey swear homage to their elder brother, Henry the 'Young King' but Richard would only swear if it was made clear that Aquitaine was his. The 'Young King' would not accept this caveat and the family went to war again with Henry II and Richard facing up to the 'Young King', Geoffrey and a host of rebel lords. The death of the 'Young King' in June 1183 caused the rebellion to collapse and now Henry II sought to establish a new family settlement by which his youngest son, John, got Aquitaine. Again Richard was now being asked to give up the duchy he had spent so much energy and money on and he would not agree. Richard emerged triumphant from his battles with John and Geoffrey and in December 1184 Henry II called his 'boys' together to be reconciled. Geoffrey died in August 1186 and now Henry II only had two sons to quarrel with.

By the strange rules of medieval hierarchy Henry II, though possessed of most of what we would call modern day France, was obliged to do homage to the King of France for his territories. King Philippe II was Henry's lord and Henry owed him obligations but the reality of Henry's power meant that Henry's fealty to the French king was mostly symbolic. King Philippe had decided that he wanted more than just the symbolic submission of this over mighty family. The Angevin empire was too powerful and his principle policy would be to work to break it up, and annex it, bit by bit, to the French crown. To this end, and with consummate skill, Philippe would develop the policy begun by his father, Louis VII of dividing the sons of Henry II from their father. This policy saw its greatest success when Philippe began negotiating with Richard directly in 1188 resulting in Richard joining with him to make war against Henry in 1189.

Henry's death at Chinon on 6th July 1189 brought the conflict to an end. Other than for a couple of lordships Philippe confirmed Richard as the heir to Henry's continental domains and Richard left to be crowned King of England in Westminster Abbey on 3rd September 1189. The celebrations were marred somewhat by anti- Jewish demonstrations in London and, after Richard left England, these spread outside the capital culminating in a massacre of 150 Jews at York in March 1190. In 1187 in a swift reaction to the news of Saladin's capture of Jerusalem Richard had been the first prince north of the Alps to take the cross and now he needed money to turn his promise into reality. After making suitable arrangements for the government of England while he was away Richard began to sell offices and titles to fill his war chest. At this time contemporaries believed he would sell anything to raise money and he was reported to have said that he would have sold London if he could have found a buyer. In 1190, having taxed England and all his other realms heavily to pay for it, he set out for Jerusalem.

Richard met up with the army of Philippe of France and having agreed to share all the spoils of war equally between them they then split up to make their separate ways to the Holy Land. Richard stopped off at Sicily where he had some business with King Tancred, who had held Richard's sister Joanna in close confinement, ever since the death of her husband, William II, King of Sicily. Richard wanted Joanna's dower as well as a legacy that William II had left to Richard's father to help fund a future crusade. Richard easily took the city of Messina by force and Tancred agreed to give Richard large sums of gold to get him, and his army, off his island. In among his money dealings with Tancred Richard promised to give Tancred's daughter in marriage to his nephew, Arthur of Brittany, who he declared was his heir presumptive.

While on Sicily Richard was forced into a difficult confrontation with Philippe. He had been betrothed to Philippe's sister Alice since 1169 and Philippe was now impatient that he should marry her. But Richard's mother was on her way to Sicily with a new bride for Richard, Princess Berengaria of Navarre. Richard had agreed to this match before he left France with the aim of gaining an alliance with Sancho VI of Navarre. Sancho's territories bordered Richard's south western domains and his support would help Richard keep the peace in Aquitaine. Since childhood Alice had always been held as a ward by Richard's father Henry II. Henry had kept her close to him, so close that he is suspected of having fathered at least one child with her. Henry had always procrastinated when pressed to give Alice to Richard, as agreed with the French, and Richard had never really seemed too bothered to press his suit. Now Richard refused to take the 'soiled goods'. He confronted Philippe with his father's behaviour with Alice and threatened to make public that Alice was Henry's mistress. Philippe caved in and released Richard from his vow, but he never forgave Richard for this public slight on his family. It was a grudge that would fester. Philippe's action after the capture of Muslim held Acre, when he left immediately to return to France, perhaps reflects a simmering hostility to the great warrior who had spurned his sister.

Soon after Richard's fleet left Sicily a great storm blew up and the ship carrying Joanna and Berengaria was forced into Cyprus and was in danger of being taken as booty by Isaac the self-proclaimed Emperor of Cyprus. Richard had to stop and conquer yet another island, this time with the help of a member of the Lusignan family. This family would later play a part in his brother John's marital affairs. Richard married Berengaria in the Chapel of St George at Limasol on the 12th May but he did not dawdle on honeymoon. By 8th June 1191 Richard was with the army that had been besieging Acre for the last two years. Replenished with Richard's and Philippe's forces Acre capitulated in July and the banners of the French and English kings were raised over the city. These banners were joined by those of Leopold duke of Austria who had led a small German contingent. Richard's soldiers soon tore them down. Saladin had agreed a massive ransom for the captured soldiers and citizens of Acre and Richard and Philippe had no intention of sharing the spoils with a third party.

Philippe soon cut short his 'crusade' and left Acre for France to claim lands in Artois. One chronicler commented that Philippe had been *'like a hammer tied to the tail of a cat'* as far as Richard was concerned. Leopold of Austria also left to go home. Richard might now be free to campaign in the Holy Land as he liked, but he had now made two enemies and they both went home before he did. Saladin did not make payment of the ransoms agreed at Acre by the due date and Richard, keen to move on to Jerusalem, decided that he could not afford to feed and guard 3,000 prisoners, so he had them slaughtered. Saladin's mounted archers harried Richard's forces all the way to Jaffa and attacked them at Arsuf in a battle that the crusaders would have lost but for the leadership and courage shown by Richard. After this internecine quarrels between the great lords within the army and the huge logistical problems of actually taking and holding Jerusalem saw the crusade start to crumble. In July Richard was again before the walls of Jaffa which Saladin had captured. Once more the chroniclers report of Richard's outstanding military prowess as he led his troops against the city. But it was not enough. Both sides were weary of war and in September 1192 Richard agreed a three-year truce with Saladin under which Christian pilgrims would be granted free access to Jerusalem.

Sick and disappointed that he had not recovered the Holy City Richard prepared to go home. It was getting late for sea travel in the Mediterranean and after surviving shipwreck on the Istrian coast Richard decided to risk a land journey through the territory of his old enemy, Leopold of Austria. Although disguised as pilgrims Richard and his followers were caught near Vienna by Leopold's men. Eventually Richard was transferred to the custody of, yet another enemy, the Emperor Heinrich VI who had already written to Philippe of France saying *'We know this news will bring you great joy'*. Early 1194 Richard was freed after a ransom of 100,000 marks had been sent to Germany – the taxpayers of England being bled yet again to pay for it. He returned to England for just two months before sailing off again to recover ground in Eastern Normandy and the Loire Valley that had been lost to France while he was in prison. From May 1194 until his death in April 1199 Richard was at war somewhere in his French dominions. His brother John's various deals with France now had to be unravelled. Richard's formidable tactical and strategic skills gave him victories in many of the campaigns and he brought King Philippe to the negotiating table to agree a five-year truce in January 1199.

While these negotiations were in progress Richard went south to reconnoitre the castle of Châlus. While riding around the castle without his armour he was hit in the shoulder by a cross-bow bolt and the wound turned gangrenous and Richard died. A number of English and French historians put out a more interesting story, less creditable to the great crusader. They reported that a peasant in the Limousin found some buried treasure (a pot of Roman coins) and took it to his lord, Achard of Châlus. By the time Richard heard about this, 'tabloid like', the horde of coins had turned into a golden statue resembling an emperor sat at a table with his family. This was too much of a temptation for Richard and he decided that, as it was within his territory, he should have it. In March 1199 he besieged the little castle of Châlus. The garrison there was thought to be no more than fifteen poorly armed men. It was not long before the lord Achard saw the writing on the wall and offered to surrender the castle, and the treasure, if he and his men were allowed to leave unharmed. But Richard was not for turning.

His pride had been hurt by this disobedience and he swore that he would take the castle by storm and riding about in a fairly cavalier fashion (no body armour) he personally set about seeking out the weakest point in its defences. Hardly believing his luck a crossbowman on the parapets above him took a pot shot at the king and wounded him in the left shoulder. Richard regarded this as little more than a scratch and returning to his tent urged his supporters to press on with the attack. The castle soon fell and the men inside were all hanged except one, the crossbowman, who was found using a just frying pan as a shield, was spared. There was no sign of the treasure, coins or golden emperor. The murdered inhabitants of that little castle took that secret (whatever it was) to their graves. The 'scratch' turned out to be a bigger problem than Richard expected. The doctors had difficulty removing the iron arrowhead, which had penetrated deep into the king's shoulder, and their subsequent rough hacking about caused the wound to inflame and grow putrid. Soon blood poisoning and gangrene set in. After a few days Richard realised that he was dying and wrote asking his mother, not his wife Queen Berengaria, to come to him. He also made a will bequeathing all his dominions to his brother John, rather than to his nephew Arthur as he had declared in Cyprus, plus three quarters of his treasure. The other quarter was to go to his servants and the poor.

He called the fatal crossbowman to him and asked him why he had wanted to kill him. The man was unrepentant. He said that Richard had killed his father and his two brothers and now he had come to kill him. He was glad to see that the king was dying and invited him to take what revenge he might. In a rare fit of generosity Richard forgave this brave and forthright man and ordered that he be released with 100 shillings in English money. However the man was not released and after Richard died he was flayed alive and hanged – a king's pardon isn't worth much from the grave! On 6th April 1199, eleven days after receiving his wound, Richard, perhaps for the first time in seven years, made his confession, received communion and the last rites and died in the evening, with his mother, Queen Eleanor, by his side. Seven years earlier, in the autumn of 1192, Hubert Walter had gone on a pilgrimage to Jerusalem and there talked with Saladin, the great Arab general who had dubbed Richard 'The Lionheart'. Saladin noted that *'I have long since been aware that your king is a man of honour and very brave, but he is imprudent, indeed absurdly so, in the way he plunges into the midst of danger and in his reckless indifference to his own safety. For my own part, however powerful a king I might be, I would like to have wisdom and moderation rather than an excessive boldness'.*

Whichever of the stories about his death are true, Richard had gone carelessly to Châlus and now he would join his father in the crypt at Fontevrault. Indeed Richard had asked to be buried at his father's feet, in the abbey, in contrition for having rebelled against him. His mother saw to it that his wish was carried out and with royal pomp Richard was buried as he wished, his heart was sent to Rouen and his brains and entrails to Charroux in Poitou. Eleanor also ensured that Richard, with so many sins to answer for, would get ongoing spiritual support by granting the nuns of Fontevrault money for new habits. She also gave the whole community there the revenues from one of her towns near Poitiers to support their kitchen and *'for the weal of the soul of my very dear lord'*. The twelfth century thus came to end with the death of a real-life hero; flawed, stubborn, reckless and ruthless but a hero who was recognised as such in his own lifetime. In less than ten years his even more reckless brother John would lose those favoured lands that Richard, his father and Eleanor had spilt so much blood to keep from the kingdom of France.

Richard lived to be King of England for less than 10 years and died aged forty-one. Despite coming down in popular history as a fearless King of Albion he spent only six months in England and that was only to raise money to leave it to go on crusade, rather than to add to the good government of the realm. His heart was always in his continental dominions, particularly Aquitaine. One argument put forward for his brief sojourn in England is that, protected by the English Channel, it was the least threatened of his domains while the others, more contiguous with his enemies on the continent, required so much more of his time and energy. This may have been true but, whatever Richard's other qualities, his devotion to England was limited to that of a continental tax collector. The founding of religious houses by a king is often a mark of his involvement in the wider community of his kingdom, all the religious house founded by Richard were located in France

JOHN (born 1167 reigned 1199-1216)

John was born at Oxford on Christmas Eve 1167. He was the fourth and youngest son, of Henry II and Eleanor of Aquitaine. Not long after his birth Henry and Eleanor began to drift apart but John was forever a favourite of his father. With three brothers in the pecking order before him John's chances of gaining a significant part of his father's great empire were slim and his father gave him the nickname 'Lackland'. His elder brother Henry the 'Young King' had been given England and Normandy, Richard had been given his mother's inheritance of Aquitaine, and Geoffrey had been given Brittany. John only managed to pick up some castles and they were all scattered around lands that his brothers controlled.

There was a legend in the family of the counts of Anjou that one of them had married a woman who was the devil's daughter, Melusine. Her parentage was supposedly discovered when she refused to attend a full mass. One day the count surrounded her with armed guards forcing her to stay while the host was raised and she flew, shrieking, out of a window and was never seen again. From this time on the family of Anjou, the Angevins, were known to some as 'the Devil's brood' destined to wrangle among themselves, brother against brother and son against father. If the efficacy of this legend was to be measured in the number and ferocity of quarrels within one family Henry's family would score high marks.

Henry II could only find something to settle on John by taking lands from one of his brothers. John's prospects seem to improve when Henry, the 'Young King', died in 1183 and Henry II offered Richard England and Normandy so that John could have Aquitaine. But Richard was his mother's favourite and she wanted him to keep Aquitaine and he, devoted to her, and the vast lands of Aquitaine, would not give it up. Richard rebelled against his father in what would prove to be the first of a number of armed clashes among the 'brood'. It was a clash that John, creating a precedent that he would build on for the rest of his life, lost!

In 1185 Henry struck on the idea that as none of his other sons had any rights to Ireland John could have that and he sent him there. Henry was also concerned that an over-mighty subject in Ireland, Hugh de Lacy, was enjoying a bit too much freedom. After six months John was back with his father, having alienated both the natives and the Norman settlers by his cavalier approach to the government of the country. He made large grants of land to his own band of followers in total disregard of local custom and Irish rights. One story had him entertaining himself by laughing at the shaggy beards of the Irish chieftains. Gerald of Wales, a royal clerk, accompanied John to Ireland and noted that, *'... being himself young and little more than a boy, followed the council of young men whom he took with him, who were utterly unknown in Ireland and themselves knew nothing, whereas he rebuffed the honest and discreet men whom he found there, who knew the customs and habits of the country, treating them as though they were foreigners of little worth'*. Clearly John hadn't inherited any of the modest 'statesmanship' genes of the Angevins. Perhaps this was the beginning of the 'troubles' in Ireland that would haunt relations between the two neighbours for the next 800 years.

John remained lord of Ireland but he still hoped for better things. His hopes were raised when his brother Geoffrey, count of Brittany, was killed in a tournament. He might have expected to gain Brittany from Geoffrey's death but he was thwarted again as Geoffrey had left his wife bearing a son, who would become Arthur of Brittany. Arthur would live just long enough to know the evil of his uncle John.

John had been the apple of his father's eye but after Henry II's fortunes declined in 1189, during his wars with Richard and Philippe of France, John quickly switched to the winning side. It was John's name at the head of the list of rebels that Henry read as he lay dying. When Richard I succeeded Henry II in 1189 he was generous to John, giving him six counties in England, the county of Mortain in Normandy and the honour of Lancaster. Since the age of nine John had been betrothed to Isabella of Gloucester, his second cousin and a wealthy heiress. In 1189 Richard approved the marriage, although the pope did not, and John got his hands on more lands. The lack of a papal blessing left John's marriage in a convenient twighlight zone, allowing it to be declared void if a better prospect turned later.

Soon after Richard left for the Holy Land in July 1190 John returned his brother's generosity by seeking to gain control of England, despite his brothers' demand that he should stay away from England for three years. When Philippe returned to France from the Holy Land, furious at his treatment by Richard, he whetted John's appetite for treachery even more by offering to help John take control of all the Angevin lands on the continent. John pulled back from this offer only after his mother, the newly released Queen Eleanor, persuaded him that to follow Philippe could mean that John might lose everything. But now there was even better news. In early 1193 John heard that Richard had been captured and was languishing in a German prison. Now John could really start to take over. He arrived in England but could get little support from the English barons most of whom felt that taking arms against a crusader king was too treacherous even for them. In January 1194, in order to get, and keep, Philippe's support John ceded him the whole of eastern Normandy except for Rouen. He and Philippe then tried to bribe the Emperor Heinrich VI to either keep Richard in prison or to sell him to them. John's record of treachery between 1189 and 1194 led the chronicler, William of Newburgh to call him *'nature's enemy'* and his arch duplicity during these years alone would have been enough to mark him out as a prince of infamy.

John was lucky to have a brother who, though ruthless with his enemies, could also be magnanimous to his family. After his release from Germany in 1194 Richard contemptuously forgave John. He regarded the twenty-seven-year-old as a child led astray by others and later restored his estates to him. After this John had the good sense to lie low until his brother died in 1199, naming him his heir. England now had a king whose greatest gift was to make enemies and lose territory. It could have been so different. Without his hyperactive father breathing down his neck, without his brothers swaggering about showing off their great domains John could have just heaved a sigh of relief that he had survived them all and striven to make something of it. Though not devoid of redeeming features (his tirelessness in dispensing justice in England is well recorded) you have to struggle to find them among the many stupid deeds of this the youngest son of Henry, the builder of empires.

As king, John made many mistakes. His first big mistake, within a year of becoming king, was to ditch his wife Isabella of Gloucester and marry Isabella of Angoulême. That 'twighlight' marriage arrangement now came in handy. This twelve-year-old girl was already betrothed to Hugh of Lusignan who, outraged at this assault on his pride, appealed to Philippe of France for justice. Although it made a lot of sense strategically for John to control Angoulême the powerful Lusignan family had aided him in the past and this insult to them was bound to provoke a military reaction. After failing to attend a summons by Philippe to answer for his behaviour the French king pronounced that all John's lands on the continent, except Normandy, could now go to Arthur of Brittany. The later collapse of the Angevin empire can be traced back to this one supremely stupid and selfish act and the rebellion in Poitou that it provoked. John was a notorious lecher and some stories even having him ravishing the wives and daughters of his barons. He had at least seven illegitimate children but he had no children by his first wife Isabella of Gloucester. His second wife Isabella of Angoulême provided John with a son and heir (later Henry III) in 1207 and later she bore him another son and three daughters.

From his accession as King of England in April 1199 until 1203 John would be involved in trying to secure his continental inheritance as Philippe of France joined Arthur of Brittany, the Lusignans and other discontented barons in alliance against him. In July 1202 John's eighty-year-old mother, Queen Eleanor, was trapped by Arthur and the Lusignans at the castle of Mirebeau in Anjou. John, for once, emulating of his swift-footed father, covered the 80 miles from Le Mans to the castle in less than 48 hours surprising the besiegers and capturing Arthur and more than 200 barons. This was John's greatest military success. Instead of building on it to make friends and keep his allies sweet John's talent for fermenting discord surfaced again. He refused to let his supporters have a share in the fate of the prisoners who, even by the standards of the times, he treated in a cruel and inhuman way.

By the spring of 1203, rumours that he had murdered his nephew, Prince Arthur, some said by his own hand in a drunken fit, damaged John's reputation even further and gave Philippe of France a good excuse to invade Normandy and turn the populace against him. After losing control of several castles, including the strategically important Castle of Gisors, during 1203, John sailed for England in December, gaining a new nickname, 'Softsword'. John had spent three-quarters of the first four years of his reign on the continent and now he retreated back to England but, just like Richard I, it was only to raise money to win back his continental lands. The morale of his supporters left in Normandy and elsewhere plummeted and King Philippe now seized the initiative. By the end of 1204 nearly all of John's continental possessions were in Philippe's hands.

John returned to France in October 1206 but failed to retain Anjou in the face of Philippe's advancing armies and was forced to agree a two-year truce with him, just managing to hold on to some south western parts of his father's once great empire. If John was ever going to raise an army big enough to defeat Philippe he would need serious funds and so he spent the next five years in England extorting money from whoever and wherever he could. In doing so he alienated large sections of the population while the royal revenues grew and grew reaching unprecedented levels by 1212. In 1214 John used this cash to put together an expensive alliance against France. Together with the counts of Flanders and Boulogne John would launch a two-pronged attack that would force Philippe to split his army. This plan came to grief on 27th July when John's allies suffered an overwhelming defeat at the Battle of Bouvines. On 18th September 1214 John and Philippe agreed a five-year truce, rumoured to have cost John 60,000 marks. John returned home to England beaten yet again and with very empty pockets.

By now, exhausted by war and wasted by taxes, the barons in England could see that they were tied to an oppressive loser who would only dish out more of the same if they didn't act. Military success in France might have saved John but serial military defeats and the loss of territory turned the barons from grumbling malcontents into serious rebels. In May 1215 the barons captured London and forced John to come to terms. Magna Carta of 17th June 1215 was hardly a charter for democratic liberty. Its detailed clauses reveal it to be more of an agreement between the king and an already very privileged class. It was also agreed by a king who was buying time. There is little in this 'arrangement' that gives more rights to the growing towns or the burgesses of the emerging merchant class let alone the farm labourer or the bricklayer. But its future influence rested less on its early thirteenth century detail than on the limpet-like myth that it created. It became a touchstone and talisman for future lawyers and statesmen who, often ignorant of the detail, accorded it promises, justifications and principles that those clanking barons neither stated nor would ever have encouraged. Rather it established a habit, in certain times of crisis, of codifying the behaviour of English kings, each of which opened the door to further periodic revisions of custom and law. At each of these critical periods the idea that the government of the country should not be conducted to the damage of the governed gained a little more ground. Magna Carta was important because it came to mean much more than it ever said.

In 1215 neither barons nor king intended to abide by this 'talisman'. John got the pope to declare it null and void and then went off to enlist a mercenary army just to make sure that the barons never got to enjoy its terms. The barons for their part elected Louis of France (King Philippe's son) as an alternative king, helped him invade England in May 1216 and joined him in riding unopposed into London. During that same year, on 9th October, after a hard days riding, John was welcomed by the citizens of the prosperous seaport of Lynn.

Happy to rest, the king settled down to an extravagant feast after which he seems to have contracted dysentery, perhaps as a direct result of fatigue and over indulgence. According to the Cistercian, Ralph of Coggershall, this ailment was brought on by the sin of gluttony *'for he could never fill his belly full to satisfaction'*.

It certainly looks like this attack frightened John, for the next morning he made a gift to Margaret daughter of William de Briouze, for the sake of the souls of her mother and brother. Early in John's reign William de Briouze, once one of John's closest supporters, was in debt to John for 5000 marks and couldn't or wouldn't pay him back. John, unlike most of his predecessors who often used a debt to keep a baron on side, was ruthless at collecting money owed to him. William managed to escape, first to Ireland and then to France but John captured his wife and his eldest son and they disappeared. It was generally believed that he starved them to death in one of his prisons during which suffering the mother was forced to eat the flesh of her dead son.

John left Lynn on 11th October 1216 and made his way north through the fen country to Wisbech, losing some of his baggage in a famous but obscure drowning incident near the Wash, where some of his household effects, his holy relics and other contents of his chapel were lost.It seems that several members of his household were also sucked into the quicksand at the point where the Wellstream meets the sea. His servants seem to have been in too much of a hurry; they didn't wait for the tide to fully recede. John was in poor spirits at this time being preoccupied with the continuing rebellion by some two thirds of his barons and the invasion and occupation of London and the eastern counties by Louis. His mood was melancholy as he sat down to dinner at his next halt, Swineshead Abbey.

The chronicler Matthew Paris says that the king *'fell into such deep despondency on account of his possessions having been swallowed up by the waves that being seized of a sharp fever* [probably a recurrence of the dysentery] *he became seriously ill'*. But he aggravated the discomfort of his illness by continuing to overeat, *'for that night by indulging too freely in peaches and copious draughts of new cider he greatly increased his feverishness'*. John seems to have spent the night in pain and the next day, unable to ride a horse, he was taken by horse-litter to the castle of Sleaford where he spent another sleepless night before being taken to the bishop of Lincoln's castle at Newark.

The Abbot of Croxton, who had some medical skill, was fetched to tend him here but his principal task now was to hear the king's confession and administer the last rites. John was obviously suffering from some sort of gastric condition – possibly the perforation of a gastric ulcer. This would account for the acute pain and collapse followed by peritonitis. John's was not a sudden death and, like his father, he had plenty of time to organise his last wishes. Before he died on 19th October he was able to name his son Henry as his heir and dictate a brief will. *'First that I desire that my body be buried in the church of the blessed Virgin and St Wulstan at Worcester...'*. Despite the monks of Beaulieu Abbey begging to have John's body for burial, Worcester was a pragmatic choice. Beaulieu was the only monastic abbey that John had founded but currently it was in the hands of his enemies while Worcester was still controlled by his own troops. John may also have been numbered among those English kings robbed on their deathbed. A priest passing through Newark to join in masses for the dead king later informed the Abbot of Coggeshall that he had seen men leaving the city loaded with loot. Obviously not all of King John's treasure was lost in the Wash!

The Abbot of Croxton took John's intestines away and his body was then borne in a funeral convoy of armed mercenaries across the country to Worcester and there buried as he had requested between the shrines of the Saxon saints Oswald and Wulfstan. Though certainly not a godly man John had occasionally spoken fondly of St Wulfstan. The two saintly shrines have long ago disappeared but the bold Purbeck marble effigy of John (the oldest carved effigy of a monarch in England) remains in the middle of the chancel and shows him lying with his head on a pillow supported by small images of St Oswald and St Wulfstan. This effigy was probably carved sometime around 1232 when, in the presence of his son Henry III, John's body was transferred to a new sarcophagus. The effigy itself probably served as the lid to his stone coffin. The shallow 'sockets' on the hands, the collar and the sword of the effigy were once filled with imitation jewels. The box tomb below the effigy with its quatrefoils and coats of arms is a later fifteenth century addition. Unlike his father and brother, and despite his seemingly endless wars on the continent, John had spent much more of his reign in his English kingdom and unlike them he was buried in an English church near an English saint. From this time onwards England would be the resting place of choice for English monarchs.

History has generally put John down as a 'bad' king. In many ways he was but, as medieval chroniclers do when they get the bit between their teeth, a sort of tabloid frenzy took over later and 'bad' has become 'monster' and 'monster' has become 'devil'. In this way one story had it that a monk killed John with a dish of poisoned peaches after he had heard the king boast that he would soon raise the price of a halfpenny loaf to twenty shillings. When asked to taste the peaches first the monk is supposed to have complied before rushing from the room so that his own eventual drop to the floor wouldn't give the game away.

John's desire to be buried close to the bones of St Wulfstan is also reputed to have been a device to trick St Peter into letting this serial sinner into Heaven. Accompanied by such a venerable saint how could he refuse? However the story that he ordered his body to be wrapped in a monk's cowl, also to aid his slipping through the pearly gates unrecognised, did have foundation, for when his tomb was opened in 1797 his body (in a remarkable state of preservation) was found to be so wrapped with the monks cowl covering robes of crimson damask. A workman present at this opening seized the opportunity to steal one of the king's thumb bones. A local Worcester story has the man using it as bait and selling the fish he caught as *'fresh fish caught with King John's thumb'*. The thumb, that put the seal to Magna Carta, somehow turned up again shortly after and was mounted on gold in a little glass case near the tomb.

John inspired neither affection nor loyalty; men never really trusted or liked him and his poor ability as a commander sealed his fate as the least notable of the first Plantagenet trilogy. Nearly all the contemporary chroniclers of John's reign agree that, even by the standards of the time, John was a cruel king. His treatment of Arthur of Brittany, the Briouze family and other prisoners certainly show a man who used cruelty as policy, perhaps assuming that such a reputation would deter those who might rebel against him. As a king who had to deal with rebellion for much of his reign, this policy clearly didn't work.

John's European policy would have dominated the headlines of daytime TV today. He did not just hand back part of a 'rebate' to Europe, he lost Normandy, Maine, Anjou and Poitou, huge swathes of what we call modern day France. But in reflecting on this loss we should note that from that time on, despite various attempting by warrior kings to get bits back, England was all that a future king or queen had. No longer just the annex to a huge continental empire, England was now the key arena of power. The development of an English culture, language and tradition distinctly separate from that of northern France was accelerated by future monarchs, who now had to put governing the English at the very top of their agenda. Isabella of Angoulême, John's one time twelve-year old bride, lived on until 1246, well into the reign of her eldest son King Henry III. All those years ago she had entranced John by her beauty and their marriage was certainly a success as far as producing a healthy male heir was concerned. She returned to France within a year of John's death where, in 1220, she married the son of the man she was betrothed to in 1200, also named Hugh Lusignan, before John stole her away. She is buried near her father and mother-in-law at the abbey of Fontevrault where her unusual wooden effigy can still be seen.

Henry III (born 1207 reigned 1216-1272)

The eldest son of King John and Isabella of Angoulême, Henry III was born at Winchester on 1st October 1207. His father later handed the boy over to the guardianship of Peter des Roches, bishop of Winchester. He would supervise Henry's education until he was fourteen and become a close friend and advisor to the young prince. Henry was reckoned to have had a good education for the times, speaking with unusual *'gravity and dignity'*. As a child Henry saw little of his father but was close to his mother, Isabella, who, nine months after King John's death in 1216, deserted her children, and left England to re-marry in France. In 1209, despite knowing of its failure to secure the throne for his grandmother, Matilda, King John ordered that his nobles take a general oath to support Henry after his death. A wily and intelligent king, John must have thought that his son's situation would be more propitious than Matilda's. As it happened John's sudden death in 1216, in the middle of a rebellion, couldn't have been less propitious.

Henry was only *'a pretty little knight'* of nine years old when news reached him of his father's death. William Marshal, earl of Pembroke, the great and noble knight who had served both Henry II and Richard I was proclaimed regent. Henry was initially crowned in the abbey church of Gloucester on 28th October 1216 with a plain circlet provided by his mother. Still in the midst of the rebellion against his father, Henry benefited from the fact that many of the barons involved, although opposing King John, had no animosity against his infant son. Prevailing sentiment would also have disapproved of depriving a boy of his legitimate inheritance, especially a boy who was English. Following the line adopted by Henry I, in distributing his coronation oath, William Marshal and his council decided to issue a modified form of Magna Carta. This would demonstrate the new regime's good intentions and possibly gain the support of those barons who might be wavering in their rebellion.

It had the desired effect. A number of rebel barons promptly defected from French Louis to Henry. Later two victories, in Henry's name, one at Lincoln led by William Marshall and one at sea, off Sandwich, saw Louis's bid to be King of England brought to an abrupt end and he was bribed to go home. A child king, in the hands of priests, Henry was not prepared, indeed, was never prepared, to rule a complicated set of domains. Historians have generally regarded Henry as a poor specimen of the Plantagenet strain and he has come down to us as fickle, simple, incompetent and totally lacking in wise judgement. Henry was crowned again (he is the only English king to be crowned twice) at Westminster Abbey on 13th May 1220, the day after he had laid the foundation stone of the new Lady Chapel at the abbey built in response to the popular cult of the Virgin that took hold across Europe in the 13th century. Henry's coronation seems to have been notable for its concord and tranquillity, although all the Jews of London were locked up in the Tower for the day, possibly to prevent a repeat of the anti-Jewish riots that occurred at the coronation of Richard I.

After William Marshal's death in 1219 a council confirmed a triumvirate of notables to govern the country but this led to the factionalism that inevitably accompanies the control of a minor. It wasn't until January 1227, in his nineteenth year, that Henry declared himself of full age, although he still did not really rule. Henry's policy of appeasing his magnates by regularly re-issuing charters, that provided him with some short-term cash, in return for reducing his longer term royal prerogatives, led him into more or less constant debt to one group or another. He was a king who delighted in the splendour of majesty. He loved to build, and he was often excessively generous to his friends and family, but his resources were never enough to support his ambitions. He would be dogged by financial problems throughout his reign. In 1234 church leaders threatened Henry with excommunication if he didn't stop the mismanagement and corruption that at the centre of his government that was damaging the struggle with Prince Llywelyn Ap Gruffudd of Wales. Henry complied and the year 1234 is really the year when he began his personal rule, it was also the year that he began looking for a wife.

In 1236 Henry married Eleanor of Provence. He was twenty-nine and she was twelve. Although not rich Eleanor was beautiful, intelligent and later, very political. Her family, the counts of Provence were also very well connected. Her elder sister, Margaret, had married King Louis IX of France and her mother's family, the counts of Savoy, controlled strategic territory in northern Italy that was important to the pope. Eleanor brought an uncle, William of Savoy, with her to England and he soon headed a council of twelve to help Henry govern the realm. William avoided the factionalism that was endemic at Henry's court and his wise council helped Henry improve his finances. Unfortunately William was called away on Savoy family business in May 1238 and never returned to England. In that year another marriage, that of Simon de Montfort to Henry's widowed sister, Eleanor, took place. Their earlier liaison had been something of an embarrassment to Henry and so he arranged that the marriage take place in secret in his private chapel at Westminster. In February 1239 Henry created Simon earl of Leicester and, on 17th June of the same year, Queen Eleanor bore Henry a son, Edward, named after Edward the Confessor. The production of a healthy male heir always lifted an English queen's influence a few notches and from now on Eleanor would be Henry's chief advisor.

Eleanor unashamedly used her influence to aggrandise her family. Another uncle, Peter of Savoy, arrived in England and joined the king's council while yet another, Bonfiace, was made Archbishop of Canterbury. Henry had never given up hope of recovering his father's lost domains on the continent and his first move was to regain his family's lands in Poitou. Other than Henry no one else was really very enthusiastic, yet with insufficient money and poor military resources, he insisted on making the expedition. His allies on the continent were few and far between but he did enter into an alliance with his mother, Isabella of Angoulême, and the family of her second husband, Hugh de Lusignan. Despite this the expedition floundered. Poor financing, failed promises of support, poor generalship and his near capture by the French, at one point, led to Henry returning home on 9th October 1243 empty handed. He was lucky that there was no rising of the barons in England as happened after his father's great defeat at the Battle of Bouvines. This was partly due to Henry's policy of giving out lavish gifts and hospitality to the great men of the realm at the expense of all other groups. He seemed to believe that if he kept the earls and the barons happy everything else would fall into peaceful place! He ignored the growing class of merchants, country knights and minor churchmen. His ongoing generosity to his barons also ignored the cost of his Poitou adventure, around £80,000, of which he still owed around £15,000.

Henry's second son, Edmund, was born on 16th January 1245 and, later in the same year, Henry began his great work of re-building Westminster Abbey to replace the original abbey of Edward the Confessor. This would be a huge Gothic structure, and its construction would be a continuous drain on funds from the royal treasury. This is, more or less, the abbey that we see today and it stands as the principal monument to Henry's artistic tastes and religious piety. Henry's piety stands out as a constant in his generally inconsistent character and although he used his religious projects to celebrate and bolster his kingship his piety was genuine. His use of religious symbolism for propaganda was highlighted when he managed to obtain a phial of Christ's blood from the Christian knights in the Holy Land. In October 1247 he personally carried this phial in a stately procession the one mile from St Paul's to Westminster where with great pomp he presented it to the abbey. His bishops celebrated it as an even greater relic than the piece of the holy cross acquired by Louis IX. In March 1250 Henry took the cross and vowed to go on crusade to the Holy Land. The saintly French King Louis IX was already there and Henry set about raising money and trying to reduce his household costs, to finance the venture. It all came to nothing. Henry had invested Simon de Montfort as lieutenant of Gascony in 1248 and now the territory was in open rebellion against

Simon's harsh rule. Speedily gathering up knights and cash, including the money he had raised for his crusade, Henry landed in France in August 1253. He was supported by his mother's relatives, the Lusignan family, and this campaign proved reasonably successful but at a huge cost. Again Henry's obligations, by way of the pensions and concessions that he gave to his supporters, grew beyond his ability pay and he had to incur more debt. At this time Henry also needed the southern border of Gascony kept secure and to this end, and incurring yet more costs, his son Edward was married to Eleanor, the half-sister of Alphonso X of Castile.

In February 1254, while still in France, Henry requested that the pope consider his son, Edmund, as a candidate for the Kingdom of Sicily. This was to be a major financial and political error. The pope wanted 135,000 marks for the nomination and Henry was broke and no one in England was much interested in securing Sicily. Resentment against Henry's excessive concessions to his, now vastly extended, family of Savoyards, Lusignans, his son lord Edward and Simon de Montfort grew into outright hostility. The factionalism that had dominated his minority had now returned in a new guise. Henry's indulgence towards those whom he hoped to keep the peace had seriously backfired on him and he was now too weak to contain them. In May 1258 Henry was forced to accept that a committee of 24 should be formed to secure the political and financial reformation of the realm. Their first move was to make peace with Louis IX of France and recognise his sovereignty of Normandy. Later in June Henry gave over all his powers to a royal council and his mother's 'second' family, the Lusignans were chased out of England. In December 1258 Henry knelt before Louis IX at Paris, in recognition that the bulk of his family's once extensive lands in France now belonged to the French king. From 1258 onwards continuing problems with Prince Llewelyn Ap Gruffudd of Wales, discontent along the Welsh Marches, the setting up of rival councils and investigations into the behaviour of Henry's officials saw his rule disintegrate. During 1260, perhaps seeing in Simon the strength that his father lacked, even Henry's son, Edward, joined with Simon de Montfort in revolt against Henry.

This alliance did not last but in 1263 Simon was able to successfully portray Henry as no longer fit to rule without being governed by a council. He proclaimed that Henry had pursued expensive and unpopular policies, that he had filled his court with aliens and had squandered his treasure on extravagant building projects and aggrandising schemes such as the failed, though still costly, Sicilian affair. He also declared that Henry had put himself above the law by breaking oaths and not correcting the oppression of his favourites. In December 1263 Henry sailed to France to meet Louis IX, who had been asked to arbitrate between the king and the English barons. Not surprisingly Louis found in favour of his brother-in-law. The barons were in no mood to accept what they saw as a biased judgement by a king for a king and in early 1264 the political struggle broke out into open war. On 14th May 1264 Simon, although greatly outnumbered, captured both Henry and his eldest son Edward at the Battle of Lewes. Shortly afterwards he called the first English Parliament that included two knights and two burgesses from a number of boroughs and shires, as well as the usual bishops and barons. For a year Simon carted Henry around with him while he ruled England with his new parliament. Ironically it was 'aliens' hogging the top positions that the barons had rebelled against but now a 'foreigner' was leading them. Simon was also a harsh and exacting leader and tensions soon arose. Contrary to popular belief Simon's Parliament did not attract the bulk of those who were entitled to attend and this severely weakened his authority, as did his rapprochement with Prince Llywelyn Ap Gruffudd of Wales. This latter 'betrayal' provoked rebellion by the lords of the Welsh Marches and it was while he was on his way to suppress it that Simon was cornered at Evesham.

Henry's son Edward had escaped from captivity in May 1265 and had spent the next three months pledging government reforms and gathering together a formidable army. On 4th August 1265 he skilfully surrounded Simon's army at Evesham. Before the battle Simon had dressed Henry in his own armour and then had him surrounded by a circle of his men. During the battle Henry was wounded in the shoulder and could well have been killed if he had not shouted out *'I am Henry of Winchester your king, do not kill me'*. It was a pitiful scene with Henry in danger from both sides. An enraged Edward triumphed over Simon and he and most of his followers were slaughtered. In fierce retribution for his treatment of the king, Simon's body was dismembered and decapitated, and his testicles were hung on either side of his nose. The estates of 254 rebels were confiscated and distributed among Henry's family and their supporters. From this point on Edward would take over much of the day-to-day government of the realm, before leaving on crusade in 1270. Henry's younger son Edmund, having failed to gain the kingdom of Sicily, was made earl of Leicester, and was given all of Simon's lands.

The cost of all this had been great and, for a time, Henry even had to pawn the jewels he had collected to adorn St Edward's shrine in Westminster Abbey. However, despite this blip in his veneration of St Edward, Henry achieved his great dream of moving the saint's remains to their new shrine on 13th October 1269. Amid splendid pomp and ceremony Henry, his two sons Edward and Edmund, and Henry's brother, Richard earl of Cornwall, carried St Edward's body on their shoulders to the new shrine that had cost so much of Henry's time and treasure. In August 1270 Henry lost the key figure who had helped him retain, and keep control of his kingdom, when his son Edward left England to go on crusade to the Holy Land. This was a severe blow to Henry. He fell very ill in March 1271 and, although he recovered, he never really regained his full strength and, in 1272, his most important councillor, after his wife, his brother Richard earl of Cornwall, died after suffering a stroke.

The boy king of nine was now sixty-five. It had been a long, if not particularly memorable, fifty-six years of kingship. When the end came the king was physically weak and suffering from some form of senile dementia. He was visiting the abbey at Bury St Edmunds in November 1272 when he seems to have suffered a mild stroke. After resting for a while he felt well enough to call a council but as Holinshed relates *'his sickness again renewing he broke the assembly and with all speed hastened to London. His sickness so increased upon him that finally he departed his life at Westminster on 16th day of November'*. It is more than likely that Henry suffered a cerebral thrombosis, and feeling that he might be close to death, *'hastened to London'* in order that he might die at Westminster, near his new abbey and the shrine of Edward the Confessor. The short, stout, ungainly old man with the blinking left eye *'who had buried all his contemporary princes in Christendom twice over'*, died without his eldest son Edward, who was still away on crusade, to console him.

A charter, dated in 1230, and now among the Westminster Abbey archives, records that Henry, like many monarchs before and after him, made early provision for his funeral. The Canon of Oseney recorded the event noting that, *'on the following Sunday (the feast of St Edmund) Henry was buried with honour in West Church his body adorned with the most precious robes and the royal crown ... borne to his tomb in a portable coffin by the more noble persons of the kingdom... he shone out with greater splendour and glory when dead than alive'*.

A later Patent Roll notes a payment *'for an image using 300 lbs of wax for a funeral procession of Henry III';* suggesting that Henry III's may have been the first royal funeral in England at which the corpse was hidden from public gaze inside a closed coffin with the king being represented by a wax image arrayed in royal robes and ornaments. This latter point is debatable. Some scholars believe that it was at the funeral of Edward II that the first image or effigy of a king was used to impersonate the corpse over a closed coffin. Before his death the king had asked that, at his funeral, the earl of Gloucester should, in full sight of all those present, place his bare hands on the coffin and swear fealty to the absent heir-apparent, the future Edward I.

Because his final monument was not ready at the time of his death Henry III was first buried in the small vault before the high altar originally used in 1066 for the grave of Edward the Confessor (Henry would have been so pleased). It was this vault (see above) that archaeologists, using low frequency radar, discovered in November 2005. Henry's body was probably embalmed, as when it was moved to its final resting place, in 1290, beneath a beautiful gilt-bronze effigy just to the north east of Edward the Confessor's shrine, it was found to be complete, with its luxuriant beard still intact. It was Henry's wish that his heart should be buried alongside his Plantagenet ancestors at the abbey Church at Fontevrault. However, it remained at Westminster for 19 years until December 1291 when it was formally handed over to the Abbess of Fontevrault who just happened to be visiting England at the time. Henry's grave was opened in November 1871, under the supervision of that great Victorian tomb-opener, Dean Stanley, to reveal a hard oak coffin lying inside a marble tomb as arranged by his son Edward I. The coffin was still covered in its original cloth of gold. Although meaning to open it to check on the physical condition of the king's body some feelings of discretion seem to have prevailed. Instead, Dean Stanley and his companions stopped, hesitated and in the end did not disturb it. We do not know if Henry intended to start a fashion by being buried on this raised 'tumulus' around St Edward's shrine but, as we shall see later, it certainly caught on.

The Re- Building of Westminster Abbey

Henry's legacy was to be that of a great builder. His patronage of art and architecture enriched the Great Hall at Winchester as well as new building works at Wells, Lincoln, Peterborough and Salisbury cathedrals. But his greatest achievement was the re-building of Westminster Abbey. An obsessive admirer of Edward the Confessor Henry took the latter's great Romanesque church and transformed it into an even greater French-Gothic one. In 1241, as part of his plan to rebuild the abbey, Henry ordered the building of a magnificent new shrine behind the current High Altar to take the body of Edward the Confessor.

In order to leave the Lady Chapel standing, which Henry III had constructed in his youth, the high altar was moved westwards to its present position. A mound of earth (the last funeral 'tumulus' to be built in England) was then built, between the high altar and the Lady Chapel. It was on this mound that the new tomb of the Confessor was to be fixed. It would be constructed in London and made out of the purest refined gold and precious stones by the most skilled goldsmiths. It would take time though (28 years) as Edward's body would not be moved there until 1269. It still lies there today – the only major English saint whose body still rests in its shrine, just a few feet away from his original tomb. That new mound of earth, with Edward's tomb at the centre of it, would become the last resting place of five kings and four queens of England. Only the base of Henry's magnificent fabric of purbeck marble decorated with mosaic now remains. Above this base stood the golden shrine, enclosing the Confessor's coffin, decorated with eleven small gold images of kings and saints and many valuable jewels.

On 6th July 1245, the new shrine to St Edward now well under way, Henry began the extraordinary job of demolishing the huge and solid Romanesque structure of the original Westminster Abbey. This work eventually occupied 400 workmen in high summer, falling to around 100 in midwinter. Henry lived to see the completion of the whole Choir and east end of the church. Edward's shrine had cost him around £1.8 million and the abbey would cost him £14.5 million, at today's values. Future kings, Richard II, Henry V, and Edward IV would have to dig deep to keep the project going. Between them they would spend a further £8.8 million, at today's values, to complete Henry's great vision; 250 years after Henry had started it. In total, the abbey cost just over £25 million, at today's values. The special taxation measures that Henry set up to gather in cash to pay for his abbey, and his other projects, formed one of those grievances that had made him unpopular with barons and commons alike. Given that there was never an original budget, it would be difficult to declare the kind of overspend that so often accompanies the construction of many UK government buildings, but there would be constitutional ramifications for Henry and his successors.

The re-building of Westminster Abbey and the Parliament of Simon de Montfort represent two related but opposite sides of Henry III's reign. One side was Henry's almost reckless and extravagant devotion to the arts and the fame of an English saint irrespective of the cost. The other side developed out of frustration with the continuing exercise of arbitrary power by an incompetent king. Part of this frustration was the enormous exactions that were made on the nobility, and the people, to fund Henry's lavish expenditure on unsuccessful expeditions to France, on furthering the claims of his many relatives, and on building his great abbey. Ironically, though part cause and effect of a medieval constitutional crisis, Parliament and abbey remain cordial neighbours to this day, 750 years after they were forged in opposition to each other. Even more ironic was the choice of Sir Charles Barry's Neo Gothic design for the new House of Commons in 1840. This design drew its inspiration from the tall pillars, arches and spires of the gothic style imported by Henry III to re-build the abbey in the mid 13th century. Parliament and abbey, as well as being neighbours, now shared the same suit of clothes. Not a bad legacy for a so called 'simple king.

EDWARD I (born 1239 reigned 1272-1307)

Edward I was born on 17th June 1239, the eldest son of Henry III and Eleanor of Provence. He was named after Edward the Confessor and was the first prince to be born at Westminster. The widespread celebrations at his birth were tempered somewhat after Henry III announced that he expected all his nobles to bring him gifts to record the event. *'God gave us this child, but the king is selling him to us'*. Edward was soon given his own household and knightly companions. Letters survive from his father showing concern over the quality of food and wine available to his son, and charging that Edward should always have an ample supply of lampreys. There seems to have been some concern over Edward's health when he was young but these did not continue and he grew to be strong and fit, and seems to have enjoyed excellent health for most of his long life. He was very tall for his times reaching the impressive height of 6ft 2ins. He was athletic and lithe with long arms and legs (he was often styled 'longshanks'), and his hair, silver blonde as a boy and dark in middle age turned bright, milk white when he was older. Although he had a slight lisp he was recorded as being fluent and reasonably persuasive in his speech.

In 1254, aged fifteen, Edward was married to Eleanor the half-sister of Alfonso X of Castile and became a faithful and devoted husband. Although an alliance born out of the military need to protect his father's Gascon borders, their marriage seems to have been a particularly happy one. Eleanor accompanied Edward on many of his travels and even went with him on crusade. Alfonso had been keen that his new son-in-law should be a man of means and so, at his marriage, Henry III granted Edward, Gascony, Ireland, the earldom of Chester and various other estates in Wales, Bristol, Stamford and Grantham. This gave Edward a degree of independence although he and his father often disagreed over policy in Gascony.

Edward's early years were spent observing the factionalism that beset his father's court and government. For a few years he fell under the influence of his mother's Savoyard relatives but later changed over to support his father's Poitevin half-brothers, the unpopular and harsh Lusignans. In 1258, when Edward's uncle by marriage, Simon de Montfort, emerged as leader of the baronial reform movement, Edward put his support behind the anti-de Montfort Lusignans, but later abandoned them and in 1261 he briefly joined with Simon against his father. This alliance was brief and Edward was with his father in France in early 1264 to hear the arbitration of Louis IX at Amiens. Louis supported Henry III against the barons and, unknowingly, lit the fuse for civil war in England. Despite Edward's effective command of the king's cavalry at the Battle of Lewes, in May 1264, the battle was lost. Henry III was captured and Edward had to give himself up to Simon de Montfort. In keeping with his status as the heir to the throne Simon kept Edward under tight surveillance rather than in a locked prison. At the end of May 1265, while out riding, Edward eluded his guards at Hereford and made his way to Roger Mortimer's castle at Wigmore on the Marches. Simon's autocratic rule had begun to alienate many of his previous supporters and men flocked to join Edward. In early August 1265 Edward, having had the bridges across the River Severn destroyed, to prevent Simon reaching his other forces, defeated Simon at the Battle of Evesham. The civil war rumbled on until Edward reduced the final rebel stronghold in the Isle of Ely in 1267.

During these years Edward had gained a reputation as a brave and effective soldier but he also gained a reputation for, changing sides when it suited him and being unreliable and untrustworthy. This behaviour may have resulted from the extraordinary dimensions of the crisis he faced in dealing with Simon de Montfort and the reforming barons. Nonetheless from this period on men were always wary of Edward's word and he continued to give them good cause, often proclaiming one set of rules but changing, or amending them, whenever he could profit from the change. Edward was conventionally pious and at Northampton in 1268, together with some other notables, he took the cross. Louis IX of France and his sons had pledged to go on the eighth crusade in 1267 and perhaps Edward felt that a son of England's king should also take up the cause. The project was not particularly popular in England and only got off the ground after a loan from Louis IX. Nonetheless, accompanied by a small force of around 255 knights, Edward left England in the summer of 1270. On his arrival at the siege of Tunis Edward found that Louis IX had died of dysentery. The crusaders agreed to move on to Sicily and then go on to Cyprus. Edward was the only leader to keep to the plan and, after calling at Cyprus for provisions, he arrived at Acre in May 1271. Once there Edward was involved in only two small campaigns before, against his will, a truce was made with the mamelukes in May 1272.

In June 1272 a Muslim attempted to assassinate Edward with a poisoned dagger. Edward managed to disarm the assassin, grab his knife and kill him but not before he, himself, had been stabbed in the arm. The master of the Temple attempted a remedy but the wound continued to putrefy. Although a romantic story has it that Edward's wife, Eleanor, saved him by sucking the poison from the wound, it was an English doctor, who had the good sense to cut away the decaying flesh, who saved his life. The crusade had turned into a lost cause but Edward perhaps enhanced his own reputation by staying on longer than any of the other leaders. But this had been an expensive affair and Edward had had to raise more money by way of loans from Italian bankers. In total the trip probably cost him in excess of £100,000. Financial acumen was not, and would never be one of Edward's strong points. He began his journey home and received the news of his father's death when he arrived in southern Italy. This news injected no change or sense of urgency to his plans. He took his time coming home, dawdling through Italy, visiting his mother's family in Savoy, calling on Philippe III, the new King of France, and then stopping off in Gascony to deal with a rebellion. He arrived in England on 2nd August 1274 nearly two years after his father's death. After all the turbulence of the Barons wars during his father's reign this slow progress showed Edward's great faith in the ability of his family and the royal councillors to keep his estate safe for him.

In his will of 1253 Henry III had urged his son to complete his great work on Westminster Abbey but Edward had seen this project suck the royal treasury dry and, already in serious debt himself, he decided to put things on hold for a while. Edward I, and his wife Eleanor of Castile, were the first king and queen to be jointly crowned in the abbey, on 19th August 1274. But the church hardly enamoured itself to the king when conspiracy and slack management led to Edward's treasure, stored in the abbey, being steadily pilfered. The abbey was not going to get much patronage after that. Rumours of silver goblets and royal rings turning up in the Thames, and at a London brothel, prompted Edward to order an inspection of his treasure. The ringleader and a number of lay accomplices were hanged while large numbers of monks were imprisoned, briefly, in the Tower of London where, following this incident, Edward also transferred the bulk of his treasury.

One of Edward's first acts, after his coronation, was to set up commissioners to enquire into the state of his inheritance. They would tour the whole of England to report on the workings of local government, including who owned (or claimed to own) what, and to note any abuse of the law or local power. Edward, perhaps with one eye on his debts to those Italian bankers, was particularly concerned to know what rights and lands might have been lost by the crown. His commissioners reported back to him in March 1275. Although they found many individual examples of extortion and corruption, within the huge mass of material they collected, they had had some difficulty pinpointing exactly what royal rights had been usurped.

Despite the immense scale of the enquiry, it was no Domesday Book, and provided Edward with little by way of important information that would help him out financially. The ambiguity resulting from this endeavour may have been one motive for the nine great

Parliamentary statutes that were passed during Edward's reign. The first of these was the Statute of Westminster in 1275 and this was followed by eight more up until the Statute of Quo warranto ('by whose authority') in 1290. The turmoil and opportunism among the barons during Henry III's reign had resulted in many abuses and unlawful seizures of land and this latter statute was aimed at clarifying the rights of lords to exercise jurisdiction over the areas that they claimed. After much debate the statute set out that anyone who could prove that his family had exercised franchisal rights continuously since 1189 could have them confirmed. The promulgation of these statutes represented an unprecedented volume of legislation over such a short time. The clerks working on these legal documents must have been working overtime! These statutes covered almost every aspect of property, criminal and commercial law, regulating the Crown's relationship with all levels of estate owners, be they secular or ecclesiastical. Much of this legislation clarified the relationships between lords and their tenants and guaranteed the agreed terms underlying gifts and the transference of land from one owner to another. Other provisions dealt with fraudulent bailiffs, regulating grants of land to the Church and the registration and recovery of debts. Arrangements for public security, including the widening of roads and cutting back the undergrowth near towns to reduce the cover available to robbers, were supported by measures setting out the arms that free men could bear to help prevent crime.

As well as being an energetic lawmaker Edward was also a very fertile king producing fourteen children, mostly girls, with his first wife Eleanor of Castile. However, only one son, Edward of Caernarfon (the future Edward II) survived to adulthood. But it was as a soldier king that Edward I would be mostly remembered and his first great trial of arms would be in among the mists and mountains of Wales. He'd made a start when, as lord Edward, he led an attempt to deal with Welsh incursions into English held lands between 1256 and 1257. At this time the Welsh princes occupied Anglesey and the, almost inaccessible, region around Snowdonia, an area much smaller than the one we call Wales today. From here, taking advantage of the disruptions in England under Henry III, the Welsh sallied forth and plundered those areas occupied by both the Welsh and Anglo Normans to the south and east of them.

After some twenty years of continuing Welsh incursions into the border counties of England Edward decided to act. In the summer of 1277 he managed to cut his father's old enemy, Prince Llywelyn Ap Gruffudd, off from his supply base in Anglesey and quickly forced him to surrender. In 1282 the Welsh rose again and Edward again invaded. This time the campaign itself did not go so well for Edward and one of his forces suffered heavy losses after an ambush in north Wales. However, Llewellyn's death in a skirmish ended Welsh resistance, leading to the complete conquest of north Wales by April 1283. Edward now claimed the country as his own. He disinherited most of the Welsh aristocracy, organised north Wales into shire counties and gave new lordships to his followers. He also began the ambitious castle-building programme that, in their ruins, still stand as a symbol of his conquest to this day. After the first Welsh war new castles were built at Flint, Rhuddlan, Builth and Aberystwyth. These were later joined by castles at Conwy, Caenarfon, Harlech and Cricieth. Many of the designs for these castles were taken from castle builders in Edward's mother's lands of Savoy. The Savoyard builders did not build to a standard pattern but details of windows, scaffolding and even the measurements of the latrine chutes suggest a strong connection. Caernarfon was a particularly magnificent structure, with its polygonal towers and dark stripes of masonry decorating the walls mimicking the Theodosian walls of Constantinople. It was an expression in stone of the old Welsh legend that the father of the Roman Emperor, Constantine, had been buried at Caernarfon. In 1301 Edward chose Caernarfon to announce that his son would henceforward be known as Prince of Wales, a precedent to be followed by every English monarch who had an eldest son. Building so many castles on the Welsh coast meant that, should they ever be besieged from their landward side, they could be supplied, unhampered from the sea.

The year 1290 was an important one for Edward. In that year he seems to have pleased everybody, attracting gifts from both Parliament and the Church, for being the first king in Europe to expel the Jews and seize their dwindling assets. They had been heavily and repeatedly taxed by Edward's father and no doubt those who still owed them money were pleased to see their debts disappear with them as they went. Their place was taken by Italian bankers and wool exporters, who loaned cash to the king in exchange for trading privileges. It was also the year that his beloved wife Eleanor of Castile died. The king was very much affected by her death and, although he remarried and lived on for seventeen more years, this was a deeply felt personal loss from which he never really recovered.

As complete as the conquest of Wales seemed rebellion broke out again in 1287 and 1294. The latter involving a series of successful Welsh assaults drew Edward back to Wales with an army of over 30,000 men and cost him around £55,000. His crusade of 1270 and his Welsh wars drained money from the royal revenues and in 1275 Edward negotiated with Parliament to levy a novel customs duty of 6s and 8d on every sack of wool exported from England. Customs duties like this provided the kind of ongoing security that Edward's Italian bankers liked. In 1284 Edward managed to reorganise some of his finances and commissioners were sent round the country to enquire into debts owed to the crown. Whatever the taxes raised, whatever the customs duties imposed, the crowns income in Edward's time would never keep up with the expenditure of a king who nearly always had an army to feed. Edward's French war of 1293-1303 was basically fought to retain his control of Gascony. It was a messy affair involving expensive payments to his allies and peace with the French was not finally agreed until 1303.

After helping the Scots pick John Balliol as their king in 1292 arrogant Edward began treating Scotland like a big shire county that he could dominate at will. This encouraged the Scottish lords to seek an alliance with King Philippe IV of France. It was the old enemy again, this time making friends on his northern borders and Edward was quick to march north. During his first campaign in Scotland in 1296 Edward captured Berwick and defeated and captured John Balliol at the battle of Dunbar. Balliol was taken to the Tower of London where he remained for several years before being exiled to France. Edward now declared himself King of Scotland and returned to London with the Stone of Scone, the ancient coronation seat of the kings of Scotland. He later had a special coronation chair made especially to contain it. Other than after a robbery, by clumsy Scottish Nationalists in December 1950, the Stone remained in King Edward's chair until 1996 when it was thought politically correct to return it to Scotland. It will be 'loaned' to Westminster Abbey for the crowning of future English monarchs. In 1297 earl Warrene, Edward's lieutenant in Scotland, suffered an ignominious defeat by William Wallace at the battle of Sterling Bridge. One of the English commanders, Cressingham, was killed and skinned by the Scots. Edward returned to Scotland for the second time with a huge army, around 30,000 strong, whose archers and cavalry easily defeated William Wallace at the battle of Falkirk in July 1298. Despite this victory Edward had not gained control of Scotland, only the areas around the castles that the English occupied in the south of the country. In early 1306, after having joined with Edward during 1301-02, Robert Bruce, probably disgruntled at the poor rewards he had gained as Edward's ally, made a bid for the Scottish crown and raised an army against Edward. He achieved some success against English forces in May1307.

Late in 1306 the chroniclers describe Edward as having developed 'a dysentery', the passage of blood and mucus in his stools perhaps indicating the onset of cancer of the rectum. Edward I, like William the Conqueror and Henry II before him, was rarely out of a suit of mail. His campaigns against the Welsh and his unfinished campaigns against the Scots had taken their toll on the health of the tall, handsome, healthy prince who had returned from the

Holy Land in 1275. By mid 1307 his illness became more acute, he became weak, lost weight and was forced to travel in a litter. His started his third invasion against Scotland in 1307 but his body, possibly much weakened by the cancer, could not equal the mental, almost manic, willpower that drove him on to Scotland. By the time he had passed Carlisle and on to the small town of Burgh-on-Sands he was near to death. It had been a mistake for him to travel so far and when his servants came to him at noon on 7th July 1307, to lift him from his bed for him to eat; he died in their arms, just within sight of the Scottish border. Although his health had been poor for some months before his death it is a testament to the mental and physical capacity of this sixty-eight-year-old man that he was able to undertake a campaign that involved marching almost the whole length of England.

As he lay dying, Edward is supposed to have required of his son that his flesh should be boiled off his bones and that those same bones should be kept and carried at the head of the English army until Scotland was finally subdued. His heart was to be sent to the Holy Land and two thousand pounds in silver was to be made available to support the 140 knights who were supposed to accompany it. Edward's body had to be taken south but for sixteen weeks his body lay at Waltham Abbey by the tomb of Saxon Harold. Then, four months after his death, he was buried in Westminster Abbey between his brother, Edmund Crouchback, and his father Henry III. The story of keeping Edward's bones to frighten the Scots was given some credence by various sources reporting that Edward's tomb was opened every two years so that the wax of the cerecloth covering the king could be renewed and the condition of the corpse inspected for when it was needed. Some yearly accounts do indeed exist from 1339 until the fifteenth century for wax to be used at Edward's tomb. Perhaps, like those European myths of 'the king who will return,' Edward's skeleton was to be pulled up and placed in front of an English army sweeping across Scotland and so it needed to be kept in good condition just in case?

In 1174, during the reign of George III, Edward's tomb was opened and examined in the presence of some senior clerics and certain Fellows of the Society of Antiquaries to test if Edward I's body had ever been removed for 're-waxing'. They found that his remains rested in a Purbeck marble coffin arrayed in coronation ornaments, with a crown and two sceptres. The innermost covering was indeed made of the very finest waxed cerecloth, superimposed over the body so closely that it revealed its exact form. They deduced from this that the remains of Edward I had not been disturbed or removed since their burial in 1307. So those old accounts didn't refer to anything inside the coffin. It is more likely that these accounts of expenditure on wax were for numerous 'wax' lights to burn around the tomb on each anniversary of the king's death, as was also the case for his Queen Eleanor, (see below). Sir John Ayloffe, who reported on the opening of Edward's tomb, noted that '*the corpse did not receive the least violation or injury; neither was it despoiled of any of its vestments, regalia or ornaments*'.

But everyone had had a good look, '*...the top of the coffin, and the stone slab covering the tomb, were restored to their proper places, and fastened down by a strong cement of terrice before the Dean retired from the chapel*'. Edward's black Purbeck box-tomb looks somewhat plain and crude besides the fine gilded bronze monuments close by. It is without mosaic, carving or effigy but it was not always as plain as it now appears and some traces of the original gilding can just about be seen. A sixteenth century inscription around the tomb is still visible. '*Edward primus Scottorum malleus hic est. Pactum serva 1308*': '*Edward I, hammer of the Scots, is here. Keep your promise 1308*'. Whoever put the inscription there was not so gifted in chronology, as Edward died in 1307 not 1308. Given the unfinished business in Scotland at the time of his death it might better have read 'Hammer of the Welsh', as, unlike the Scots, they were never to recover from his 'hammering'. Dean Stanley reported that a massive wooden canopy originally stood over the tomb until, during a later midnight funeral, the assembled mourners had to use some of the wood from it to defend themselves against attack by a mob.

One episode, often forgotten or ignored, in Edward's life is that in 1299, when he was sixty, and she was only seventeen, he married Margaret of France, the sister of the French King, Philippe IV. This marriage was part of the peace settlement with France that was eventually concluded in 1203. Although over forty years older than Margaret, he fathered three more children with her, during their eight years together. She remained in England after Edward died in 1307. She died in 1318 and was buried in the Church of the Franciscan Greyfriars in Newgate, London, where her niece, and successor as queen, Isabella of France, would also to be buried.

Nineteenth century historians dubbed Edward I the 'English Justinian' in recognition of the great range of statutes noted above. However his often arbitrary behaviour towards his nobles and his lifelong reputation for untrustworthiness have occupied more space in twentieth century histories. He was certainly a man, who though preaching the limits of the law to others often ignored it himself. The 'Song of Lewes' written during the Barons' war against his father reported Edward as being treacherous and untrustworthy, '*the lying by which he gains his ends he calls prudence*'. Although coming down to us as a great lawmaker there were many instances when Edward bullied his subjects unlawfully and others where he manipulated the law to enrich himself and his family. Nowhere was this more apparent than in Edward's manipulation of inheritance among his nobility, including bullying them, even on their deathbeds, to make lands over to him or his family. Edward was notoriously greedy and many of those who opposed him often did so out of disgust at the poor rewards they had been given in return for their allegiance. Certainly no angel, Edward was a tough character, stern, often uncompromising, harsh and brutal. He had seen what procrastination and weakness had done in his father's time and he was not going to see it repeated. Unfortunately his tough policies did not come cheap and he would leave his son a legacy of royal debts valued at around £200,000.

Eleanor of Castile

Edward's beloved Queen Eleanor died long before him in November 1290 near Lincoln. The tender angels of the hard warrior's nature emerged when Edward wrote: '*my harp is turned to mourning, in life I loved her dearly, nor can I cease to love her in death*'. He erected twelve beautiful 'Eleanor Crosses' (including Banbury Cross) at each point that her funeral cortège halted on its way to Westminster via Charing. Only three of these original crosses remain: namely Waltham, Geddington and Hardingstone. As was often the practice with medieval monarchs, bits of Eleanor were scattered about. Her entrails were left at Lincoln, her heart was deposited in the Blackfriar's monastery in London and her body was first placed in Edward the Confessor's original grave (now becoming a kind of holding vault) until she was moved to a fine tomb, at the foot of the monument to her father-in-law, Henry III. It was ordained that each year on the anniversary of her death (St Andrew's Eve) 100 wax lights were to burn around her grave and that this should be done forever. For a long time after this each new Abbot of Westminster, as part of accepting his office, had to publicly declare in the Chapter House that he would solemnly keep up this 'Eleanor' service. Three royal personages were now united with the Confessor on his burial mound, but the son of Edward I and Eleanor would not be joining them.

EDWARD II (born 1284 reigned 1307-1327)

Before engaging with his foolish and unfortunate son, we should note that at his death Edward I had left the wars in Scotland a bit like an unfinished Vietnam with many of his victories proving illusory as far as long-term gains were concerned. The wars had been going on for many years, were still not resolved, and at Edward I's death it looked as if Scotland could never be won. That sixteenth century inscription around his tomb, declaring Edward as the 'hammer of the Scots', suggests a king who had successfully defeated the Scots. The truth was that right up until the late fourteenth century and beyond, living in the northern counties of Cumberland and Northumberland was a dangerous and uncertain existence. It was more like living on the edge of a continuous terrorist threat than as part of a nation protected by the king's writ.

For many years the Scottish used the northern counties of England as a convenient bank, extorting money from the northern English to help fund their wars against the southern English. Indeed the 'Black Rents' they extorted from both lords and their tenants gave rise to the term 'Blackmail'. On Midsummer Day 1314 (seven years after Edward I's death) the army of Edward II was decisively defeated at Bannockburn by a Scottish army only a third the size of his, led by Robert Bruce. By the summer of 1315 a vast area of the north of England, equivalent to about 20% of the whole kingdom, was paying tribute to the Scots. This victory by Robert Bruce left the 'Scottish question' open for nearly 400 years until the peaceful Act of Union in 1707 brought the two old enemies together.

The Edward II who lost at Bannockburn was a great disappointment to his father. No great soldier he, his world revolved around fashion, frippery and all the amusements that a privileged life could bestow. A king at 23, Edward was born on 25th April 1284, the fourteenth child and fourth son of Edward I by Eleanor of Castile. The three elder sons John, Henry and Alphonso had all died young while their surviving brother, Edward, was tall, strong, golden haired and as good-looking as his father had been in his prime. But inside this fine Plantagenet shell there was no statesman, no warrior and no lawmaker. Instead there was a self-obsessed playboy addicted to amusement and aggrandising his amusing friends. His father certainly had some early forebodings particularly about his friendship with Piers Gaveston whom the old king banished from the court not once but twice.

Gaveston, the handsome son of a Gascon knight, had been a member of Edward's household since 1300 and the two young men had become close friends. Soon after his accession, Edward II restored Gaveston to court and lavished favours on him, including the earldom of Cornwall, a title normally reserved for the sons of kings. Edward's insult to the great earls by avoiding or ignoring their councils and his use of patronage to aggrandise Piers and a small coterie of idlers sealed his fate. By ignoring the traditional avenues of preferment reserved for the old aristocracy Edward was showing his contempt for them and they would not stand by and watch Gaveston reap their entitlements forever.

In January 1308 Edward married Isabella, the daughter of King Philippe IV of France, at Boulogne and during the same year rumours began to circulate that, even though married, Edward loved Gaveston more than his new queen. Much has been made of Edward's homosexual relationship with Gaveston and later the young Despenser, on whom he lavished even greater wealth. But other than for vague hints by chroniclers there is no solid evidence for this. As foolish as Edward was he was not going to provide categorical evidence of a sexual relationship with another man. Having said that Edward's outrageous behaviour in sending his father-in-law's wedding presents back to England, as gifts for Gaveston, was an outrageous insult to Isabella and her father redolent of the kind of reckless affection that only a besotted lover would indulge in. Such exhibitions make it hard to doubt that Gaveston and Edward were not sexually involved. If they were, and if Edward's servants at court new about it, such an exhibition of his affection towards another man would have added yet another layer of horror to the offence already felt by the martial masculinity of the older aristocracy.

Edward I had been a tough ruler and on his death there were certainly some barons who, kept in their place by the old Edward's powerful personality, would want to get back some of the power that had become centralised around a strong king. As luck would have it his son was just the person to give them the chance and the battle lines between weak king and strong nobles were soon drawn. Edward II was one of the most unsuccessful kings ever to rule England. With warmongering factions roaming the country, repeated political failure and some of the most horrific violence seen in the medieval kingdom there were few redeeming features to his reign. It has to be said that his legacy was not an easy one. His father's castle-building spree in Wales, the armies raised in France to secure Aquitaine, and three campaigns to take Scotland had left Edward II with massive debts. Edward I had had to call frequent Parliaments in order to expand the forms of taxation he needed to fund his great projects. And the wage bill was huge. No armies of a comparable size to those raised by Edward I would be seen on English soil until the Civil War in the seventeenth century. During Edward I's time a much more representative House of Commons (building on the initiatives of Simon de Montfort) emerged as a key element in the decision-making process and Edward II would have to deal with them.

In 1311 the barons sought to check Edward II's obsession with Gaveston by issuing the 'Ordinances' which demanded more control over royal appointments and that Gaveston be exiled for good. Edward agreed to their terms but within two months Gaveston, seemingly unaware of the danger he was in, was back flaunting himself at the king's Christmas court, and in 1312 his enemies captured and killed him. In 1314 the humiliation of Bannockburn forced Edward II to acquiesce in the government being taken over by a council led by his cousin, Thomas of Lancaster, an avaricious schemer but an incompetent organiser. Around 1317, Edward became involved with another fortune-seeking male favourite, Hugh Despenser. Hugh's father, also a Hugh, was close to the king and a sworn enemy of Thomas of Lancaster. These Despensers, father and son, were Marcher lords drawing their power from lands held on the borders between England and Wales. They were greedy and ambitious for land and power and they were just as wily at getting money and grants of land from the infatuated king as Gaveston ever was. In 1321 a combination of the other Marcher lords, in union with Thomas Lancaster, who resented the expansion of Despenser power in South Wales, forced Edward to exile his new friends. But a year later the king fought back with much greater resolve and this time the king's men triumphed over Lancaster at the battle of Boroughbridge, cut off his head and hanged two-dozen nobles, all in the name of revenge for Gaveston. It was an unprecedented judicial bloodbath and one for which Edward would pay dearly. But for now the Despensers were called back and Edward was, for once, victorious!

After this Edward and the Despenser family were on a high, with both the king and his two favourites enriching themselves with scant regard for law or justice. But in 1323 trouble in Gascony led to war with France a year later and in 1325 Edward sent his wife, Isabella, to Paris to negotiate with her brother, King Charles IV. Isabella was twelve years old when she married Edward and gave him two sons and two daughters, testimony at least to his bisexuality. But his close relationships first with Gaveston and then the younger Hugh Despenser had tested her patience to the limit and, despite her husband's pleas for her to return, she refused to leave France. Isabella now became a magnet for the discontented and there was no one more discontented than Roger Mortimer of Wigmore, another great Marcher lord. He had been captured by Edward in 1322, escaped from the Tower of London in 1323 and made his way to Germany and later to France. He now saw Isabella as his route to taking his revenge on the king and the Despensers and, to the horror of the French court, Isabella openly took him as her lover.

Isabella's eldest son, Edward, (later Edward III) had arrived in France in September 1325 to do homage to the King of France for Aquitaine in the name of his father. Isabella refused to let him return to Edward II and, with Mortimer, prepared to invade England. Isabella's brother King Charles IV of France, shocked by her behaviour with Mortimer, forced her to leave his court and she moved on to stay with the count of Hainault (in Flanders). The count agreed to provide Isabella with mercenaries for her invasion in return for her son Edward marrying his daughter Philippa. Isabella agreed and on 24th September 1326 Isabella, Mortimer and Prince Edward invaded England with a modest force. They landed at Orwell in Suffolk and faced no resistance. The two Despensers were soon caught and executed, the elder at Bristol on 27th October 1326, and the younger at Hereford on 24th November. King Edward was captured and first taken to Monmouth Castle where the great seal needed to call a Parliament was taken from him on 20th November 1326. On 16th December the king was taken, under guard, to Kenilworth Castle.

In January 1327 the Parliament that had been called by Mortimer, in Prince Edward's name, accepted that as he was *'incorrigible without hope of amendment'*, Edward II should be deposed. Edward, still at Kenilworth, and under great pressure, agreed to abdicate in favour of his fourteen-year-old son. Although Prince Edward was officially proclaimed king, in place of his father, on 25th January, and crowned at Westminster Abbey on 1st February 1327, it was Roger Mortimer who now took up the reins of power. The young king was entirely surrounded by Mortimer's servants and, at this time, Edward III was no more than a cipher doing whatever Mortimer instructed. The former king was moved from Kenilworth Castle on 2nd April 1327, transferred to the custody of Thomas Berkeley and John Maltravers, and imprisoned at Berkeley Castle, on the banks of the River Severn in Gloucestershire. While he was there a number of plots and conspiracies to free him were uncovered and Mortimer and Isabella became nervous lest one day, one of these should succeed.

While young Edward III was under their control, but without his knowledge, it is generally believed that Mortimer and Isabella made plans to murder his father and sometime in September 1327 they issued a direct order to Thomas Berkeley for the deed to be done. The killing of Edward II, if he was really killed in 1327, is the first royal murder since Saxon times. He will later be joined by Richard II, Henry VI and Edward V. Although he was executed, some would maintain that Charles I was also murdered, he was certainly deposed. The particular story of Edward's gruesome murder at Berkeley is one of fact mixed with myth mixed with horror.

On 21st September 1327 servants of Thomas Berkeley after trying, and failing, to starve Edward II to death in a stinking dungeon, eventually placed a heavy door over the weakened king. Thus immobilised a hollow animal horn was placed in his rectum so that a hot copper spit could be put into his body to burn the walls of his bowel. The animal horn would ensure that no burning would appear on his flesh, and by causing death via the failure of internal organs, no other marks of the murder would be seen on the body, should it have to be displayed in a public place, which was the usual form after the death of a medieval king. This account of Edward's death, derived from a selection of earlier chronicles, was written up 20 years after the event by one Geoffrey de Baker but none of the chroniclers who record the death of Edward II had first hand knowledge of what really happened at Berkeley Castle in 1327. They simply built on the rumours of the king's murder that were circulating at the time they were writing. Give or take a gruesome detail here and there, the Geoffrey de Baker chronicle has been taken as a reasonable record of what occurred, and it was too good a story to bother digging around for another.

On 23rd September 1327 Edward III was at Lincoln, 110 miles from Berkeley castle, when he received the news that his father had died. The letter implied that his death was from natural causes, after an illness brought on by grief at his deposition. The next day Edward III, wrote to his cousin, the earl of Hereford, and noted that *'my father has been commanded to*

God'. Mortimer refused a request for Edward II to be buried with his father and mother at Westminster Abbey and instead ordered that he should be buried in the abbey of St Peter at Gloucester, now Gloucester Cathedral. Edward II's body was embalmed in the usual way, the whole body, including the face, being covered in cerecloth. Then, after being watched over by servants loyal to Mortimer, the ex-king's body was taken to Gloucester Abbey where it would lie in state under a magnificent hearse for the next two months. No expense was to be spared over the dead king's obsequies. Eight hundred gold leaves were ordered for gilding the image of a leopard on the cover draped over the coffin and four great lions gilded, and dressed in the royal arms, were placed at the four corners of the hearse. A wooden effigy of the dead king, wearing a copper crown and dressed in his own robes, lay on the sealed, wooden coffin. The funeral took place on 20th December 1327 and was attended by Mortimer, Isabella, Edward III and several hundred more mourners. Given the winter gloom that must have pervaded the abbey at that time of year the spectacle of hundreds of candles, around the hearse, lighting up the effigy of the dead king, placed high up within the structure, must have made an impressive sight. Queen Isabella, still bearing some affection for the king she had displaced and allegedly murdered, had Edward II's heart enclosed in a silver vase which she intended to have buried with her. The dead king's coffin was then taken from the hearse and buried in a tomb on the north side of the nave. But was it really the body of Edward II who was lowered into that grave?

An Alternative Ending?

Another story emerges from a letter, to Edward III around 1336, written by an Italian papal notary, one Manuel Fieschi. This has Edward II being forewarned of the murderous intent of his jailers and orchestrating an escape from Berkeley after killing a porter. Fearful of Mortimer's and the queen's wrath at letting their prisoner escape, the servants responsible for carrying out the murder, substituted the porter's body for Edward's and reported to the queen and her lover that the king was dead. The escapee is supposed to have fled to Ireland and then to France, where the pope received him at Avignon. He then went on to Cologne and then to Italy, where he became a hermit. When Edward III was visiting Koblenz in 1338, a man calling himself William le Galeys appeared, claiming to be the king's father but no one there seemed to take this very seriously.

Yet another version of Edward II's survival after 1327 is that recently set out by Ian Mortimer, in the English Historical Review (see Sources). After nearly 40 pages of forensic examination of the contemporary evidence for Edward II's murder at Berkeley, Ian Mortimer concludes that Edward II was not murdered in 1327. His verdict is that Thomas Berkeley fabricated the ex-king's death, on Roger Mortimer's orders, for political purposes. Those purposes being to keep the old king alive, but confined in prison, so that he could better control the new king, Edward III. Thus if Edward III began to show signs of shaking off Mortimer's control Mortimer would wheel Edward II out to prove that the son had illegally taken the crown from his living father. Mortimer must have thought that the confusion resulting from such a revelation would ensure his role as the power behind the throne. If so this was a dangerous idea. The threat of exposing a living Edward II, like the threat to use a nuclear weapon, was only valuable as a threat. Once used it would be as damaging to Mortimer as to Edward III, possibly even more so. It would not be difficult for Edward III to prove that Mortimer was the master mind behind the deception which he, as a young boy of fourteen and in Mortimer's power, could not influence or control.

This theory corresponds with the tenor of the Fieschi letter but differs in the sense that it was Edward's captors, rather than the efforts of Edward II himself, who arranged for him to stay alive. Ian Mortimer rests his case on three main planks. His first plank is that no one other than Roger Mortimer's servants or retainers confirmed the identity of the corpse before it was embalmed and completely covered in cerecloth. The embalming was done within a few days of Edward II's supposed death and no one, attending the court at Lincoln, could have got there to see it before it was covered up. Thus there was ample time for another body to be substituted and at no time, after the corpse left Berkeley for Gloucester, was it open to view.

His second plank was that during 1330, three years after Edward II's supposed death, the earl of Kent, Edward II's half-brother, aided by a number of nobles, set in train plans to release Edward II from Corfe castle where he clearly believed him to be alive and kept as a prisoner. Indeed, knowledge of the ex-king's survival seemed to be quite widely accepted in 1330, the Mayor of London even preparing new clothes for Edward II in anticipation of his release. Roger Mortimer prosecuted the earl of Kent for treason and made no secret of the fact that Kent was being tried for planning the release of *'Sir Edward, sometime king of England, your brother, who was put down out of his royalty by common assent of all the lords of England ...'*. The pretence of Edward's death was thus exposed for all to see! A letter from Kent to Edward II in Corfe castle was read out, *'I have the assent of almost all the great lords of England, with all their apparel, that is to say with armour, and with treasure without limit ...'*. This evidence of a clear intention to rescue a man that Parliament had condemned to confinement secured Kent's conviction. The poor man now broke down and pleaded for his life. His plan to save his beloved brother had enmeshed him in Mortimer's own complex web of deceit and his trial had exposed the lie of Edward II's death in 1327. The young king Edward III must have been mortified that he had gone along with this great deception, breaking the rule of Magna Carta that no man should be wrongly imprisoned. Who knows what this future flower of chivalry was thinking as the young king sentenced his uncle to death?

Mortimer had only seven months to enjoy his ascendancy. In November 1330 he too would be executed as Edward III broke away from his evil mentor and became a real king for the first time. What Edward III could not escape from was that if his father, Edward II, was indeed alive he had joined, however unwittingly, in keeping an anointed king, in jail, in secret, for more than two years. Ian Mortimer's third plank is that Edward III never punished those supposedly responsible for his father's murder because such punishment would only open up the question as to whether murder had really been done?

If Edward II was alive after 1327 and after Mortimer's death in 1330 the question remains that, with Mortimer, the chief jailer, dead, what happened to Edward II? This is where the 'alternative ending' becomes less clear. The Fieschi letter is the only source to claim that Edward II was definitely alive after 1330. The letter describes Edward II travelling around Europe before turning up in Italy where he lived as a hermit under the protection of an Italian family with connections to Edward III and the English crown. The William le Galeys who turned up at Koblenz in 1338 was not punished as an impostor indeed his guardians were given expenses for keeping him. The Italian connection suggests that Edward II may have died in the autumn of 1341, 14 years after his supposed murder, and that he was buried in an unmarked grave somewhere in northern Italy.

Whatever the truth, for seven hundred years, a body believed to be that of Edward II, has lain beneath a tomb in the north ambulatory of Gloucester Cathedral. A splendid alabaster effigy (one of the finest in England) of Edward II, authorised by his son Edward III, rests on a tomb chest of oolitic limestone clad in Purbeck marble. Despite his woeful performance as a monarch, the ingrained English respect for the divinity of kings made this tomb at Gloucester a place of veneration for thousands of medieval pilgrims. It was the rich offerings of these pilgrims that helped Abbot Adam de Staunton's architects turn the once dark Romanesque choir of Gloucester into the splendid perpendicular structure that we see today. Edward II had done something right after all. One thing we should note, with regard to the certification of royal corpses. After the funeral of Edward II royal funerals were always carried out with the face exposed before burial to enable clear identification of the deceased.

The reign of Edward II was a struggle from day one. He inherited a costly and unfinished war with the Scots, huge debts and lords and magnates who were desperate to get back some control and influence after the iron grip of Edward I. To counteract the latter Edward II began building a wall of favourites around him who were outside baronial control and who, depending on him entirely, would be loyal to him alone. Edward's intoxication with these men, whom he cosseted and protected to such an extent that no lasting compromise between him and his enemies was possible, was a fatal flaw. It proved to his enemies that his personal pleasures and preferences were more important than the exercise of responsible government. Although many of their agendas were less than laudable, it gave his opponents enough of a stump of the moral high ground to proclaim that he was not fit to rule. The crux came after the execution of Gaveston and the fierce civil war and executions of 1320/21, after which, one chronicler recorded, that no noble condemned to death was allowed to speak in his own defence. Political violence had become a commonplace and no one, including the king was safe. The turbulent 1320s and 1330s of Edward II's reign set a template for violence against lords and kings which would emerge again during the reign of Richard II and during the violent dynastic squabbles of the mid 15th century.

When Edward II's wife Isabella of France died in 1358 she was buried at the Franciscan church in Newgate, London wearing her wedding mantle. An alabaster effigy of Isabella clutching Edward II's heart to her breast was destroyed when the priory was made a parish church around 1550. During the 18th century this beautiful, intelligent and learned woman gained the epithet 'She Wolf of France' and one story has it that the great power given to the chessboard queen is directly attributable to the power once held by Isabella over England. Isabella was pious and assiduous in her pilgrimages to English shrines and her enthusiastic collecting of relics. Her love of books, particularly and her love of chivalric tales is attested by the more than thirty books in her library when she died. Her role in the politics of the time was complex. She was marginalized by her husband and eventually turned against him. To the male chroniclers recording the times that was unforgivable, they rarely spared a line in an illustrated manuscript to highlight the indignities heaped on a woman. During her time with Mortimer she was reported as still being fond of the king she had helped displace and possibly murder. Perhaps she had some affectionate memories of an Edward who has been lost to us among the scandals and controversies over Gaveston and Hugh Despenser?

EDWARD III (born 1312 reigned 1327-1377)

Edward III was born at Windsor on Monday 13th November 1312, the eldest son of Edward II and Isabella of France. King Edward II was so pleased to hear that his line would continue that he granted the man who brought him the news the extraordinary sum of £80 a year for life. Breaking with established tradition Edward II then named his twelve-day-old baby earl of Chester a title normally given to royal children in their late teens. Clearly this son was a joy to his parents and a blessing to the realm. That realm would be plunged into civil war from 1320 onwards and the eight year old earl of Chester would have seen the start of it as his father and his Despenser favourites were defeated in 1321. He would then have seen his father regain strength and confidence and defeat his enemies at Boroughbridge in the following year. He would certainly have heard of the unprecedented violence that his father instituted in the aftermath of that battle, including the public beheading of Thomas, earl of Lancaster, the king's own cousin and a member of the royal family. Closer to home, he would have seen the way his father deprived his mother of her income and freedom following the Despenser ascendancy.

Small incidents often have big consequences and so it was in 1324 when a quarrel concerning the right of an obscure abbey to build a fortified town on their land in Aquitaine sparked a small war in France that Edward II had to respond to. Despite Edward's deteriorating relations with his wife he sent Isabella to negotiate with the French king, her brother, Charles V. It was in France that Isabella met Roger Mortimer an implacable enemy of the king and the Despensers. They became lovers and together they began to plot their mutual revenge. At this time Charles V was insisting that Edward II do homage for his lands in Aquitaine, a chore that Edward had been putting off. At first Edward wanted to go to France to do this himself but he was persuaded by the Despensers that they would be in mortal peril if they lost the king's personal protection. Edward eventually agreed that he should stay in England and, as an alternative, made his son duke of Aquitaine so that he could go to France to do the required homage on his father's behalf. Young Edward then left England and joined his mother. Once in her hands Isabella was not going to let her son go and the final break between the queen and her husband was sealed. Hardly anyone now remembers the name of the abbey of Saint-Sardos that precipitated this great rift and the eventual undoing of an anointed king that was its consequence. Isabella and Mortimer now made their way to Hainault to secure a mercenary army to invade England, and to agree that Prince Edward should marry Philippa, the youngest daughter of count William of Hainault, within two years.

Mortimer and Isabella, dressed in widow's weeds to mark a woman in distress, landed in England on 24th September 1327 and after this, royal power just evaporated from Edward II. Hugh Despenser the elder was caught at Bristol and summarily executed, despite Isabella's pleas for clemency. Prince Edward would probably have seen the younger Hugh Despenser dragged through the streets of Hereford on 24th November with verses from the bible written on his body. For maximum dramatic effect he was then hanged on a gallows fifty feet high. He was then cut down before he was dead and his heart and penis were cut out and thrown on a fire. Young Edward was getting to see at first hand how his nobles waged war! Edward's father was captured later, on 16th December 1327, and taken to Kenilworth castle where he was forced to abdicate in favour of his son.

Mortimer and Isabella had carried out the first invasion of England since 1066; they had secured the king, kept the goodwill of the people and only spilt the blood of a couple of hated royal favourites. The fourteen-year-old Edward III was crowned on 29th January 1327 at Westminster Abbey under conditions never seen before. He was the first king to be crowned king by parliamentary decree, the first son to be crowned king while his father was still alive and kept a prisoner and Isabella was the first queen to help organise the displacement of her husband to make all this possible. There is no evidence to suggest that Edward III was a reluctant player in the deposition of his father, but for three years the young king could not act independently and was plainly subservient to a duopoly made up of a regency council of barons, and Roger Mortimer. In January 1328, as agreed with count William of Hainault, Edward III married his daughter Philippa at York.

Mortimer aimed to run the country using the young Edward as a front for as long as possible. But, aged 17, the young king came out from behind to make the front a reality. During a council called in October 1330 at Nottingham, Edward's friends entered Nottingham castle by way of a secret tunnel and seized Mortimer in the hall of the queen's lodgings. Mortimer was then taken to the Tower of London and, just to be sure, masons walled him up in a room to ensure that he did not escape. Edward III lodged in the room next door. A month later Mortimer was dragged, bound and gagged to be charged before parliament with a long list of crimes. He was then hanged at Tyburn wearing the same black tunic he had worn at Edward II's funeral at Gloucester in December 1327. We cannot be sure, at this point, whether Edward III believed this his father was dead or alive. If he did believe him to be alive he was determined to maintain the fiction of his death by indicting all those supposedly involved in his murder, though most of them were, handily out of the country. Queen Isabella was allowed to retire to Castle Rising in Suffolk as long as she stayed quiet and out of politics. The 'true' reign of Edward III had begun. And it was to be, for a time at least, a splendid one. It was a reign best seen in two parts.

The first part was a story of political stability, martial success in France and the celebration of knightly chivalry. Thanks partly to Edward's adroit accommodation with the still novel institution of parliament, the nation enjoyed one of the longest rebellion-free periods in its history. In 1328 Charles IV of France, the last of the direct Capetian line, died without a male heir. Edward could make a credible claim to the throne of France through his mother Isabella, who was Charles' sister, so in 1338 he announced his claim, beginning the 115 years war with France that lasted on and off until 1453. There were a number of early failures but Henry of Derby's whirlwind campaign to recapture Gascony in 1345 injected Edward with new energy and zeal and in early July 1346 he landed in France with an army made up mainly of foot soldiers and longbowmen. A very unchivalrous orgy of rape, burning and pillage soon followed. August 1346 found Edward and his army on the defensive at Crécy but the over confident French cavalry, waiting until just before sunset to attack, rode into cloud after cloud of English arrows, leaving the flower of their youth piled up in front of the English army. It was a momentous victory against overwhelming odds.

From Crécy Edward made his way to Calais. He needed a bridgehead in France from which he could safely supply his troops during further invasions. Calais was a strong defensive town, almost impregnable, it was the nearest port to England and it was well protected from the weather to facilitate supplies all year round. In 1347 Edward settled down for a long siege of the town. The French assembled an army to attack him but Edward's position looked impregnable and they went away again. After 11 months and being forced to eat their cats and dogs for lack of supplies, the Calais garrison gave in. Edward agreed to accept their surrender only if six leading members of the town came out, with ropes around their necks, carrying the keys to the castle and the town, for him to do as he wished with them. They did as they were asked and prostrated themselves before Edward who then ordered them to be beheaded. Everyone was shocked at this, not least because of the message it would send out to any French armies that might conquer an English held town. The story goes that Queen Philippa begged Edward to relent and he did. The incident of the 'six burgers of Calais' has been passed down to us as the victory of a humanitarian queen over a ruthless and unfeeling warrior. But Edward had gone to the wire on this kind of thing before; it was a kind of theatre that allowed him to look both tough and magnanimous, not a bad message for a supposedly chivalric king to send out. Much to the discomfort of their French allies'

Scottish military action across the borders in England, meant to draw resources away from France, had not been very successful. In October 1347, before Calais had surrendered, the Scottish king, David II, had been captured at the battle of Neville's Cross near Durham and taken to London as a prisoner. In many ways Calais was a greater victory than Crécy. Handily close to England it remained the key English base in northern France for the next two hundred years. It even sent MPs to the English Parliament between 1536 and 1558, the latter year being the year that the French took it back.

Back at home in England Edward would face an enemy that no sword or armour was proof against. In 1348 the plague crept into England via a Genoese ship, killing over forty percent of the population. The plague would strike again in 1361/62, 1368/69/ and 1374/75. The human devastation these visitations caused in the towns and villages of England fuelled price rises, demands for higher wages and disrupted the once fixed patterns of social and economic relations for many years to come. The end of Edward's reign saw many employers struggling to hold down wages and many workers seeking to push them higher to secure a better life for themselves and their families. The seeds of the Peasants' Revolt in 1381 came with a flea on a rat. After his victories in France during 1346 and 1347 and, despite the plague ravaging his kingdom, the year 1349 found Edward busy creating the Order of the Garter.

Despite the brutal carnage that his armies had wreaked in France, Edward III was much taken by the chivalric romances. He wanted to emulate the knightly, if largely fictitious, behaviour embodied in the cult of St George and King Arthur. A key element of this was the still formal, but new-style, tournament of single combat rather than the mock battles of the earlier century. At a tournament, held at Windsor, on St George's day 1349, Edward announced the formation of a new order – the 'Order of the Garter'. The twenty-six knights who attended and took part in that tournament became its first members and were supposed to be *'co-partners both in peace and war'*. Edward was probably building on the more informal 'Companionship of the Garter' that his son, 'the Black Prince', had founded in 1348. The choice of a 'garter' as the symbol for Edward's new order was probably based on the garters often worn (over his armour) in his youth, by the great warrior, friend and cousin of the king, Henry, duke of Lancaster.

The charming story, much repeated, is that the Garter symbol and its famous motto, *'Honi soit qui mal y pense' (evil to him who thinks it evil)*, stems from Edward III picking up the countess of Salisbury's garter at a ball after the fall of Calais. The king is supposed to have chosen the motto to rebuke those onlookers who saw some ulterior motive (evil thoughts) in his action. As good a story as it is this is probably a myth. Mid 14th century women did not wear garters. It would be consistent with Edward's serious approach to ceremonial of this sort that the motto was more than a casual piece of whimsy. Perhaps he was making a comment on those killjoys who felt that it was unfeeling and ungodly to hold a great tournament at the height of the worst plague to hit England. Tournaments were often associated with a heightened sexual freedom among the combatants and the ladies who attended. Plague and sex, disgusting!

Edward III had used a personal motto before to 'frame' one of his great spectacles and this one was also enigmatic. In 1342 he held one of the largest tournaments of his reign involving more than 250 English knights and he had a personal motto, *'it is as it is'* embroidered on just about every piece of cloth used at that event. One theory is that this motto signified that Edward's father, Edward II, thought murdered at Berkeley Castle in 1327, but possibly still alive somewhere in Italy after that time, was now, at last, truly dead. Emphasising the second 'is' of the motto those of Edward III's court who knew of the secret would understand its meaning and could join with him in celebrating his freedom from the living ghost of his father.

In 1356 the king's eldest son, Edward 'the Black Prince', using the same military tactics his father had used at Crécy, won another great victory against the French at Poitiers, this time carrying off the French king, John, to join King David II of Scotland for a well-earned rest in captivity. Two enemy kings, one at Windsor and one in the Tower: not a bad haul! A treaty of 1360 confirmed Edward's rule over Calais and Aquitaine in return for him dropping his claims to the crown of France. His victories at Crécy in 1346 and Poitiers in 1356 represent the high water mark of Edward's military career. But winning is one thing, 'keeping' is another, and maintaining English rule in territories as far away from England as those in Aquitaine proved too difficult and too expensive. By 1374 all that England held in France was Calais and a smaller strip of southwest France than that which Edward had inherited in 1327. Another 'victorious' king, Henry V, would follow Edward in the next century; and his successes would also wilt under the unforgiving sun of French harassment.

As well as a highly successful warrior abroad, Edward III was also a successful peacemaker at home, garnering continued and faithful support from the baronial classes throughout his reign. A key component of his policy was the marriage of his children to the sons or daughters of great lords in order to make the baronage a huge extension of his own family. Thus the great families of Mortimer and Lancaster were made faithful family members rather than disgruntled outsiders. Or, as President Lyndon Johnson was to say, in another political era he got them *'inside the tent pissing out rather than outside the tent pissing in'*. Giving his great magnates the opportunity to test out their valour on French soil and share in the distribution of the loot thus acquired did him no harm either.

The second and least illustrious part of the king's reign really starts with the death of his wife Queen Philippa after a long illness in 1369. They had been married for 41 years and, despite her many years of illness, she had been making preparations for her tomb as early as 1362. Edward felt her loss most dearly. She had been with him during those early and dangerous days when he was ruled by Mortimer, she had been the force that kept the peace between her quarrelling sons and she had been his oldest and closest companion. After her death Edward may have suffered a minor breakdown. Certainly his libido now seemed much stronger than his martial stamina and he resorted to a succession of mistresses. The most notable of these was Alice Perrers. His mental grasp on events may have been affected by his doting on her, as one chronicler noted that during the final years of his life Edward III *'had no more discernment than a boy of eight'*. He certainly became reclusive, more withdrawn and less involved in the work of royal administration. Later the death of his first and favourite son, Edward, 'the Black Prince' in June 1376, after six years of debilitating illness (probably dysentery), affected Edward greatly. It was 'the Black Prince' who at sixteen had engaged in frontline combat at the battle of Crécy and it was he who a decade later defeated the French King John at the battle of Poitiers. Until his illness in 1370, the king had relied on his eldest son to keep order in Aquitaine and his death was a great loss both personally and militarily. The embalmed body of his son lay in state in Westminster hall for nearly four months before it was moved for interment to the cathedral at Canterbury, close to the tomb of St Thomas Becket. It is entirely possible that Geoffrey Chaucer himself, as a minor official in the royal household, took part in the long funeral procession from London down through Rochester to Canterbury.

Edward III first seems to have been taken seriously ill in September 1376, three months after the death of his son; but with the aid of a diet of broth and bread dipped in goat's milk, he made a full recovery. His relations with Parliament, once so convivial now broke down completely. The 'Good Parliament' of 1376 fiercely attacked the king and those hangers-on who were corrupting the good of the state. Chief amongst these was his grasping mistress Alice Perrers, who had secured the promotion of her husband as Governor of Ireland and was involved in the financial scandals that were rocking the court. But senile Edward was now beyond responding to calls for better government. In April 1377 he was at Windsor for his last celebration of St George's day. Here, in a festival of irony that we can appreciate in hindsight he knighted both the future Richard II and Richard's eventual supplanter, Henry Bolingbroke, John of Gaunt's eldest son. On 21st June 1377, deserted by his family and irritated by a priapism and shingles, in addition to serious arterial trouble, Edward III died at his Palace of Sheen.

This palace, near the present day Richmond Park in London, grew from a manor house used by Edward I to escape the noise and bustle of London. Part of the palace would later be pulled down by Richard II in his desperate grief at the death there of his wife, Anne of Bohemia. In 1497, a fire destroyed most of the rest and Henry VII rebuilt it and called the new palace Richmond after his own family name. This new palace became the occasional resort of many English monarchs. After the death of Charles I in 1649, Parliament had it surveyed and over the next 10 years it was mostly demolished and the stones used for other buildings. The French historian Jean Froissart, a friend and frequent guest of Edward III, describes a pathetic deathbed scene at Sheen not unlike (less the sexual excitement) those experienced by William the Conqueror and Henry II:

'Shameful to relate, during the whole time that he was bed-ridden, King Edward had been attended by that infamous whore Alice Perrers, who always reminded him of things of the flesh .... When she realized that he had lost the power of speech and that his eyes had dulled, and that natural warmth had left his body, quickly that shameless doxy dragged the rings from his fingers and left'. A priest who found him some hours later gave him a crucifix to hold and heard him say *'Miserere Jesu'* in sign of repentance before expiring. He was sixty-four and had reigned for over fifty years.

The anonymous Chronicon Anglie also gives a key role to the *'infamous whore'*. He notes that the king grew weak *'not of the kind that is believed to be usual in old men, but which is said to attach itself for the most part to youths given to lechery'.* Noting that the *'old man's chilliness'* makes him more vulnerable in this than *'the young man's heat'* he declares that the king's natural fluids and nutritive heat were exhausted by all this desire *'and his virility failed'.* His weakness was thus directly attributable to *'his desire for that wanton baggage Alice Perrers',* not least as shortly before his death this *'courtesan along with her daughter Isabella had lain with him all night long'.* Medieval chroniclers (often misogynistic monks) love a scarlet woman and though these colourful stories are probably true in relation to the proximity of Alice Perrers to the king during his last days, it seems unlikely that Edward's death was directly related to venereal disease contracted from his mistress. She is known to have born him a son and two daughters and none of them are recorded as having inherited a venereal infection.

Less colourful, but more likely, is that Edward died from a circulatory disorder leading to a cerebral thrombosis that damaged the right side of his brain. The effects of this can clearly be seen on the face of his wooden death mask portrait. The carving shows a mouth that is twisted from some form of facial paralysis such as often follows a stroke. This would be commensurate with reports of his decline and dotage. Edward's is the earliest surviving death mask of an English monarch and formed part of the plaster and linen effigy that was carried on the bier during his funeral. It can still be seen today on display in the Undercroft museum at Westminster Abbey. His body was taken from Sheen in solemn procession to Westminster Abbey for burial. The journey took three days and poor men clad in black, all bearing torches, accompanied the coffin. In all, an astounding one thousand seven hundred normal sized torches were used, plus three hundred larger ones that were placed close to and around the tomb. Fifteen large candles also added to the brightness of the scene. Fear of fire must have been a real concern during these torch and candlelit rituals. Later Edward was buried with proper pomp and dignity: the expense of his household, shortly to be disbanded, rose to £566 for the day of the funeral.

His splendid bronze tomb was constructed 10 years later. Not the effigy of a great warrior, like that of his son 'the Black Prince', old Edward's days of glory on the fields of France were too faint a memory for that, but that of a noble and dignified old man with flowing locks (despite his near baldness) and the beard of an Old Testament prophet. The sword and shield that Edward used in France were kept near his tomb until the time of Elizabeth I. Dryden notes that young men might freely take them and wield them about in sport. *'How some strong churl would brandishing advance The monumental sword that conquer'd France'.*

Longevity proved to be the undoing of Edward III's reputation, as at his funeral little remained of his French conquests except the fortresses at Bayonne, Bordeaux and Calais. His real legacy is better represented by the small, delicately carved effigies of his children set in niches around his tomb. In a recent biography of Edward III, Ian Mortimer calculates that as thirteen of Edward III's children survived to adulthood, producing around fifteen hundred descendants by the year 1500, his genes are now probably shared by all but about one percent of the white population of the UK. Edward III was the first English king to grant dukedoms based on English territory and the progeny of these royal dukes - Lionel duke of Clarence, John of Gaunt duke of Lancaster, and Edmund Langley duke of York - would bedevil, complicate and muddy the dynastic struggles of England for the next one hundred years. It was their great-grandchildren who would be directly responsible for what Sir Walter Scott in his 1829 novel 'Anne of Geierstein' first called 'The Wars of the Roses'. But at Edward III's death the start of these struggles was 22 years away, as the first son of his first son, Richard II, would be peacefully crowned king despite being a child of just ten years old.

The symbolism, badges, emblems and heraldry of Edward III's Knights of the Garter seem far away and irrelevant to us now. But these, and even earlier symbols, refuse to die. The white rose, a badge supposedly worn by David II of Scotland when held prisoner in the Tower by Edward III, was later taken up by Charles Edward Stuart during his Jacobite rebellion of 1745. In 1999 it was also worn by Scottish nationalist MPs when Queen Elizabeth II opened the new Scottish Parliament in Edinburgh. The shirts of the English football and cricket teams still carry the three lions 'passant guardant' chosen by Richard the Lionheart on his return from captivity in 1195. These 'irrelevant' old symbols hang around for a long time and once a year the present day Knights of the Garter still walk to their service in St George's Chapel Windsor wearing cloaks, garters and badges that would have warmed the heart of Edward III.

RICHARD II (born 1367 reigned 1377-1399)

Richard II, often referred to as 'Richard of Bordeaux', was born on 6th January 1367 at Bordeaux in his father's duchy of Aquitaine. He was truly very well connected. He was a great, great grandson of Edward I on his father's side and a great-grandson of Edward I on his mother's side. His father was Edward, the famed 'Black Prince', his mother was 'Joan the Fair maid of Kent', a daughter of that Edmund earl of Kent who was born to Edward I by his second wife, Margaret of France, when he was 64 years old. This was the same earl of Kent who tried to release (the dead?) Edward II from captivity in 1330 and was executed for his pains.

Richard spent the first four years of his life at his father's court in Bordeaux. His elder brother, Edward of Angoulême, who had been born in 1364 died there after which Richard and his family moved back to England. As Edward III fell into decline Parliament, fearing that Richard's powerful uncle, John of Gaunt, might harm him and seize the throne, required Richard to appear before them in 1376 so that they *'might see and honour [him] as the true heir apparent'*. Richard succeeded as King of England on 22nd June 1377, at the age of ten, on the death of his grandfather Edward III. His father Edward the Black Prince had died the year before, so he lost his father and grandfather in quick succession. A series of councils governed the country between 1377 and 1380 and various servants of Edward 'the Black Prince' exercised some control over the boy king. Even during these early days Parliament registered concerns over the seeming extravagance of the royal household. The hangover from Edward III's military commitments in Calais and the Scottish border required heavy taxation and three unpopular poll taxes were levied between 1377 and 1381.

It was the activities of the poll-tax collectors in south Essex in May and June 1381 that sparked off the Peasants' Revolt. The demands of the peasants, particularly those seeking the emancipation of serfs, were rooted in the social and economic tensions that rose out of the swinging mortality caused by the great plague. In early June bands of rebels from Kent joined those from Essex and several thousand entered London. Having retired to the Tower of London with his councillors the fourteen-year-old king heard of the destruction being caused by the rebels in the city. He decided to ride out to meet them at Mile End on Friday 14th June. In this, unlike his household knights, who stayed in the Tower, he showed great personal courage. Richard offered the rebels charters of freedom and a pardon for their rebellion if they went home. Richard's proud bearing drew respect from the rebels who assured him that they sought no harm to him, only the evil councillors who had misled him. They were ready to disperse when Richard received news of another rebel group, who had broken into The Tower and murdered the king's chancellor.

On the next day, 15th June, Richard confronted the rebels again, this time at Smithfield, and asked their leader, Wat Tyler, why they would not go home. Tyler replied that they would not disperse until their demands were met. Angry at Tyler's impertinence, the Lord Mayor of London rode forward and struck him, killing him on the spot. Sensing the danger that they were now all in Richard boomed out to the rebels, *'I am your leader: follow me'*, drawing the rest of the mob away from the melee around Tyler and giving royal reinforcements time to arrive. Although he agreed a pardon for the leaders of the revolt they were later arrested and executed. Whether Richard broke his word intentionally or whether he was forced to break it by others is not known. Either way the rebels gave up and those who survived the executions, dispersed, and went back to their towns and villages.

Previous kings of England had sought marriage alliances close to home, in France or Spain. But in Richard's case his government believed that an alliance with Anne of Bohemia would be just the bulwark that England needed against the weight of France. Anne was the daughter of the late Emperor Charles IV and sister of the emperor-elect and King of Bohemia, Wenceslas IV. This was the time of schism in the church. England and the empire recognised Pope Urban VI, in Rome, while the French recognised his rival, Clement VII, in Avignon. Building on such concord, with a marriage, could extend English influence in central Europe and cement a valuable alliance. Anne came to England in May 1381 and was married to Richard in the following January. In the end the alliance with the empire, did not bear fruit despite Richard having to pay £16,000 to Anne's father. Although Anne never bore Richard any children their relationship seems to have grown into one of genuine affection.

At the time of the Peasants' Revolt the young king had seemed to show great promise, but, as he matured, cultivating the art of diplomacy took second place to more aesthetic interests. Sensitive, refined and artistic of temperament, he loved books, literature, fashion and fine food – he insisted that spoons be used at court. He fostered the fashion for wearing shoes with elongated toe pieces and is thought to have invented the handkerchief. More substantially, his interest in architecture led to the construction of the beautiful hammer beam roof in William Rufus' Westminster Hall. He was also garrulous, highly-strung, capricious and quick tempered. By the time he was nineteen he was attempting to rule via the favourites he had personally appointed to his household. This large and expensive group was openly despised by key members of the 'larger' aristocracy who soon challenged Richard, making it clear that an earlier king, Edward II, had been deposed for behaving much like Richard was now. Like that doomed monarch, Richard had little understanding of the deals and compromises that were an essential aspect of 14th century politics.

By 1387 Richard was still lavishing patronage on his courtiers and friends, the wars in France were going badly and in 1386 Charles VI of France was even planning an invasion of England. Parliament insisted on establishing a commission to control all the king's finances for a year and to conduct a thorough review of royal finances. Richard saw all this as a major assault on his royal prerogative and he decided to embark on a nine-month progress around England to put as much distance between him and the interfering commissioners as possible. During his time on the road Richard quizzed various judges about the legality of parliament's commission and all of them declared it illegal to infringe his prerogative, against his will, and declared those who did so to be guilty of treason.

Richard returned to London in November 1387 determined to enforce his will but was met with three earls, Gloucester, Arundel and Warwick who demanded an indictment of treason against five of his favourites. Richard played for time, while his supporters raised forces in Cheshire. These three earls, calling themselves the lords appellant, were later joined by John of Gaunt's son, Henry Bolingbroke, earl of Derby and Thomas Mowbray, earl of Nottingham. Their forces easily routed Richard's Cheshire army at the battle of Radcote Bridge on 20th December 1387 and Richard was forced to call a Parliament which he knew would put his favourites on trial for treason. Richard was detained in the Tower of London for a time and his unpopular counsellors were either executed or exiled. Those judges who had suggested to Richard that encroaching on the royal power was treason now all found themselves charged with the same offence and were lucky to survive. They were exiled to Ireland!

The lords appellant did not seek to institutionalise the power they had assumed in 1387 and by 1389 Richard had resumed responsibility for the conduct of the government. In the years that followed, Richard appeared to have heeded the lessons of 1387 and became more cautious in his dealings with his nobles. The amnesty was not to last. Richard's devotion to an idea of kingship, similar to that that would later be known as the Divine Right of Kings, grew more and more, particularly after the death of his wife, Queen Anne. Anne had been devoted to her husband and had often been successful in calming Richard's impetuous nature. Theirs was a marriage, though originally a union for state reasons, which turned into a real love affair. Unfortunately, Anne died of the plague in 1394 at the palace of Sheen. Richard was so affected by her death that he had a whole slice of the palace pulled down. He then had the graves of two grandchildren of Edward I moved from the Confessor's

Chapel in Westminster Abbey in order to release this site for his queen and himself. Like Henry III, Richard was a dedicated follower of Edward the Confessor and when in England always left a special ring at Edward's shrine. Anne's funeral, a dramatic night time affair, was celebrated at enormous cost with hundreds of wax candles being brought in from Flanders and the leading nobles being summoned to attend by an insistent and imperious letter. Illuminated by hundreds of torches, the like of which had never been seen before, Anne's body was laid before the shrine of the Confessor.

The earl of Arundel, who arrived late for the funeral, having already missed the lying in state, then had the temerity to ask the king if he could make an early exit as he had some pressing business to attend to. Richard, suffused with grief and outraged at such insensitivity, seized a mace from a verger and struck Arundel who, bleeding from the blow fell to the floor. Notwithstanding his status, Richard's act of sacrilege had polluted the sanctuary with blood and the churchmen present promptly suspended the funeral. In September 1396, aged twenty-nine, Richard married the seven-year-old Isabella of Valois, daughter of King Charles VI of France. Isabella, as a child, was a queen in name only, being cared for by servants at Windsor where Richard occasionally visited her. When Henry IV became king, he sent her back to France, less her jewellery, where she married Charles, duke of Orleans and died in childbirth aged twenty. Her younger sister, Catherine of Valois, would later marry Henry V and her husband Charles would be imprisoned by him in the Tower of London for twenty-five years.

In September 1397, seemingly out of the blue, Richard decided to rid himself of the original lords appellant. He had the tardy earl of Arundel executed, the earl of Warwick exiled to the Isle of Man and his uncle the duke of Gloucester murdered while in captivity in Calais. In 1398 he banished Henry Bolingbroke for ten years after Henry quarrelled with Thomas Mowbray duke of Norfolk amid charges and counter charges of treason. Henry was heir to the mighty John of Gaunt, third son of Edward III, duke of Lancaster and Richard II's uncle. After Gaunt's death in the same year Richard increased Bolingbroke's banishment to 'life' and confiscated his lands. These were the great estates of the duchy of Lancaster and Richard was keen to bring them back to the crown. Later, Richard left for a campaign in Ireland. While he was away the aggrieved Bolingbroke landed in Yorkshire, initially just seeking to secure his inheritance as duke of Lancaster. But by the time Richard arrived back on the mainland in south-west Wales, a tide of discontent had swept England and Bolingbroke was being urged by many nobles to seize the crown. Richard was captured by subterfuge after leaving Conway Castle and taken to London.

By 2nd September 1399 Richard was held in the Tower of London. Bolingbroke's motives now became crystal clear. He established a committee to declare clear reasons why King Richard could be set aside. This committee conveniently concluded that Richard's *'perjuries, sacrileges, sodomitical acts, dispossessions of his subjects, reductions of his people to servitude, lack of reason, and incapacity to rule'* were just grounds for his deposition. On 29th September a deputation of lords, including Bolingbroke, visited Richard in the Tower where he was forced to abdicate after a reign of twenty-two years; he was just thirty-two years old. The deputation put it out that Richard simply repeated a promise to abdicate that he had already made at Conway. Other sources suggest a different response and one has Richard denouncing his fellow countrymen as having *'exiled, slain, destroyed and ruined so many kings, so many rulers, so many great men'*. He was deposed by Parliament the next day amid a reading of thirty-nine accusations against him. Parliament later accepted Henry Bolingbroke as their new king, Henry IV. There is little certainty about what happened to Richard next. Before Christmas 1399 he was taken first to Knaresborough and then to Pontefract Castle in West Yorkshire for safekeeping. It is believed that he died there in early 1400. He was certainly dead by 17th February.

Various minutes from the General and Exchequer Council early in 1400 seem unsure whether Richard is alive or dead and suggest that if alive he be securely guarded and safely locked up or *'if he be dead'* to be shown openly so that the people could *'have knowledge of the fact'*. That the king and his council were actively involved in the details of Richard's last days is shown in at least two recorded exchequer payments. One to a clerk sent to Pontefract Castle on *'secret business, by order of the King'* and another to a valet of Sir Thomas Swynford (a brother-in-law of Geoffrey Chaucer) coming from Pontefract to advise the king's council *'of certain matters which concern the kings advantage'*.

Like his great grandfather, Edward II, before him, Richard disappeared behind the secret walls of a castle with few witnesses prepared to attest as to how he met his end. So it is difficult to know exactly how he died. What is certain is that Richard died within the precincts of Pontefract castle on or near the 14th February 1400. The chronicler Holinshed (furnishing great drama for Shakespeare) has Henry Bolingbroke sighing (much as Henry II did over Becket) for a *'faithful friend that will deliver me of him'*. In this version one Sir Piers of Exton takes up the challenge and leaves *'with eight strong persons'* to relieve his master of this great worry. Holinshed reports that, at Pontefract, Richard was first deprived of his food taster, giving rise to the suspicion that he might have been poisoned, and that Exton and his confederates later entered his cell and fought with Richard. The deposed king responded by fighting valiantly killing four of the assassins before succumbing to the stroke of a pollax delivered across his head by Exton himself.

Despite this dramatic report Richard's death remains an enigma. Some sources refer to him being starved or starving himself to death and this is of course possible. He certainly was stubborn enough to refuse food and launch a 'hunger strike' and if he did his jailers might be all too happy to let him get on with it. Given the reference to food and food tasters in some of the contemporary sources Richard may well have been poisoned. A common way to be rid of enemies from time immemorial, it is as likely as any other cause, given that his corpse showed no outward signs of the wasting that deliberate starvation or a hunger strike would show. A natural agent such as the lethal 'death cap' mushroom could have been systematically mixed in with his food and would certainly have killed him over a ten-day period. It is all a matter of conjecture, but die in that castle he did; a healthy 33 year old man with no known prior ailments or illnesses. On 17th February instructions were given for Richard's body to be transported from Pontefract to London, stopping at all the notable towns on the way so that it could be viewed by large numbers of people. Edward Hall says that Richard's body was *'embalmed and seared and covered with lead al save his face (to the entent that all men might perceive that he was departed out of this mortal lyfe)'*.

As £80 (a considerable sum) was spent just to bring the corpse to London it must have been attended with some degree of state. His body arrived in London on 6th March and rested for one night in St Paul's, where it was again shown to the people after the Office of the Dead and again in the morning after mass. According to John Harding, Henry IV and many lords were present at this scene and offered up some eight or nine pieces of cloth of gold to place on his coffin. Later Richard's body was taken to Westminster Abbey, where all these rituals were repeated, and where those present expected Richard to be interred in the tomb he had prepared earlier next to his wife Anne. Long before he died, Richard had ordered his own tomb to be built in Westminster Abbey. He designed it so that his effigy lay beside that of Anne, grasping her hand in his. The tomb was completed while he was still alive, with two effigies in copper gilt decorated with the ostrich feathers and lions of Bohemia, the eagles of the empire, the leopards of England, the peascods of the Plantagenets and the sun rising through the black clouds of Crécy. As we have seen earlier, the wishes of kings with regard to their own funerals are often no more than that, as after their deaths the living decide who goes where and when, especially when the decision is in the hands of a usurper.

In a move that surprised all those present in Westminster Abbey, Richard was not buried there. Instead Henry IV had Richard's body was taken from Westminster to the Dominican Friary in the royal manor of Kings Langley, Hertfordshire, where he was buried without pomp or state in early 1400. John Harding notes *'But then the kyng, him fast to Langley sent. There in the Freers to be buried secretment'*. Perhaps Henry (like his ancestor William the conqueror) thought the *'secretment'* necessary. A grand funeral might resurrect the idea of Richard as a wronged and supplanted monarch. Any burial, even a quiet one, in Westminster Abbey would attract some attention and later the tomb and its gilded effigies might take on the role of a shrine attracting the disaffected and causing the name of Richard of Bordeaux to be tossed about among mobs or groups who wished to see the old days back. Curiously, Richard's golden effigy rested there in Westminster Abbey, by that of his wife, but he was not lying beneath it.

Richard's body remained at Kings Langley for 13 years until Henry V, who had been knighted by Richard and had fond memories of him, had it brought back to Westminster Abbey amid great pomp and had it solemnly re-interred alongside Anne. Perhaps Henry V also felt some of the guilt that haunted his father and this act provided some release or as we might say today 'closure'. Another reason for Henry V's action may be to confirm that the corpse at Kings Langley was definitely that of Richard II. Various rumours had circulated in 1400 that it was Richard's chaplain Maudlin, whose likeness to the king was well known, who was buried there. How this story gained any kind of credence is not known as Maudlin had been executed a month before Richard died. At the relocation of Richard's body to Westminster, many who had known Richard recognised his features and certified that it was indeed the body of the unfortunate king. By a strange irony of fate the banners and displays of arms that had garnished the funeral of his usurper Henry IV were borrowed from the Prior and Convent of Canterbury to do honour to King Richard on the day of his burial at Westminster.

One old servant of the courts of Edward III, Richard II and Henry IV didn't have to wait for his place in Westminster Abbey. Geoffrey Chaucer, author and civil servant, died eight months after Richard in October 1400 at his tenement near the Lady Chapel of the Abbey. He is buried at the entrance to St Benedict's Chapel, giving rise to an area of the abbey that will forever be known as Poets' Corner. Originally his tomb was just a leaden plate with an epitaph written by an Italian poet hung on an adjacent pillar. The present marble tabletop tomb was originally erected by a minor poet, Nicholas Brigham, in 1556, with a portrait of Chaucer painted on the wall above it. Richard II and his wife were both patrons of Chaucer's work and from 1378 onwards Richard had given Chaucer a twenty-pound annuity. In 1389 Richard appointed Chaucer as Clerk of the King's Works and he probably passed by the earlier royal tombs many times as he went about his duties. Eventually both he and his unfortunate king found rest under the same roof.

Richard II had a real affection for Westminster Abbey. His coronation in the abbey, arranged and supervised by his uncle John of Gaunt, is the first of which there is a detailed contemporary account. It was celebrated with unusual formality and splendour. He was married to his beloved Anne of Bohemia there and it was there that he was supposed to have consulted a respected hermit on his way to confront Wat Tyler and the rebels at Smithfield. His portrait, hung in the abbey for more than 600 years, is the oldest contemporary representation of any English sovereign and can still be seen hanging at the west end of the Nave. Dressed in his coronation robes, it shows us the curling mass of auburn hair, the large heavy eyes, the long thin nose, the short tufted hair under a beardless chin and the soft melancholic expression of a troubled youth. This portrait is probably not anything like a true likeness of Richard. It is more of an icon of majesty and the trappings of the kind of kingship that Richard believed in. A vivid representation of the sanctity of the royal prerogative that eventually led to his destruction.

Few people seek to disturb the bones of a famous author, but a king, that's another matter! Richard II's remains were much manhandled in the mid 18th century, when scholars from Westminster School and others started putting their hands in the holes in the lower panelling on the south side of the tomb that were once covered by decorative metal shields. At that time two skulls and two copper gilt crowns were found. The small cleft that was visible on the side of one of the skulls was pronounced to be the opening of a suture from length of time and decay. It was also in such a part of the head that it would have been clearly visible when the body was exposed had it been caused by the stroke of Exton's pollax. The contents were examined again in August 1871 when a pair of shears, long forgotten and left by the plumber who assisted at the interment in 1413, was also found.

A king, delicate, cultured and fastidious in life, in death becomes the plaything of schoolboys and curious onlookers. A beautiful tomb in the great abbey was not always a safe haven for the body of a king. Queen Victoria, on visiting the abbey one day, expressed her regret at the neglect of the effigies of Edward III, Richard II and Anne. She was particularly concerned to see that there was no support for their heads and later gilt cushions were made for all three.

HENRY IV (born 1366 reigned 1399-1413)

Henry IV was the only son, and sixth surviving child of John of Gaunt, duke of Lancaster, and his first wife, Blanche, the youngest daughter, but sole heir of Henry, the first duke of Lancaster. Henry was born at his father's castle at Bolingbroke in Lincolnshire around 7th April 1366. He was the first king since the Conqueror to be born in England of English parents. His mother Blanche died of the plague in 1368 when Henry was only two so he never knew her. Later Henry joined the household of Gaunt's second wife Constance of Castile, and later still the household of Gaunt's mistress, and third wife, Catherine Swynford, who Gaunt married in 1396. When he was eleven years old Henry began using the courtesy title of earl of Derby, borne by his maternal grandfather. Henry was a first cousin of Richard II and was one of those nobles with Richard II during the peasant's revolt of June 1381. While Richard was out negotiating with the rebels Henry was dragged out of the Tower with some others who were murdered by the mob. Henry only just survived *'in a wonderful and kind manner'* aided by one John Ferrour of Southwark, a man who Henry had to pardon, twenty years later, for his role in the January rebellion of 1400.

Henry wore a short forked beard and always kept his red hair short. As a young man he enjoyed vigorous health. He was fit, energetic, powerful, an excellent swordsman and he was probably the most accomplished English jouster of his time. As well as being skilled in the martial arts he was also very devout, well read and an accomplished musician. All in all a textbook Christian lord with everything to live for. Henry was married to Mary Bohun at her home in Rochford Hall in Essex around 5th February 1381. Mary's sister, Eleanor, was already married to Gaunt's brother, Thomas of Woodstock. Mary, who called herself Plantagenet, was the daughter of the earl of Hereford and a descendent of King Henry III. Mary was eleven years old at the time of her marriage and later bore Henry four sons and two daughters. The birth of their eldest son Henry (later Henry V), was followed by Thomas (duke of Clarence), John (duke of Bedford) and Humphrey (duke of Gloucester). All four grew to manhood prior to Richard's deposition in 1399 and it must have looked to Henry IV then that the House of Lancaster would not easily come to grief. But in fact all of his sons were dead by 1435. The only heir to the House of Lancaster would be Henry V's weakling boy. Mary died in 1394, aged 24, giving birth to their sixth child, Philippa, five years before Henry became king and Henry went into mourning for a year. She is buried in the chapel of the Old Trinity Hospital in Leicester. Henry had no children by his second wife, Johanna of Navarre, who survived him by 20 years. It is she who is buried beside him in Canterbury Cathedral.

Henry was present at the Parliament that censored Richard II in October 1386 and that set up a commission to enquire into the king's affairs. Although a moderating influence, he also joined the other lords appellant in the campaign to defeat Richards 'Cheshire' army in 1387, and was one of those who confronted Richard II in the Tower during the same year. Henry then joined, arm-in-arm, the other lords appellant, dressed all in cloth of gold, to pursue charges against Richard's courtiers in the Parliament of February 1388. Richard would never forget his 'loving' cousin's behaviour. In 1392 Henry made a pilgrimage to Jerusalem. He enjoyed his tour around Europe and spent more than a week in Palestine visiting the holy places and making offerings. He returned to England in September 1393. In 1397, in a shock move, Richard II arrested the three original 'appellants' who had humiliated him ten years before. Henry was naturally apprehensive that he too would be caught up in the king's vengeance. Henry was made earl of Hereford in September 1397 but was still wary that Richard might seek to harm him. Into this atmosphere of nervous distrust walked Thomas Mowbray, now duke of Norfolk. On a ride from London to Windsor in December 1397 Mowbray told Henry that Richard planned to seize or kill Henry and his father and to disinherit himself and others in revenge for Richard's defeat at Radcote Bridge in 1387.

Henry is not reported as saying anything to Mowbray in return for this information but he did tell his father who then told King Richard. This conversation between Mowbray and Bolingbroke was destined to precipitate a chain of events that would set both men on a course that neither of them sought, nor could have imagined. In 1398 the king's council considered the various accusations that Mowbray had made and decided that the matter should be decided by combat, between Henry and Mowbray. As the combatants prepared for battle, Henry beginning his military exercises and employing armourers from Milan, the king decided that they should not fight. Instead he banished them both, Henry for 10 years and Mowbray for life, with effect from the 20th October 1398.

Richard promised Henry that his inheritance would be safe should his father die while he was in exile but two days after Gaunt's funeral, in February 1399, Richard revoked this promise and changed Henry's exile from 10 years to life. Henry began his exile in Paris where he was warmly received by King Charles VI (the mad) of France. He was made comfortable there and he hoped to move south to visit his two sisters, Katherine, Queen of Castile, and Philippa, Queen of Portugal, at some time in the future. After Gaunt's death and Richard's annexing of the duchy of Lancaster Henry's plans for a European holiday were put on hold. On 1st June Richard II arrived in Ireland accompanied by most of his closest supporters. Towards the end of that month Henry left France and sailed to England. He landed at Ravenspur, on the northern tip of the Humber estuary around 4th July, with just a handful of his own retainers. He hoped to find more supporters in England and to capitalise on Richard's absence in Ireland. Henry's motives have been much debated. His first declaration was that he came only to claim his rightful inheritance of Lancaster that Richard had stolen from him. But Henry knew Richard well enough to know that breaking his exile and returning home in arms would not be acceptable to him. For Henry to survive, without constant fear of a vengeful attack on him, he would have to achieve an on-going supremacy over Richard, perhaps as vice-regent or, he would have to replace Richard entirely.

Henry met no significant resistance and he had no hesitation in executing three of Richard's closest councillors at Bristol at the end of July. Richard arrived back from Ireland on 25th July with a force of about 7,000 men, but he found a country largely supportive of Henry. With a few friends he rode to Conway castle in north Wales. Henry outmanoeuvred Richard by taking the king's personal stronghold of Chester and when Richard was tempted out of Conway by promises of safe conduct he was taken, under guard, to Flint castle where, a fully armed Henry met him, and no doubt made clear the reality of the king's position. By 2nd September Richard was lodged in the Tower of London while Henry paid his respects at his father's tomb in St Paul's. Henry based his claim to the throne on Richards's misgovernment, Parliament's approval, his Plantagenet lineage back to Henry III, and the support of most of the great magnates of the realm.

Henry was crowned King Henry IV in Westminster Abbey on 13th October 1399. He was possibly the first English king to be anointed with oil, supposedly given to Thomas Becket by the Virgin Mary, and he may also have been the first to have been crowned in Edward I's seat with the Scottish Stone of Scone tucked underneath it. On the 15th October, keen to secure his new throne for his descendants Henry had his eldest son, aged twelve, invested, in Parliament as Prince of Wales. Parliament was keen that Richard should be punished for his crimes and the ex-king was taken, under strict guard and in secret, first to Leeds Castle in Kent and then to Pontefract Castle in Yorkshire. Plots to depose Henry and restore Richard were uncovered in early 1400 and these may have prompted the moves that eventually resulted in Richard's death.

Given the records available we cannot tell for certain if Henry gave the order for Richard II to be killed at Pontefract but, given the many reported signs of Henry's subsequent guilt concerning Richard, it seems a reasonable presumption. While a deposed king lived he would always be a magnet for any group disaffected by the new king's policies. It wouldn't be wise to keep an old king alive while a new king struggled to forge his place. Richard II had no children and had publicly announced that his heir should be Roger Mortimer, earl of March and grandson of Lionel, duke of Clarence, the second son of Edward III. After Roger's death in Ireland, before Richard, in 1398, his seven-year-old son, Edmund Mortimer, became heir presumptive to the English throne. Bolingbroke's action in seizing the crown in 1399 disrupted this dynastic plan. Although young Edmund kept his life under the new regime he spent thirteen years of that life imprisoned at Windsor (the full length of Henry IV's reign) only being released in 1413 by Henry V.

Henry may have started off well as king, acclaimed by Parliament (to whom he owed his election) and nobles alike, but things soon started to go wrong. At some point after his arrival in England Henry seems to have promised to reduce taxes, a promise widely believed by those that heard it, to mean that there would be no taxes at all. Even with the huge resources of the duchy of Lancaster to help him rule this was clearly a promise too far! Henry also had to reward those who had helped him to the crown and to buy the support of Richard's retainers. This resulted in a massive increase in the cost of the royal household, costs that Henry was never really to get under control. Ironically Henry had often accused Richard II of waste and extravagance but the Parliaments of 1401 to 1406 regularly laid the same complaint against him. Lack of money continued to plague Henry and his constant requests for cash or loans from his nobles soon generated a deep disillusionment with his government. As early as 1401 the bishop of Lincoln comparing the welcome that greeted Henry's accession with present troubles noted that, *'joy has turned to bitterness, while evils multiply themselves everywhere, and hopes of relief fades from the grieving hearts of men'*.

Citing the excessive cost of the royal household, excessive annuities and misspent taxes, Parliament forced Henry to accede to their demands for royal cutbacks, making it difficult for Henry to reward those lords who had helped him to the crown. This particularly hurt the powerful northern-based Percy family. Henry Percy earl of Northumberland, his son Henry (known as Hotspur) and Thomas Percy, earl of Worcester, despite being given many castles, and many important offices of state, still felt they should have been better rewarded. They eventually rebelled and joined with the Welsh insurgent Owen Glyn Dwr to put Edmund Mortimer on the throne. On 21st July 1403 the king, together with his eldest son (later Henry V), faced the rebels at Shrewsbury. It was the only battle that Henry IV every fought and it was a brutal and severe affair. At first Hotspur's Cheshire archers drove back the royal vanguard wounding the Prince of Wales in the face. But as the battle raged Hotspur was killed and the rebel cause collapsed. Thomas Percy was caught and executed while Henry, earl of Northumberland got off with a parliamentary pardon. Despite being pardoned Henry Percy continued to move in and out of rebellion and in 1405 he failed to come to the aid of his co-rebel, Richard Scrope, Archbishop of York. After surrendering his arms, Scrope was executed outside York on 8th June 1405, the only pre-Reformation English bishop to die in this way. Northumberland was eventually killed in battle near Tadcaster in 1408. Henry IV's victories against these northern rebels eased both his financial position and his relations with parliament but they took a terrible toll on both his mental and physical health. The death of Archbishop Scrope affected him badly. Killing such a senior churchman, however justified, weighed heavily on his mind. He now had an archbishop and a king to feel guilty about.

After 1405, a king who, only six years earlier, had been renowned for his fitness and martial prowess was hardly ever capable of leading his troops in person. He became weak and progressively affected by a horrible skin disease that he first thought might be leprosy. Although confined to the covered parts of his body, it smelt awful and gave him continuous discomfort. Some contemporaries saw the disease as a divine judgement on Henry for killing Archbishop Scrope. In April 1406 Henry complained of a leg injury possibly causing him circulatory problems as he was too ill to attend Parliament. His skin disease was probably a form of dermatitis and through its progress over a number of years it may have left the king more open to infection by reducing his immune system. More dangerously, Henry is also reported to have suffered from some kind of epileptiform condition that led to periods of unconsciousness or semi-coma that sometimes left his doctors unsure as to whether the king was alive or dead. These attacks may well have had their origin in some form of kidney failure and together with his skin disease may account for the illness that dogged him for so many years. The autumn session of Parliament in 1405 insisted on a financial reform programme to be guided by a small, executive council headed by the Prince of Wales. As heir to the throne the Prince now became the focus of attention. He cultivated his own followers and, taking on more of the work of government as his father's health deteriorated, eyes were turning to him as the future king.

In June 1408 Henry suffered a seizure at Archbishop Arundel's manor at Mortlake on the Thames. To the distress of those present the king remained unconscious for several hours and gave the appearance of being dead. At the end of the year Henry was ill again and made a will in English, in January 1409 that occasioned reflections on a sinful and misspent life. In the last two years of his life Henry hardly left London except to visit Becket's shrine at Canterbury. He was visiting the tomb of another saint, Edward the Confessor, in 1413, when he suffered a fit that left him unconscious. He was carried into a room at the abbot's house at Westminster. This room was decorated with tapestries depicting the history of Jerusalem and had thus garnered the name the Jerusalem Room. A fortune-teller once told Henry that he would visit Jerusalem before he died and when the king, in a moment of lucidity, asked where he had been taken and was told he was relieved. Aware that he was close to death, it symbolised in some way the truth of the prophecy and gave him some comfort. His sins having weighed greatly on him all his life this slight, this final coincidence, perhaps gave him confidence that he would after all be received by his maker with forgiveness. Various stories have come down to us about 'Prince Hal' prematurely picking up the crown as Henry lay in a semi-coma in the abbot's lodgings. In one of these the king wakes up to find the crown missing and his son has to bring it back to him, explaining that he thought that his father had died. The king, not far from death now, is supposed to have chastised the prince, asking him what right he had to the crown when he himself had none. To this the Prince is supposed to have replied, that, as his father had held it and kept it by the sword so would he.

Henry died on 20th March 1413 after exhorting his son to follow a path of righteousness and piety and to reflect on how a mighty prince can be brought as low as he was brought now. According to J. H Wylie, '*the king's body was washed, brained, bowelled, and embalmed in a mixture of myrrh, aloes, laurel-flower and saffron, and wound in cerements of waxed Rheims linen, leaving the face alone exposed. They then clothed it in a long robe reaching to the heels, with a royal mantle over it. The thick brown beard was smoothed over the throat and chin, the crown was placed upon the head, the hands were strapped with cerecloth sewed about each thumb and finger, and dresses in gloves richly broidered with orphreys. The right middle finger wore a gold ring, the right hand held a golden orb with the cross resting on the breast, while the left hand lay at his side grasping a sceptre of gold which reached to the left ear. The legs were cased in silken galogs or buskins (reaching to the thigh) and the feet were shod with sandals*'.

The body then lay in state at Westminster Abbey for a time before being '*stripped again, lapped in lead chested in a rough elm hutch, packed with haybands to steady it, and taken down the Thames to Gravesend in a barge arrayed with lamps accompanied by eight vessels having on board the Prince of Wales, his brothers John and Humphrey and a crowd of barons, knights, bishops, abbots and other notables*'. At Gravesend the body was put on a horse-bier covered in cloth of gold and drawn by road to Canterbury. Henry had asked to be buried at Canterbury rather than at Westminster. Richard II was not yet buried there so it was not a wish to avoid being near one in whose death he had connived. More probably he wished to further exculpate his many sins by being buried close to Saint Thomas Becket, the intercessor. The funeral cost 500 marks which '*accords well with the extravagant vanities of candlesticks, torches and such other items of display that characterized the pompous funerals of that age*'.

Henry's second wife, Joan of Navarre, died twenty-four years after Henry and it was she who commissioned the altar tomb over his grave with a full-length figure of her husband in gilt and painted alabaster, robed and crowned as he would have looked when he lay in state. After her death in 1437 her own figure was placed by her side beneath a beautiful fan-vaulted canopy. Her body in its lead coffin lies altogether within the area of the base of the tomb while the grave of her husband extends for about a third of its length beyond it to the west, implying that the base structure was not placed in its present position until after 1437. It has to be said that this tomb looks rather sad today with its broken and clipped hands. The effigy of the king shows us an almost benign face with a wry smile; his beard is parted and his gown clasped at the neck. Both king and queen have angels holding up their red pillows and Henry rests his feet on a smiling lion. On the wooden canopy above we can just make out the faded colours of the arms of England and Navarre. One gets the impression that this tomb is very much an also-ran for visitors to the Cathedral. The top attraction is the splendid copper gilt effigy of Edward 'the Black Prince' located between two pillars directly opposite. Henry IV is the only English king to be buried in this ancient cathedral. His son Henry V, returning to England victorious from Agincourt, stopped at Canterbury to pay homage at the tomb of Thomas Becket. During these devotions the irony that the bones of his father lay just a short step from the tomb of the Black Prince, whose son his father had usurped, may have crossed his mind. Henry IV's tomb and leaden coffin was opened in 1832 largely to disprove a storey that it had not been buried at the time of his death but thrown into the Thames. In the brief moments before the air rushed in to turn him to dust '*the face of the deceased King was seen in complete preservation*'.

Henry was 46 when he died and he had reigned for 13 years. Almost from the start of his reign he was beset by rebellion and things just got worse. The more he overcame his enemies to secure his throne the more he suffered. Getting the crown had been relatively easy; keeping it for his descendants became a torment almost from the start. Henry's reign has always seemed a wretched affair when compared to some others but he did reign in difficult times and, being elected by Parliament, was always aware that he was much more of an 'elected' monarch than any of his predecessors. All three of the main players in Parliament, the Church, the Lords and the House of Commons wanted something in return for granting him the crown. The Church insisted on a heresy hunt and the persecution of the Lollards, something Richard II had always resisted; the Lords (as usual) wanted plunder in Wales, Scotland and France and when they didn't get as much as they expected turned on the king himself; the commons saw their chance to put a brake on royal expenditure.

In Shakespeare's two plays, Henry IV parts one and two, Henry is portrayed as a man harassed by rebellious barons, at odds with his councillors and plagued by a wasting body, all as divine retribution for his usurpation of the true king. In the drama God punishes the once strong and healthy man for his monstrous deeds. In this, Shakespeare gets very close to the truth. In the last years of his life Henry IV was a sad shadow of that Henry earl of Hereford who went into exile in 1398. In 1399 Richard II annexed the duchy of Lancaster and incorporated it into the crown. This unlawful 'theft' by the king prompted Henry's return to England, and resulted in Richard's eventual usurpation. Henry, as heir to that great duchy, by seizing the crown now confirmed the two parts as one. Richard II had brought the duchy of Lancaster back to the crown and Henry, by seizing the crown, had brought the crown to Lancaster, a dynastic marriage that remains in tact to this day. There is still a post in the English cabinet (a kind of jack of all trades) called 'Chancellor of the duchy of Lancaster'.

HENRY V (born 1387 reigned 1413-1422)

Henry, first son of Henry Bolingbroke (later Henry IV) and Mary of Bohun, was born in the chamber of the gatehouse of Monmouth Castle (then part of the duchy of Lancaster estates) in 1387. This location gave rise to the name 'Henry of Monmouth' by which he was sometimes known. The son of a third son of Edward III Henry was not destined for the crown and so little is known of how or where he spent his youth. Henry's mother died when he was seven-years-old and his father was often away. He probably spent some time on the estates of his maternal grandmother, Joan, countess of Hereford. Henry was joined by his brothers, Thomas, duke of Clarence, John, duke of Bedford, and Humphrey, duke of Gloucester and two sisters, Blanche and Philippa. After his father was banished in 1398 Henry's position might have been precarious but Richard II seems to have treated him well granting him £500 a year for his maintenance. Henry was with Richard in Ireland when his father landed at Ravenspur in July 1399 and persuaded Richard that he had nothing to do with the events that were unfolding. Although he was not used by the king as a tool in any of the negotiations with his father, Richard still kept him confined in Ireland, at the castle of Trim, north-west of Dublin.

Once Bolingbroke had secured the throne Henry returned to England and he was present at his father's coronation in October 1399, carrying the sheathed and blunted sword of justice in the procession. A nervous King Henry IV determined to show the world that he intended to promote and continue a new dynasty, soon had his son created earl of Chester, Prince of Wales, duke of Aquitaine and duke of Lancaster. Prince Henry was slim and very tall, standing around six feet three inches. He had a ruddy complexion on a lean face, was clean-shaven and his portrait shows us that he had a prominently pointed nose. His dark hair was cropped tightly in a ring above his ears; perhaps it made it easier to get a helmet on?

His military training began in 1401 when Henry, together with Henry Percy (Hotspur), attempted to subdue the rebellions in north Wales led by Owain Glyn Dŵr. The mountainous terrain was difficult and raids into rebel held territory were expensive and largely unproductive. Henry was getting his first taste of how successful guerrilla warfare could be. Hotspur's family, the Percy's, disaffected with Henry IV, then rebelled against the crown and began an alliance with Glyn Dŵr to depose Henry IV. In July 1403 the fifteen-year-old Henry joined his father in the viciously contested battle against Hotspur and his family at Shrewsbury. Hotspur was killed in the battle and the Percy rebellion largely dissipated. But Glyn Dŵr was still at large and the Welsh revolt kept Henry in martial occupation for several more years until he captured the key area around Aberystwyth, late in 1408. The Welsh rebellion had gradually died out by 1410 but Glyn Dŵr, though defeated, was never captured. He would be the last of the Welsh leader to call himself Prince of Wales. This early military command in Wales was a forging house for Henry. Here he learned the importance of effective command and efficient organisation, together with ensuring a regular supply of money and equipment to keep his troops happy. When he became king, Henry worked to reconcile himself to the Welsh by issuing pardons (they had to be paid for), and by making inquiries into acts of oppression by royal officers within the principality. The number of Welsh soldiers who fought for Henry in France is a testament that some of these efforts bore fruit.

From the age of around eighteen onwards Henry was an active, energetic and intelligent, if somewhat arrogant, member of the King's Council. The great issue of the times was his father's finances and Henry was as keen as anyone to reorder the royal income and expenditure. It was during this time that stories of his differences with the king's 'older' advisors and his impatience to succeed his sickly father gained ground. In 1410 Henry replaced Archbishop Arundel as leader of the council but the renewed background chatter urging Henry IV's abdication in favour of his son lead the king to sack him, and recall

Arundel, a year later. During this time the younger Henry began gathering around him people he could rely on, including his Beaufort half-uncles, the children of his grandfather John of Gaunt by Catherine Swynford.

The controversies surrounding an inconclusive expedition to France during Henry IV's time, lead by his younger son Thomas duke of Clarence, resulted in considerable polarisation at the court with the growth of a number of factions and the Prince of Wales surrounding himself with armed retainers. Henry IV's death clearly saved an ugly situation from getting worse and Henry V succeeded peacefully to his father's crown in 1413 at the age of twenty-five. Given the uncertainties that had dogged Henry IV's reign it is surprising that there was no opposition to his son's accession. Perhaps the anticipation of putting the last years of the sickly old king behind them and welcoming a young, fresh, virile king tempered any thoughts of drastic regime change. Henry V was crowned at Westminster Abbey on 9th April 1413 and he now settled down to build fences with old foes. In an early propaganda move to 'bury' some old grievances Henry even re-buried Richard II in pomp alongside Richard's queen, Anne of Bohemia at Westminster Abbey. Henry retained some affection for Richard who he had travelled with to Ireland in 1399, and who had knighted him.

In 1413, in another conciliatory move, Henry released Edmund Mortimer, fifth earl of March, and nominated heir of Richard II, from his incarceration in Windsor Castle. It was this Mortimer, who keen to prove his loyalty, informed Henry V of the 'Southampton' plot of 1415. This plot, to kill Henry V, was led by Richard Plantagenet, earl of Cambridge, (Mortimer's brother in law) to put him (Mortimer) on the throne. On Henry V's death Mortimer was trusted enough to be elected a member of the Council of Regency that oversaw the minority of Henry's one-year-old son Henry VI. He died of the plague in 1424 ending the male line of the famous Mortimer clan. However their family name would not stay hidden from English history for long. A claim to the throne would emerge later in the century based on the female line of Mortimer. It would be central to the demands made by the Yorkist side in the 'Wars of the Roses'.

Within two years of being crowned Henry skilfully tied up any latent aggression in his nobles by initiating yet another war against France. France was ruled by the (mad) King Charles VI, or rather by a group of rival princes who took control during the king's regular periods of incapacity. Henry, voicing his claims to lands in France that had been ceded to Edward III, sent ambassadors to Paris to make his point. The French ambassadors, who came to England in reply, ostensibly to head off Henry's invasion plans, brought Henry and his nobility the dauphin's gift of a box of tennis balls, *'be-cause he shulde have sumwhat to play with-alle, for hym and his lordes'*. They seem not to have understood the English sense of humour. Henry V had dreamed of reclaiming the old Anjou-Normandy-Maine 'empire' of Henry II and, immune to any afflictions of self-doubt, he set sail for France in August 1415. He took a fleet of 1500 vessels and an army of around 10,500 fighting men, plus all the support materials and personnel that his early days in Wales had taught him to carry.

Within a few days Henry had besieged Harfleur and blockaded it from the sea. Henry's active use of artillery, *'harde & grete gune-stonys, for the Dolfyn to play with-alle'*, eventually had its effect on the plucky resistance of the town, and it surrendered on 22nd September 1415. After installing a large garrison there Henry moved off, with around 6,000 men, to march on Calais. The army which left Harfleur, and marched through Normandy, was weak, weary and riddled with dysentery. Aware of the dangers of low morale Henry actively rode among his men to encourage them as, many times, it looked like they might collapse and just stop where they fell. After a little over two weeks, with the French harrying them at every step, Henry realised that, whatever the state of his army, he would have fight the French in a pitched battle.

On the 25th October, the feast day of Sts Crispin and Crispinian, the battle took place near the small village of Agincourt. It is difficult to imagine this scene now without thinking of the rousing speech that Shakespeare's Henry V makes to his troops before the battle. But we should think instead of the filthy wet state of the land in front of the English after a night of heavy rain. Again, as at Crécy in 1346, an overconfident French army launched a frontal assault and again they were overwhelmed by the power of English archers. The heavily armoured French were soon wallowing in the mud as the arrows of the highly disciplined English bowmen showered over them in hailstones of steel. Ironically the French were badly served by their superior numbers as the dead blocked their way forward and the wounded that turned back ran into those troops coming forward. It was not long before panic set in among the French and large numbers of them were killed by English archers who ran among them in hand-to-hand fighting, having run out of arrows. The French suffered appalling casualties (around six thousand dead) while Henry's victory was achieved with less than four hundred killed.

The next day Henry, and his now victorious army, moved on to Calais where they arrived on 29th October. At Agincourt Henry V had achieved in a single day what his father Henry IV had spent thirteen years failing to achieve. All England united behind their king, and he returned home in November 1415 to a hero's welcome. Parliament voted Henry tunnage and poundage for life, along with some other taxes, while London welcomed their hero with rejoicing and a French-style formal reception. Only two-and-a-half years after his coronation Henry was basking in the sunshine of his subjects' love, a warmth that his father had never enjoyed. Victory, on foreign soil, over the old enemy had clearly made him master of his kingdom. English domestic policy would now take a back seat as Henry spent the next five years building on his victory at Agincourt. The once so welcoming Parliament was now confronted with heavy demands for financial support to consolidate the victories of 1415. The French soon blockaded Harfleur and it was only relieved in August 1416 when, Henry's brother, John duke of Bedford, destroyed the French ships surrounding the port. With none of his diplomatic initiatives with France bearing fruit Henry was back on French soil in[t] August 1417. He brought an army of some 10,500 men including a large contingent of archers and after nearly one and half years of gruelling battles and sieges across Normandy the great city of Rouen finally fell to Henry in January 1419.

After a series of unsatisfactory negotiations with the French, the assassination of John duke of Burgundy, in September 1419, changed the dynamics of French politics as his heir, Philip the Good, was more inclined to accept the English position. By the Treaty of Troyes in May 1420, Charles VI was to keep France during his lifetime but Henry was recognised as his heir and would marry the French king's daughter, Catherine of Valois to seal the pact. They were married on 2nd June 1420 at Troyes when Henry was thirty-two and she was nineteen. Many Frenchmen would not accept the Treaty of Troyes or stand by and see the dauphin disinherited in favour of an English king of France. Aided by the forces of Burgundy Henry set out to quash the discontented and reclaim some key castles that they held near the upper reaches of the Seine. The campaign was a success and in December 1420, the dauphin, having failed to appear in Paris to answer charges with regard to his part in the murder of John duke of Burgundy, Henry was legally confirmed as heir to the throne of France.

After an absence of three and a half years, Henry returned to England in February 1421 to crown his new queen, make a royal progress through some important cities and conceive an heir. A time perhaps to enjoy the pleasant tedium of domestic life after the hard years in harness? If so it was all too brief. As noted earlier an English king does not easily keep order in the lands of France when he is away across the water. News of the death of his younger brother, Thomas duke of Clarence, in Anjou, after a clash with a Franco-Scottish force, sent Henry back to France in June 1421. Clearly Agincourt was no more than the start of a long slog of sieges, battles and marches to come. Enmeshed in a gruelling winter siege of the strategically important town of Meaux, just 30 miles due east of Paris, Henry, and his army, were tired, weak and dispirited by the time the town and castle surrendered in May

1422. The opposition to the Treaty of Troyes was taking a harsh toll on English treasure and morale. During the winter of 1421 Henry had received the news of the birth of his son, also named Henry, at Windsor, despite his firm instruction that the child should be born at Westminster. He would never see his son but Catherine did come to visit her husband in May 1422 when the first signs of Henry's illness became apparent. Henry was probably suffering from severe fluid loss or had contracted dysentery, the unwelcome companion of so many of his soldiers during his French campaigns. Whatever it was Henry could not shake it off and in July he had to be carried in a litter to the siege of Cosne on the upper Loire. He never made it to Cosne and, clearly very ill was taken instead to the castle of Vincennes, south east of Paris. He died there in the early morning of 31st August 1422, after struggling to clarify his will, legacies to his wife and the church, his funeral arrangements and all things needed to provide an effective Council of Regency for his nine-month-old son and heir.

Thomas Walsingham noted that the king *'from having an old distemper, which he had contracted from excessive and long continued exertion, meanwhile fell into an acute fever with violent dysentery. This his physicians did not venture to treat by any internal medication, but forthwith gave up hope of his life...'.* Those words *'did not venture to treat'* and *'gave up hope'* suggest that Henry, although suffering from dysentery, was also suffering from something else which the surgeons did not feel capable of fixing. Dysentery alone was something that his surgeons would have often treated, and sometimes cured. The length of time it took Henry to die suggests that he may have had a long term illness like cancer of the rectum. This would fit in with both the length of his illness and his growing weakness. Perhaps he died suffering from both? In one months time his old enemy Charles VI of France would also be dead and Henry V, had he lived, would have been proclaimed King of France in his stead. Now, that proclamation would have to be made for a nine-month old child. The dispossessed dauphin (the future Charles VII) was unlikely to stand by and watch that without taking up arms again!

Henry wrote his will in the third year of his reign and seems to have given quite detailed attention to where he wanted to be buried. Although he died in France, and the cities of Paris and Rouen are supposed to have offered serious sums of money to secure his body, his well-known attachment to Westminster Abbey prevailed and sumptuous arrangements began to be made for his funeral. The journey to England would be long so the king's body was embalmed and packed into a lead coffin ready for the journey. First, he was taken to the church of Our Lady in Paris, then to rest in state in Rouen and then on to the church of St Wulfran in Abbeville. From there a ship took his body, his queen, his servants and lords all dressed in mourning, to Dover. The party arrived in Dover around 31st October exactly two months after his death. One Simon Prentot was paid £300 12s 6d for seven 'herses' one each for resting at Dover, Canterbury, Ospringe, Rochester, Dartford, St Paul's London and Westminster *'for the funeral of the most excellent prince and lord King Henry the fifth, brought from the parts of France...'.* The average cost of these 'herses' was just under £43 but the last, for Westminster, complete with two hundred torches, ran to just over £53 so it was probably a little more splendid than the rest. The long procession moved on to London where it was met by fifteen bishops, many abbots and a great body of clergy.

The solemn obsequies were performed in the presence of Parliament, first at St Paul's, and then at Westminster Abbey. As his funeral procession passed through London, men from the great city guilds stood at key doorways holding lighted torches accompanied by priests who censed the corpse as it passed by them. In total the guilds provided two hundred and eleven torches with the Mercers and four other big guilds providing twelve torches each while the smaller ones offered up less. The Hatters could only scrape together the cash for two but the *'Chamberlain at the cost of the commonality provided each torch-bearer a gown and hood of blanket'.* Henry's coffin supported an image of the king made of boiled leather painted, robed and crowned. The crown was of precious gold; the robe was of purple furred with ermine and in his one hand he held a golden orb with a cross on it while in the other he held a sceptre. It must have looked a glorious sight as it was joined by one thousand more torches for the final journey into the abbey. His funeral was the grandest of any English king to date. The conscription of large numbers of poor men to attend the funeral procession of a king was a popular form of symbolism perhaps to ally the dead king with 'all' his subjects. It certainly had the effect of providing a large number of men with free cloaks and hoods that they would otherwise never have been able to afford. Some also managed to keep bits of the valuable wax from the large candles that they had to carry.

As the ceremony neared its completion the sombre scene was enlivened by the clatter of horses' feet echoing across the abbey as three fully armed horsemen, on chargers richly draped in the arms of France and England, rode straight up to the high altar. There, they had their arms and banners seized from them to signify that they served their master no longer and must therefore give up both their arms and his colours. Henry's body arrived at Westminster on 6th November 1422 and he was buried the next day. When it came to the building of the king's tomb at Westminster the abbey authorities were put under some strain to accommodate Henry's precise wishes. The extreme eastern end of the Confessor's Chapel previously devoted to the storage of sacred relics had to be completely cleared out. The relics were eventually placed in a chest between the tomb of Henry III and the Confessor's shrine. Henry had ordered that a separate Chantry be built above his tomb, where masses might forever be offered up for the good of his soul. His wish was that it would be high enough up for the people far down in the abbey to see the priests officiating there.

All this meant building a new stone platform that would have a grave set in it and a monument placed over it. This idea of a platform built above ground with a space in it to take the dead king was very unusual in England. Today this platform runs over the steps leading to the Henry VII Chapel. Henry V's shield, helmet and saddle were hung above his tomb and his effigy was cut from solid oak and plated over with silver gilt. The head, now just a strangely shaped wooden block, was made of solid silver and once rested on two pillows. The main outline of the king can still be seen wearing the gown, hooded tippet and mantle that formed his parliamentary robes. The carefully carved feet were worked from separate pieces of oak and pegged on to the trunk. At the time of its creation it must have been a wondrous thing to see, all that silver glistening in the half-light of the abbey. Seeing it today (not easy, as it requires special permission from the abbey Vergers) it looks a sad remnant of its reported grandeur. Two gold teeth from the face were stolen in Edward IV's reign and robbers carried off the rest of the silver at the time of the dissolution of the Monasteries. Henry VIII must have been peeved to miss that little haul.

Like King Richard I, Henry V became a real hero and a European-wide legend in his own lifetime. He was deeply religious. His piety often showed itself in his reluctance to accept credit for his victories which he always put down to God's agency. A sombre man of action, a French observer noted that he looked more like a priest than a soldier; he radiated a calm and order that belied his steely determination when fixed upon a course that he believed in. Notably, Henry encouraged the use of English in both speech and writing; he encouraged the translation of Latin works into English and by using English in letters, sent out under his own seal, he really initiated the concept of the 'King's English'. When not encased in armour he liked music and loved hunting. He was a man of few words but of many victories, it is hard not to contemplate what might have happened had his reign lasted twenty years rather than just nine?

Catherine of Valois

Henry V's wife Catherine of Valois holds a curious place in the history of English monarchs. Within a short time of Henry V's death in 1422 she had little to do with her son,

Henry VI, and was only associated with him at ceremonies or special occasions. She was more or less exiled to Wallingford Castle north-west of Reading and well away from London. The wars with France continued and perhaps, she being French, the Council of Regents thought she might be a risk to have around the court. Isolated and lonely, she fell in love with Owen Tudor, a Welsh Clerk to her Wardrobe. In 1428 Parliament reacted to rumours of their relationship and forbade Catherine to marry without the king's consent. They may have already been married by this time, they may have married in secret afterwards or they may never have got married. No one can be sure.

Whatever their legal status, Catherine had five children by Owen, one daughter dying in infancy. In 1436 Henry VI's council, frightened by the political fallout that both parents and children might cause, forced the lovers to separate and Catherine, now seriously ill, went to Bermondsey Abbey where she died a year later. In 1452, and without causing a scandal, Henry VI legitimised their children. After various adventures, Owen Tudor, a staunch Lancastrian, was captured at the battle of Mortimer's Cross and summarily beheaded in the market place at Hereford in 1461. Two of their sons played an important part in the dynastic struggles of the fifteenth century: Jasper Tudor who later became earl of Pembroke and duke of Bedford, and Edmund Tudor who was made earl of Richmond. This Edmund Tudor married the ambitious Margaret Beaufort. Her restless family were descended from the famous affair between John of Gaunt and Catherine Swynford whose children were later legitimised by Richard II in 1397. Later Henry IV, interfering with this Act of Parliament, literally and unlawfully wrote a new clause in between the lines of the Act, excluding the Beauforts from the succession. This interference was confounded when Edmund's son by Margaret, Henry Tudor, became Henry VII, the first king of the Tudor dynasty.

Catherine of Valois was buried in Westminster Abbey but only in a rude coffin in a 'badly apparelled' state. The wooden funeral effigy, which was carried at her funeral, still survives in the Undercroft Museum at Westminster Abbey. She was not to rest in peace. The slab that rested on top of her tomb was accidentally, or deliberately, destroyed during the destruction of the Lady Chapel by her grandson Henry VII, when building his own grand mausoleum. Perhaps he wanted any obvious memorial to his dubious ancestry removed. At this time she was placed on the right side of her husband, Henry V, where she 'continued to be seen, the bones being firmly united, and thinly clothed with flesh, like scrapings of fine leather'. With the coffin lid on her tomb left loose anyone passing by it could view her corpse, and many did. It became a sort of tourist attraction. For a few pence a Verger would slide the lid off and let you have a peek.

Samuel Pepys noted in his famous diary, 'On Shrove Tuesday 1669, I to the Abbey went, and by favour did see the body of Queen Catherine of Valois, and had the upper part of the body in my hands, and I did kiss her mouth, reflecting upon it I did kiss a Queen: and this my birthday and I thirty-six years old and I did kiss a Queen'. Catherine of Valois was the daughter of a French king, the wife of an English king, a mother to one English king and a grandmother to another one. Not a bad record for a woman so quickly relegated to the back pages of history and who after her own death was left as a tourist attraction by her grandson. Her body was eventually properly interred in a vault under the Villiers' monument in the Chapel of St Nicholas, in Westminster Abbey at the time of the Duchess of Northumberland's funeral, in 1776.

HENRY VI (born 1421 reigned 1422-1461, 1470-1471)

"Hung be the heavens with black, yield day to night!
Comets importing change of time and states,
Brandish your crystal tresses in the sky,
And with them scourge the bad revolting stars
That have consented unto Henry's death!
King Henry the Fifth, too famous to live long!
England ne'er lost a king of so much worth. "

(William Shakespeare, Act 1, Scene 1, first part of King Henry VI)

Woe to that king who follows a military hero. The dandy Edward II had to walk in the steel clad footsteps of Edward I; the gentle aesthete, Richard II had to follow those two great warriors Edward III and Edward the Black Prince. In 1422 the eight-month-old Henry VI, packed with the genes of a French king known to be mad, had to totter behind the footsteps of the shining light of the age, his father King Henry V. While Henry V had to loiter with ill-concealed impatience to take on his father's crown Henry VI had it thrust on him before he could walk. Henry VI was born at Windsor on 6th December 1421, the only son of Henry V and his wife Catherine of Valois. The accession of a child king never bodes well and this child king proved no exception. The question of who should rule England, and France, during his long minority had, to some extent, been answered by Henry V's will. The dead king's brother, the duke of Gloucester was to be Henry VI's custodian and protector while responsibility for the, as yet incomplete conquest of France, was to be given to Henry V's other brother, John duke of Bedford. These arrangements were altered in December 1422 to declare Bedford as Regent of all English held France, while Gloucester was named 'protector and defender of the realm and chief councillor for the king' while Bedford was abroad.

The child king lived with his mother during the 1420s and they lodged mainly in royal residences near London. Henry seems to have been a normal, healthy child brought up and educated by members of Henry V's old establishment and taught the usual accomplishments expected of a late medieval king. In 1428 Richard Beauchamp, earl of Warwick, a loyal companion in arms to Henry V, was made *'governor, tutor and master'* of the young king. His brief was to teach him *'good manners, letters and languages'*, all in the context of Christian courtesy and virtue. Henry's grandfather Charles VI of France had suffered from ungovernable fits of insanity and Henry would be afflicted by something of the same. But none of this was known when Henry was a child. Henry's mother Catherine of Valois, the queen dowager, had entered into a relationship with Owen Tudor, a Welsh squire and from 1430 onwards Henry ceased to reside regularly with her.

As a young boy Henry was occasionally paraded about London on ceremonial occasions and would, as he grew older have been aware of the tensions that were growing among his various uncles as to whom should be doing what with the king. Despite their quarrels the 'protectorate' of Henry VI was generally characterised by stable government in England while Bedford continued the war in France with some success. In 1429 the tide turned against him when Joan d'Arc's appearance revitalised the downcast French nobility and revived both their morale and their erstwhile lagging fortunes. After the fall of Orleans to the French Charles VII was crowned, at Rheims, with Joan at his side on 17th July 1429. This prompted Henry's advisors to also plan a coronation in France. But first Henry had to be crowned King of England. This was done in November 1429 when, at seven-years-old, Henry was anointed with holy oil and crowned king in front of all his nobles, in Westminster Abbey. In April 1430, at great cost, and at some danger to himself and his entourage King Henry VI crossed over to France to repeat the ritual. The military situation in France was such that

Henry had to stay at Rouen for over a year. Although the great inspiration of the French, Joan d' Arc, had been captured and burnt at the stake in May 1431, Henry was not able to go to Paris to be crowned, King of The French at Notre Dame, until December 1431.

After his coronation in France Henry was hastily moved back to Rouen and then sent back to England where he arrived in February 1432. He would never visit France again. While he was sailing home, Henry's erstwhile ally, the duke of Burgundy, concluded a truce with Charles VII. Henry's French coronation had obviously done little to cleave his allies to him. It was a turning point in English fortunes. From now on, with Bedford exhausted and disillusioned, the initiative would lie with Charles VII. With Burgundy's complete desertion to Charles VII in September 1435 the English cause was almost lost. Bedford's death on 15th September 1435 brought an end to the dreams of Henry V. Even the thirteen-year-old Henry VI, who had wept on hearing of Burgundy's desertion, knew that these were mortal blows from which his armies would not recover.

After 1432 Henry continued his education and the earl of Warwick noted that he was growing to understand his 'hiegh and royal auctoritee and estate'. Indeed, the signs looked good. Henry was tall, healthy, serious minded, fluent in English and French, interested in reading, hunting and education. Contemporaries report him as personable, perceptive, well educated, a natural scholar and even precocious. He was regarded as elegant and good looking with exemplary manners. He was also exceptionally pious and unworldly and he immersed himself in readings on religion rather than the exertions of the tilt yard. This sensitive and intelligent boy was surrounded by the growing conflict between his uncles, Gloucester and Cardinal Beaufort, who strove to dominate and control him. Some idea of Henry's growing interest in religion can be garnered from his stay at the abbey of Bury St Edmunds in 1433/44 during which he asked to be admitted into the abbey's fraternity. By 1437 Henry was ruling in fact as well as in name. It soon became clear however that Henry detested violence of any kind, he hated war, its misery, its expense and its waste and was more inclined to support his uncle, Cardinal Beaufort, in wanting an honourable peace with France. His views were not held by all his advisors but some were acknowledging the near impossibility of maintaining England's rule over northern France and Gascony and the peace party at court gained momentum after 1439.

At home Henry steered his energies towards his love of education and his desire to see it spread beyond its traditional precincts of Oxford and Cambridge. Henry was an admirer of King Alfred who had also promoted education and literacy. In 1440, when he was eighteen, Henry founded Eton College by the Thames at Windsor, providing for seventy scholars to receive a free education. Seventy scholars still receive a full grant to study at Eton today but now they gain admittance by competitive examination. Henry did not just hand out the charter for Eton he laid the foundation stone and personally modified the plans for the buildings. No previous king of England had endowed such a public grammar school of this kind or size, or showed as much interest in the scholars as Henry did. A year after Henry founded Eton he founded King's College Cambridge, first for twelve students and then later for the seventy scholars from Eton who could move on complete their education there. From its foundation until 1873 King's College admitted only Etonians and they gained their degrees without the inconvenience of sitting university examinations. In the matter of these foundations Henry's motives were as pure as any king's could be. He wanted to see improvements in both the lay and ecclesiastical pool from which his court and the church could draw from. He saw all of this work through a lens of piety and Christian virtue and, unusually for a king, from the standpoint of compassion, humanity and sensitivity to the human condition that he believed were the foundation stones of Christianity.

These contributions to late medieval education still preserve Henry's name but the shadow of a martial father is so much darker when it falls on one who has absolutely no interest in military matters, and thus it was with Henry VI. His piety made him a good man but a poor king. Had he been the son of a well-to-do London hatter he would have lost himself in a remote monastery or college somewhere. But he was born to be a king and there was no escape. At court he was a bit on the prudish side; he was generous to a fault and quick to pardon offenders who should have been watched more carefully. Henry's most intimate advisor was William de la Pole, earl of Suffolk. Suffolk had risen steadily through the offices of Henry's household and after he masterminded Margaret of Anjou's journey to England to marry Henry in 1445 his position at court seemed unassailable.

A greedy and ambitious man he now used his influence to aggrandise his family and friends on an outlandish scale. He also secured his marriage to the richest heiress in England, Henry's relative, Margaret Beaufort. Henry's generosity in rewarding his friends and household servants soon outran his budget and he fell into debt. In an unheard of level of patronage he often made life grants to his servants without asking for any payment in return. He also spent freely on a new establishment for the queen and he repaired and maintained a large number of royal palaces around London at considerable expense. The feisty fifteen-year-old Margaret of Anjou, a lioness compared to her mild husband, would never forget Suffolk's part in arranging her marriage. She needed allies as her marriage to Henry was unpopular. Although the niece of the Queen of France she brought no dowry with her, she was not her father's heir and anyway the duke of Anjou was poor. Her marriage to Henry took place at Titchfield Abbey in the New Forest on 22nd April 1445. Not long after the wedding it emerged that the surrender of Anjou and Maine, to Margaret's father, had been part of the marriage settlement.

By 1450 England faced political and military crisis as parliament denounced Suffolk and other royal servants for wasting the king's revenues, abusing his trust and exploiting the king to the impoverishment of the crown. Henry defended him and only banished him for five years. Suffolk fled but was killed as he tried to board a ship to leave England. Rebels from Kent attacked London throughout the summer of 1450 with Henry oscillating between concessions and executions. Margaret, based at Greenwich, managed to buy some time by pardoned one group of rebels in July. Margaret was a great counterweight to Henry. She was a warlike queen, as happy on the battlefield as at the court, but her skills at diplomacy could be put on a torn postage stamp and she was most definitely guilty of aggravating the quarrels that were to come. Henry, no doubt in thrall to her strong will, was devoted to her but the lack of an heir after eight years of marriage sent the wrong signals to a number of ambitious contenders for the throne.

These included Richard duke of York, who was descended from both the second and the fourth son of Edward III, and Edmund duke of Somerset, who was descended from the Beaufort clan. The quarrels of these mighty subjects, also dramatised by Shakespeare in the famous scene of rose plucking in the Temple garden, gave rise to those wars later commentators called 'The Wars of The Roses'. This was pure drama but, as usual, Shakespeare got the tenor right. These nobles grew to hate each other so much that they would commit the most violent and vicious acts on each other's children, fathers and brothers over the next fifteen years. The vicious retributions exacted by Edward II on his enemies was emerging as a template for the violence of another age.

Poor Henry VI couldn't handle any of this. His weakness encouraged conflict among his nobles and in the end it was his incapacity to rule that brought so many calamities to his realm. He was also ill. In August 1453, without warning, Henry suffered a severe mental collapse accompanied by severe physical impairment. It seemed as if *'his wit and reason were withdrawn'* and that he had *'no natural sense or reasoning power'*. Henry was helpless. He required the support of several servants to attend him day and night, to feed him and to help him move from room to room. He was in a state of paralytic melancholia, depriving him of memory, speech and reason. This first attack lasted nearly eighteen months until Christmas 1454. A second attack in the autumn of 1455 lasted until February 1456. During these long bouts of mental instability he would sit totally still, unaware of people and things around him. When he was presented with his newborn son early in 1454 he looked at him just once without a word before casting down his eyes once again. One report, probably malicious, has him looking surprised at seeing the child and exclaiming that *'it must be the son of the Holy Ghost'*.

The loss of Castillon in France in 1452 brought the three hundred years of English rule in Aquitaine to an end. This was a defeat from which Henry's government would never recover. The festering disputes around the court concerning the loss of France, the control of the sickly king and the nomination of a protector and heir, would now be settled by steel on steel. Somerset was an early victim when he was killed at the first battle of St Albans on 22nd May 1455, the opening salvo of 'The Wars of the Roses.' Four years of uneasy manoeuvre followed before Queen Margaret decided that only military defeat would silence York. In the summer of 1459 she routed him at Ludlow in Shropshire and forced him and his eldest son Edward earl of March (later Edward IV) to flee the country. The roller coaster ride of battles that make up the Wars of the Roses is too complex to enumerate here. Suffice it to say that after many battles Edward IV, son of the impatient, but now dead, duke of York declared Henry unfit to rule and was crowned in London on 4th March 1461. Henry and Margaret's armies were destroyed at the battle of Towton on 29th March 1461 and they both fled to Scotland. Henry VI, after spending a year wandering around the north of England was captured in July 1465 and *'brought as a traitor and criminal to London, and imprisoned in the Tower there; where like a true follower of Christ he patiently endured hunger, thirst, mockings, derisions, abuse and many other hardships'*. He would stay there for five years.

The wheel of fortune turned just one more time for Henry in 1470 after Edward IV had been defeated and forced to flee abroad. On 3rd October 1470, bewildered and *'mute as a crowned calf'* Henry was rolled out for one more time and called 'king' this time as a puppet of that great turncoat Richard Neville, earl of Warwick (the 'Kingmaker'). He was to reign again for less than eight months before a rejuvenated Edward IV returned to England. He defeated Queen Margaret's army at Tewkesbury in Gloucestershire in May 1471, killed her seventeen year old son Edward, and executed a number of prominent Lancastrian lords. He then took Queen Margaret with him, as his prisoner, to London on 21st May 1471 and within a few hours Henry VI, back in the Tower of London, was dead. The official version of his death put out on 23rd May was that Henry died of *'pure displeasure and melancholy'* after hearing of the defeat at Tewkesbury. It seems much more likely that he was murdered, probably stabbed to death by his guards, on the order of Edward IV in the Wakefield or the Lantern Tower. Edward, now a worldly twenty nine, wanted a speedy end to the symbol, however weak, that might give his enemies a cause to continue the conflict that had occupied him since he was seventeen.

On 22nd May Henry's body was taken from the Tower; first to St Paul's and then to Blackfriar's, where his face was exposed for a whole day so that people could see him. Stories of blood gushing from his nose signifying that he had been the victim of a barbarous murder were soon circulating. Later at night and with *'more swords and staves than torches'* about his coffin he was carried by water in an unlit barge *'without singing or saying'* past the Magna Carta island of Runnymede to the abbey at Chertsey in Surrey, for which he had declared some affection. This abbey had a church that was 275 feet long and was one of the grandest in the land, the whole complex occupying around 9 acres of rich meadowland by the Thames. It was dismantled on the orders of Henry VIII in 1537 and many of the stones removed to build a home for his ex-wife Anne of Cleves at Oatlands.

At the abbey, trusted soldiers from Calais guarded his coffin and more than £15 was spent on wax, linen and spices for his interment. Edward IV clearly intended his old enemy to rest in peace at Chertsey, well away from the court and the politics of London. It was not long, however, before a number of miracles were reported at this tomb and large numbers of pilgrims began to visit it. This was not the plan. It may have been this undesirable attention by pilgrims or simply an act of kindness that prompted Richard III in 1484 to have his body moved from there to St George's Chapel Windsor, ironically close to the tomb of Henry's old adversary Edward IV.

Even when he was not altogether in touch with this world, Henry developed an interest in where he would spend the next. Between the Battle of St Albans in 1455 and the Battle of Wakefield in 1460 Henry VI took to wandering about Westminster Abbey at all hours of the day and night seeking out a suitable place for his tomb. On one occasion he and Abbot Kirton walked around Edward the Confessor's Chapel together by torchlight. The abbot suggested various locations in the abbey including moving the tomb of Eleanor of Castile to accommodate Henry. Henry demurred at this and then fell into one of his *silent fits*. On seeing the neglected coffin of his mother, Catherine of Valois, Henry was asked if it should perhaps be more *'honourably apparelled'* and his own body laid between it and the altar of the Chapel. He fell silent again. When he eventually spoke he asked the abbot to name the kings among whose tombs he stood.

Then it was suggested that the tomb of Henry V (his father) should be pushed over to one side and his own placed beside it. Again he demurred *'Nay let him alone; he lieth like a noble prince. I would not trouble him'*. The abbot then explained that the relics, once moved to make way for his father's tomb, could be moved again. At this suggestion Henry became more animated and he marked out with his foot seven feet and then taking a staff pointed to the spot saying *'Here methinks is a convenient place'*. The master mason of the abbey then marked out the limits of the grave, the relics were removed and workmen were paid to set them up somewhere behind the altar. They toiled in vain *'the great trouble came on'* and Henry's dear wish to be buried near Edward the Confessor was thwarted by events and the circumstances of his death.

Later the 'name' of Henry VI would be needed to serve a new king. After the battle of Bosworth in 1485 Henry VII was looking for ways to link himself with the House of Lancaster that would give him more credibility as a claimant to the throne than his tenuous bloodline would suggest. What better way to join himself with the last king of the House of Lancaster than to plan a sumptuous tomb to receive the body of Henry VI; and while he was about it plan his own tomb to be near or, better still, inside this great monument. Two saintly men together! After the death of Henry VI, Edward IV, had begun using dynastic symbols to cement his hold on the crown but serious dynastic propaganda was definitely a Tudor invention! Henry VII had married Elizabeth, the daughter of Edward IV, so he had made his peace, and a clear connection, with the House of York, the great 'tomb project' would seal his link with the House of Lancaster.

By the late 1490s the memory of Henry VI had garnered a serious following of those who wanted to pray at his tomb or even his image. At York Minster it took the archbishop himself to stop people making special offerings to just a small image of Henry in the rood screen. None of this was lost on Henry VII. He promptly set about seeking the canonization of Henry VI, and his first thought was to prepare a new tomb for him at Windsor. In 1494 he started work on a new chapel located to the east of St George's Chapel to house the new tomb. This was on the site a chapel built by Henry III and then rebuilt by Edward III to house the Knights of the Garter.

All this was put in train, only to be interrupted by noisy petitions from the two abbeys of Chertsey and Westminster. Chertsey claimed that Richard III had seized Henry's corpse by violence and that it should be returned to its original resting place. The monks of Chertsey were missing the cash and gifts that those pilgrims had brought. Westminster claimed that all those midnight visits by Henry underlined his wish to be buried near Edward the Confessor. Feelings were running high, so much so in fact that a special Council was held at Greenwich to adjudicate. They decided in favour of Westminster, but Windsor, perhaps pleading that possession was nine tenths of the law, would not accept the decision and went to law.

Henry VII ignored their pleas and went ahead with plans for a great tomb at Westminster and £500 was spent to begin moving Henry's body. Pope Julius II granted a license for this, declaring that Henry's enemies had contrived to belittle his miracles and leave him in obscurity. Henry VII sat down with his architects to plan a new chapel at Westminster. It would be a wonder, greater even than Edward the Confessor's shrine. Some records in the abbey even suggest that Henry VI's body was actually removed from Windsor to some *place undistinguished'*, but the wills of both Henry VII and Henry VIII indicate that it remained in the south aisle of St George's Chapel. The proposed great tomb house at Windsor was left only three parts built on Henry VII's death in 1509. Now covered in wall-to-wall Victorian gothic it is the Chapel where Queen Victoria created a memorial to her beloved Prince Albert.

The canonization of Henry VI that the pope had promised never happened. Henry VII was notoriously parsimonious and perhaps the pope asked for too much cash up front. The great new chapel at Westminster, however, did get built; not for Henry VI, but for Henry VII himself. At Windsor legions of unwanted architects retired and the body of Henry VI remained buried beneath a simple tomb under an arch on the south side of the altar. Nearby is a fifteenth century octagonal alms-box bearing the royal initial 'H' where all those faithful pilgrims would, and still can, place their offerings. In 1910 this tomb was opened for examination and the bones of a strong man, around five feet nine inches tall and aged between forty-five and fifty-five at his death, was found. The broken skull bones were thought to be small and thin in proportion to the stature of the man. The body had been dismembered when first placed in its coffin and moving it from one grave to another had clearly affected its condition. Against his warlike father's desire, saintly Henry had been born at Windsor and there his body stayed, despite the wishes of so many to move him somewhere else.

EDWARD IV (born 1442 reigned 1461-1470, 1471-1483)

Edward IV was the eldest son of that proud Richard duke of York who opposed the reign of Henry VI and began the struggle for the crown that eventually brought an end to the Royal House of Lancaster so painfully conceived by Henry IV. Edward was born in Rouen in Normandy on 28th April 1442. His mother was Cecily Neville, youngest daughter of the huge family fathered by Ralph Neville 1st earl of Westmorland and blood aunt to Richard Neville earl of Warwick (the 'Kingmaker'). His father was descended from Anne Mortimer a daughter of Edward III's second son Lionel duke of Clarence. This combination of Plantagenet and Neville blood put Edward at the centre of a noble clan that could count on support from many quarters.

Little is known of Edward's childhood but he does not seem to have spent time outside his family circle, in the house of a great lord to learn the ways of nobility as many sons of his rank were. He was probably created earl of March, a hereditary title of the Mortimer clan, in late 1445. At seventeen Edward was definitely with his father at Ludlow castle in Shropshire and was at the Yorkist defeat at Ludford Bridge in Ludlow in October 1459. After this he went with his uncle, the earl of Salisbury and Salisbury's son, Richard Neville, earl of Warwick, to Calais while his father went to Ireland. In 1460 Edward, Salisbury and Warwick invaded England and gained possession of Henry VI after defeating his army at the battle of Northampton. Over that summer the earls ruled London in the king's name and when York arrived back in England his place as heir to the throne after Henry VI's death was agreed. Queen Margaret was not going to stand by and see her son disinherited and she soon raised forces to oppose York and his sons.

The duke of York was cornered and killed at the battle of Wakefield on 30th December 1460 and Edward, as head of the family, became the leading contender to replace Henry VI. After defeating a Lancastrian army, lead by the earls of Pembroke and Wiltshire, at the battle of Mortimer's Cross on 2nd February 1461 Edward joined forces with Warwick and entered London on 26th February where Edward was declared king on 4th March 1461. But battles still needed to be fought. Edward marched north to meet and defeat Henry and Margaret's' much larger army, at the bloodiest battle of the war, at Towton on 29th March. After a tour through the northern counties Edward returned to London and was crowned King Edward IV in Westminster Abbey on 28th June. After Towton Henry VI and Margaret escaped to Scotland but Henry later entered England hiding at a variety of locations in the north. Edward thus started his reign with the ex-king still alive and roaming around the north of England actively supported by the Scots and Lancastrian sympathisers. Edward began his reign by embracing some of his old enemies in an attempt to bring some normality to government after the factionalism of the last ten years. In general this policy worked and in July 1465 Henry VI was betrayed and captured in Lancashire.

Edward is the first, and last, king in English history to lose his throne, go into exile, invade his own kingdom, destroy his rivals, regain his crown and then reign in comparative peace for another twelve years. His reign divides neatly into two distinct parts: 1461-70, and 1471-83, the eight-month gap being accounted for by his short period of exile in Burgundy. After the bloody conflicts of the last six years, Edward needed to build fences and, unlike his predecessor, he was just the man to do it. Six foot four inches tall, blonde, good looking and with a military bearing, he looked every inch a king. He wore the latest fashions and had his head, legs and feet cleansed at least every Saturday night. Edward was also a master of 'spin'. He loved to be seen by people, was a snappy dresser, engaged well with people of all classes and revelled in the showmanship of being a king! The justification for his seizure of the throne from Henry VI was his noble ancestry and he used many different forms of propaganda to help bolster his image. His personal badges of a sun in splendour and the three crowns were widely promulgated. Few people might have got to see the king, but they saw him in such symbols, and Edward's supporters, like those of a modern day claimant to the leadership of a political party, saturated England with badges and symbols that advertised his claim to the throne. Most importantly, Edward also brought to the table his military success at Mortimer's Cross (1461), Towton (1461) and Tewkesbury (1471). A late medieval king was still measured by such things and the memory of the havoc wreaked by the docile Henry VI was still fresh in peoples minds.

Edward started well; he promised Parliament in 1467 that he would *'live off mine own and not to charge my subjects but in great and urgent causes'*. He began the process of putting crown business in the hands of competent salaried officials rather than selling crown offices off to scavenging courtiers, and he promoted trade by becoming a successful wool trader himself. In the 1460s Louis XI of France was at loggerheads with Burgundy and Brittany. Edward favoured an alliance with Burgundy rather than with France but Richard Neville, earl of Warwick, Edward's richest and most powerful supporter, preferred an alliance with the French. In the end Edward triumphed and his youngest sister, Margaret was married to duke Charles, 'the Bold', of Burgundy. Warwick still harboured hopes of marrying Edward off to a princess of France.

But Edward's weakness was women. He was an inveterate womaniser with a bit of a taste for older ladies. But one woman (such a one as Henry VIII would also encounter), Elizabeth Woodville, the widow of Sir John Grey, a Lancastrian who had been killed at the second battle of St Albans, would not yield to Edward. She wanted a ring and surprisingly Edward agreed to her terms. This was a serious mistake. In May 1464 he married Elizabeth, a widow with two sons, five brothers and six unmarried sisters. That Edward kept the marriage a secret, even from his closest advisors, for four months suggests that he foresaw trouble arising from it. It was certainly the main cause of the initial breakdown of trust between him and Warwick, who was busy negotiating a marriage alliance between Edward and a French Princess at the time.

The largely unmarried Woodville clan would greedily gather in gifts, honours and appointments, to the dismay of the older aristocracy. They would become the new rich, despised and hated by the old rich for flaunting their new honours under the protection of their great ally, the king. One outrageous example of their quest for status was the marriage of the queen's brother, the twenty year old John Woodville, to the extremely wealthy Dowager Duchess of Norfolk, a three-time widow of nearly eighty, a match that, even in that age of opportunistic and bizarre contracts, shocked nearly everyone at court. Edward was a great pragmatist, others might be shocked by his finding wealthy husbands and wives for Elizabeth's family but by connecting them to some of the most powerful families in the realm he was also linking himself more securely to the English nobility. However unpopular she may have been with the old nobility Elizabeth was at least fertile. She gave Edward two surviving sons and seven daughters, five of whom survived to adulthood. Once within the bosom of the Woodvilles and his various mistresses, Edward settled down to a life of leisure and pleasure. Meanwhile, frustrated at losing the diplomatic coup of an alliance with France and feeling excluded from the new circle of advisors that clustered round the king, Warwick became disaffected. He was supported by Edward's brother, George duke of Clarence, who nurtured dreams of becoming king. Initially these two dissidents confined their activities to lending covert support to uprisings against Edward in the north and midlands.

Later, from Warwick's base at Calais, they moved into overt opposition. In July 1469, Warwick led a group of Lancastrian nobles back to England. Clarence was with him and now, against his brother's express wish, he married Warwick's daughter Isabel, They caught Edward off guard, he was captured and sent to Warwick's castle at Middleham. But the pair of rebels had not organised their rebellion very well as their attempts to rule in the king's name while the king was a prisoner did not play well with Londoners. Eventually Edward was released and arrived back in London in the middle of October. Despite the death of the queen's father and brother John, who had been beheaded at Coventry by Warwick and Clarence, Edward resumed his usual policy of forgiving most of those who had opposed him. This policy may have been resented by the queen and it certainly did not placate Warwick and Clarence who, in the spring of 1470, instigated yet another rebellion, this time in Lincolnshire. The rebellion failed and Warwick and Clarence fled to France where they entered into negotiations with Margaret of Anjou for the restoration of Henry VI. In September 1470 they invaded England with a large French and Lancastrian force. They were supported by some leading English nobles such as Jasper Tudor and Lord Stanley. Edward was in the north when they arrived and moved south slowly hoping for support from Warwick's younger brother, John Neville, who had remained loyal to him before. His trust was misplaced as John defected to the rebels. Edward, his brother the duke of Gloucester, and the lords Howard and Hastings, fled to Edward's sister, Margaret in Burgundy, leaving Warwick to enter London unopposed. Warwick wheeled the ragged Henry VI out of the tower to be king yet again, shattering Clarence's dreams in the process, and giving him a good reason to consider defecting to his brother. Elizabeth Woodville had stayed in England, finding sanctuary in Westminster Abbey, where she gave birth to Edward's first son, the future Edward V, on 2nd November 1470.

The duke of Burgundy was, at first, reluctant receive his brother-in-law. As part of the price of French support Warwick had agreed to help Louis XI of France invade Burgundy and the duke needed more time to prepare. This changed when Louis declared war on Burgundy in December 1470 and, with nothing to lose, the duke helped Edward with his plan to invade England. In March 1471 Edward landed in England a few miles above Ravenspur, near where Henry Bolingbroke had landed seventy-two years before. Later in April, joined by Clarence, Edward's forces had grown to such strength that he was able to enter London unopposed on 11th April to be reunited with his queen and his new son. On 14th April, the same day that Margaret of Anjou and her son landed in England to support Warwick, Edward defeated (and killed) Warwick at the battle of Barnet. Edward, now back in vigorous military form, moved quickly to intercept Margaret before she could cross the River Severn and join with her Welsh supporters. He met and defeated her at the battle of Tewkesbury in May where her son prince Edward was killed. Edward IV had decided that Henry VI would always be a magnet for Lancastrian discontent and, without further ado, he had Henry murdered in the Tower on the night of his return to London. A sad king had come to a sad end! With his enemies vanquished, the ex-king and his heir dead, and a healthy male heir of his own, Edward's authority would now be unchallenged for the next twelve years.

His policy again rested on a plank of reconciliation with old enemies and the distribution of patronage to those who he regarded as loyal and trustworthy. Unfortunately his brother, Clarence was not a beneficiary. He objected to Edward endowing their brother Richard, duke of Gloucester, with half of the great Warwick estates after Richard married Anne Neville who was part heiress to these with Clarence's wife Isabel. In the end he was accused of plotting against the crown and Edward did not hesitate to have him executed (see below). Edward tried, on the whole successfully, to maximise his income from the crown estates and from royal wardships or ecclesiastical vacancies rather than by constant recourse to parliament. His recourse to using benevolences, really enforced gifts from his subjects rather than loans, to help fund his French and Scottish wars was less popular, although one wealthy widow is recorded as having doubled her contribution in return for a kiss from the king!

Edward's growing security in England led him to cast his eyes overseas. Louis XI of France had supported Edward's enemies and Edward was now determined, in alliance with his brother-in-law, the duke of Burgundy, to get some revenge. Hopes were high and the king left England in July 1475 with a well-equipped army of 10,000 men hoping to meet his brother-in-law, Burgundy, with a similar number. But Burgundy came with nothing at all.

Families! Another ally, the duke of Brittany, also failed to turn up and Edward's 'revenge' melted away. Instead, on 29th August 1475 Edward met Louis XI on the bridge at Picquigny on the Somme to seal the terms of a seven-year truce. Afterwards there was much feasting and the French king later reported that he had seen off his enemies with *'venison pies and good French wine'*. In fact he had seen them off with a big bribe. All this merry Anglo-French concord was achieved by Louis paying Edward £15,000 down and promising him an annual pension of £10,000. Many of the English nobles, including Edward's brother, the duke of Gloucester, saw this as a buy-out that stained the honour of English arms. Other than having to deal with the plotting of *'false fleeting perjured Clarence'* the post Picquigny years were spent gorging at huge feasts, making three more daughters, supporting William Caxton and his novel printing press, and being attended on by his favourite mistress, the divorced wife of a London mercer, named Jane Shore. Edward the great soldier and dandy was now lazy and corpulent. Polydor Vergil notes how in later life the king began to *'slyde by lyttle and lyttle into avarice'*. Perhaps he was laying down some examples that his grandson, Henry VIII could follow? Contemporary chroniclers agree that Edward was losing his good looks and running to fat as early as 1475 but they all note his excellent memory and general good health. His sudden illness during Easter 1483 thus took everyone by surprise.

Edward IV was taken ill at Windsor on 30th March 1483 after accompanying a group of courtiers boating on the Thames. He later travelled in some discomfort to his palace at Westminster. News of his illness reached all parts of his kingdom so speedily that on the 6th April a report reached York that the king was dead, and a dirge was duly sung in York Minster. This was slightly premature as at that time Edward was still alive. Indeed, Edward lingered on for ten days and had enough time to make various codicils to his will and express his wishes for the governance of the country after his death. He named his brother Richard duke of Gloucester to be protector of his son and called lord Hastings and the queen's relatives, who had been openly quarreling, to his bedside, and begged them to be reconciled. They did so with a transparent grace that would fold in on itself moments after Edward's last breath.

On 9th April, 1483, Edward died at his palace at Westminster, aged forty. His son, Edward V, the new king, being then twelve, was holding his Court and Council of the Marches at Ludlow Castle. At the time of Edward's death, Richard, duke of Gloucester, was two hundred miles away at Middleham Castle in Yorkshire. Opinions differ concerning Edwards's final illness and its cause. Some ascribe it to acute indigestion and Edward's delight in rich food (he often took an emetic after dinner so that he could start all over again) lends some credence to this diagnosis; others point to the damp spring air around the River Thames; others to a stroke of apoplexy and others to venereal disease. His early death was probably the cumulative effect of all of these plus the toll taken on his body by so many days and nights spent in the hard company of arms and armies.

The details of Edward's funeral give an insight into the kind of pomp, ritual and ceremony attending the funeral of a late medieval king in England, at least of one who died in his bed. After the king's death, his body was *'laid upon a board all naked, saving he was covered from the navel to the knees'* and placed for twelve hours in the Palace of Westminster while the Mayor of London, aldermen, priests and nobles came to pay their respects. At dawn the next day the king's remains, wrapped in waxed cloth, were taken to the Chapel of St. Stephen in Westminster Abbey, wearing a crown and dressed in a full suit of gold armour. He lay here, in state, for eight days guarded every night to prevent desecration by intruders.

After the lying in state, the corpse, still with the crown on its head, was placed on a movable wooden stand, covered by a broad pall of black cloth of gold. Now ten bishops and two abbots came into the abbey, followed by lord Howard carrying Edward's own banner. Other canopies and banners followed and behind these came a line of nobles, some of whom stopped to touch the king's bier from time to time. The royal hearse stood in the abbey topped with an image of the king clothed in full royal regalia. Knights clad in black mail with visors closed, and carrying bare swords, filled the choir and the nave. Other ecclesiastics in long white robes knelt around the coffin while more priests carried burning candles of black wax several feet in length. Finally the bier with the king's image on it was placed on the hearse, and the funeral cortège left the abbey for Windsor. Lord Howard, wearing a mourning hood and still carrying the royal banner, lead the procession on a horse dressed in black velvet trappings bearing the king's arms. The cortège halted at Charing Cross for the chariot to be censed and another stop was made at the nunnery of Syon House, near Windsor, where Anne de la Pole, a niece of the dead king, lived.

The body lay under guard in the Syon House church till the following day, and at Eton the cortège stopped again for the body to be censed by the Bishops of Lincoln and Ely. At Windsor the body was censed for the third time, after which it was brought into the king's own foundation, the impressive, but yet to be completed St George's Chapel. Here a 'marvellous well-wrought hearse' awaited it. The coffin of the dead king was again guarded overnight. The next day the assembled bishops sang the Mass, and a requiem was sung by the Archbishop of York. After this an armed knight, all in steel, bareheaded and carrying an axe, rode on horseback to the choir door, dismounted, and was led inside to make his traditional offering as 'the man of arms'. The peers then offered their traditional gifts of cloths of gold.

The king's remains were then taken from the bier and placed in the marble tomb that Edward had prepared some time before, on the north side of the altar. The chief men of his household, again following tradition, now threw their staves 'in token of being men without a master and out of their offices' into the grave. The heralds then cast their coats of arms into the grave and were then re-clothed in other royal coats of arms. Edward's own gilt suit of armour, surmounted by a cloth of crimson velvet with the arms of England and France embroidered on it, was hung above the tomb together with a banner displaying the royal arms. Edward had made serious plans for his tomb well before he died. Indeed the tomb he prepared under the most easterly (and holiest) arch between the north aisle and the altar was almost integral to the growing fabric of the new chapel. In his will of c1473, Edward laid down elaborate details for his tomb and a chantry chapel to be built above it. Hardly anything of the tomb and monuments he so carefully stipulated remain, but the beautiful, and large, chantry chapel above it has survived and has been adapted to various uses over the ages.

Sutton, Visser-Fuchs and Griffiths note 'A cadaver in whatever form, lying on black marble, within a shining black marble arch, with armorial escutcheons in coloured enamels and metals, the text presumably in brass letters, would have been very impressive'. It is likely that not all of Edward's hopes for the formal design of his tomb were actually carried out. His military achievements, the surcoat, sword and belt, helmet and cap of maintenance were, however hung over his tomb. This feature may have been inspired by the two warrior-tombs of Edward 'the Black Prince' at Canterbury and of Henry V at Westminster. Both of these tombs had their military achievements hung over them and for both some remnants survive. Nothing survives of those that hung above Edward IV's tomb. One Captain Fogg, a Cromwellian soldier, plundered some items in October 1642. He also helped himself to all the rich plate on the chantry altar.

The chantry chapel over the north aisle was completed with an altar and two bay windows in stone looking down over the high altar and choir. In 1519 Henry VIII replaced the stone window nearest the altar with a wooden one and it is said that Catherine of Aragon watched the annual Garter services from up here. This little vantage point would be used by many more queens in the future. Edward also requested that there should be room in the chantry chapel for thirteen persons to pray for his soul. He also wanted an image (whether kneeling or recumbent is not specified) of himself in the centre of the chapel in silver gilt, or at the least copper gilt, as a reminder of who they were all praying for. If it was ever completed nothing of this effigy now remains. One striking component of the tomb that has survived is the elaborate iron gates hung on two ornate towers made by the Cornishman, John Tresilian, between 1477 and 1484. These gates, once part of the railings around Edward IV's tomb, were later removed from their original position and are now placed in front of the screen on the choir side of his tomb.

Between 1782 and 1792 George III instituted major repairs to St George's Chapel. During the repaving of the north aisle on 13th March 1789, workmen came upon the entrance to Edward IV's burial vault. The chamber contained Edward's lead coffin with the sparse remains of Elizabeth Woodville's wooden coffin on top of it. Edward's coffin was removed and opened before a group of worthy observers including Sir William Herschel the famous astronomer. The skeleton was complete and measured at six feet three and a half inches or 192cm. The workmen involved in the discovery made their find known to the townsfolk of Windsor, many of whom flocked to the tomb and pinched various bits of the king's remains as souvenirs. The large quantity of Edward's hair found intact seems to have been particularly prized and many later commentators and correspondents had either seen or owned some of it. The black tomb slab that lies over Edward's grave today was placed there in 1787.

What we see of Edward IV's tomb today is a shadow of what he planned. The founder of this beautiful chapel obviously had a very clear idea about the kind of monument that he wanted and although part of his plan seems to have been carried out, his proposed effigy in the chantry chapel and some other work was probably downgraded or forgotten as the dynasty changed in 1485. It is unfortunate that the route of the tour round St George's Chapel today inclines visitors to turn right out of the north aisle into the choir just before they reach the slab that now marks Edward IV's grave. Many of them thus miss the last resting place of the man who founded, and began building, this magnificent chapel, one of the finest examples of fifteenth century fan vaulting.

George duke of Clarence

Edward's younger brother, the unstable George duke of Clarence, was executed for treachery in February 1479. His life had been one deception after another and no one was really surprised by the king's final exasperation when he approved his execution. After a roller coaster ride of treasons and quarrelling with his family, Clarence had the temerity to ask Edward in 1477 for permission to marry (his wife, Isabel, having died in childbirth) Mary, the heiress of the duke of Burgundy – an inheritance far too important to drop in Clarence's unsteady lap. Edward's refusal sent Clarence off to mutter further treasons against his brother and he was arrested, attainted of treason in parliament and sentenced to death. Elizabeth Woodville, who hated Clarence for the part he played in the death of her father and brother, John, in 1469, helped Edward overcome any reluctance he may have had about signing his brother's death warrant. The old story, repeated by Shakespeare, is that Clarence was drowned in a butt of Malmsey wine. There is no contemporary evidence for this except that Clarence's daughter, Margaret Pole, did wear a model of a wine cock (tap) on her wrist in remembrance of her father.

We know that Clarence died in the Tower of London and was eventually buried in Tewkesbury Abbey in Gloucestershire, a foundation within the manors inherited through his wife Isabel Neville. On the floor of the ambulatory in the abbey is a grating covering a small vault where (unusually in England) some of Clarence's bones and those of his wife are preserved in a glass case. She died before him and we must assume that there once was some sort of monument in the abbey covering both graves that was destroyed at the dissolution of the monasteries. After this their bones were probably collected up by sympathetic monks and put in this small case. When I first visited the abbey in the 1970s it was still possible to visit this vault, small candle in hand, to see the modest remains of this once proud brother of a king. Today a lock and chain bar the way to all but those with a direct line to the key holder. Given that Clarence is supposed to have been drowned it is an irony that this little case had to be set high in the wall of the vault to avoid the flooding that periodically besets the lower reaches of the abbey. He would certainly have been swilling about in that vault during the devastating floods that afflicted Tewkesbury in July 2007.

Elizabeth Woodville

The funeral of Edward IV's wife, Elizabeth Woodville, is an interesting contrast to the pomp that accompanied the interment of her husband. Living on well into the reign of Henry VII she was the mother of Henry VII's Queen, Elizabeth of York. She died at Bermondsey Abbey on Friday 8th June 1492, leaving a brief will noting that she had no worldly goods to leave to her daughter (the queen) or any of her children, other than her blessing. Having started off well with her new son-in-law, King Henry VII, their relationship deteriorated and Elizabeth, the once great scooper up of wealthy partners for her family, seems to have fallen foul of Henry by allegedly flirting with treason.

She is thought to have requested that her funeral be an austere affair *'without pompes entering or costlie expensis'*, her main wish being that she be buried with her late husband, Edward IV, in St George's Chapel Windsor. By now she was comparatively poor and given that the estate of the deceased generally paid for the funeral the austerity was perhaps less to do with piety than the economic reality of her later life. During the late evening of the 10th June (Whit Sunday) her body was conveyed by river from London up the Thames to Datchet where it was taken quietly (perhaps even secretly) through what was then known as the 'Little Park' to Windsor and St George's Chapel. She was met by a single priest and seems to have been buried almost immediately in a coffin resting on that of her husband. Over the next four days various people including three of her daughters arrived to mourn her. Masses and requiems were sung and offerings were made but only a dozen old men were assembled to hold some second hand torches and candle ends around her hearse - a clear indication of a low level of ceremony. When Edward IV's tomb was opened in 1789 only a few fragments of both Elizabeth's skeleton and her wooden coffin were found lying on top of the king's lead one. Her estate didn't run to the luxury of a lead casing.

Edward IV had invigorated the monarchy. His claim to the throne was drawn from his ancestor, the second son of Edward III and, more importantly, by success in battle. He was one of the first kings to understand the role of the merchant class in England and he worked hard to fund his affairs without constant recourse to parliament, to centralise government around the king and to put men in his service who he promoted by merit rather than by title. It is now accepted by most historians that Henry VII followed closely the practices and policies developed by Edward IV and the year 1485 is no longer considered to be an instant gateway into the modern era. More than half of Edward's councillors, still alive in 1485, were used by Henry and so continuity and refinement rather than revolution characterised the first Tudor regime.

EDWARD V (born 1470 reigned 3 months- April 1483-July1483

Edward V, born on 2nd November 1470, was the eldest son of Edward IV and his wife Elizabeth Woodville. His father was in exile when he was born and so his birth, in the sanctuary of Westminster Abbey, was at a precarious time for his mother and his family. When Edward IV reclaimed his throne he made his son prince of Wales and earl of Chester on 26th June 1471 and he got parliament to recognise him as his heir seven days later. From 1476 onwards Edward was based, with his council, at the Yorkist castle of Ludlow. He and his council were to be the main agent of royal authority in Wales and the marches. Edward was at Ludlow when his father died.

The accession of a twelve-year-old boy to the throne after nearly twelve years of peace under his well-established father should have gone relatively smoothly but the brutality of the 'Wars of the Roses' among the English aristocracy was real and its memories were still vivid. One historian, J. R. Lander, has argued that the amount of fighting was very small, estimating that there was only about thirteen weeks of actual conflict over thirty-two years. Against this view should be set the fact that between 1455 and Edward IV's reclaiming of his throne in 1471 twenty-six peers of the realm had been killed in battle and thirteen executed. Six of Edward III's direct descendants in the male line had met a violent death, and violence, enmity and jealousy were never far from the surface among the great lords of late medieval England. So instead of 'smooth' the death of Edward IV was followed almost immediately by a furious struggle for power over the boy king. In itself this was nothing new.

Although the death of King John in 1216 had seen the peaceful accession of his child heir Henry III despite the country being in the middle of a civil war, the deaths of Edward III and Henry V prompted serious power struggles to control a child king however, none of these resulted in the child's death. In 1483 the conditions were typically medieval in that one group, the newly-ennobled Woodvilles, sought possession and control of the boy king while another group, the old nobility, led by the king's brother, Richard duke of Gloucester, sought the same. The stage was set for a 'grab the boy' drama.

At Edward IV's death on, 9th April 1483, Edward was at Ludlow under the guardianship of his maternal uncle, Anthony Woodville, earl Rivers, while his paternal uncle, Richard duke of Gloucester, (who had been named Protector in a codicil to Edward IV's will), was two hundred miles away at his castle in Middleham in Yorkshire. The race was on to secure the 'body' of the young king. The queen got off to a good start. While Gloucester was still in the north she quickly persuaded the king's Council to pass a resolution replacing Gloucester's Protectorship with a Council of Regency controlled by her family and friends. In parallel with this she arranged for Edward V to be brought to London as quickly as possible for a speedy coronation after which any protectorship would lapse anyway and she would then definitely be the power behind the throne.

In mid-April, while still at Middleham, Richard received news from lord Hastings of his brother's death, and the queen's machinations. Ominously there was no official word of the king's death from the court at Westminster so Richard despatched letters to earl Rivers at Ludlow and to the queen and the Council in London. Around 20th April Richard set off for the south with around 300 armed retainers, planning to meet a new friend and ally, Henry Stafford second duke of Buckingham, at Northampton. They met there on 29th April after the king and his retinue had left. Earl Rivers doubled back to see Gloucester to explain that the king had gone on to Stony Stratford, to better provision and accommodate his retinue. On the morning of 30th April Gloucester, suspicious of all this haste and, determined to secure the protectorship, had Rivers arrested and then moved on to Stony Stratford to meet the young king and arrest two more of the queen's adherents. The old nobility had dealt with the new and after resting for a time back at Northampton the two dukes escorted Edward V to London.

The news of all this reached the queen on 1st May 1483 and she immediately took sanctuary in Westminster Abbey with her younger son, the ten year old Richard, duke of York. Gloucester, Buckingham and the young king entered London unopposed on 4th May, the day the queen and her 'Council' had set for the new king's coronation. The old nobility had won round one but they couldn't hang on to the 'body' forever without moving towards a proper coronation. In the late fifteenth century a boy of twelve was almost an adult and so the coronation was now planned for 24th June. In a surprise move Gloucester arrested a number of Edward IV's leading councillors and executed Edward IV's closest friend, William Lord Hasting. It is generally believed that Gloucester decided to make his pitch for the crown by the second week of June 1483. On 10th June Richard wrote to the city of York for military aid against the queen and her clan, 'which have intended and daily doth intent to murder and utterly destroy us,' and by 22nd June his supporters were putting forward arguments for his accession.

In making this move Gloucester seems to have been much encouraged by the young duke of Buckingham. Richard's claim was based on three foundations. The first was to do with the legitimacy of King Edward IV. This story was once thought to be just a piece of classic 'usurper' propaganda on the part of Gloucester but a newly discovered entry in the cathedral registry of Rouen dated 1441 puts Richard duke of York, Edward's father, on military service from 14th July to 21st August 1441 at a location several days march from Rouen. Edward was born on 28th April 1442 and, calculating back, it would seem that the duke was not in Rouen at the time of his conception. In addition, Edward's christening was a very quiet affair conducted in a side chapel while that for the duke's second son, Edmund, prompted a huge celebration encompassing the whole of the cathedral. As intriguing as this discovery is, the fact remains that the duke of York never repudiated Edward in his lifetime and so, under English law, Edward IV was York's legal son and heir whether he, or someone else, fathered him.

Robert Stillington, Bishop of Bath and Wells, raised the second foundation, one more in keeping with Edward IV's lecherous lifestyle. He declared that he had knowledge that Edward had previously been contracted to marry one lady Eleanor Butler, a widow and a daughter of the famed warrior John Talbot, earl of Shrewsbury. In the eyes of the church such a contract, although often entered into in a cavalier fashion by some noblemen, was as solemn as a marriage vow. If true, this would make Edward's marriage to Elizabeth Woodville invalid and all his issue, including Edward V, illegitimate and thus ineligible to inherit the crown. The third foundation was the well oiled justification of 'who wants a child king when a strong soldier and administrator of the blood royal is on hand willing and able to replace him'. This later idea was always a winner with the nervous merchants and traders in London (what we would today call 'the City') whose profits might well be disturbed by a contested or unstable minority. The result of all this busy propaganda was that Elizabeth Woodville was persuaded to release Edward V's ten-year-old brother, Richard, duke of York, from the sanctuary at Westminster, to join Edward in the Tower 16th June. On 26th June Edward V was declared a bastard and Gloucester, 'by request of Parliament,' seized the crown. While all this was going on the two princes were kept hidden in the royal apartments in the Tower of London and Gloucester was crowned King of England on Sunday 6th July 1483.

The permanent disappearance of the two princes after the summer of 1483, together with Richard's failure to show them in public to scotch the rumours of their deaths seems pretty conclusive proof that he had had them secretly murdered in the Tower. The contrary argument that having had them debarred from the crown because of their illegitimacy Gloucester had no need to dispose of them is a thin one. Their survival, wherever they were located, would always be a magnet to those who were wedded to the blood of Edward IV (however tainted) or who might nurse future grievances against the new king.

Thus, secretly and behind closed doors, arose another of the great 'whodunits' of English history – the mystery of the murder of the two princes in the Tower. How they actually died is unknown but if they weren't suffocated while they slept in the White Tower they have been a thousand times since in performances of Shakespeare's Richard III. The White Tower was later the lodging of Sir Walter Raleigh when imprisoned by King James I. He used to take his exercise on the battlements leading out from the tower and here, no doubt, the young princes did the same. However the princes died no more is heard of them – impostors arose later but of the real sons of Edward IV no more would be heard. During the 1650s Oliver Cromwell ordered that the old royal apartments to the south of the White Tower be demolished. This job was never finished and Charles II later decided to clear the site. As part of this 'clearing' process workmen were busy breaking down an old turret and its staircase that led to a royal chapel higher up in the White Tower. On 17th July 1674 when working deep under the base of the staircase (at ten feet below ground level) the workmen found a wooden chest containing the bones of two children along with bits of rag and velvet around them. The bones were immediately declared to be those of the two lost princes.

After two hundred years, subsidence probably accounted for the great depth of the chest but if this was the two princes they had been very carefully hidden. This was a recess under a private stairway only used by monarchs and their families to access the royal chapel above. Alison Weir in her book 'The Princes in the Tower' draws particular attention to the pieces of velvet that survived. Velvet was invented in Italy during the fifteenth century and was not made in England until the sixteenth century. During the fifteenth century it was restricted by both cost and social convention to a few wealthy nobles so the discovery of this fragment suggests that these two children had died after the invention of velvet, probably sometime late in the fifteenth century, and were definitely from wealthy stock. Charles II ordered that the royal surgeon examine the bones. Using the limited forensic knowledge of the day he confirmed that they were the bones of the two princes. Four years later Charles II commissioned Christopher Wren to provide a white marble urn for the bones and it is that urn that we see today in Westminster Abbey, located just a short step from the monumental tomb to their sister, Elizabeth of York, and her husband, Henry VII

In 1933 George V gave permission for the urn to be opened and the contents examined. It was found to contain parts of the skeletons of a boy of about twelve and a boy of about nine years old. While admitting some difficulty in assessing the evidence, the two medical experts confirmed that the bones were consistent with the sizes and ages of the two princes in 1483. Forensic science (radiocarbon dating, chemical testing etc.,) has made remarkable progress over the last seventy odd years and a much better judgement on the nature, age, cause of death etc., of the persons entombed there could be made now. However I understand that the Dean and Chapter of Westminster have resisted all requests for further testing and remain reluctant to ask Queen Elizabeth II for permission to disturb the bones again.

Another little mystery associated with the princes surfaced during the last century. In December 1964 demolition workers in Stepney in London discovered a small lead coffin that was easily identified from the inscription on it as being Anne Mowbray, daughter of the last Mowbray duke of Norfolk, who was married to Richard duke of York in 1478, when she was only five and he a few months younger. She had died at Greenwich in 1481 just three weeks before her ninth birthday. She was a great heiress and Edward IV had taken a lot of trouble to arrange the match for his youngest son. Anne's body had originally been taken from Greenwich in an elaborate river procession to Westminster Abbey, where she was buried amid great pomp. It is thought that her body had then been moved during building works in Westminster Abbey in 1501. It was then taken, possibly at the instigation of her mother, the Duchess of Norfolk, to the abbey of the Minoresses, known as the Minories, around the same time. Unlike those of her husband, enough of her remains were found to confirm them as being those of the young princess. On the order of Queen Elizabeth II, she was re-interred in the Henry VII Chapel in Westminster Abbey close to her original resting place, and not far from the supposed bones of her young husband. She was the last royal person to be laid to rest in the abbey in a chapel that was not even built when she was alive.

RICHARD III (born 1452 reigned 1483-1485)

Richard III, born on 2nd October 1452, at Fotheringhay castle in Northampton was the youngest surviving child of Richard duke of York and Cecily Neville. Mary Queen of Scots would end her life in the same place one hundred and thirty-five years later. Being the youngest son of Richard Plantagenet, duke of York there is not a lot of contemporary evidence for his early life and character but what there is, up until June 1483 generally paints him in a reasonable light. As the son of Richard duke of York there would be no expectation that Richard, or for that matter his brother Edward IV, would need to be trained for the crown. But their lives would be those of privileged aristocrats, moving around the castles and estates of their father who was a great landowner and an important member of the ruling elite, being a direct descendent of Edward III, albeit through the female line.

In 1461 Edward IV created Richard duke of Gloucester. The nine-year-old duke was then sent for 'nobility' training to the household of, his cousin, Richard Neville earl of Warwick at Middleham castle in Yorkshire. He may have remained there until late 1468 when he was sixteen, an age when he could be deemed to have come of age. Richard stayed loyal to his brother, the king, when Clarence and Warwick rebelled in 1469, and he went with Edward IV to exile in Burgundy. After his restoration in 1471, Edward granted Richard many honours for his loyalty and he started to emerge from the shadow of his brother to take on some of the great offices of state. As a youth Richard had been a witness, and sometimes a part, of those great struggles between York and Lancaster that saw his father and brother, Edmund, killed when he was eight. He fought his first battle, at Barnet, with distinction aged nineteen and gained further honours by commanding the vanguard at the decisive battle of Tewkesbury in 1471. After this Richard received more gifts of lands from his brother. These had often been collected up, after others had forfeited them, in order to give Richard and income rather than any particular regional influence. He later swapped some of these lands with other great magnates to give himself more of a concentrated power base.

In 1471, against his brother, Clarence's wishes, Richard married Anne Neville, daughter of Richard Neville earl of Warwick and sister of Clarence's wife, Isabel. He was thus able to claim part of the huge Warwick estates that Clarence had hoped to keep for himself. As part of Warwick's rebellion against Edward in 1470, he had arranged for Anne to be married to Henry VI's son, prince Edward of Lancaster, who was killed at the battle of Tewkesbury. Anne and Richard were not strangers; they had known each other since they were children, during Richard's time at Middleham. In 1473 Anne bore Richard a son, whom they christened Edward. He would die soon after being created Prince of Wales in April 1484. From 1475, after receiving more grants of lands, forfeited by the king's enemies, Richard emerged as the pre-eminent force in the north-east and far north-west of England, the only northern areas outside his sphere of influence being Lancashire and Cheshire. Throughout Edward's second reign Richard was constable and admiral of England and was active in both capacities, including presiding over the trial of the Lancastrian lords captured after the battle of Tewksbury.

After Edward swapped his armour for the pleasures of London and Windsor, Richard retired to the north to rule over it, in Edward's name, as an almost independent entity. Richard was well employed by Edward and he became an able administrator, hard working and conscientious in his rule there, inspiring loyalty in many and the sincere devotion of his closest aids. The Croyland chronicler gives Richard a favourable review, noting that he was daring, quick and alert with an overweening mind, a sharp wit and *'courage high and fierce'*. Dominic Mancini was rather more gushing: *'Such was his renown in warfare, that whenever a difficult and dangerous policy had to be undertaken, it would be entrusted to his discretion and generaliship. By these arts Richard acquired the favour of the people, and avoided the jealousy of the Queen, from whom he lived far separated'*.

Much has been written about his physical description. Being short with dark hair he is thought to have resembled his father more than Edward IV did. Most contemporaries agree on his short stature, small body, delicate arms and limbs and general feeble appearance. Later reporters (mostly Tudor writers) turned 'delicate' and 'feeble' into a vile hunchback who was born deformed with a shrivelled and withered arm: just the kind of man to go around murdering everybody who got in his way. The earliest portrait of him dated c1516-22 (a copy of an original believed to have been painted from life) hangs in the collection of the Society of Antiquaries in London and shows no sign of any deformity. He does look preoccupied, stern, thin lipped and pinched, certainly not a man likely to be the life and soul of the party. Edward IV was probably glad that he stayed in the north. Although less of a sensualist than Edward, Richard did find the time to father a number of bastards and he arranged marriages for two of his daughters before he died.

From 1475 onwards Richard rarely visited London, spending most of his time pacifying the lawless northern counties and dealing with an almost continuous spate of Scottish incursions. In 1482 his campaigns against the Scots culminated in the recapture of Berwick and an unopposed entry into Edinburgh. Edward rewarded this victory, and the ten years of loyal service behind it, by making Richard's wardenship of the West March a hereditary office. This almost created a state within a state – a very powerful office and one that Parliament confirmed just two months before Edward IV died. That early death changed everything. Richard's movements thereafter and his role in usurping the throne have been outlined above in the brief story of Edward V. Richard clearly believed that the Woodvilles, using the boy king as their puppet, would change the balance of power in the land. That they would alter the rights and privileges of the old nobility (including himself) and provoke dissent and probably rebellion as they seized more titles and offices and emptied the royal treasury into their own pockets.

In May 1483 Richard may have believed that he needed to protect his position as protector by playing up the fear of the political instability that Woodville control of a young king would cause. But as May turned to June he began re-formatting these concerns into a justification for him seizing the crown. His identification of other 'traitors', outside the Woodville clan, like Edward IV's closest friend, lord Hastings, underscores this change of direction. Once he had decided what he was going to do, like the efficient military commander that he was, Richard moved quickly towards his own coronation. It was probably this speed of action that left many of the lords and citizens unsure of themselves with regard to the fate of the two princes. Richard was also careful to demonstrate that he was a force for continuity rather than change hardly altering any of the personnel involved in central and local government. As London showed no inclination to contest his claim to succeed Edward IV he may have become overconfident. He seemed to believe that his only enemies at that time were the Woodvilles and their allies, but it was a deceptive peace. It was a lull, but a storm was already brewing among some of his supporters and that discontent would re-ignite the hopes of Henry, earl of Richmond, sheltering in exile across the sea in France.

Richard remains, for good reason, the prime suspect in the murder of the two princes. Although the principal citizens of London went along with acclaiming him king, most Londoners probably believed that Richard had done away with the princes. Nevertheless, having this belief humming away in the background was not a good foundation on which to start his reign. However, pomp and ceremony, like bread and circuses, can paper over discontent for a time. Richard's coronation, on 6th July 1483, was a glittering affair, attended by nearly all the peers of the realm including Lady Margaret Beaufort, wife of lord Stanley, and mother of a little known exile named Henry Tudor. Only three months later, in October 1483, the greatest supporter (and one of the greatest beneficiaries) of Richard's rise, Henry Stafford, second duke of Buckingham, started a rebellion in support of Henry Tudor, who was purportedly on the high seas coming to join him. The English weather turned out in force and heavy rain caused Buckingham's army to melt away, leaving the duke to be taken, without a fight, and quickly executed at Salisbury. Henry Tudor and his little fleet did set sail but they failed to land on English soil; Henry went back to Brittany and this revolt was over.

But Richard's confidence of June 1483 was evaporating. He now knew that there would be more to come. His usurpation must have been profoundly shocking to his contemporaries. It is difficult to understand for instance why men rebelled against him as early as 1483 given that he had kept most of Edward IV's servants in office. The drift of the disaffected away from him over the next two years suggest that unhappiness with his usurpation emerged gradually among his subjects but that it did, over time, prick mens consciences into supporting an alternative candidate. With his only male heir dead, Richard was not the certain prospect for a stable, trouble-free dynasty that he once was. His wife was sick and he must have known that Elizabeth Woodville had promised her eldest daughter by Edward IV, Elizabeth of York, to Henry Tudor, should he successfully defeat Richard at some time in the future. During the summer of 1484, Richard almost succeeded in extraditing Henry Tudor from the court of duke Francis I of Brittany, but Henry just managed to escape to the even more hospitable bosom of Charles VIII of France. The year 1485 started with the death of Queen Anne in March and found Richard watching and waiting for the inevitable invasion. It came on 7th August when Henry Tudor landed at Milford Haven in South Wales. Over the next fifteen days Henry marched unimpeded across Wales and central England. He gathered supporters as he went and met up with lord Stanley (his stepfather) and Sir William Stanley at Atherstone in Staffordshire on 20th August to gain assurances of their support. At this time the most Henry got was a 'we'll wait and see'. He finally met up with King Richard's army at Bosworth field a few miles west of Leicester on 22nd August 1485.

This battle has entered the pantheon of English battles as a defining moment in the dynastic history of the English crown. As a scrap it was a poor affair, more like a big melee. Ironically its most significant feature was those who, while present, did not fight or who changed sides to be with the winner. The earl of Northumberland (ostensibly leading Richard's rearguard), who was a Percy may have been angry over his families diminished status in the north when Richard was in charge. Whatever his reason he simply stayed still and watched the battle. The two Stanley brothers, one of whom (lord Stanley) was married to Henry Tudor's mother, the formidable Margaret Beaufort, switched sides when they thought Richard was losing. In a way the two-hour battle of Bosworth was a metaphor for Richard's life after 1483 with its mix of suspicion, loyalty, treachery and personal courage. Personal friends deeply loyal to him stayed by him and perished, two lords supposedly of his colours changed sides when they saw that Henry could win, another lord stayed put and just watched while Richard made a courageous dash to try and end the battle with one desperate blow.

Soon convinced that the Stanley's' meant to 'wait and see' and that Northumberland was not going to support him, and with only eighty of his personal bodyguard, Richard charged down from the hill where he had placed his standard. He rode straight into the group of soldiers protecting Henry, killing his standard bearer and unhorsing the huge Sir John Cheney. At this moment, William Stanley's men, who had ridden across the line of battle, arrived to support Henry, and Richard, now vastly outnumbered, was dragged from his horse and hacked to death. He *was killed fighting manfully in the thickest press of his enemies'*. He was 32 years old and he would be only the second and last king of England to lead his army into battle and die on a battlefield: (King Harold II in 1066 being the first).

To the south of the main battlefield is a hill, still known as 'Crown Hill.' Here lord Stanley is supposed to have placed a crown taken from the helm of the dead king (legend has it that he retrieved it from a thorn bush) and placed it on Henry's head to the acclaim of the soldiers and lords present. While this was going on Richard's body was stripped naked, despoiled and derided with a felon's halter about its neck. He was then thrown over a horse, which one of his own heralds was forced to ride, and taken to Leicester.

For two days his body lay exposed to view in the house of the Grey Friars close to the river Soar. It was then rolled into a grave without stone or epitaph. Ten years after the battle Henry VII disbursed £10 for an alabaster tomb to be placed over Richard's grave. At the dissolution of the monasteries, the church of the Grey Friars in Leicester was plundered, Richard's tomb was destroyed and his remains thrown into the river Soar. His stone sarcophagus was used as a horse trough in Leicester for a number of years. Thus ended the last of the thirteen Plantagenet kings who had ruled England for 330 years.

Despite reigning for just 26 months, Richard III has become one of the most controversial of all our controversial monarchs. The plots, schemes and actions of those two years and the months that preceded them have occupied historians, professional and amateur, in ecstasies of claim and counter claim. The Richard III Society (Fellowship of the White Boar) still maintain a website that puts forward the case of a much wronged man, brother and king. Others see him as a villain whose hand is seen in a variety of diabolical murders, who stole a crown and murdered two beautiful boys in the Tower of London. Yet others see him as having no more and no less of the ruthless temperament of an opportunistic fifteenth century prince. It is now generally recognised that the very effective propaganda of Henry VII and the later Tudors had its greatest victory in blackening the character of this the last Plantagenet to in order to justify a change of dynasty that had little foundation in law. It is these Tudor voices that shout out the history of this king and it is they who provided the principal sources for Shakespeare's famous play 'Richard III'. This great 'drama', for drama is what it is, has done more than anything else to shape the popular perception of this two-year king down the ages and has been taken as history by many who should have known better.

HENRY VII (born 1457 reigned 1485-1509)

Henry VII was born at Pembroke Castle on 28th January 1457, the son of Lady Margaret Beaufort and Edmund Tudor, earl of Richmond. Edmund was one of the sons of Queen Catherine of Valois and her Welsh lover Owen Tudor. Henry's father had died, probably of the plague, three months before he was born. By the time Henry was four, the House of Lancaster, to which he was linked was losing its grip on the crown. In 1462 the Yorkist king, Edward IV, put young Henry into the wardship of his great Welsh supporter William, lord Herbert. Herbert brought him up in Ragland Castle and intended to marry him to his eldest daughter. Those plans died with Herbert when he was executed in July 1469 prior to the restoration of Henry VI. The brief return of Henry VI brought young Henry an audience with the old king and this was an occasion later remembered as one where Henry VI prophesied that Henry Tudor would one day wear the crown. Henry then spent most of his time with his uncle, Jasper Tudor, earl of Pembroke. After Edward IV's successful return in 1471 Jasper and Henry were besieged in Pembroke Castle. Uncle and nephew managed to escape and left Wales, taking a ship from Tenby. They intended to escape to France but, after a stormy voyage, they found themselves at the mercy of Francis II, duke of Brittany.

As Edward IV consolidated his position in England Francis of Brittany tightened his grip on his guests and they were more or less kept under house arrest. In 1474 Jasper and Henry were separated and in 1476 Francis agreed to surrender Henry to Edward IV but Henry's departure from St Malo was delayed by illness and Francis II countermanded his orders. Henry took advantage of the confusion to take 'sanctuary' at a church in the town and Edward IV's men had to return to England empty handed. But it had been close! After the usurpation of the crown by Richard III in 1483 Henry's prospects changed dramatically. The direct Lancastrian line had been extinct since 1471, other potential claimants had died or been killed, leaving only Henry as a credible candidate through his Beaufort blood line. Henry's mother, Margaret began plotting for her son's return and Elizabeth Woodville promised Henry the hand of her daughter, Elizabeth, if he should gain the crown. After 12 years of exile things were certainly looking up! But they wouldn't go smoothly. Buckingham's failed rebellion against Richard III in October 1483, left Henry at sea with an army but with storms tossing him about until he made landfall back on the French coast. Nonetheless Henry put a brave face on it and on Christmas day 1483 he took an oath in Rennes cathedral to marry Edward IV's eldest daughter, Elizabeth of York, and to rule jointly with her.

This was good propaganda for all those Yorkist supporters who had been alienated by Richard III. In early October duke Francis' treasurer was just about to conclude a deal with Richard III, to hand Henry over to him in return for English archers for Brittany to use against its enemies, when Henry, forewarned slipped out of Brittany and moved to France. Yet another dramatic escape! These memories of house arrest and near capture would haunt Henry all of his life and may account for his perennial nervousness and almost total distrust of the English aristocracy. The French saw more mileage in helping Henry than Francis of Brittany had and on 1st August 1485, well supplied with materials, money, men and ships Henry sailed down the Seine to begin his invasion of England. Henry had received many promises of support from leaders in Wales and so it was to Milford Haven that he set his course and it was there that he landed on 7th August. Henry marched through Wales and through the midlands gathering more forces as he went and eventually met King Richard on that fateful field near Market Bosworth on 22nd August, arriving as earl of Richmond and leaving as King Henry VII.

After his victory at Bosworth Henry did keep his word and marry Elizabeth of York but he never ruled jointly with her. Henry was twenty-eight and she was twenty. Henry made much of how their union brought peace and now healed the wounds of past dynastic struggles. Although allied for the purest of pure political reasons, Henry and Elizabeth did grow very fond of each other. Henry VII was the first king of the house of Tudor. His claim to the throne rested on conquest and his descent from the Beaufort 'bastards' of John of Gaunt by Catherine Swynford. Throughout his life Henry, who had been born in Wales and had spent all of his youth there, carefully cultivated a romantic link with those origins and later used many Welsh symbols and other dynastic badges to adorn buildings, the liveries of his servants, charters and his famous chapel and tomb in Westminster Abbey.

There were others who had a greater claim to the throne than Henry Tudor but he had not sailed across the channel to put them on the throne. In the end it was Parliament who, gently skipping over questions of legitimacy and descent, simply enacted that the *'inheritance of the crown...was rested and remained in the person of Henry ... in the heirs of his body, perpetually with the grace of God so to endure, and in none other'*. Parliament's decree was remarkably prescient. The crown has remained linked to the heirs of Henry Tudor notably through his daughter Margaret Tudor. In 1503 she was married to James IV of Scotland. One hundred years later, in 1603, her great-grandson James VI of Scotland became James I of England making Margaret Tudor the grand dame of the British royal family, for whom she is a direct ancestor.

Sequestering the tools and instruments, the badges, prophecies and genealogies, used by Edward IV, Henry VII set about cementing his claim in a war of active propaganda that is an object lesson to any twenty first century student of public relations. We have seen (under Henry VI) how he appropriated the name of that saintly king, planning a great tomb for them both, and how he married into the House of York to ensure that his descendents had a better bloodline to celebrate than he did. From rocky foundations he was to build a monarchy that would stave off all competitors, ending the kind of internecine warfare that had brought him to the throne and Elizabeth of York cooperated magnificently. She gave birth to three sons and four daughters, but only their second son, Henry, (later Henry VIII), and their daughters, Margaret and Mary, would outlive their parents. Elizabeth died in 1503 shortly after the birth of a daughter, Catherine, who also died within days of her mother. Henry was overcome with grief and *'privily departed to a solitary place and would no man should resort unto him'*.

His long exile and the vicissitudes of fortune that dogged his early life left Henry suspicious of the English nobility, whom he hardly knew and whose loyalty he could only test at the risk of their possibly fatal duplicity. Forever cautious this left him reliant on a small circle of tried and trusted allies. This 'careful' approach included continuing Edward IV's policy of using efficient bureaucrats and lawyers who owed their careers directly to him rather than from privilege bestowed by birth. The various rebellions during the early part of his reign exacerbated his paranoia. 'Plantagenet' was still a word to stir men's hearts and there were still too many of that name living to disturb his sleep. Shortly after Bosworth, he sent Clarence's ten-year-old son, the earl of Warwick (a clear contender for the throne despite his father having been attainted), to the Tower. Henry wasn't above locking children away either! John de la Pole, earl of Lincoln (a son of Edward IV's sister, Elizabeth Duchess of Suffolk) had escaped after the battle of Bosworth and also was still at large. Henry's insecurity took human form when he established, for the first time in England, an armed bodyguard, the lineal ancestor of the present yeoman of the guard. In modern times these colourfully attired men guard and reside at the Tower of London. Henry also apparelled them in splendid uniforms, as befitted those close to the body of the king.

In 1486 an impostor, Lambert Simnel, gained support, pretending to be the young earl of Warwick. He was captured after the battle of Stoke, in 1487, during which the earl of Lincoln, who had supported Simnel well knowing him to be an impostor, was killed. Later another pretender, Perkin Warbeck, this time posing as Richard duke of York, one of the princes in the tower, gathered a following around him, including that same Sir William Stanley who had defected from Richard III at Bosworth. Stanley and others were executed, and Warbeck eventually gave himself up and was lodged in the Tower. In 1499, plagued by plots to release Warwick, Henry had both Warbeck and Warwick executed. Thus the list of executions began that would become a key instrument of Tudor policy. Edmund de la Pole, Lincoln's brother, after various adventures, also ended up in the Tower where he remained until Henry VII's death. Henry VIII executed him in 1513. Henry VII created very few new peers. Indeed, the numbers of the peers actually dwindled during his reign, from fifty-five to forty-two, and it cost those that were left dear to be among their number.

Henry used a number of unpopular devices to intimidate the nobility. Any lord that crossed him and then returned to favour only received a part of their estate when initially pardoned. They would only get the rest back after a period of good behaviour. Another of his schemes, for both raising money and keeping nobles in their place, was to force them to sign a 'bond' which bound them to observe certain strict conditions, the breaking of any of which meant a forfeit of money to the king. Yet another forced 'bond' (a recognizance) acknowledged a debt to Henry that would be waived only after a period of good behaviour. In these matters Henry decided if the terms of the 'bonds' had been met: he was both judge and jury. This genius for amassing money and using royal prerogatives rather than calling parliaments (it sat for only ten months during his nearly twenty four year reign) gained Henry few friends.

Henry's foreign policy was aimed at alliances that would gain him freedom from expensive wars. His greatest success was to persuade (doggedly over many years) Ferdinand of Aragon to allow his daughter, Catherine of Aragon, to marry his eldest son Arthur. The wily Ferdinand waited until he saw all of Henry's rivals put away before he would allow the marriage to be confirmed in 1501. Catherine brought with her a regal dowry that Henry was loath to forgo when Arthur died suddenly. Henry's obsession with money and his detailed involvement in his accounts and state papers made him unpopular as a royal figure who was expected to look and behave more like a king than an accountant. No surprise then that many courtiers were tickled by the story that his pet monkey once shredded one of his principal notebooks. During the last years of Henry's life many believed that he had become unduly rapacious in gathering in money from his subjects. He had steadily expanded his royal estates until they yielded over £40,000 a year, nearly double the income that they had provided for Richard III, while a revival in European commerce increased his annual customs income to a similar figure.

After 1503 Henry's health began to deteriorate. His vision was failing and the physic of the time offered no remedy. For a king who practised daily accountancy this would have been very frustrating. Always on the skinny side, he began to lose weight and his teeth were giving him trouble. The chronicler Polydore Vergil described them as *'few, poor and blackish'*. Henry had long been afflicted by gout and also suffered a discharge into his breast that wasted his lungs at least two or three times a year, especially in the springtime. In March 1509 Henry retired to his new palace at Richmond, built on the fire-damaged ruins of the old Royal Palace of Sheen. By 24th March his 'springtime' cough became much worse and on 31st March 1509 he made his last will. He hung on until Saturday 21st April 1509, when he died in an agony of pain and penitence, probably of chronic pulmonary tuberculosis.

On his deathbed, he had urged his second son, Henry VIII, to marry Catherine of Aragon (still a widow after seven years) in order to keep the dowry she had brought with her, and cement the alliance with Spain. This he duly did. Henry VII could not have imagined, devout Catholic that he was, that within this last wish would lie the seeds of the greatest religious change in English history. By 1509 tensions among the nobility had built up to such an extent that news of Henry's death was kept from the new king for two whole days while the old aristocracy attempted to reposition itself at the centre of government. Although the royal coffers were full when he died many people, including the pious Thomas More, rejoiced to hear of Henry's death, and the two ministers most closely involved in his financial exactions were executed by Henry VIII soon after.

At Henry's funeral thousands of pounds were spent on masses for his soul and alms for the poor. The procession began at Richmond Palace, his coffin being drawn by seven horses, each covered in black velvet with the arms of England set on both sides. Knights bearing banners walked on each side of the horses and all the great nobility of the realm followed behind. A likeness of the king was carried on the coffin, crowned and dressed in his Parliamentary robes, accompanied by hundreds of torch-carrying mourners. At the door of St Paul's, it was met by the Bishop of London, to be carried inside by twelve soldiers (a heavy lead coffin lay inside the wooden one) to lie before the High Altar where knights and heralds guarded it all night.

The next day, after three long masses, everyone retired to lunch before setting off again via Fleet Street and Charing Cross to Westminster Abbey, where the two archbishops received it, censed it and had it carried inside, where a solemn dirge was sung in the company of eighteen bishops and abbots. After this the corpse was again left overnight, guarded as before. The next day many rituals involving presentations of the king's armour, helm, shield and crown were carried out until the second son of the earl of Surrey rode into the abbey, fully armed, to present himself to the coffin before being disarmed and dressed in a black gown. The Bishop of London then gave a long sermon before the coffin, covered in a black velvet pall with a satin cross of white reaching from one end to the other, was laid in the vault. The chief men of Henry's household then cast their staves of office into the vault, after which all the heralds removed their coats and hung them on the side of the herse while they cried *'The noble King Henry the seventh is dead'*. They then retrieved their coats and cried out *'God send the noble King Henry VIII long life'*.

Well before his death, Henry VII commissioned two projects that were to cast their spell on Westminster Abbey and its visitors for the next five hundred years. The first was a new Lady Chapel to replace that founded by the child Henry III in 1220; the second was the construction of a magnificent tomb within it to stand over the grave of his wife and himself. This would be a tomb to celebrate not the end but the beginning of a new dynasty. Initially Henry VII resolved to exploit the fashion for devotion to the memory of Henry VI by seeking his canonisation and re-planting his body at Westminster in the easternmost part of the new chapel where the RAF chapel is today. There, set in stone, the bones of the last king of the House of Lancaster would be linked eternally with the tombs of a new dynasty – the Tudors. The costs of canonising Henry VI demanded by Pope Julius II set the bar too high for Henry VII but his project for the new Lady Chapel, although still very costly, was not going to be abandoned for lack of a new saint. Henry joined with the clever Abbot Islip to plan this *'wonder of the world'*, one of the last great glories to be built in the abbey.

The old Lady Chapel, complete with a tavern called the 'White Rose' attached to its outside walls, was duly demolished and on 24th January 1503 Abbot Islip laid the first stone of the new. One of Henry's master masons was Robert Vertue whose brother, William Vertue, had worked on the vaulting of St George's Chapel Windsor. Stone from Kent, Reigate, Yorkshire and Caen in Normandy was gathered and the intricate lines of the Chapel's fantastic fan-vaulting rose from its foundations. Music in stone! The normally parsimonious Henry spent £34,000 on this great project in his lifetime, and his executors added at least another £20,000 more. This would represent an expenditure of around £19 million at today's values! Raising the floor of the chapel so high over what is virtually a basement storey suggests that the substructure was planned for more funerary vaults than for just the founder and his wife. Not to be beaten by Edward the Confessor, Henry VII also died just as his great project was completed.

The body of Elizabeth of York, who had died about one month after the laying of the new foundation stone in 1503, was placed in one of the abbey's side chapels until the new chapel was sufficiently advanced for her to be buried within it, and Henry joined her in 1509. Despite there being a slight misalignment between the vault and the elaborate tomb above it is clear from the careful construction of the stone-walled vault below ground that this burial space was intended from the first foundation. The vast tomb we see today was completed in 1518 by the Florentine sculpture Pietro Torrigiano, who once broke Michelangelo's nose in a fight. While he worked on the tomb he was said to have enjoyed the occasional tussle with any Englishman who cared to test his mettle. The effigies of the king and queen are executed in gilt bronze protected by a magnificent bronze screen adorned with saints and Tudor badges.

This tomb with its striking Italianate ornaments of saints and angels is rightly regarded as one of the first great monuments of Renaissance art in England. But this was not all that Henry wanted his heirs to remember him by. In his will he ordered that a gold-plated statue of himself (similar to the one Edward IV had desired at Windsor), kneeling in full armour and holding the crown that he won at Bosworth, should be placed on top of the shrine to Edward the Confessor. Like Edward IV's kneeling statue, this extravagant, not to say vainglorious, request was not carried out. For three hundred years the Henry VII chapel would be the usual burial place of English monarchs and their families. In a society that remained, despite the later Commonwealth, firmly monarchical, this gave a unique aura to Henry's chapel, an aura strong enough to endure both changes of dynasty and religious practice.

Arthur Prince of Wales

Identifying Winchester with Camelot and wanting to extract the most from his Welsh heritage, Henry VII sent his wife to Winchester to have their first child and had the son, thus born, christened Arthur in 1486 at Winchester Cathedral. Later, Arthur was sent to Ludlow to preside over the Council of the Marches as Prince of Wales and was soon betrothed to Catherine of Aragon, whom he married much later at St Paul's Church London in April 1501. Arthur's short life and the even shorter period of his marriage to Catherine of Aragon (about 18 weeks) had a momentous impact on the future of religion as it was to be practised in England. The question of whether Arthur and Catherine of Aragon consummated their marriage during those 18 weeks became the crux of the great question over whether Henry VIII had taken his brother's wife unlawfully. According to Leviticus: *'It is an unclean thing; he hath uncovered his brother's nakedness; they shall be childless'.* All of Catherine's children by Henry VIII all died except for one (later Mary I), but she was a deeply pious woman and maintained to her dying day that she and Arthur had never consummated their marriage and that the statement to that effect outlined in the terms agreed by Pope Julius II's dispensation for her to marry Henry VIII was true.

Some commentators suggest that Arthur and Catherine were regarded as being too young to cohabit at Ludlow and did not sleep together but, as he was fifteen and she was seventeen, this sounds unlikely. Many noble women were bearing children at fourteen during this period. We know that Henry VIII wanted to divorce Catherine for failing to produce a son, and later because he had fallen under the spell of Anne Boleyn. But the issue of the consummation of Catherine's previous marriage was the catalysing issue, and there is no doubt that Henry began to believe that he had sinned against God and that he was being punished for it by Catherine producing dead children. Arthur died, aged fifteen, on 2nd April 1502, and his body was carried in a great procession from Ludlow to Worcester Cathedral. After a sumptuous funeral on 25th April 1502 his coffin was placed under a hearse richly decorated with wax images. In 1504 a fine chantry chapel was built over a simple granite tomb just to the south of the high altar. The reformation of the monasteries caused by his brother's split from the Church of Rome brought an end to the use of such chapels and the statues and images decorating Arthur's chapel were badly defaced by the image breakers. Interestingly, while other monuments were being damaged after the break with Rome, a new tabletop tomb was constructed to enclose King John's coffin in the choir at Worcester, perhaps reflecting some fellow feeling for John, a well-known opponent of the papacy.

HENRY VIII (born 1491 reigned 1509-1547)

The second and only surviving son of Henry VII and Elizabeth of York, Henry VIII was born at Greenwich on 28th June 1491, strengthening his father's claim to initiate a dynasty that carried the blood of both York and Lancaster. His father is said to have shown him little affection as a child, focussing his attention on his eldest son, Prince Arthur, who was five years older than Henry. The Spanish ambassador noted that Henry *'was so subjected that he does not speak a word except in response to what the King asks him'*. After Arthur's death some of this 'subjection' was probably due to over protection of an only son and heir to shield him from bad influences and not least, given Arthur's early death, communicable diseases. Henry was a strong, good-looking lad, who loved a variety of sports including jousting, tennis, hunting, archery and wrestling. He was a musician and a tireless dancer. He had a fair complexion with hair inclining to ginger and at twenty-one his waistline was a slim thirty-two inches. In his late twenties he grew the beard that we know so well from his portraits. Like his grandfather, Edward IV, he stood six feet two inches tall, and also like him, he was extrovert, affable, charming and full of energy, with a great interest in weaponry and the business of war. The scholar Erasmus, who met the eight-year-old Henry, found him well read, curious and learned in French and Latin. This, then, was the charming young man who would turn into the self-indulgent and ruthless grotesque of his later years.

Following his father's wish, and his own inclination, Henry married Arthur's widow Catherine of Aragon on 11th June 1509. He was then eighteen and she was twenty-four, already an 'older' woman as far as childbearing in the early sixteenth century was concerned. Henry inherited a government system that revolved around his father in detail as well as strategy. This was not how Henry VIII would work at the business of being a king. He had many other interests and therefore delegated, inconsistently, most of the administration to a royal council or, when he found one, to a sort of chief executive, such as Cardinal Wolsey or Thomas Cromwell, and sometimes, again inconsistently, to both council and chief executive. This muddle was handy for Henry. Claiming ignorance of unpopular acts done in his name was a favourite trick – and who was going to contradict him?

There were many strands to Henry's thirty-eight year reign. hree strands, that inevitably merged and mingled with each other at various times, are covered here. One strand was his colourful personal life; another was his strong desire to play the role of arbiter in European affairs. His agent in both these was initially Cardinal Wolsey. The last was his wish to stabilise his new church settlement. His main agent in this, until his downfall in 1541, was Thomas Cromwell. Henry has often been portrayed as a great womaniser. Compared with some of his ancestors and many kings to come he was quite moderate. A shy young man, before his marriage he only had four or five mistresses. Lady Anne Hastings and Jane Popincourt came before the beautiful Elizabeth Blount from Kinlet in Shropshire, with whom he had a healthy son, Henry Fitzroy, who died in 1536. Another was Mary Boleyn, sister of his future wife Anne Boleyn and another, may have been, Madge Shelton. This was hardly a cast of thousands!

Henry's move to play a key role on the European stage came first through his desire to resurrect the hundred year's war with France. His French wars of 1512-1514 are famous for gaining little at great cost, bringing only Boulogne by way of conquest. In 1514 Henry sealed a temporary peace with France by marrying his younger sister, Mary, to the decrepit French King, Louis XII. In 1520 Cardinal Wolsey orchestrated the splendour of the 'Field of the Cloth of Gold' where Henry joined King Francis I of France for a four-week summit designed to secure peace and have a party. Some raids into northern France in 1522 and 1523 in support of the Emperor, Charles V, used up the last of Henry's war chest and more or less signalled the end of Henry's military posturing in France. Wolsey's diplomacy had sought to put Henry on an equal footing with the Holy Roman Emperor, Charles V, (Charles I of Spain and Catherine of Aragon's nephew) and Francis I of France. Both these rulers sat on annual incomes that dwarfed Henry's and his quest to 'be like them' would leave his son with huge debts.

After his divorce from Catherine of Aragon, the matter of Henry's Supremacy over of the Church of England, and what it really meant, took centre stage. The smaller and then the larger monasteries were dissolved between 1536 and 1540 (Waltham Abbey being the last to surrender) filling the pockets of the king as they went, but there was little change in daily church practice. Henry was supreme head of a national church in England and while it retained most of its medieval Catholic organisation, what it lacked, in line with Henry's fuzzy middle way, was a firm confession of faith. It was his subject's allegiance to him, as head of the church in England, rather than to the pope, in Rome, as head of a universal Catholic church, that was important to Henry. But the genie was out of the bottle.

Many of Henry's advisors, including his second wife Anne Boleyn, were finding comfort in the reformist ideas coming from Germany and northern Europe. Their emphasis on independence from the pope, but not their radical theological position, accorded well with Henry's own wish to assert more control over the church. Thomas Cromwell, a closet radical, guided a series of measures through Parliament that basically added believing and thinking as the king did about religion to the list of duties owed by a subject to the crown. As Thomas More and Bishop John Fisher discovered, the severest punishment would be meted out to those subjects who did not conform. As head of the church, Henry's Catholic orthodoxy swung one way and then another depending on the allies he needed at home or abroad. That he initiated a huge reform of the church is not in doubt, but it would be his son who turned it into a revolution.

Henry confiscated and then converted Cardinal Wolsey's old house at York Place, in to the grand Palace of Whitehall, which covered twenty-four acres and was one of the largest palaces in Europe. Around the same time he acquired the neighbouring site of the Hospital of St James and re-built it as St James' Palace where his initials 'H.A.' can still be seen in the brickwork of the clock tower. The fates of Henry's six wives fill metres of bookshelves and we shall touch on them only briefly here and note their deaths and burial sites later. Henry's marriage to Anne Boleyn (1533) produced yet another daughter, Elizabeth, later Elizabeth I, and this together with Anne having made an enemy of Thomas Cromwell sealed her fate. Eleven days after Anne's execution in May 1536 Henry married the 25-year-old, modest, pale-faced and gentle Jane Seymour. This marriage brought Henry both joy and tragedy. Jane died shortly after giving birth to Henry's only son, Edward VI, in October 1537. After 28 years of waiting for a son Henry had achieved his dream, but at the cost of the life of his young queen.

During 1540 Henry was casting about for a protestant alliance that would help him against Francis I and the Emperor Charles V should they ever decide to invade England. Cromwell arranged for him to marry the protestant Anne of Cleves. Henry had only seen her as presented to him in a portrait by Holbein and this turned out to have been excessively flattering. When Anne arrived in England, she spoke no English, was decidedly unattractive and lacked any sort of accomplishment. Henry dubbed her *'a Flanders mare'*. It was too late to reject her and so for political reasons Henry went ahead with the marriage in January 1540. Not being sexually attractive to Henry and, not being able to converse very much, the bride and groom made do with playing cards on their wedding night. Henry divorced her six months later. This Anne was the unknowing instrument of Thomas Cromwell's downfall as his enemies used Henry's displeasure over the Cleves affair to have him attainted for treasonable heresy and he was executed in July 1540. Henry's next wife was the 16 year old, and, very skittish, Catherine Howard. She was a daughter of the younger brother of the duke of Norfolk and Henry married her in July 1540. At 49 Henry had lost the muscular physique of his youth. He was now fat, swollen faced and unattractive and Catherine looked elsewhere for sexual gratification. She began an adulterous relationship with her old flame, Francis Dereham, and also a young man named Thomas Culpepper. Henry enraged by her betrayal, wanted to cut her head off himself, but in the end let the executioner do it, in February 1542, while regretting *'his ill luck in meeting with such ill-conditioned wives'*. His last wife Catherine Parr, who he married in July 1543, and who at the ripe old age of 33 had already buried two husbands, became the companion that his later years and his many ailments needed. The only one of his wives to meet his expectations she made a comfortable and loving home for his son and two daughters and nursed the king assiduously throughout his last years. After Henry's death in 1547 she married her old flame, Thomas Seymour, brother of Jane Seymour, and died in 1548 of complications after giving birth to his child.

In his youth Henry had been physically strong but he had suffered from a number of illnesses during his life including smallpox and malaria. He also collected a number of injuries from jousting and other sports. One of these occurred in January 1536 (a few days before Anne Boleyn miscarried again) and left him unconscious for two hours. All this affected Henry's mental state and stirred doubts in him about the direction of God's will. God had prevented him from having sons by Catherine of Aragon and now he was doing the same with Anne. After Anne's execution in 1536 he began complaining of chronic migraine headaches, acute insomnia and painful sore throats, and he suffered the onset of the painful leg ulcers that would eventually cripple him. He became prematurely grey and abnormally obese and developed a strange growth on the side of his nose. After 1546 his legs became so swollen that he was unable to walk unaided and his sight was starting to fail. In January 1547 he became too weak to stand or sit and spent the last eight days of his life propped up in bed.

A popular misconception is that Henry suffered with, and died of syphilis. This may well have come about because Catherine of Aragon and Anne Boleyn both suffered a number of miscarriages and stillbirths and miscarriages can be a common feature of syphilitic conception. Without proper treatment syphilis can reappear up to thirty years after initial transmission and Henry's blind rages, severe headaches, contradicting orders on succeeding days, and his body's inability to recover from leg ulcers certainly point to syphilis as a component in the illnesses that contributed to his death. Set against this is that he was never known to have been given mercury, the common treatment for syphilis at the time. Given that Henry had a child by each of four women (Catherine, Anne, Jane and Elizabeth Blount) none of whom caught the disease, and had sex with at least another two, who also lived free of it, this diagnosis is doubtful. The illness that caused his death was probably a mosaic of ailments that had built up over time. Today we would probably collect his symptoms under the umbrella of Cushing Syndrome, named after the American endocrinologist Harvey Cushing who reported it in 1932. This disorder, most common in middle age, is caused by the delivery of excessive levels of the hormone cortisol directly into the bloodstream prompted by over activity of the adrenal gland (just above the kidneys) or by over activity of the pituitary gland due to a pituitary tumour. The symptoms of this disorder include insomnia, high blood pressure, rapid weight gain, a puffy 'moon face', skin that becomes thin and bruises easily, muscle weakness, excess sweating and brittle bones prone to fracture. Another common sign is the growth of fat pads along the collarbone and on the back of the neck today called a 'buffalo hump'. In his later years Henry was known to have had a humped upper back. It would also account for the slow healing of Henry's leg ulcer. Mental change is also common with sudden and unpredictable mood swings being commonplace. The sufferer becomes paranoid and deeply suspicious of everyone around them. Afflicted with chronic fatigue, the victim becomes quarrelsome and often unnaturally aggressive, as in Henry's reported fits of blind rage.

Although we can't be absolutely certain, these symptoms accord well with the descriptions that have come down to us of Henry's condition during the last five years of his life. That he displayed irrational anger and aggression is confirmed by his signing of death warrants for both his wife, Catherine Parr and his good friend Archbishop Cranmer, and his later sorrowful admission to them of the threats they unknowingly faced while he was in a rage. On 26th December 1546, physically very ill but of sound mind, Henry made a few alterations to his will naming his only son Edward as his heir, to be followed, should Edward have no heirs of his own, first by Mary and second by Elizabeth. This reaffirmed that his two daughters (both once declared bastards) would come out of the shadows to stay in line to inherit the crown. During January 1547 Henry's illnesses became worse and he began to move in and out of consciousness. On 27th January he asked to see Thomas Cranmer, the friend who had arranged so many of his matrimonial and religious matters. By the time Cranmer arrived, Henry was fading fast and had lost the power of speech. In reply to the Archbishop's request to confirm that he truly repented all his sins, the king squeezed his hand tightly and this was taken to mean that he did. Henry's illnesses lasted for years rather than months. He had been on a slow conveyer belt, exhausting and painful, as he moved towards death. His last wife, Catherine Parr, had carefully tended his ulcerous leg but she could not cure him. He died a mass of rotting flesh amid the horrendous stench of his bursting leg ulcers on 28th January 1547 aged 55 at his palace at Westminster.

For three days Henry's body lay within his apartments in the Palace of Westminster while the members of his council prepared for the new King Edward VI. Henry VIII died on 28th January 1547 Henry eschewed the vault of his father at Westminster Abbey and willed that he be buried in St George's Chapel, Windsor, next his third wife Jane Seymour. Like that of his maternal grandfather, Edward IV, sixty-four years earlier Henry's funeral procession would have to make the long journey from Westminster to Windsor. Three elaborate hearses had to be constructed and fitted out with the usual quota of impressive candles. One would hold the coffin in the palace chapel at Westminster, one would do the same at Syon, the mid resting place on the journey, and the last would be built for St George's Chapel. London cloth merchants did tremendous business in providing 33,000 yards of black cloth and 8,085 yards of black cotton to hang in the chapels and for the hooded cloaks of the mourners. On the evening of 2nd February Henry's great coffin was moved from the private apartments into the Palace Chapel beneath a hearse festooned with eighty-two foot-long square tapers and various heraldic decorations. As usual a wooden rail enclosed the hearse, containing seats for the twelve chief mourners to sit and reflect while the dirge was sung.

The next phase in the choreography of a monarch's funeral was the distribution of dole to as many poor people as possible, in the hope that they would all go away and pray for the soul of the dead king. Over 21,000 claimed the privilege of being poor on 7th February 1547 and the doling out (from two doorways) went on from noon until six in the evening. This day-long chore is somewhat ironic. As part of his church 'reforms' Henry had decided that it was only ancient precedent and charity that justified saying prayers for the dead. He believed that at best, they could only reduce some part of the pain of death, it being a condition about which nothing was known. His father, Henry VII, had laid out in excess of £50,000 in pious works to ensure the repose of his soul. Henry VIII, despite his rejection of the word purgatory, as not being mentioned in any scripture, did hedge his bets by leaving assets worth £600 a year to St George's Chapel. A massive gilded chariot was then prepared to carry the coffin and the now mandatory effigy of the king, prepared and dressed in sumptuous robes.

But the way to the grave also had to be cleared and an order went out to tidy and mend all the highways between Westminster and Windsor. Wayward trees that might collect a pennant or two in their branches were cut down, narrow roads were widened, hedges cut down, bridges checked and scores of boards painted with bright heraldry were delivered to all the parishes through which the cortège would pass. Early on the morning of Monday 14th February, the procession was ready to set off from Charing Cross. Henry's coffin was carried out from the chapel by sixteen yeomen of the guard under a rich canopy of blue velvet fringed with silk and gold. The effigy was placed on top of it looking *'exactly like that of the king himself and he seemed just as if he were alive'*. The procession would eventually stretch out for four miles and be attended by over a thousand horsemen, including many nobles carrying colourful banners and hundreds more, on foot, carrying torches. Two carts followed behind carrying spare torches to replenish those that burnt out. Priests stood at the doors of their churches dressed in their best vestments, censing the corpse as it passed by.

The cortège reached the church at Syon at about 2pm and the coffin was taken inside to rest on another hearse, and a watch was set over it for the night. There it lay guarded and undisturbed but for the process of its own decomposition. During the night putrid matter leaked out of the coffin and it was reported that stray dogs wandered into the church and licked it up. During 1534 a friar is supposed to have preached a sermon against Henry declaring that *'the dogs would lick his blood as they had done Ahab's'*. There is nothing like a prophecy seemingly come true to make a good story. One version of the 'accident' was that the coffin collapsed due to its great weight, fracturing the wooden outer coffin and cracking the lead shell inside. Another account has the lead casing being broken open by the shaking of the carriage on the road from Westminster and that the plumber who came to solder the broken joint was followed in by a dog who did the macabre 'licking'. It was over two weeks since the king had died and, given his poor physical condition, his body would be in an advanced state of putrefaction. Like many stories of this type there is probably a grain of truth in one or other of the versions.

Newly soldered or not, the king's coffin set off again early on Tuesday morning towards Windsor. At the town, it was greeted by scholars from Eton College dressed in white surplices carrying tapers and singing psalms. Inside the chapel the coffin was placed in a thirty-five foot high gilded hearse surrounded by thirteen pillars all holding candles, using an estimated 4,000lb of wax! Henry's widow, Catherine Parr, looked down on these obsequies from Catherine of Aragon's window in Edward IV's chantry chapel. The next day, Wednesday 16th February, the ceremonies continued and the traditional knight in armour rode into the choir of the chapel and laid his weapon on the altar. After this the notable mourners made the usual offering of fine palls and the conservative Bishop Gardiner, who Henry had fallen out with just before his death, preached the sermon. Then sixteen yeoman of the guard using five strong linen towels, which they kept as their fee, slowly lowered the coffin into the vault next to the body of Jane Seymour. After reciting the burial service, Bishop Gardiner threw in some earth and the officers of Henry's household all broke their wands of office and threw them into the grave, signifying that their master was dead and their office (for now at least) was redundant. Garter King of Arms then cried out for God to give *'good life and long to the most high and mighty Prince our sovereign lord King Edward VI...'* followed by a blast of trumpets that brought the funeral to an end. Various items, such as cushions, an iron chair and the blue velvet cloth of state used during the funeral, were then handed out to royal officers as gifts or 'fees' and then everyone retired to dinner. Later that day the lords of the Privy Council rode back to London. The new king was to be crowned in three days time and it was time to think of the living and, not least, how living could be made better.

Wolsey's Monument

In 1524, well before he fell from Henry VIII's favour, Cardinal Wolsey commissioned an Italian craftsman, Benedetto de Rovezzano, to build a tomb for him that would stand in the centre of the old St George's chapel that lay to the east of Edward IV's new Chapel. It was to be made of black and white marble, it would be four feet high and it would stand on a base nine feet long and eight feet broad. On the corners of the base there were to be four graven and gilded copper pillars nine feet high, on each of which an angel would stand carrying a candlestick. Round the tomb the figures of more angels were to carry

Wolsey's personal emblems whilst four children bore his arms. On top of all this would be an effigy of the Cardinal.

After the Cardinal's fall, Henry VIII appropriated, what had already been built of this tomb for himself and engaged the same Italian, Benedetto, to finish it off. An altar was to be added to the tomb and the whole massive structure was to be surrounded by an enclosure with doors built into it. During 1536 Henry became heavily involved in affairs of state, including the Pilgrimage of Grace. No more work was done on the tomb after that time and it remained incomplete. Benedetto was said to have ruined his eyesight from the glare of the furnaces in which he cast his metals. Not to be put off Henry's will still specified that this monument should be completed and then placed over his grave. It is assumed that he intended that his body and that of Jane Seymour would be placed in a new grave, in what was then known as the Wolsey Chapel (now the Albert Memorial Chapel) and the sarcophagus placed over it. It was not to be, and his body remained in, what Henry had assumed would be only a temporary vault, with the body of Jane Seymour beneath the choir of St George's Chapel without a monument or even an inscribed stone to mark the spot.

There he would remain forgotten for over two hundred years until discovered by those lords charged with finding a resting place for Charles I in 1649. During the night before Charles I was buried, a Cromwellian soldier is said to have jumped into the open vault, broke a hole in Henry's lead coffin (the outer wooden one had decomposed) found nothing of value and left with part of the velvet covering and a piece of bone which on his apprehension he claimed he took to make a handle for a knife! The great sarcophagus remained unused and unloved in the Wolsey Chapel until 1804 when George III set his workmen to build a huge tomb room in the space below it. At this time the 'old' sarcophagus was moved to facilitate the new excavations and was left lying around the chapel until early in the 19th century. Then someone had the bright idea that it could accommodate another great ego, lord Nelson, who died at the battle of Trafalgar in 1805. The unfinished pride of a cardinal and king thus found a final home in the crypt of St Paul's as the tomb of that much loved naval hero.

Henry's direct heirs, Edward VI, Mary I and Elizabeth I had no children and his only other son, a healthy bastard by Elizabeth Blount, whom he named Henry Fitzroy, died before him in 1536. Thus, despite the great footprint Henry VIII left on English history, the present royal family has no direct link with him.

Henry's Six Wives

Catherine of Aragon (exiled by the king in 1520) died in 1536 aged 51 at Kimbolton castle in Huntingdonshire. An autopsy revealed a *'completely black and hideous' tumour grown around her heart'*. This may have been a secondary from a melanotic carcinoma but Catherine's supporters chose to believe that she died of slow poisoning. Henry refused to spend more than was *'requisite or needful'* on her funeral and she was buried in Peterborough Abbey (now Cathedral). Apart from the king's niece, Lady Eleanor Brandon, no representative from the royal family was present. She would have to wait until the 20th century for the markings on her grave to be changed to read 'Queen of England'.

Anne Boleyn was executed in 1536, aged 36, on Tower Green just four months after her predecessor died. Her witticism that *'Catherine of Aragon is my death and I am hers'* proved all too prophetic. Thomas Cromwell, her erstwhile ally, wanted her dead, and so concocted a catalogue of lies about her behaviour that sealed her fate. The executioner was brought over especially from France and she was buried in the Chapel of St Peter ad Vincula* in the Tower of London. I believe that Anne was the true passion of Henry's life and that, despite the birth of his son by Jane Seymour later, he never really got over executing Anne.

Jane Seymour died in October 1537, aged 30, nine days after giving birth to the future Edward VI, not of puerperal fever as has often been suggested, but from an internal haemorrhage possibly resulting from parts of the placenta being left in her womb. This is something an experienced midwife would surely have spotted had they not been banned from the childbed by Henry's physicians. She is the only one of Henry VIII's wives to be buried with him in the vault under the choir in St George's Chapel.

Anne of Cleves died in 1557 (10 years after Henry VIII) as a convert to Catholicism, aged 42, after a pleasant life as Henry's official 'sister.' She was interred by Queen Mary's restored Catholic monks on the south side of the altar in Westminster Abbey. After her hearse was dismantled it was found that during the night the monks had '*spoiled it of all velvet cloth, armes, baners, penselles and all the majesty and valens, the wyche was never sene afore so done*'. Not much of a testament to the moral basis of Mary's new monastic vision!

Catherine Howard was executed in 1542, aged 20, on the same block used for the execution of Anne Boleyn, and her remains joined those of that earlier queen in the vault of the Chapel of St Peter ad Vincula.

Catherine Parr died at Sudeley Castle in Gloucestershire in 1548, aged 36, of puerperal fever, very soon after giving birth to a daughter, Mary, by her fourth husband lord Thomas Seymour. She was buried in St Mary's Chapel at the castle. Her grave was rediscovered in 1782 after the English Civil War had left both the castle and the Chapel in ruins. Her lead casket was opened and her body was found to be 'uncorrupted'. However, lack of proper care with her coffin after the exhumation led to the degradation of her remains and it was not until 1817 that she was reinterred by the then Rector of Sudeley. The plaque next to the tomb was copied from the original inscription found on her lead coffin. The effigy on the tomb was made in Victoria's reign.

*The Royal Chapel of St Peter ad Vincula was erected in the reign of Edward I in 1272 on the site of an earlier church built by Henry I in 1100. Around 33 notables are buried in the vault beneath this chapel in the Tower of London and 20 of these either died here or were executed during the reign of the Tudor monarchs. As well as Henry's two queens, Lady Jane Grey (the nine day queen), John Fisher Bishop of Rochester, Sir Thomas More, Thomas Cromwell, Henry Grey duke of Suffolk, Thomas Howard duke of Norfolk, Robert Devereux earl of Essex and James duke of Monmouth are also buried here. During the 19th century Queen Victoria had the Tower vault opened and tidied up. The two Tudor queens and all the other residents were found to be still in place amid the broken coffins and dust of ages. As one might expect from a queen dedicated to funerary protocol, Victoria had all the various bones collected up, sorted out and put in neat urns.

EDWARD VI (born 1537 reigned 1547-1553)

Edward VI was born at Hampton Court on 12th October 1537 the only son of Henry VIII. Henry had gone through two wives before his third, Jane Seymour, provided him with a son at the expense of her own life. Henry's desire for a son had grown into one of the great obsessions of English dynastic history. A woman had not ruled England since the brief reign of Queen Matilda in 1141 and the chronicles told Henry that she was a disaster. So a son was needed, and a large part of the first twenty-eight years of Henry's reign were spent trying to get one, while the last ten years were spent worrying about him. The irony of all this was that the desperately sought-after boy, although robust enough when he was young, would die before his sixteenth birthday. Then it would be those girls, whom Henry had alternately loved, hated, disowned, debarred from the throne and then reinstated, who would follow.

Until he was six Edward was brought up by a group of women, carefully selected by his father, who moved him around various residences away from the foul air of London. Henry's concern for the security, health and hygiene of his son is apparent in the detailed instructions that he set down for the care of his boy. Of his two half-sisters, Mary (twenty years older) and Elizabeth (four years older), Edward is thought to have preferred Mary. After his father's marriage to Catherine Parr, family life moved up a notch as she brought all of Henry's children to court, creating something approximating to a true family atmosphere for them. Catherine had a great affection for Edward and encouraged him in his studies and his letters to her clearly show how much he appreciated her care.

In order to bring the Scots into Henry's, rather than France's orbit, the treaty of Greenwich, in 1543, betrothed Edward to Mary Queen of Scots, then seven months old, but this bit of marriage diplomacy failed and so the on/off wars with Scotland would continue. Catherine Parr was a committed evangelical and Edward's tutors, one of whom (John Cheke) was close to the queen, were energetic proponents of evangelical reform. The queen, always careful to mute her protestant ideas in front of her husband, would have been delighted that Edward was being taught and brought up by protestants. Catherine Parr's hand in the formation of Edward's ideas for the subsequent religious changes in England is something that receives little notice, but it was profound. Edward was a conscientious student and, had he lived long enough to rule by his own hand might have shown a degree of intelligence and learning greater than any king of England before or since. Edward continued his education when he became king through a carefully scripted agenda of history, French, Latin, Greek and classical reading. His surviving notebooks and his 'chronicle', a kind of journal, are a unique record of both his curriculum and his views on current events, many of which he was directly involved in.

Carrying the desperate hopes and burdens of Henry VIII, this precocious boy succeeded his father on 28th January 1547, aged nine. Henry VIII knew well the pitfalls of a minority and his will was packed with arrangements that shouted his royal commands from the grave. In it he nominated sixteen executors to govern England during his son's minority plus a further twelve to be called on as and when required. In the heated religious atmosphere of the day, eight of these executors might be described as 'traditionalist' (pro-Catholics) and eight were 'anti-traditionalist (pro-reform) thus neutralizing one another and preserving Henry's eccentric religious middle-way. He also decreed that their named membership could not be changed and their decisions had to be taken by a simple majority vote. In this way Henry hoped to reduce faction, number packing and the chance of some regent emerging to take on royal authority. All of this care and attention came to nought, as three days after Henry's death Edward Seymour, earl of Hertford, was proclaimed lord protector (an office Henry had deliberately avoided) and governor of the king's person *because he was the king's uncle on his mother's side.* This powerful 'protectorate' was set to last until Edward was eighteen, when he would assume all regal powers himself. He would, however, die well before that. Later the young king made Hertford duke of Somerset, John Dudley became earl of Warwick, and Thomas Seymour (another brother of the late queen) became baron Seymour of Sudeley. Somerset then named a new and expanded board of executors to take in those whom Henry had left out. All these men were committed to advance church reform, and so Henry's son was to be guided not by a balanced council, as Henry had wished, but by dyed-in-the-wool reformers. If there were room in his vault for any turning Henry VIII would surely be turning now!

Edward's coronation oath was full of the changes to come. No more promises to protect the clergy and uphold law and liberty. Instead *'Your Majesty is God's Vicegerent and Christ's Vicar within your own Dominions'*. From now on the crown would decide what constituted law and liberty. Both Church and Parliament would now be expected to consent rather than decide. At his coronation, Archbishop Cranmer had urged Edward to *'see Idolatry destroyed' and 'images removed'*. These were the first shots of the protestant reformation, and evangelicals everywhere took heart and braced themselves - the war against the Antichrist had begun in earnest. As early as July 1547, shrines and candles were banned and in 1548 any images, be they in stained glass, wood or stone, were also banned. The age-old tradition of telling stories on church walls and windows was replaced by plain glass and lime wash. Out went other storytelling devices – mystery plays, holy day pageants, maypoles and all religious processions. The chantries were also banned, their income, left pay for priests to pray for the souls of the dead, was appropriated and the schools they supported closed. There would not be another such dramatic change to church life and furniture until the Commonwealth of the 1650s.

Edward's reign can be divided into two very unequal parts. The first, the protectorate of Somerset, lasted from 1547 until 1549; the second under John Dudley the 19th earl of Warwick (later 1st duke of Northumberland) as great master and lord president lasted from 1549 until Edward's death in 1553. Somerset, a member of the evangelical grouping at court, virtually ignored the king's council to monopolize power for nearly two years. He renewed war with Scotland that then triggered war with France. The costs of maintaining garrisons on two fronts, even with a disastrous debasement of the coinage, the sale of chantries and a tax on sheep, nearly bankrupted Edward's treasury. But Somerset's nemesis was the attempt to enforce the use of Cranmer's new Book of Common Prayer in 1549. This prompted a serious rebellion among the country gentry starting in the West Country and spreading across England. At the same time the forced enclosure of common land led to Kett's rebellion in Norfolk, which was routed by that gruff old soldier, the earl of Warwick. These great disturbances led to Somerset's fall in October 1549 and the rise of his competitor for control of the king, Warwick. Although Somerset was pardoned in 1550 and released from the Tower, he could not stand being just a support player and he began intriguing against Warwick, who had him executed in January 1552 on exaggerated charges of treason.

Warwick, who in October 1551 was created 1st duke of Northumberland, had a slightly longer tenure as the king's 'controller', maintaining his position partly by satisfying Edward's growing desire to be active in government and to influence decisions himself. From 1550 Edward became personally engaged in politics particularly with regard to the radical religious changes being put in place by his government. His growing independence is seen in his personal involvement in confronting his half-sister Mary over her refusal to conform to the new liturgy. Although greedy for himself and his friends, Northumberland ended the costly wars with Scotland and France, handing back Henry VIII's only serious war prize, Boulogne, in the process. He also started rebuilding, the debased coinage, although this was fitful and piecemeal, and began the climb back from the ruinous financial policies of Somerset, adopting deflationary policies and paying off the whole of Edward's overseas debt. By rationalizing the procedures of the King's Council and reforming government finance and administration, he set up models that first Mary and then Elizabeth would continue to develop. He seems to have developed into a serious evangelical protestant up until abjectly surrendering himself back to Catholicism on the scaffold.

Around March 1553 Edward VI probably drafted his 'Devise' for the succession. This serious change to his father's last will and to the Act of Succession as approved by Parliament in 1544 seems to have been brought about by Edward's worry that his two sisters, as well as bearing the taint of illegitimacy, might marry foreigners and thus undermine the laws of England, or, worse, undo his programme of protestant reforms. Originally this 'Devise' envisioned the crown passing to a succession of protestant males under a complicated scheme involving a 'governess' role for their erstwhile mothers and a council of twenty. As he neared death Edward changed this messy hierarchy in order to favour Lady Jane Grey exclusively. Lady Jane was the granddaughter of Henry VIII's younger sister Mary and the daughter of Henry Grey, Marquess of Suffolk. This branch of the family had been referred to in Henry VIII's will as coming into the line of succession only *after* his daughters, Mary and Elizabeth and their heirs. This key change was almost certainly made after Northumberland's son, Guildford Dudley married Jane (against her will), on 21st May 1553 and certainly not later than 10th June 1553 when the doctors gave Edward three days to live. Eyewitnesses would attest to seeing the duke of Northumberland initiate the changes. Although Northumberland's hand was clearly at the king's elbow, Edward sincerely regarded Jane as his true sister in religion. It was she, not his sisters, who could be relied on to carry forward his religious reforms.

Sir Edward Montague, Chief Justice of the Common pleas, told Edward that the execution of such a change after his death would be treasonable. Edward, in no mood for lectures on the law, commanded Montague and all the other judges to accept it. Montague complied but in return demanded the king's pardon as only Parliament could overturn the Act of 1544. Edward replied that Parliament would ratify it at its meeting in September. The king died well before September on the evening of 6th July 1553 at his palace of Greenwich, praying to the last that England be defended against popery. It all happened too fast for Northumberland, who needed more time to garner support for Lady Jane Grey. His failure to capture Mary Tudor at her country residence in Suffolk in order to neutralise her bid for the throne left him out on a limb and a clear candidate for the scaffold.

The surgeon who opened Edward's chest found '*the disease whereof his majesty died was the disease of the lungs, which had in them two great ulcers, and were putrefied*'. Such cavities in the lungs indicate the reactivation of tuberculosis typical of that seen in adolescents. It is likely that Edward had close contact with someone who already had tuberculosis before 2nd April 1552 when he complained of being ill from measles. Measles suppress immunity to tuberculosis and so from early April 1552 Edward's ability to fight it was probably weakened. By Christmas of 1552 he was showing the first signs of the disease and a bad cold in February 1553 may have hastened his decline. The Venetian envoy who saw him in March 1553 noted that although Edward still looked handsome he was clearly near death.

In order to gain more time for his plans, one story has Northumberland dismissing Edward's doctors and installing a woman quack doctor in their place who administered 'astringents' which brought on a temporary improvement but possibly slowly poisoned the king through the levels of arsenic they contained. Edward's suffering reached such a pitch during this treatment that he was heard to whisper to his tutor '*I am glad to die*'. This account of Edward's death has his legs and arms swelled, his fair skin darkened, his fingers and toes became gangrenous and he lost his hair and his nails. A further embellishment to this story has it that Northumberland, worried that the state of the young king's body would give rise to suspicion of poisoning, had some other poor lad put to death, spiriting Edward's body away to an unknown grave and replacing it in the royal coffin with the unfortunate substitute. The report of the surgeon, who did the post mortem noted above, never once mentions that the body he is dealing with is any other than that of the king, who he knew.

Edward was buried on 6th August 1553. He was encased in his lead coffin immediately after his death and it is this haste that might have given rise to the rumours noted above. On his coffin was fastened a leaden plate bearing an inscription reciting that he was 'on earth under Christ of the Church of England and Ireland the supreme head' and recorded the precise hour in the evening when he died. Edward lay unburied for a whole month due to the long negotiations between Mary and her ministers as to the mode of his funeral rites. He may have wished to be buried next to his father at Windsor but, for reasons still unknown, he was to go to Westminster, to the Chapel of his grandfather, Henry VII. An effigy, now lost, of the young king was made by Nicholas Bellin of Modena in wax and wood in the style of Pietro Torrigiani's tomb of Henry VII. Edward was brought from Whitehall Palace to Westminster Abbey the night before his funeral 'without cross or light.' The procession from the Palace to the abbey was a mass of black velvet. Beside the banner of his mother Jane Seymour fluttered the banner of his half-sister's Catholic mother, Catherine of Aragon. He may be going to his maker as a radical protestant but a reminder of that most Catholic of his father's wives would accompany him. Hard won concessions from Mary, who was a bitter enemy of the protestant cause, allowed Edward's funeral service to be conducted according to the Reformed Protestant Church. This was the first time this service was used over the grave of an English monarch and the last and saddest role of his public ministry that Archbishop Cranmer, who had baptised and crowned Edward, was destined to perform.

The new queen, Mary Tudor, stayed away from the funeral and instead, with her Catholic priests, attended a requiem mass in the Tower of London under the auspices of Bishop Gardiner. It is one of the many paradoxes of Edward's funeral that the body of the first protestant King of England should be placed in a grave near the entrance to Henry VII's vault and topped by an altar built for the chanting of the very masses that he had been the chief agent in abolishing. The dynastic statement of laying the boy so close to his grandfather must have outweighed the irony of laying the protestant prince under Torrigiano's rich, and very Catholic, altar canopy. Yet another paradox was that this altar, all there was of a memorial to Edward VI (that most puritan of princes), was the only altar in Westminster Abbey to be totally destroyed by the Puritans in 1643. After this no monument marked his grave and he had to wait until 1866 to have his name inscribed on a stone over his vault.

Edward's illegal nomination of Lady Jane Grey would send an innocent young woman to the scaffold and cause little or no hindrance to his Catholic sister ascending the throne. That Antichrist so reviled at Edward's coronation would now be warmly embraced at Mary's. Fires were going to burn! A learned, maturing renaissance prince cut down in his prime or an inconsequential pawn in the hands of greedy nobles who manipulated a boy-king for their own ends? The jury is still out on these hectic six and a half years. One thing is certain. Although his reign was light on socially minded reforms, other than for a few well-known grammar schools, Edward helped set in train one of the great transformations of English society and culture, namely the Protestant Reformation. The die was cast and, other than for Mary's brief crusade to restore Catholicism, no church, no priest and no bishop would ever be the same again. Elizabeth I would eventually restore Edward's structures, liturgy and doctrinal statements with hardly any amendment going on to form the basis of the Church of England as it is today.

MARY I (born 1516 reigned 1553-1558)

Queen Mary the first Queen Regnant of England since Matilda, was the only surviving child of Catherine of Aragon, the first wife of Henry VIII. She was born on 18th February 1516, when her father was 24 and her mother 31 years old. Her childhood swung in cat and mouse fashion from beloved daughter and princess to hated imp of disobedient popery. When she was fifteen, Henry banished her mother from court, and after July 1531 Mary was not allowed to meet or see her. These were stressful times for the once-happy, healthy and privileged teenager. Her world was turning upside down. She suffered a number of physical and psychological ailments including feverish illnesses, indigestion, anorexia, sleep disturbance and depression, much of which was linked to her being denied the company of her mother and the spasmodic mental pressure applied by her father,

Catherine of Aragon had urged Mary to *'speak few words and meddle nothing'*. It was not advice she was capable of taking. Clinging ardently to her original status and her mother's faith, she came perilously near to danger during both her father's and her half-brother's reign. When Henry had her sent from court to satisfy his new wife, Anne Boleyn, she refused to be demoted to just a 'lady', and with a stubbornness inherited from her father, insisted on being called 'princess' until Henry broke up her household and planted her among the hated Boleyn's at Hatfield House. In March 1534 the Succession Act made her illegitimate, and her half-sister, of six months, Elizabeth by Anne Boleyn, became the new heir to the throne. Mary became seriously ill twice in 1535, the court physicians noting grief and despair at her own and her mother's state as a likely cause. In January 1536 Mary's mother died, prompting even deeper bouts of melancholy. In June of the same year Mary, not broken but humiliated, surrendered to her father's will and signed a paper admitting that her mother and father were never married, that she was not a royal princess and that Henry was indeed the Head of the Church in England. Her mother's death and this forced testament exacerbated her already poor physical and mental health.

Although taking its toll on her health, Mary was learning how to dodge and weave through an awful maze of defiance, resistance and self-protection. But the roller coaster was far from over. After Anne Boleyn came Jane Seymour, with whom she got on well. Anne of Cleves' reign was too short to affect her and, although not close, she seems to have had no problems with the doomed Catherine Howard. Her salvation came with Catherine Parr, who embraced her warmly (there was only four years between them) and they became good friends during the last three years of her father's life. Only on Henry VIII's death did Mary learn that her father had reinstated her in the order of succession and left her considerable estates in East Anglia. For the first time this gave her some measure of economic independence, a place where she could cultivate followers of her own and enjoy the life of a landed magnate. Mary was happy to see her brother crowned king as, despite their religious differences, she loved him and happily bought into the convention of the time that 'men' were the natural choice for kings. This conviviality was short-lived. At the age of ten her half- brother had written to Catherine Parr urging her to prevail on Mary to give up foreign dances and merriments, which *'did not become a Christian princess'*, not a crime we now associate with the dour and sober Mary. But the sombre queen of later years was once a playful young woman enjoying music, dancing, minstrels, gambling at cards and buying jewellery and fashionable clothes.

More seriously, she was later summoned to London by her brother, King Edward to explain why she flouted the law by still holding the Catholic mass in her household. Mary replied that she would sooner he took away her life than her religion and was bold enough to lecture the king in front of his council *'Riper age and experience will teach Your Majesty much more yet'*. Not a little irritated, Edward is supposed to have replied that *'You also may have something to learn, none are too old for that'*.

Mary did not stand entirely alone. Behind her (albeit at some distance) stood her powerful cousin Charles V, Holy Roman Emperor and King of Spain. He had threatened to make war on England if Mary was not allowed to practise her mass and a game of compromise, threat and more compromise between brother and sister ensued throughout the last three years of Edward's life. Sometimes defiant, sometimes compliant, Mary walked a grim tightrope, with her servants being harassed and even imprisoned for their perceived connivance in her disobedience. After Edward's death, Northumberland miscalculated the nobility's appetite for disturbing the lawful processes as set out in the 1543 Act of Succession. As many prominent men surprised him by rallying to Mary's side, the bumbling plan to crown Lady Jane Grey collapsed and Mary entered London on 3rd August 1553 clad in purple velvet and satin to scenes of joyous relief and celebration. Her support came from both protestants and Catholics and drew on a deep vein of respect for the law in the English psyche that saw naked injustice in Northumberland's machinations and that upheld her legitimate right to ascend the throne.

Mary saw it differently. God's hand was on the tiller. She had been saved and chosen to bring England back to the true faith; it was a miracle and she would not let God down! She would also only marry a man that God would approve of. As a child Mary had been promised as a bride to a number of European princes, including the Emperor Charles V. He now ordered his son Prince Philip, later Philip II of Spain, to take up that old promise on his behalf and become a suitor to Mary. She was delighted to be so courted and a marriage treaty was signed in November 1553. Mary may have rejoiced at this proposal to join up with her mother's kinfolk in Spain but many in the country disapproved. They knew that Mary would bring back the pope and all his works, but a Spanish consort having a hand in England's affairs, not to mention its treasury, was a step too far.

In January 1554, Sir Thomas Wyatt, at the head of a large band from Kent, boldly fought his way to London, and for a moment Mary stood in great danger. Eventually the rebellion was crushed and Wyatt and many other leaders were executed. Mary's half-sister Elizabeth, suspected of being in league with Wyatt (son of that poet and courtier Sir Thomas Wyatt the elder who once loved her mother), was promptly sent to the Tower. No evidence being found to incriminate her, she was soon released and sent off to Woodstock so as not to get in the way when bridegroom Philip arrived. Wyatt's move also rang the death knell for Lady Jane Grey. Until this time she had resided quietly in the Tower but Wyatt's rising had fuelled that old ghost so familiar to Mary's ancestors: that such a prisoner would only be a magnet for future rebellion. She was executed, the sad victim of a plot by men who used her royal ancestry to secure power and privilege for themselves.

Parliament reluctantly went along with the Spanish marriage; Philip was a reluctant groom, whose main aim was to get England involved in his war with France; many of the Queen's Council were also reluctant; sadly only Mary was really enthusiastic. Nonetheless, in July 1554, just a year after her victorious entry into London, Mary was married to Philip in Winchester Cathedral. The Venetian ambassador reported that the queen was of '*low stature, with red and white complexion, and very thin: her eyes are white and large and her hair reddish; her face is round, with a nose rather low and wide; and were her age not on the decline,* [she was 38 years old at the time] *she might be called handsome rather than the contrary, and she had no eyebrows*'. If this marriage made sense to Mary, fantasising in her closet, it was deeply resented in the wider world of her realm. There the old English hatred of foreign meddling was quick to surface and the taint of Spain and Spanish Catholicism made it more difficult for Mary to implement the restoration of the Catholic Church in England. In tragic irony, Mary would now start that desperate quest for an heir that, after her own birth, had so obsessed her father. At twenty seven Philip was eleven years younger than his wife so hopes were high of impregnation. Not very tall, dignified, haughty and dull, his duty lay in attending to his new wife but his heart lay in his continental domains. It would be these (to

Mary's great distress) that would draw him away from her for long periods. If he was lukewarm in his affections for her, Mary was clearly besotted with him.

Besotted she may have been but by the start of 1555 it was clear to Mary that her seven-month old marriage was not going well. She was convinced that this was due to God's displeasure at the heresies still being practised in England. Something had to be done to get God on her side again and so the burnings began. On 4th February 1555 a priest called John Rogers was burnt at the stake at Smithfield in London. Another two hundred and ninety people followed him, including Archbishop Cranmer. John Foxe's hugely influential and graphically illustrated *'Book of Martyrs'* notes how both high and low were caught up in Mary's hunt for heretics: virgins, infants, servants, labourers, wives, artificers and gentlemen as well as five bishops and twenty one divines all went to the stake. Contrary to expectations, Philip seems to have gauged the political impact this would have on Mary better than his wife. Although he burnt five heretics in the Spanish Netherlands for every one of Mary's, he strongly counselled against fierce persecutions in England.

The public burning and humiliation of Archbishop Cranmer in Oxford backfired when at the last he thrust the hand that had signed his recantation from protestantism into the fire so that it would burn first for its transgression. Mary's linking of heresy with treason, against the advice of her very Catholic husband, and her violent punishment of those who were so labelled, gained her the name Bloody Mary and it is that name, as tenacious as a humped back and a withered arm, by which she has best been known. Although she restored the Catholic religion she could not persuade the country gentry to give up the gains they had made at the expense of the monasteries, and her own attempts to found new religious houses were limited. For Mary's Catholic 'reformation' to work it was critical for her to destroy the economic basis for protestantism in England. But it was not to be. Parliament, amid colourful scenes of 'packing' and the chamber door being bolted from the inside, refused to approve the confiscation of the estates of those protestants who had been exiled or simply fled abroad; the heretics would still be able to draw their cash!

In September 1554 Mary had reported feeling a child move in her womb and by December was writing to her father-in-law declaring *'it to be alive'*. By April 1555 Mary had withdrawn with her women to her birthing chambers at Hampton court. The physicians and midwives were all assembled and a child was expected by 9th May. A peasant woman 'role model' of similar build and age who had given birth to healthy triplets a few days before was brought to Mary to prove to her that it could be done. A series of letters with dates left blank from Mary to the pope, Charles V, the King of France and other princes announcing the birth were also prepared but by September 1555 it was all over. The pregnancy had been a phantom and after all the well publicised birthing arrangements, Mary was now something of a joke in London, with rumours circulating that she had been pregnant with a lapdog or a monkey. Mary was probably suffering from secondary amenorrhoea (absence of menstrual periods). Amenorrhoea can be caused by hormonal changes due to emotional stress, depression, loneliness and severe deprivation during childhood. This would certainly accord with Mary's early history. It can also be caused by a disorder of the ovary such as polycystic ovary or an ovarian tumour. Amenorrhoea may also cause prolactimona (a benign tumour of the pituitary gland). Mary had mistaken a swollen abdomen caused by a tumour for pregnancy. She was thirty-nine and would be unlikely to be able to conceive again. Her pregnancy had given her renewed leverage with Parliament and her programme to restore the Catholic Church. Now with no heir on the horizon the prospects of a long-term future for her programme looked bleak and power began to ebb away from her.

Mary's husband Philip, had more pressing matters on his mind than phantom pregnancies and burning heretics, and in the summer of 1557 he achieved his principal objective in marrying Mary by getting her to declare war on France. Within six months Calais, which England had held for more than two hundred years, was lost. This symbol of the old English claim to the crown of France was now of little value but its loss was a national humiliation that added to Mary's woes. After spending just over three months 'visiting' with Mary, Philip again left England on 6th July 1557. He would not return. He may have been pleased to leave and is said to have complained of *'a horrid stench that emanated from her nose'*. In the autumn of 1557 Mary again believed that she was pregnant and during the next six months there was a repetition of the 'pregnancy' of 1555. By the end of May 1558 intermittent fever set in and in August she was reported to be *'suffering from low fever and dropsy'*. This fever could well have been induced by the influenza that carried off so many people in the epidemic of 1558. Mary's health gradually declined over the autumn and, on 29th October Philip, was told that his wife was now *'grievously ill and her life is in danger'*. He stayed away and sent one of his council to visit the queen. Philip had spent less than 18 months of their 52-month marriage in England, and this must have affected Mary's mental state. In early November her depression and general malaise was accompanied by severe headaches, fever, an almost total loss of vision and her periods of confusion were becoming more frequent.

In hindsight we can deduce that she was suffering from some kind of fever, probably influenza, together with an abdominal abnormality, most probably an ovarian cystic tumour, that caused her abdomen to swell as it would in pregnancy. The signs of an ovarian tumour and the phantom pregnancy suggest that she was dying of a progressive prolactimona aggravated by chronic anaemia possibly caused by the regular bloodletting she had been subject to. On 6th November 1558, urged on by Philip's representative, Mary publicly acknowledged her half-sister Elizabeth as her heir. Ten days later, during the night of 16th November, Mary moved in and out of consciousness. When awake she reported having dreams of heavenly children happily playing, and talked of Philip and Elizabeth, who she felt sure would marry after her death. Her confused dreams and visions continued long after the administration of the final sacraments. Eventually her eyes fixed on the host, her lips moving in prayer and, fully conscious to the end, she died at 7am on 17th November 1558. She was forty-two and had reigned for only five years. Her friend Cardinal Pole, Archbishop of Canterbury, and architect of her Catholic revival, died on the same day.

Elizabeth the half-sister, whom she disliked and distrusted and who had once loomed so large as a threat to Mary's state, was immediately proclaimed queen, and formally accepted as such by Mary's council and, even the Spanish ambassador. Londoners seemed relieved that Mary had gone – those screams above the flames of Smithfield were still warm memories. *'All the churches in London did ring, and at night men did make bonfires and set tables in the street, and did eat, and drink, and make merry for the new Queen'*. Mary's body lay in state at St James' Palace for over three weeks. Her heart and bowels were buried in the Chapel Royal at St James' but her corpse was given a full Catholic funeral in Westminster Abbey. It would be the last such funeral in Latin to be held there, although Elizabeth did allow a dirge and requiem mass to be sung in the abbey for the Mary's cousin, Emperor Charles V, who died a few days later. Mary's hearse, bearing a grand effigy of the dead queen in her royal robes adorned with wax angels and escutcheons, was taken to the abbey on 13th December and her funeral mass and burial took place on the next day. The processions and heraldry for Mary were those as for a king as she was the first Queen Regnant to die on the throne. Thus helmet, sword and armour were all carried before her hearse on the journey to Westminster Abbey as had been done for all her male ancestors before her. *'Ladies riding all in black trailed to the ground, and a hundred poor men in good black gowns bore long torches with hoods on their heads, and arms on them. And all the way chandlers having torches to supply them that had torches burnt out'*.

Bishop White of Winchester, who had crowned Mary at her coronation and a man who could expect little sympathy from the new regime, preached the eulogy in Latin. *'She restored to the Church such ornaments as in the time of the Schism were taken away and spoiled. She found the realm poisoned with Heresy, and purged it'*. In for a penny, he foolishly pressed on: *'Our late sovereign hath left a sister, a lady of great worth, behind her, whom we are bound to obey, for a living dog is better than a dead lion'*. Elizabeth's Latin was as good as his and the tactless man was placed under house arrest as he left the pulpit.

Mary was the first occupant of the north aisle of Henry VII's chapel. After the officers of her household had broken their staves and cast them into the grave no monument was placed over it. Instead it was filled in with rubble and left as an oblong plot. One final indignity remained. The various altars that Mary had re-erected in the abbey, or which had survived the hammers of Edward VI's wreckers, were ordered to be broken up by Elizabeth and the stones and fragments from these were left piled on Mary's grave for the whole of Elizabeth's reign. Shards of rubble and the broken symbols of her great vocation were all that marked her tomb. Forty-five years would elapse before an epitaph would mark the memory and last resting place of this unhappy queen. The festive atmosphere continued even as Mary was being buried as cheery souvenir hunters went to work. *'The people plucked down the Cloth, every man a piece that could catch it, round about the church and the arms to'*.

In her will Mary had asked that her successor keep up the old religion, pay off her debts and bring her mother's body from Peterborough, to be buried beside her in Westminster Abbey. Queen Elizabeth certainly paid off all her debts, but, as expected, she restored the protestant religion and, as the daughter of the woman who had (briefly) displaced Catherine of Aragon as Queen of England, she did not find it politically expedient to bring the body of Mary's mother to Westminster.

Mary's early death at forty-two left a country at war, recovering from two years of poor harvests, famine and a flu epidemic. Much of this was out of her control but, like Richard III, Mary's history was to be written by the victors and she would suffer, almost immediately, from the virulent anti-Catholicism of those writing for her successor. Elizabeth I would reign for forty-four years and wear out her welcome; but Elizabeth would benefit from Mary's 'experiment' that a woman on the throne was no better and no worse than a man. She would also learn from her sister's choice of a husband. Elizabeth would face many pressures to marry foreign princes and perhaps Mary's experience was not far from her mind as she refused them all.

ELIZABETH I (born 1533 reigned 1558-1603)

Elizabeth I was Henry VIII's second daughter and the only child of his second wife, Anne Boleyn. She was born at Greenwich on 7th September 1533. Yet another disappointing girl for her son-obsessed father! Her childhood, like that of her half-sister Mary, would swing from adored princess to despised bastard. She was only two and a half years old when her mother was executed and it is likely that she hardly saw or remembered her. But the consequences of her mother's failure to bear a son for Henry VIII she would always remember. Six weeks after the execution of her mother, Henry persuaded Parliament to declare Elizabeth illegitimate and thus began the merry-go-round of suspicion, intrigue and status change that would hang over her during the reigns of no less than three monarchs, Henry VIII, Edward VI and Mary I.

These youthful trials, like those endured by Mary, probably contributed to the vacillation and circumspection for which she became famed after she became queen. After Henry's death, Elizabeth moved in with his widow, Catherine Parr, who had married, an old flame, the handsome Thomas Seymour. During her time with them as a girl of fourteen, Seymour is reported to have flirted with Elizabeth, entering her bedroom before she was dressed, climbing into bed with her and indulging in much rumbustious 'love play.' Eventually Elizabeth was moved away but rumours persisted that she had once been pregnant by him. How these teenage memories affected her attitude towards men and sex in later life it is difficult to tell, but her attitude to her own marriage and her later vindictiveness towards others near her who married or wished to marry may have some link with it.

Elizabeth was nineteen when her half-sister Mary became queen and was now in much more peril than she had been under her protestant brother. The Venetian ambassador reported that her *'figure and face are very handsome, and as such an air of dignified majesty pervades all her actions that no one can fail to suppose she is a queen ... her manners are very modest and affable'*; not quite what Mary would want to hear! Elizabeth now had to dodge and weave through the religious changes being implemented by her sister. Though reluctant, she complied with Mary's wish and attended mass. This pragmatism would be her saviour over the next five years. Her friend and advisor, William Cecil, Secretary of State under Edward VI, urged her to keep out of inflammatory politics and, despite her holding to this, Wyatt's rebellion of 1554 put her in further danger as Mary had her sent to the Tower of London on suspicion of aiding him. Although Wyatt and his supporters were tortured to declare her involvement they said nothing to incriminate her and she left the Tower after two months. To her surprise Elizabeth's new brother-in-law, Philip of Spain, emerged as an unexpected ally. He found her more attractive than his wife and began to see her as an insurance should Mary suffer an early death. Mary's deathbed worries about his attraction to Elizabeth look like being well founded. On Elizabeth's peaceful and unopposed accession, Philip, hardly in deep mourning for his late wife, promptly suggested that they should get married. Elizabeth politely refused.

Elizabeth was at Hatfield House when she heard of Mary's death and her own accession. Under an ancient oak tree in the park there she is supposed to have received the news by quoting from Psalm 118. *'This is the Lords doing and it is marvellous in our eyes'.* It was a kind of miracle. She had survived the execution of her mother and the terrors and suspicions of Mary. Like Mary, after the Lady Jane Grey affair, Elizabeth really believed that God had delivered her safely through all those uncertain and dangerous times. Her subjects were equally pleased that she had survived. The historian John Strype caught the mood of exultation. *'She rusheth not in at the first chop, to violate and breach former laws; to stir her people to change what they list, before Order be taken by Law. She hangeth no man, she beheadeth none, she burneth none, spoileth none'.* At York she was greeted as a true sovereign *'of no mingled blood of Spaniard, or stranger, but born mere English here among us'.*

Elizabeth was crowned on 15th January 1559 amid much popular rejoicing. *'Such was the shout and noise of organs, fifes, trumpets, drums and bells, that it seemed as though the world had come to an end'.* The religious world was certainly in turmoil. With no Archbishop of Canterbury and with many bishops dead, too old, infirm or still espousing the 'old faith', Elizabeth had to fall back on the very junior Owen Oglethorpe, Bishop of Carlisle, to place the crown on her head. Later, ostracised by his fellow bishops, he was said to have died of remorse. The difficulties over the coronation presaged further problems. Parliament's tortuous renewal, by only three votes in the House of Lords, of the new protestant Religious Settlement, and the refusal of bishops to take the oath of supremacy, set Elizabeth on course to a breach with Rome. William Cecil, an enthusiastic protestant, had also secured the introduction of Cranmer's radical 1552 version of the Book of Common Prayer. This raised more problems and some Catholic Bishops, refusing to use it, found themselves in the Tower.

All this was pain and grief to Elizabeth, who though a protestant, was like her father more akin to what we would call an 'Anglo-Catholic'. She appointed both Catholics and protestants to her Council and in religious practice her real feelings were often difficult to gauge. Unlike most protestants of her time she was not too keen on sermons and urged restraint on the numbers of preachers sent out to any one shire. The centre of her personal religion was the private act of prayer and she preferred the old church's code of celibacy for clergy. She sanctioned making the sign of the cross during baptism and liked to see her priests dressed in the old, ornate vestments. In November 1559, zealous protestants were shocked to see candles and a crucifix reappear in the Royal Chapel. But these few signs represented all there was to be of the old ways.

These Catholic 'appearances' could not hide the real doctrinal changes that were taking place. In 1570 Pope Pius V finally excommunicated Elizabeth and announced that *'Whosoever sends her out of the world only does not sin but gains merit in the eyes of God'.* This declaration of war, prompted the Privy Council to draw up a counter measure, a 'Bond of Association'. This 'licence to kill' signed by hundreds of protestant nobles and gentry basically empowered the signatories to pursue and destroy anyone found to be implicated in an assassination of Elizabeth. It was a game of very violent tit for tat. Although Mary Queen of Scots was not mentioned by name, she was clearly the target. Whatever Elizabeth's part in this 'Bond' it would be a convenient shield for her to hide behind and to avoid any personal responsibility should Mary ever be killed. She was her father's daughter!

The politics of Elizabeth's time mixed marriage, religion, the succession and foreign policy in much the same way as they had for Mary. The question of Elizabeth's marriage and the production of an heir was, of course, on everyone's mind, not least William Cecil's. Parliament begged Elizabeth to consider a spouse within three months of her accession. It was early days and Elizabeth, in order to dampen their ardour, told them that she would live and die a virgin. Later she did feel a great attraction to Robert Dudley, brother of the Guildford Dudley who had married Lady Jane Grey. That Robert was already married seemed to put the idea out of court and when his wife, Amy, was found dead in mysterious circumstances, prompting a royal inquiry, the scandal made any move in that direction impossible. Perhaps Elizabeth kept Dudley close to her to confuse foreign suitors. Perhaps she did intend to marry him? Perhaps she did not – who was ever to know? Marriage to a foreign prince would inevitably mean having to take sides in one European conflict or another, and a Catholic husband would raise the same ghosts that bedevilled Mary. The question of the queen's marriage would never go away and it would never be resolved. By 1578, when the queen was 45, the biological clock had won and all the marriage games were over. Whether Elizabeth was really a virgin or not she would trade on the persona of a 'Virgin Queen' until the end!

In September 1561 a cheeky Mary Queen of Scots sent an emissary to Elizabeth to check on how she stood in relation to succeeding her as Queen of England. Elizabeth received the man politely and agreed that her cousin, the Queen of Scots, had a good claim, indeed she knew of no other with a better, but she would never declare her as her heir. During Mary's reign Elizabeth had often described herself as *'the second person'*. The one, who as heir presumptive, would always attract followers prepared to rebel against the 'first person'. She had no intention of resurrecting a second person in the shape of Mary Queen of Scots. As it happened she didn't have to. After Mary's arrival in England, many English Catholics soon saw Mary as a very credible first person (see below). On 30th May 1588 Philip of Spain's great fleet left Lisbon for the Netherlands to gather up the troops that he needed to invade England. On 9th August, complete with silver breastplate and looking for all the world the great war leader, Elizabeth addressed her troops assembled at Tilbury: *'My loving people I come among you not for my recreation and disport but being resolved in the midst of the heat of battle to live and die amongst you all.... I know I have the body of a weak and feeble woman but I have the heart and stomach of a king and a king of England too and think foul scorn that Parma or any prince of Europe should dare invade the borders of my realm...'*.

It was a Churchillian performance but, after the scattering of Philip's 'unbeatable' armada by Howard, Drake, Hawkins and Frobisher and the wholly supportive British weather in the Channel, this would mark the high point of her reign. From here on in it would be down-hill all the way as the next eight years saw war weariness, famine, food riots, high taxation, recurrent plague, rising crime, vagrancy and regular violence on the queen's highway. Her court was becoming more corrupt with even her loyal, and once incorruptible, Secretary Burghley sometimes taking bribes worth twenty-five times his salary. Elizabeth the 'Virgin Queen' was worn out and she was wearing out her welcome. The execution of her one time favourite, the dashing but stupid earl of Essex, on 25th February 1601, set a maudlin seal on what would be her last two years. In that same year Elizabeth's ministers began preparing for James VI of Scotland to ascend the English throne. Robert Cecil, the son of old Secretary William, was in regular and secret correspondence with James, using coded names for each other, and secret routes to convey their letters. This was dangerous stuff. The prospect of her death, and thus having to name a successor, filled Elizabeth with an obsessive horror. *'The name of my successor is like the tolling of my own death bell'* and *'I can by no means endure a shroud to be held before my eyes while I am living'*. Ministers found to be preparing that shroud would not be ministers for long.

Elizabeth had always been proud of her record as a strong and healthy prince. Other than a bout of smallpox in her late twenties she had walked, hunted and danced her way through her forty four year reign in robust health as a result of following an *'exact temperance both as to wine and diet'*. The winter of 1602 however found her in low spirits and in early January 1603 she caught a severe cold. Later that month she travelled in *'summer like garments'* through a very wet and cold day to her supposedly warmer palace at Richmond. On arriving, she was taken ill again and, possibly as a result of a dental infection, she had difficulty swallowing food. During February she continued her work on affairs of state but disturbed those around her by ordering that the ring placed on her finger during her coronation be filed off (a delicate matter as her flesh had grown over it) and this prompted the inevitable assumption that the 'marriage' to her kingdom, inaugurated by that ring, was coming to an end. To this sad 'portent' was added the death of the queen's closest female friend, the countess of Nottingham, on 23rd February after which Elizabeth's spirits never rose above a deep melancholy. By early March she began to deteriorate physically; she could not sleep, was feverish and would not go to bed, preferring instead to sit for days and nights on a pile of cushions laid out in one of her chambers. This was a desperate ploy to stave off the grim reaper for she feared that if she once lay down she would not get up again. The glands in her neck enlarged and she continued to have difficulty eating.

Around 21st March, and after her many protests, Lord Admiral Nottingham eventually got her into a bed, by which time she would not take food or medicine and soon lost the power of speech. After this she clung to the Archbishop of Canterbury's hand refusing to let him rise without praying further. The sensitive issue now arose of Elizabeth naming an heir. Many on her council had already made contact with James VI of Scotland to ensure his smooth succession in England and their own place in his affections. Now they needed the queen's confirmation that all this grovelling had been worth while. They thus enquired of her who she wanted to name. Was it James VI of Scotland? Elizabeth was now past speaking and all they got was the queen raising her hand to her head in a dumb show. Was this approval or just an arm-jerk of frustration? Her council had no doubt that this sign betokened her consent to James. This was just as well and all agreed that the queen had come through at the last. Elizabeth died at 3am on the morning of 24th March 1603 *'mildly like a lambe, easily like a ripe apple from a tree'*. She probably died of pneumonia following a respiratory infection complicated by a dental infection and inflammation of the parotid glands. The queen did not make a will *'...nor gave anything away, so that they which come after shall find a well stored jewell house and a rich wardrobe of more than two thousand gowns with all things else answerable'*. A collection that not even the late Princess of Wales could compete with!

The queen's body lay at Richmond for a few days before being taken at night by water to lie in state at Whitehall. Elizabeth had instructed that her body was not to be disembowelled and embalmed and there is some debate about whether this was done or not. Her body was wrapped in the traditional cerecloth *'and that very ill too, through the covetousness of them that defrauded hir of the allowance of cloth was given them for the purpose'*. As was usual for a royal funeral, everything near the queen's bier in Whitehall was then hung with thousands of yards of black cloth. Cloth of gold at £6 a yard was also requested, probably to dress her effigy, while gilt nails were used for her coffin and bullion nails for the lead inner casing. While she lay in state at Whitehall she was visited by just about anyone who could rustle up a decent set of black clothes.

A month after her death her body, enclosed in a lead coffin, was taken to Westminster Abbey, where her heart was enclosed in a casket with that of her sister Mary. Her funeral was a grand affair and the first for which a contemporary drawing. On 28th April *'the corpse ... laid on a chariot, drawn by four great horses trapt in black velvet, the picture of her old body counterfeited after life, in her parliament robes with a crown on her head and a sceptre in her hand, lying on the corpse...was roylly conveyed to the Collegiate Church of St Peter of Westminster. There were esteemed mourners in black about the numbers of one thousand six hundred persons'*. A group of poor men and two hundred and sixty six poor women led the procession, not praying for a protestant queen's soul now but still the happy recipients of a suit of clothes and the dole that was still distributed on such occasions.

Many Londoners turned out to see her final journey. John Stow, who attended the funeral wrote: *'Westminster was surcharged with multitudes of all sorts of people in their streets, houses, windows, leads and gutters, that came to see the obsequy, and when they beheld her statue lying upon the coffin, there was such a general sighing, groaning and weeping as the like hath not been seen or known in the memory of man...'* This was probably the grandest royal funeral to date with around eighteen thousand yards of various black materials being issued to anyone who was, however remotely, involved: including bargemen, spice-bag makers, bellringers and kitchen maids. The drapers of London must have been hanging about outside Richmond Palace for weeks.

Elizabeth had toyed with the idea of using Wolsey's old tomb, still lying unfinished and unused in the Wolsey Chapel at Windsor. Like the two previous grandees who had contemplated using this great lump of marble, this came to nothing. At first Elizabeth was buried in the vault of her grandfather, King Henry VII, but three years later her successor, King James I, had her body moved. A grave was dug out of the 'rubble' covering the coffin of Mary and Elizabeth's coffin was placed directly on top of it. A large white marble monument was then erected to her memory at a cost of £1485; despite James I stipulating that the work should not exceed £600. The face on the full-length recumbent effigy was probably taken from the queen's death mask. Elizabeth was the last monarch buried in the abbey to have a monument erected above her. Elizabeth's half-sister Mary has no separate monument. Elizabeth's coffin is thought to have gradually crushed Mary's - the half-sisters still wrestling with each other? The words of the Latin inscription continue the irony: *'Consorts both in throne and grave, here rest we two sisters, Elizabeth and Mary, in the hope of one resurrection'.*

In her deathbed confirmation of James VI of Scotland as her heir, Elizabeth had overridden the preference of her father in his third and final Accession Act of 1544. This declared that if all his children died childless (which they did) the crown should descend through the heirs of his younger sister Mary (the Greys) and not through the Scottish blood line joined by his eldest sister Margaret. But Elizabeth hated the Greys. During the Lady Jane saga the Greys had happily declared Elizabeth to be a bastard, and so she quietly locked her father's will, and his inappropriate last wishes, away in an iron chest far from prying eyes, hoping for it to be forgotten which it was.

During Elizabeth's last days, her young kinsman Robert Carey was present at Richmond Palace and often sat with the dying queen. Much of what we know of her last moments comes from his memoirs. His other claim to fame is that while Elizabeth was dying he organised horses to be stationed along the 'North Road' so that he could be the first to bring James of Scotland the news of Elizabeth's death and James' accession to the English throne. Within two hours of her death, and in driving rain, Carey was on his first leg of that journey, arriving at Holyroodhouse at about midnight on the third day. This epic piece of one-upmanship made him very unpopular among his peers in England and, perhaps recognising this, James does not seem to have rewarded young Carey with very much for his trouble. Perhaps James was uncomfortable imagining a young man hanging around his own death bed before speeding off to embrace his successor.

The life of Queen Elizabeth I has been acted out in biographies, films and television series to a degree rarely bestowed on other historical figures. For nearly all of these the, 'soap opera' tension between her private life as a women and her public role as a monarch has taken centre stage. But Elizabeth was a mistress of artifice. She could be, and was, so many things to her court and her people that the real woman and the real queen, despite the wealth of documentation available about her, are probably impossible to disentangle. To Elizabeth, image became everything: protection, showmanship, authority and magnificence. Reality she left behind long ago under an old oak tree in Hatfield Park.

Mary Queen of Scots

Mary was no Queen of England but, as mother of James I of England (James VI of Scotland), her closeness to the throne of England, her intemperate involvement in plots to depose Elizabeth, and her execution on English soil all give her some claim to be mentioned here. Had her first husband, King Francis II of France lived, Mary's life, as Queen Consort of France, might have been very different. But he died after just one year as king and the eighteen year old Mary was bundled back to cold, protestant, quarrelsome Scotland.

Mary Queen of Scots drew her claim to the throne of Scotland directly from her father James V. He was the son of James IV of Scotland and Margaret Tudor the elder sister of Henry VIII. Thus Margaret's granddaughter, Mary, could lay claim to the throne of England should Elizabeth predecease her. While she was Queen of Scotland, wrapped up in the confused and complex world that was Scottish politics, that dynastic detail did not seem too important, but when she married Henry Stuart, lord Darnley, a Catholic and an English subject, this particular detail became more dangerous.

Also a grandson of Henry VIII's sister Margaret, from her second marriage, Darnley now added a second dose of Tudor royal blood to any child that he and Mary might have, and Elizabeth I was furious about their marriage. After Darnley's death in suspicious circumstances, in 1566, Mary's role as queen of the Scots became fragile and after further strife, imprisonment and a third marriage, she escaped from her enemies in Scotland. Leaving her two year old son James behind she crossed the Solway to seek sanctuary in England. This move was bad for everybody concerned as the potent mix of dynastic and religious affinity made it dangerous for both Mary and Elizabeth to be resident on English soil.

While in Scotland Mary's Catholicism had been muted in the face of the protestant lords who surrounded her, but now it shone like a beacon to the large minority of Catholics who served under a protestant queen and who were forced to observe protestant religious practices. Many English Catholics believed Mary should be queen because they didn't recognise the marriage of Anne Boleyn to Henry VIII as being legal. To them Elizabeth was ineligible to inherit her father's crown. To them Mary living in England was a Godsend! All of this was very bad news for Mary. Catholics plotting to put her on the throne were bound to lose. Elizabeth's councillors, informers and security service, organised by the crafty Sir Francis Walsingham, were highly effective. Indeed they were more than capable of nourishing or even inventing plots in order to expose those they saw as a danger to their mistress the queen. The Babington Plot that eventually brought Mary Queen of Scots down is just one in a long series of Catholic plots that first Elizabeth, and then James I, had to deal with. Sir William Cecil uncovered, possibly even kindled, the Babington Plot against Elizabeth and his son, Robert, first earl of Salisbury, uncovered, and probably secretly abetted, the famous Gunpowder plot against James I.

After considerable pressure from her ministers a reluctant Elizabeth had Mary brought to trial for treason. It was a bogus affair, the result preordained. All Mary's papers had been removed, she was not allowed to see the evidence against her, she was denied legal council and, as she was not an English subject, she could not really be tried let alone convicted of treason against an English queen. During the trial Mary reminded her accusers *'Remember Gentlemen the Theatre of history is wider than the realm of England'*. She had been a prisoner in England for 19 years; she never returned to Scotland and, contrary to some reports, she and Elizabeth had never met face-to-face.

She was executed at Fotheringhay castle in Northamptonshire on 8th February 1587, aged 44. At her execution she removed her black cloak to reveal a dress of crimson-brown, the liturgical colour of martyrdom in the Catholic Church. To the distress of everyone, particularly Mary, the executioner bungled his job taking three blows to hack off her head. The first blow struck the back of her head while the next struck her shoulder severing her subclavian artery spewing blood everywhere. Mary is said to have covered her head with a gold-spangled veil after this blow, grateful, no doubt, that the last one did, just about, take off her head. More farce was to follow as when the executioner held up Mary's head to proclaim *'God save the queen'*, he was left holding her auburn wig, while the Queen of Scots' head rolled off the scaffold onto the floor. During all this, Mary's terrified pet dog, a Skye terrier, is said to have darted out from beneath her skirts hiding beneath his mistresses severed head. He pined away and died shortly afterwards. Mary had requested to be buried in France at either St Denis or Rheims, but Sir Francis Walsingham had issued strict instructions concerning the disposal of her remains that did not include transporting a Catholic martyr to France.

Keen to outwit any Catholic relic hunters, seeking souvenirs, the government had arranged that many of the items that Mary had touched were quickly burned including the bloodstained headsman's block. Her rosary beads and prayer book (now in the Russian National Library of St Petersburg) were all that survived. Later in the afternoon surgeons removed Mary's heart, and other organs, and buried them secretly within the walls of the castle. Mary's body was then embalmed, wrapped in a wax winding sheet and encased in a heavy lead coffin, said to have weighed at least nine hundredweight. Walsingham was taking no chances with possible relic hunters! As was often the case with the death of English monarchs, instructions were issued to close all the ports. This had the effect of slowing down the news of Mary's death to France and other Catholic countries. Mary's body remained, unburied, behind the locked doors of Fotheringhay castle for five months after her death.

On a hot, Sunday, 30th July 1687, in deference to the 'assumed' feelings of Mary's son, James VI of Scotland, Mary's body was taken, in the dead of night, by the light of torches, to Peterborough Cathedral for a proper burial. Some heralds, nobles and mourners had been ferried in from London to give some semblance of royal solemnity but the great weight of the coffin prevented much by way of processional ceremony. An effigy of Mary, probably modelled on her death mask, was carried in the procession and the banners of Mary I, Francis II of France and Darnley were hung on the pillars of the nave, but not a banner representing Mary's third husband, the detested Bothwell. In his sermon the protestant Dean of Peterborough took the opportunity to proclaim the day of her execution as a righteous reward for her own complicity in murder, being almost twenty years to the day after the death of her own husband, lord Darnley. The day being very hot and the corpse having remained unburied for five months, the ceremonies were not drawn out and the coffin was quickly placed in a vault in the south aisle of the cathedral. Costing no more than £321 Mary's funeral rites were not expensive, and around a third of this money was used to pay for the banquet, in the Bishops Palace, that the London courtiers enjoyed afterwards.

On his accession to the throne of England, James I was in no hurry to remedy these slights to his mother. He had already paid for, and had constructed, a fine monument to his predecessor Elizabeth I, and in 1606 a master mason was instructed to start carving a white, marble effigy for Mary that was eventually completed in 1612. In that year James ordered that his mother's remains be exhumed from the vault at Peterborough and re-interred in Westminster Abbey beneath a magnificent tomb in the north aisle of the Henry VII Chapel. There she still lies, just thirty feet from the grave of her cousin, tormentor, and executioner, Elizabeth I. The two cousins, closer in death than they had ever been in life, would probably not chuckle at the irony of their final resting place.

In 1867 Mary's tomb, and that of Elizabeth I, were opened, by order of Dean Stanley, who was on a mission to discover where James I was buried. Although James was not found in either Mary's or Elizabeth's vault, it was discovered that Mary shared her grave with at least 40 of her descendants. The once lonely queen was certainly lonely no more! This vault, built of brick and measuring twelve feet long, six feet high and seven feet wide, was packed with a vast pile of lead coffins of different shapes scattered in piles and reaching from the floor to the roof. The most poignant sight that greeted these tomb openers were the piles of very small coffins belonging to the first ten children of James II and the seventeen infants miscarried by Queen Anne. The massive coffin of Mary Queen of Scots was still intact without a break or tear after its 300 year sojourn. For once Dean Stanley and his band of investigators left well alone, forbearing to open up the sealed container of the Mary Queen of Scots. Dean Stanley wrote that *'The presence of the fatal coffin which had received the headless corpse at Fotheringhay was sufficiently affecting without endeavouring to penetrate further into its mournful contents'*.

Something of a romantic figure for later generations, Mary was a bit of a dunce when it came to understanding the give and take of good government. If she impresses at all it is mainly in her talent for wasting the considerable assets that she inherited. But in one way she triumphed over Elizabeth from the grave. It would be her DNA that would provide the next

Effigies of King Henry II and Queen Eleanor, of Aquitaine, at Fontevrault, the Loire, France. Henry II died at his castle of Chinon in 1189. The first English king to be buried at Fontevrault, he was followed there by his son, Richard I, his wife Eleanor, his daughter Joanna and two of his daughters-in-law, Berengaria of Navarre and Isabella of Angoulême. Towards the end of her life Eleanor became a nun at the abbey of Fontevrault. Her effigy is the only one of the royal group showing her reading a book.

Effigy of King John at Worcester Cathedral. This is the oldest effigy of an English king to be found in England. John died at Newark in Lincolnshire in 1216. He specifically asked to be buried at Worcester between the tombs of two saints, Wulfstan and Oswald. He was buried in a monks cowl to help hide his face as he approached St Peter and the gates to heaven believing that his disguise and being accompanied by two saints might help gain him entrance.

Bronze and gilt effigy of Henry III, son of King John, at Westminster Abbey.
Henry died at Westminster in 1272. Henry desired to be buried close to the tomb
of Edward the Confessor which he also had refurbished at great expense. Henry
undertook the re-building of the abbey and it is his abbey with some additions
that we see today.

Detail from the effigy of Edward II in Gloucester Cathedral. It is believed that Edward was murdered in Berkeley Castle in 1327 and his beautiful alabaster tomb was commissioned by his son Edward III. Popular devotion to the deposed king proved handy to the cathedral as the donations of the pilgrim's visiting the tomb funded the extensive structural re-modelling that was carried out in the mid-14th century. Recently a debate has arisen over whether Edward II was buried here in 1327 or whether he escaped his captors and lived on to be buried somewhere in northern Italy.

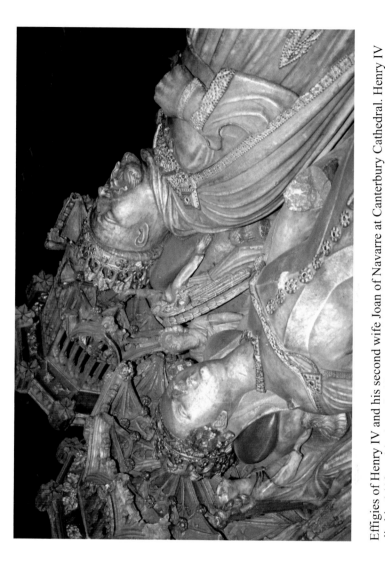

Effigies of Henry IV and his second wife Joan of Navarre at Canterbury Cathedral. Henry IV died in 1413 and is the only king of England buried at Canterbury. He lies on the opposite side of the cathedral to his uncle, Edward the 'Black Prince'. Riddled with the guilt of deposing and murdering Richard II Henry wanted to be buried at Canterbury close to the tomb and shrine of St Thomas Becket.

Gilt bronze effigy of Henry VII in the chapel that bears his name at Westminster Abbey. Henry died in 1509 and his tomb, an early example of early Renaissance art and design in England, was completed in 1518.

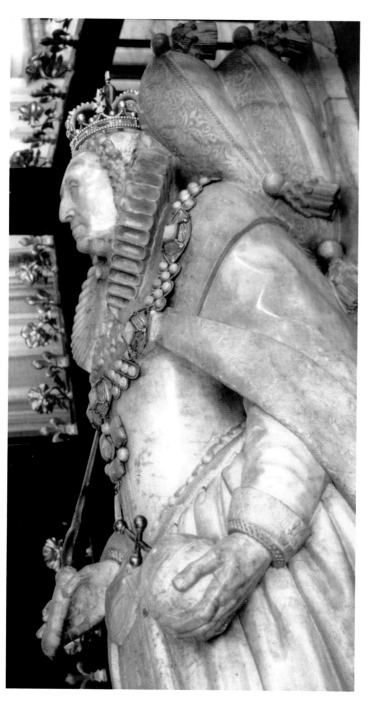

Effigy of Elizabeth I on her tomb in the Henry VII chapel at Westminster Abbey. Elizabeth died in 1603 and her tomb, ordered to be made by her successor, James I, was finished in 1606. Elizabeth's body lies on top of that of her half-sister Mary I who has no monument. The Latin inscription in front of the monument reads: *'Partners both in throne and grave, here rest we two sisters, Elizabeth and Mary, in the hope of one resurrection'.*

The south side of St George's Chapel in Windsor Castle. This chapel with its exquisite fan vaulting was begun in by Edward IV in 1475 and is contains the tombs of ten English and British monarchs: Edward IV, Henry VI, Henry VIII, Charles I, George III, George IV, William IV, Edward VII, George V and George VI. As Westminster Abbey became full of royal bodies George III had a huge royal vault built beneath this chapel which contains the remains of many members of the Hanoverian royal family.

king of England; it would be her blood, not Elizabeth's, which would flow through the kings and queens of England over the next four hundred years. The downside for Mary is that from her death onwards, with just one blip, it would all be protestant blood. It is often said that James I ordered the demolition of Fotheringhay castle as a sort of punishment to the building for hosting his mother's execution. In fact the castle 'died' gradually as local builders and landowners carried away the stones for various building purposes and it was described as ruinous in 1635, ten years after James' death. The staircase down which Mary walked to her execution is now in the Talbot Hotel at Oundle, built in 1626.

JAMES I (born 1566 reigned 1603-1625)

James I of England (VI of Scotland) was born on 19th June 1566 at Edinburgh Castle the only son of the unfortunate Mary Queen of Scots and Henry Stuart, lord Darnley. James had a somewhat unusual childhood. Baptised a Catholic, James was crowned a protestant king of Scotland at the parish Kirk in Sterling on 29th July 1567, just a year before his mother was forced to flee to England. A king before he could talk, he joined that band of ancestors who, since 1406, had come to the throne of Scotland as a minor. James was brought up, largely at Sterling castle, by a succession of Scottish 'Regents' who rarely lasted, or lived, long. Moray was shot in 1570, Lennox died in a brawl in 1571, Mar (believed poisoned) at least died in his bed in 1572 and Morton, though lasting longer than the rest, was executed in 1581 for his part in Darnley's murder fourteen years earlier. It was a strange and insecure childhood and more than once James' life was in danger. After a period of being kidnapped by two lords 'for his own good', James eventually assumed the reins of government in 1583 at the age of 17. He thus joins Mary and Elizabeth in a triumvirate of monarchs whose childhood was dysfunctional, dangerous and motherless. It was beginning to look like a prerequisite for ascending the English throne that you be denied your mother at an early age and pass your childhood in fear of your life. Modern psychologists would have had a field day!

Among his many disturbances, one thing was constant in James' life: he was brought up in the rigours of the very protestant, Scottish 'Kirk.' His principal tutor, the dour George Buchanan, believed that the way to learning lay as much with the rod as the book, and he relished using it. Buchanan was also a leading figure in the presbyterian kirk where the general assembly of the clergy, and not the king was the supreme authority. It was a world in which kings could make mistakes and be held accountable and punished. Not an arrangement Elizabeth I or her father would have subscribed to! In his early thirties James clearly felt that some re-thinking of these ideas was needed and in 1598 he wrote and published 'The True Law of Free Monarchies' where all that stuff about kings being human was dispensed with. Instead James affirmed that kings are called gods, they are appointed by God and answerable only to God. Despite his later nightmares over his beatings by Buchanan, James voluntarily developed a passion for learning and scholarship that remains unequalled by any subsequent English monarch.

James VI was to rule Scotland, as an adult, for 20 years before he also became King James I of England at 37. It was a good apprenticeship for the big one, as Scotland was a nest of civil strife and religious ferment requiring all his cunning. Scotland was not a rich kingdom and so when Elizabeth offered James a pension of £4,000 a year in 1586 to keep his borders peaceful he took the money. As well as being very useful it probably helped soften the blow of his mother's execution a year later. James made proper, decent but muted complaints to Elizabeth about it but as the most convincing successor to Elizabeth's crown there was no point in rocking the boat too much.

London greeted the announcement of James' accession with restrained joy. Elizabeth's death was a great shock to Londoners many of whom had never known another ruler. No builder of palaces, she had regularly travelled to live off the score of her great nobles and these progresses had brought her into contact, albeit briefly, with many of her subjects in the southeast and the midlands. There was also relief that the succession problem of 44 years standing had been resolved so easily and peacefully. James made a slow progress to London, stopping off at York, missing Elizabeth's funeral, and arriving in London on 7th May 1603 in triumph as the unopposed heir to his great great grandfather Henry VII and the first ruler of all Britain. The great spender with only a small treasury to ransack in Scotland now had an Aladdin's cave to play with. And he needed it. Unlike Elizabeth James came to England with a family and this meant 'households' not just for him but for his queen and his eldest son, Henry Prince of Wales. The Virgin Queen had been monarchy on the cheap compared with funding such a brood and this, when added to James' hopeless extravagance and generosity towards his favourites, would set a time bomb ticking.

Londoners saw a portly man of medium height with thin brown hair and pale blue eyes that were popping and rolling. His thin, knock-kneed legs struggled to carry his bulky trunk and the heavily padded doublet he wore to protect himself from the assassin's knife. Awkward and ugly, with a straggly beard and a slobbering tongue too large for his mouth, James cut an image all together different from the regal poise of Elizabeth. His conversation was often a garrulous stream in which bits of learning, esoteric theories and homely proverbs mingled with jolly familiarities, all in such a broad Scottish accent that very few people understood what he said. If not quite cutting the dash that people expected, James did claim to come as a peacemaker, hoping to reconcile Catholics and protestants and to end England's expensive war with Spain. To this end, and within a year of his accession, he summoned three major conferences: on peace, religion and union with Scotland. This initiative by the 'managerial' James, the James who knew how to organise and set out precise instructions to achieve a clear objective stands in clear contradiction to the loose, shambling, disorganised and spendthrift James, the James so used to informality and frankness in dealings with his Scottish nobles. But James was a man of many contradictions, a man of learning who was happy babbling nonsense, a man of religion who would waste his peoples treasure on trifles.

James' first conference on peace ending in the Somerset House peace treaty of August 1604 was a success, ending the 20 year war with Catholic Spain. Ironically, agreed without any concessions to English Catholics, this treaty left them feeling betrayed. Where once they had looked out to Catholic Europe for support, now they would have to fall back on their own resources to seek justice. And some were quick to act. At the end of October 1605 James became aware of a plot involving 'powder' to damage the whole of the government at the next opening of Parliament. James' spies let the plot run until 4th November, the day before the scheduled opening, when at 11pm, soldiers searched the cellars below the House of Lords and found a man with a nine inch match in his pocket lying among piles of coal covering thirty-six barrels of gunpowder.

His name was Guido Fawkes and he was soon lying on the rack. If the conspiracy had succeeded it would have wiped out most of the British royal family and the entire English political establishment. The conspirators were soon rounded up, tortured, and put to death, but there was no widespread persecution of Catholics and James' peace treaty with Catholic Spain held fast. For many protestants this plot, by its audacity and potential for destruction, planted the idea that there was now and forever a serious threat from an international Catholic conspiracy that they dare not ignore and must forever be on their guard against.

James had avoided destruction by 'powder' but he could not prevent the death of his eldest and much loved son Henry, Prince of Wales, probably of typhoid, aged eighteen in 1612. Two thousand mourners followed the boy's body *'at a foot's pace'* to the abbey. His effigy clothed in rich garments *'did so lively represent his person, as that it did not only draw tears from the severest beholders but caused a fearful outcry among the people as if they felt their own ruin in that loss'.* There was some public comment at the time that, for one who had been so much lamented, Henry was given no monument. Instead he was placed in a vault with his grandmother, Mary Queen of Scots, beneath the fine monument James had recently completed for her.

Young Henry's death signalled the beginning of the end for a lingering cavalier of the Elizabethan age. Though detained in the Tower for being implicated in the 'Main Plot' of 1603 to replace James I with Arabella Stuart, Sir Walter Raleigh had been protected by his friendship with Henry. Sir Walter was executed in 1618. Having brought back tobacco from Virginia, he may have been one of the first to request a last 'smoke' before he died. He is buried in the chancel of St Margaret's Church just to the north of Westminster Abbey, but the exact location is not known.

While only a claimant to the English throne, James could flatter all those religious groups in England who corresponded with him, giving false hopes to all sides of the theological divide, but as King of England he would have to choose. Crunch time came at the Hampton Court religious conference on the future of the church, in 1604. Here the more extreme aspirations of puritans and Catholics were dashed on the rocks of James' pragmatic middle way. James was delighted to be Head of the Church in England, not just one of a congregation of equals before God, as he had been in the presbyteries of Scotland. Although at heart a Calvinist, Elizabeth's ornaments and ceremonies were safe in James' hands. The only substantial result of this conference was the decision to undertake a new translation of the bible. The Authorised Version, eventually published in 1611, still stands as a rare example of a masterpiece of English prose produced by a committee; indeed a committee divided into six sub-committees.

From the moment of his accession James desired more than just a personal union of his two crowns and his wish to see a formally established 'Kingdom of Great Britain' dominated the first five years of his reign. However sensible this seems to us from the perspective of the 21st century, James' dream of one king, one law, one people was a hopeless vision at the time as the English Parliament had no intention of losing the ancient and glorious name of England in a mish mash of Scottish and English traditions. In October 1604 a frustrated James by-passed Parliament and assumed the title of King of Great Britain by proclamation, and in April 1606 insisted on a British flag to back it up. His 'Union Jack' (derived from the Latin for James, 'jacobus') would now fly from the sterns of all 'British' ships. By November 1606 the commissioners set up to pave the way for a truly united kingdom of 'Britain' reported back to Parliament, and James made his last pitch. The MPs did accept the naturalisation of James' Scottish subjects and accepted free trade between the two kingdoms but the rest was buried.

Much has been made of James' homosexuality. While still in Scotland and when only twelve years old James, 'embraced' the first of those men who would become known as his favourites. His cousin Esmè Stuart came over from France in 1579, became duke of Lennox in 1581, and enjoyed the loathing of the Scottish lords as a pro-French Catholic who got much too close to the king. Over the years three more would follow: George Gordon earl of Huntley, Robert Carr earl of Somerset; and, his only English favourite, George Villiers duke of Buckingham. Whether any of these men enjoyed carnal relations with James is a question that fascinates many historians but the evidence (occasional fondling of them in public) is thin and the question has to be left open. In 1589 James married the fifteen year old Anne of Denmark and when storms prevented her sailing to Scotland, romantic James, in a clear display of heterosexual zeal, sailed across the North Sea to bring her home in person.

At this time it was clear that James cared for, perhaps even loved, Anne and they had six children, three of whom survived to adulthood. Later, his ardour cooled, and his favourites, the most outrageous of which was George Villiers, soaked up his affections, not to mention sacks full of privileges and emoluments. Villiers became cupbearer to the king in 1614 and from then on his status and privileges increased culminating in his being made duke of Buckingham in 1623. He soon established himself as a spider at the centre of a web of patronage that pleased some and made enemies of the many more who didn't get to drink from the cup. James was not the first king of England to promote undeserving male favourites. Both Edward II and Richard II had done the same but like a modern day leader who doesn't know when to sack a favoured minister for incompetence, parliament eventually gets tired of waiting.

James' extravagant treatment of Buckingham and his other favourites set the scene for parliament's frustration with him on other fronts. No matter how much money they voted him they could see it seeping away into the pockets of the undeserving. Elizabeth's customs revenues had stagnated and failed to keep up with inflation, as had the rents levied on crown lands, many of which were now ludicrously undervalued. Without a parliamentary subsidy, James had fallen back on various royal prerogatives to raise cash, including selling honours, a practice still much discussed in modern Britain, and James even invented a new one to sell, the baronetcies. This title came above a knight but below a baronet! In February 1610 Robert Cecil put a radical scheme before parliament to help the king. He suggested a 'great contract' by which the king would give up a range of feudal dues traditionally belonging to the crown in return for a £600,000 lump sum and an annual grant of £200,000. At first it looked like Cecil might have found an answer to the interminable arguments that had plagued both king and parliament over his personal expenditure, but conservative council on both sides prevailed, the proposal fell and James dissolved his first parliament in February 1611. His second parliament in 1614 fared no better with regard to the king's finances and was dissolved after two months. His third and last in 1621 saw the king seeking peace with the old enemy, Spain, while the MPs cried for war but, contrarily, demanded a discussion of their grievances before voting supplies. The MPs were losing patience with James and went so far as to set out in the Journals of the House of Commons that their privileges were *'the ancient and undoubted birthright and inheritance of the subjects of England'*. In an uncharacteristic act of pique James went to Westminster and dramatically tore out these pages from the Journal. It would be easy to surmise that by this very physical interference with the proceedings of MPs James was setting the scene for the Civil War that his son would instigate after his death. But this was not typical of James' approach to Parliament and anyway he was in the autumn of his reign when he behaved like this. James' son, Charles I, would only be thirty nine years old when he invaded Parliament and his tyranny, if accepted, would last for much longer.

Anne of Denmark died in 1619 after suffering from dropsy and renal failure associated with anaemia. The king, detained by illness at Newmarket, was not present. Anne's funeral had to be put off until two months after her death, as there was no money to put the king's servants into mourning. It was intended that her funeral be a magnificent affair, costing three times more than that of Elizabeth I, but the public were disappointed with the general effect. The Dean of Westminster was charged to find a suitable place for her but she lies alone in a northeast recess of Henry VII's chapel.

Early in 1623 James' eldest son Charles and the duke Buckingham set off for Spain on, what would turn out to be, at doomed quest to secure a Spanish marriage. On their return to England they supported the war party in The Lords and they both grew excited as Parliament began to consider war with Spain. This was the last thing that the enfeebled James wanted. Somewhat presciently James turned on Charles saying *'that he would live to have his bellyful of parliaments'*. This warmongering 'marriage' between Charles and Buckingham upset the king and could only have aggravated his poor physical condition. From about 1622 onwards James had begun to look thin and wasted. He had suffered from kidney problems and arthritis for some time and as his weight loss continued through September 1624 he was seen to deteriorate further. He suffered from convulsions and intermittent mild fever, possibly as a result of chronic fibroid tuberculosis.

In the early spring of 1625 James retired to his great country house of Theobalds that he had acquired from Robert Cecil, in part by giving him the site of Hatfield House, twelve miles from London, in Hertfordshire. After a days hunting near there on 5th March 1625 he fell ill of what contemporaries called the 'tertian ague', a description about as specific as the way we use the term influenza today. So called because it followed a three day cycle, James' *'ordinary and moderate'* attack would be expected to run its course and he recover. But he didn't. Instead the intermittent fever became so severe that he was driven to thrust his hands into cold water and drink quantities of small beer to cool himself. By 12th March the fits that he had begun to suffer from were subsiding and the king made preparations to move to Hampton Court. At this stage, the duke of Buckingham and his mother decided to try some remedies of their own. Somehow Buckingham managed to expel all James' doctors from the sick room, after which, he and his mother began to apply medicines and plasters of their own devising to the king. Contemporary reports suggest that this was a white powder, possibly arsenic based, and a salve devised by Buckingham's mother. As time went on and James' fever got worse his physicians protested but Buckingham still kept them from the king.

Eventually James realized that he was close to death and in need of spiritual support. John Williams, Bishop of Lincoln, hurried to Theobalds to prepare James for his end. After this, James ordered everyone to move two or three rooms away from him so that he could have secret talks with his son, Charles. The king lingered on for three days more before he called for Charles again in the early hours of 27th March. James could say no more to his son, having lost the power of speech, and he died shortly afterwards. He was in his fifty-ninth year. The strange behaviour of Buckingham and his mother inevitably gave rise to rumours that the king had been poisoned, despite a post-mortem on the king finding no trace of such an invasion of his organs. Their medicines, if composed of arsenic, may have complicated an already lethal combination of ailments. As with Edward VI, tales later emerged of James' extremities turning black, his nails dropping off, and his hair falling out.

One other theory has James dying, as his son, Henry, and his mother, Mary Queen of Scots, may have done, from the accumulative effects of porphyria; his convulsions, vomiting, pain and intermittent fever are consistent with its symptoms and one doctor did report signs of the tell-tale purple urine. James had been ill for at least three years and over that time his symptoms (intermittent fever - weight loss, chest infection, severe diarrhoea, dehydration and loss of appetite) left his body in no shape to fight off the stroke that probably got him in the end. The chest infection at the heart of all this was probably tuberculosis aggravated by many years of poor diet. James was said to have always bolted his food and mixed many kinds of alcohol at one sitting. Mr Watson, one of the king's surgeons, held a post-mortem on 28th March when it was noted that: *'On opening the head it was found so very full of brains that they could not keep them from spilling, a great mark of his infinite judgement'*.

One source has James's body lying at Theobalds for eight days *'without any covering, saving a white sheet, which grieved and galled the hearts of such of his servants as could neither help nor durst control it'*. His body was then embalmed and placed in a lead coffin, shaped to the kings body, as supplied by plumber Abraham Greene at a cost of twenty shillings for the lead. A copper plate inscribing the king's magnificence was then soldered on to it. This was then placed in a wooden coffin made out of two elm trunks, so cut as to allow one half to rest on the other. On the night of 4th April James' body left Theobalds for London in a black velvet coach escorted by Charles I and other nobles. From Holborn it made its way through Chancery Lane and the Strand to Denmark House, lit by 300 torches whose flames struggled against the ceaseless rain that had plagued England all that spring. He lay there for nearly five weeks preached over by John Donne and flanked by six magnificent silver candlesticks that Charles had brought from Spain, before being buried at a private funeral in Westminster Abbey on 4th May.

He was buried, not with his predecessor Elizabeth, his mother, his wife, or his children, but deep inside the tomb of Henry VII. Perhaps James wanted to link up with another king who had founded a dynasty; the first Stuart spending eternity with the first Tudor? Getting the unwieldy coffin inside the vault involved displacing the bodies of Edward VI and Elizabeth of York, but eventually it was done. So well was it sealed over that, like his son, Charles I, after him no one could find him for 250 years. Eventually, Dean Stanley, after digging around in various royal tombs, discovered him in 1869. A black and white drawing in Stanley's *'Memorials of Westminster Abbey'* (1886) shows James' long lead coffin next to those of Henry VII and Elizabeth of York, without much space in between.

This private interment was followed by a magnificent public funeral on 7th May, with Charles I starting a new tradition by walking on foot from Denmark House behind the 'chariot'. The effigy was dressed in rich crimson velvet and the face had been carefully made from a death mask taken of James at Theobalds. Mourning cloth was distributed to more than 9,000 people, who also joined the procession. It was a long walk and, not unlike the life of the deceased, was said to have been 'a confused and disorderly' affair. The cortège, starting at ten o'clock in the morning, didn't arrive at the abbey until after five o'clock in the evening. Inigo Jones designed the royal hearse, a huge octagonal structure raised on a podium ascended by three steps. Standing female figures representing Religion, Justice, War and Peace were set on plinths, while the king's effigy reclined under a dome decorated with royal arms and allegorical figures depicting virtues in mourning.

Although Inigo Jones saved money by making the figures that supported the great canopy out of plaster of Paris and muslin instead of marble, James kept spending beyond the grave as the full cost of his funeral exceeded £50,000. The great spender and lover of court masques was right at the centre of this one – the final lavish entertainment at which he was sure to be the star. An Old Testament star at that, as during his two-hour funeral sermon an effusive Dean Williams compared James in 'every particular' to Solomon. A month before this show, another masque, a masque of death, had taken centre stage in London as Bubonic Plague resumed its march across that oft-visited city. By the time James was buried 13 parishes had been infected by it, and by August more than four thousand people had died of it. The coronation of his son, Charles I, had to be postponed until early in the following year to avoid it.

As he lay dying, surrounded by his lords baying for the blood of Spain, James had prophesied that, when he was gone, 'they should have more war than they knew how to manage'. For 22 years the 'wisest fool in Christendom' had mostly kept his countrymen out of war. Within 17 years his son would plunge them into a war that would pit his old subjects, not against Frenchmen or Spaniards, but against each other! In this James was partly complicit. James' DNA was soaked in the Divine Right of Kings and the hunger for absolute power and like all DNA this one would not give up easily. James' may have been a more intellectual, almost scholarly, vision moderated by the reality of the evolving English parliamentary system, but for his son it would turn into an emotional and religious crusade. The drama of the ambivalence of power that was acted out for the first time in plays like Othello, Volpone, King Lear and The Tempest while James' new bible was being translated would later be played out in an immense and desperate struggle on the green fields of England.

CHARLES I (born 1600 reigned 1625-1649)

Born at the dawn of the seventeenth century, in 1600, Charles Stuart was the second son of James I and Anne of Denmark, and became heir to the throne after the death of his elder brother Henry in 1612. Poor 'brilliant' Henry died in a coma after a mysterious fever. It was probably typhoid but the headaches, buzzing in the ears, delirium and convulsive fits he suffered may also have been due to the porphyria that later affected George III. At 12 years old Charles first lost Henry and then, a year later, his sister Elizabeth. She was whisked off to Heidelberg to marry Fredrick V, the Elector of the Rhine Palatine. It was this Elizabeth who may have carried the porphyria gene that passed down the Hanoverian generations to George III. Charles never saw her again.

Reserved, small, unimpressive in appearance and with a stammer that never left him, Charles had lost his two closest friends. After his mother's death in 1619 he moved closer to his father's favourite, the once-hated Buckingham. Together they went secretly to Spain in early 1623 to arrange a marriage between Charles and the Infanta Donna Maria, the daughter of Phillip III of Spain. The ensuing, but unsuccessful, diplomacy there hinted at the kind of duplicity that Charles would later use in his dealings with the English Parliament. He offered all kinds of concessions to the Spanish regarding the freedoms of Catholics in England to secure the match, seemingly immune to the outcry this would cause back in England. The Infanta on the other hand, horrified at having to betray her faith, declared that she would rather go to a monastery than marry a heretic.

The 'heretic' returned home empty handed and James, depressed at the failure of his peace negotiations with Spain, began discussions with the French for Charles to marry Henrietta Maria, daughter of King Henry IV. After his father's death Charles did marry her and again he made secret promises to the French concerning concessions to English Catholics. After the death of Buckingham in 1628 Charles and his queen became closer, and despite her reputation for being a poor judge of character, he came to rely on her more and more.

Unlike his coarse and noisy father, Charles cultivated a court that was sober, elegant, dignified and hedged about with strict rules of ceremony and etiquette. He always put some distance between himself and his courtiers and serious distance between himself and his subjects. Enclosed within such a bubble, aloof, cold and with little sense of humour, it is easy to imagine him becoming self-obsessed and dwelling on the prerogatives of a divinely anointed king. He put himself far away from the day-to-day world of negotiation and compromise that occupied the merchants, lawyers, country gentry, even the nobility, who made up his Parliament and then wondered why they didn't understand him. His love of performing in allegorical court masques was as close as he got to engaging with other people.

Charles' first three parliaments in 1625, 1626 and 1628 were not happy. They complained about the failure of his military expeditions in Spain and France, the enforcement of loans, his illegal collection of tonnage and poundage, his billeting of soldiers without payment and the imprisonment of subjects without due process. They also wanted his close friend, the militarily inept Buckingham, impeached. Infuriated, Charles dissolved Parliament in 1629, putting several MPs in prison.

It was not a good start. After 1629 he governed for eleven years without calling a Parliament, during which he raised money by various illegal means. One of these was his continued use of tonnage and poundage, a payment for each 'tun' of wine imported, and a levy on the pound sterling value of all imported and exported goods. Charles had been granted this, for just one year, in 1625 but he persisted in collecting it every year. Another illegal scheme was to impose a tax known as the 'Ship Money'. In using this Charles was resurrecting an old Tudor tax that had been levied, on port towns and counties, to support the navy in times of war. Charles was advised that there was no reason not to levy it on towns and counties throughout the country, even in times of peace, and when introduced it provided a very lucrative income for the king. The 'extended ship money' was first levied in 1634 and it raised over £2000,000 in its first year, almost 90% of the cost of keeping Charles solvent, but it was very unpopular causing riots and demonstrations and some people who protested about it or failed to pay it were put in prison.

Safely solvent Charles then entered the realm of religious controversy by seeking to enforce the English Book of Common Prayer on the Scots. Their response was to raise an army to oppose Charles and his response was to blunder about trying to put an English army together on the cheap. Wars need more money than even Charles was able to raise and after he was forced into a humiliating peace with the Scots he had to call a Parliament in November 1640 to ask for money to launch a second campaign. They were 'not amused'. Charles' arrogant and persistent misuse of his customary privileges alienated the country gentlemen, lawyers and merchants (the equivalent of today's middle England) who made up the House of Commons many of whom had come to believe that the king had been acting unconstitutionally. They quickly dismantled the apparatus of his personal rule, impeached his ablest advisor, the earl of Strafford, released those he had wrongfully imprisoned and insisted that Parliament could only be dissolved by its own consent. Frightened into signing Strafford's death warrant, Charles sacrificed a loyal and intelligent servant for his own convenience. It would haunt him for the rest of his life. Later, on the scaffold, Charles told those near him '... an unjust sentence that I suffered to take effect, is punished now by an unjust sentence on me'.

After agreeing to various concessions and compromises, Charles then lost patience with all he was being asked to yield and, encouraged by his queen to root out the worst offenders, he entered the House of Commons in January 1642 intent on arresting five of its leading members. Warned of his arrival these five escaped via a back door and Charles was left murmuring that 'all my birds have flown' and the scene was set for the first and last Civil War to be fought among the English.

After reigning for just seventeen years Charles raised his standard at Nottingham in 1642 and the English Civil war began. Its first phase ended in May 1646 when Charles I surrendered to the Scots, promising them the religious presbyterianism that they wanted and he hated, expecting them to help him renew the war with parliament. But the Scots were tired and keen to go home which they did after handing Charles over to the English. During his imprisonment, and convinced that any means were justified to secure his successful reinstatement as king, he tried to set the various parties involved against each other. He promised concessions to every group he could contact, be they Scottish presbyterians, English Anglicans, Irish Roman Catholics and even the Puritan leaders of the Parliamentary army. This behaviour harked back to his duplicity when he was in Spain and reflects the moral isolation of one insulated by wealth and privilege to such an extent that even the blaringly obvious contradictions in his mendacity are hidden from him. In the end the army, exasperated by his time wasting, duplicity and the Scots invasion of England in the summer of 1648 to put him back on the throne, insisted that Charles be put on trial for waging war on his own people. A dubious High Court of Justice pronounced the sentence that the army wanted and Charles was condemned to death.

During his imprisonment Charles had someone, probably his chaplain John Gauden, write a pious meditation on his sufferings that he titled 'Eikon Basilike' (The Royal Image). This little book, promoting Charles as a misunderstood and saintly royal martyr for the Anglican cause, became a clandestine bestseller. Little known today, it was a massive hit after his death and helped prolong the idea of an eternal, divine and sacred basis to the monarchy in England for the next 100 years. At the 'Restoration' in 1660 it could be brought out and brandished by all those seeking to prove their loyalty to his restored son. If ever a piece of printed propaganda helped establish a new regime this was it.

The execution of a king ordered by a 'committee' of fifty-nine signatories was unknown in the annals of English monarchy. On 30th January 1649, aged 48, Charles I walked out, in full view of the public, to a platform erected outside a window of the Banqueting Hall in Whitehall to meet the headsman. It was a cold winter's day and so the king took the precaution of wearing two shirts so that he wouldn't be seen, however involuntarily, to shiver on a day when he would not want to be accused of being a coward. '*I would have no such imputation*' he declared and with a cool, calm and resigned dignity he lay fully stretched out on his stomach and set his head on the block. The executioner later held the king's head aloft, probably uttering the usual cry of '*Behold the head of a traitor*'. But the crowd did not seem to enjoy the spectacle and are reported to have made '*such a groan... as I never heard before and I desire I may never hear again*'.

Thus ended the life of the second Stuart king of England. Shortly after his death two troops of soldiers arrived to clear the area. Various reports have these soldiers engaging in some macabre entrepreneurial activity: allowing people to dip their handkerchiefs (Richard II would not have approved!) in the blood near the block; selling off pieces of the block and wooden scaffold; selling lumps of bloodstained sand; and charging a large number of people for looking into the king's rough coffin.

That night the king's body lay at Whitehall. It was later moved to the large table in the Dean of Westminster's kitchen where it was embalmed by a Maidstone surgeon named Thomas Trapham, who, nine years later, after serving as a surgeon to Oliver Cromwell, may also have embalmed Cromwell's body. Trapham sewed the king's head back on his body and although pestered with numerous requests for locks of hair and other souvenirs, he swore that he was never tempted to provide them. After embalming, the body was wrapped in cerecloth and then placed in the same coffin that was seen on the scaffold. Shortly after this it was sealed inside a lead outer coffin and moved to St James' Palace.

It now became apparent that Parliament had given no thought to where the ex-king was to be buried. Charles had not expressed any particular location for his burial. A place next to his father in Westminster Abbey might have been appropriate but Parliament were not keen to hear any more 'groans' or to see any demonstrations of mourning by closet royalists during a funeral in London. '*... his burying there would attract infinite numbers of all sorts thither, to see where the King was buried; which was judged unsafe and inconvenient*'.

After some discussion, St George's Chapel at Windsor was chosen. It was inside a castle that could not be entered without permission, it was away from London and with sufficient secrecy few people would observe the final journey of the 'traitor'. Parliament decreed that the cost of the funeral should not exceed £500 and that the body of the king '*...should be privately carried to Windsor without pomp or noise*'. So, at night on 7th February, a week after his execution, the body of the king, in one of his own coaches covered in black, driven by one of his old coachman and escorted by two troops of horse left London for Windsor.

On arrival, the Governor of the Castle, Colonel Whichcote, greeted the body. He was adamant that the funeral ritual could not involve the burial service as set out in The Book of Common Prayer and clearly wanted this business over as quickly and as unceremoniously as possible. In preparation he had started excavating a grave near the tomb of Edward IV. But Charles rested that night in the king's bedchamber. Next day four lords, Richmond, Hertford, Lindsay and Southampton, who had attended the king during the last years of his life, arrived at Windsor and promptly rejected Whichcote's preparations. They wanted a more prominent position in the Chapel for their king and friend, and walked about St George's Chapel tapping the floor with sticks and stamping about to identify any hollow sound. It had been over 100 years since a royal funeral in the Chapel and no one was alive who remembered where the bodies were buried. Eventually right in the centre of the choir, opposite the eleventh Garter stall on the sovereign's side, they found what they were looking for.

After workmen opened it up they found that this was the unmarked vault containing the bodies of Henry VIII and Jane Seymour and luckily it looked like there was room for one more. This space was probably meant for Catherine Parr, Henry's last wife, but she, after remarrying and dying in childbirth, was buried at Sudeley Castle. Some of Charles' servants were concerned that their saintly master should not lie in the same vault as the man who had squandered the revenues of the dissolution that might have been '... *converted to sundry pious uses*'. But the four great lords had no such qualms. The centre of the choir would do them quite well.

The coffin of the king was still unmarked, so the duke of Richmond found a strip of lead and scratched 'King Charles 1648' on it and had it soldered to the main coffin. At that time the year was reckoned to end on the 25th March, so as far as the duke was concerned it was still 1648. The next day, just before 3pm, Charles' coffin was carried out into a snowstorm. By the time it reached the great west door of St George's Chapel a carpet of white covered the black velvet pall draped over it.

Bishop Juxon refused to extemporise a funeral service from memory. If he couldn't use the Book of Common Prayer properly he would say nothing. There would be no service and no prayers. Thus in eerie silence the coffin of King Charles I was lowered into King Henry's vault, placed on two trestles and the snow covered velvet pall thrown over it.

On the accession of Charles II, Parliament, in suitably fawning mode, began discussing with him the building of a proper memorial to his father. The lords Southampton and Lindsay were despatched to identify exactly where in St George's Chapel they had committed the old king, but they returned to report that they couldn't remember where it was. Suffering from a chronic lack of cash, Charles II may have been grateful for their memory loss as it gave him some respite from those who would press him to build a new monument to his father. Some people did know exactly where the old king was buried, as Samuel Pepys visited Windsor in 1666 and was conducted to '*where the late King is buried and King Henry and my Lady Seymour*'. Charles II did however find the money to lavish considerable sums remodelling the State apartments at Windsor. This is somewhat ironic as at the time of his father's death Windsor castle was very nearly pulled down, the relevant bill in Parliament being defeated by only one vote.

Later, in 1678, Parliament revived the idea of a monument to Charles I, and Sir Christopher Wren even designed a grand mausoleum, a circular building surmounted by a large dome, at an estimated cost of £43,000. This would have completely replaced what was then the Wolsey Chapel and is now the Albert Memorial Chapel at Windsor. This space was the site of the first St George's Chapel built by Henry III and modified many times until reaching its present form. It was a mercy that Popish Plots and other matters pushed this scheme aside as Wren's design, huge and resembling a miniature St Paul's, would have been completely out of place near the gothic splendour of Edward IV's main Chapel. Later descendents of the second Stuart king showed little interest in such a grandiose venture and Charles I's grave remained unmarked.

In the early nineteenth century there was much curiosity about the whereabouts of the 'lost King.' Why they kept losing him is not very clear. In 1813 the Duchess of Brunswick (the mother of the then Princess of Wales) died and it was agreed that she should be buried in a small vault close to that of Henry VIII. During these excavations the workmen accidentally damaged the wall to the older vault. Peering through a hole they saw three coffins. The Prince Regent (later George IV) was made aware of the discovery and '*perceived at once, that a doubtful point in history might be cleared by opening the vault*'. The 'doubtful point' presumably being the precise identity of the body in the third coffin?

The Prince Regent, his personal physician, Sir Henry Halford, and three others entered the vault on 1st April 1813. Halford published a detailed account of this event (including a winking left eye at the first moment of exposure), in various journals, confirming that it did indeed hold the body and severed head of Charles I. During this examination the severed head was actually taken out and held up to view. Like others who had opened royal tombs before him, Sir Henry couldn't resist the temptation to sneak out a souvenir. A part of the king's beard, some hair from the back of his head, part of a neck vertebra and a tooth were removed and taken to Halford's home near Leicester. It was said that Sir Henry had the piece of vertebra set in gold for use as a saltcellar. If so, the phrase 'he dined out on the story for ever' could have been made for him. Later in 1837, perhaps to ensure that they didn't 'lose' Charles I again, King William IV had a memorial stone of black marble laid directly above the vault noting that Henry VIII, Queen Jane Seymour and Charles I lie below it and it is this stone that still marks the spot in the choir of St George's Chapel.

In 1888 some disquiet arose in the newspapers about the retention of these relics by the Halford family and the grandson of Sir Henry, perhaps reacting to the outcry, decided to present them to a reluctant Prince of Wales (Later Edward VII). Eventually the Prince handed them over to the Dean of Windsor with a request that they be reunited with the body of King Charles I. Thus, at 6pm on Thursday 13th Dec 1888, six marble squares were once again removed in the choir and the vault opened to view. Those looking through the aperture saw that a smaller coffin already rested on that of the king. This contained the remains of Anne, daughter of Queen Anne (when she was Princess George of Denmark), who died stillborn at Windsor in 1696. One hour later the Prince of Wales arrived and personally supervised the lowering of the small casket holding the relics down on to the centre of King Charles' coffin. By about 9.30pm the same night the vault was closed up and the tragic king, sometimes lost, sometimes found, has remained undisturbed ever since.

Ben Jonson

When Charles became king he inherited, among other things, Ben Jonson, a playwright, masque writer, poet, boozer and brawler, from his father James I. Jonson had been a great friend of Shakespeare's and had served three monarchs: Elizabeth I, James I and Charles I. Charles knew him well. He had commissioned and appeared in a number of Ben's masques and even the humourless Charles might have cast a wry smile over Ben's last performance.

Jonson's rumbustious life ended in August 1637. He had lived in the precincts of Westminster Abbey for most of his life but the eight pounds, eight shillings and ten pence that were the total value of his possessions at his death meant that a funeral in his favourite abbey was unlikely. Some years before, Jonson had been joking with the then Dean about his lying with the poets in the abbey, noting that *'I am too poor for that, and no one will lay out funeral charges upon me. No sir, six feet long by two feet wide is too much for me: two feet by two feet will do'*. Although it was summer when he died, and many people were out of London, Jonson did get a funeral in the abbey and *'all or the greatest part of the nobility and gentry then in town'* attended it.

Later his friends collected a considerable sum of money for a monument to go over his grave, but the disturbance of the Civil War intervened and the cash had to be handed back. However, all was not lost. Later a passer by, acting on an impulse, ordered a brief inscription to be cut into the little square of marble that marked his grave in the north aisle of the nave. He gave the stonecutter eighteen pence for the work, four pence halfpenny a word, for he cut just four 'O Rare Ben Jonson'. A perfect epitaph for one who had lived such an incomparable life. Early in the nineteenth century, when the body of one Lady Wilson was being buried near this grave, the workmen discovered that Jonson's rude coffin had indeed been buried upright. His friend the Dean had taken him at his word and given him his *'two feet by two feet'*. He left the old rough writer standing; 'O Rare Ben' was still not lying down!

OLIVER CROMWELL (born 1599 Lord Protector 1653-1658)

The third man to sign Charles I's death warrant, Cromwell was an unlikely regicide. He would have been four years old when his uncle, and Member of Parliament, Sir Oliver Cromwell rode north to meet James I on his journey south to claim his crown in London in April 1603. Indeed, he might even have met the new king at Hinchinbrooke Abbey near Huntingdon, where James rested a few days with Sir Oliver, who entertained him with some serious feasting. Sir Oliver must have been aware of James' love of the hunt for, as well as a gold cup, he made the new king a present of horses, a pack of hounds and hunting hawks. Sir Oliver was clearly out to gain a few early brownie points before James I got lost among the favour-seekers of London. Stretching our imaginations a bit, James may even have petted the four-year-old Oliver; a brief link to a future tragedy unimagined by either king or boy.

The four-year-old nephew of Sir Oliver was the son of Robert Cromwell, who was the second son of a knight living in Huntingdon. Robert had no land and not much of an income. He married a widow, Elizabeth Steward, who brought with her a welcome, if small, income of around £60 per year. In 1616 young Oliver went to study law at Sydney Sussex College Cambridge, but on the death of his father in 1617 he returned home. Oliver was married in August 1620 to Elizabeth Bourchier, the daughter of a retired London fur trader with extensive lands in Essex. They produced nine children, five boys and four girls. One son died as an infant and two others died one, aged 17, while at school, the other at 21, while serving as an officer in the Parliamentary army.

In 1625 King James I died and his son Charles I became king. In March 1628, through the influence of the Montague family of Hinchinbrooke, the 30 year old Oliver was returned as an MP for Huntington. Charles I dissolved this Parliament in March 1629 and Oliver returned home. It is around this time that Cromwell seems to have suffered from a sickness that affected him both physically and mentally, prompting some sort of personal crisis or nervous breakdown, which in its turn prompted him to turn to God and convert to the Puritan (Calvinistic) faith.

As head of the house it fell to Oliver to find husbands, who would not demand extravagant dowries, for his six sisters and in 1631 he sold most of the family property (possibly to help cover debts incurred in paying those dowry's) in Huntington and moved his family to a farm near St Ives (about 4 miles from Huntingdon). His health was not good. He had suffered severe stomach cramps in 1628 and now a chest infection caused him to wear a red flannel around his throat. Cromwell's financial circumstances improved in January 1636 when his maternal uncle died, leaving Oliver holding substantial leases (worth about £300 per year) on tithes held by the Dean and Chapter of Ely cathedral. By now Cromwell's Puritan faith was strong enough to find him preaching in the houses of others as well as his own. It was a faith that would underpin all his actions from now on and his view of himself as 'God's commander' would grow more intense as the conflict with the king went on. Cromwell's religious conversion aligned him with an intricate web of leading Puritan families around Essex and London, including the family of Robert Rich, earl of Warwick. Bolstered by this support, Oliver was elected as one of the two members for Cambridge to both the Short and Long Parliaments in April and October 1640.

On 22nd August 1642 Charles I raised his standard at Nottingham and the Civil War began. In early 1643, without much military experience to commend him, Oliver Cromwell was promoted from captain to colonel. Oliver made no bones about the kind of men he wanted in his army '*I had rather have a plain russet-coated captain that knows what he fights for, and loves what he knows, than that which you call a gentleman and nothing else...* '.

In August 1643 Edward Montague, second earl of Manchester, was given command of the eastern association and he made Oliver a lieutenant general of the army in February 1644. Oliver commanded the left wing of the cavalry, including three regiments of Scots cavalry, at the great battle of Marston Moor on 2nd July 1644, receiving a nasty flesh wound in the neck before returning to lead the final decisive and victorious charge. After this Oliver was dubbed 'Ironside' and his troops 'the Ironsides'. He wrote to his brother-in-law afterwards '... *Give glory, all the glory, to God ... God made them as stubble to our swords'.* By the end of 1644 Cromwell and Manchester were at loggerheads, each accusing the other of failing to act decisively enough. These quarrels eventually lead to Parliament instituting a self-denying ordinance under which serving MPs were disqualified from military command. Despite this move Cromwell managed to remain both a soldier and an MP! At the same time, Sir Thomas Fairfax was given command of the 'New Model Army', a national force free of the regional envies and limitations that had hindered progress in the war so far.

Cromwell increased his personal prestige by driving half the royalist cavalry from the field at Naseby on 14th June 1645 and then re-grouping his horsemen to return and break the spirit of the royalist infantry. In May 1646 Charles I surrendered to the Scots, hoping to find new friends to continue the war. He was mistaken, as the Scots soon opened negotiations with the English Parliament on terms for handing Charles over to them. These negotiations went on until December 1646, when with a small down payment of the £400,000 promised; the Scots army handed the king over and then went home. Charles I was subsequently taken as a prisoner to Holdenby Hall in Northamptonshire in February 1647 and was later moved to various castles and houses.

In July 1646 Cromwell returned to Westminster where his disillusionment at Parliament's failure to prosecute the war robustly was now overlaid by a deep depression at the back-biting and factionalism that he found there. In February 1647 depression had turned to severe illness as Cromwell reportedly nearly died from an infected abscess, exacerbated by his run-down mental state. Parliament was now keen to disband the army but serious disaffection within it (the army was owed £300,000 in arrears) was growing. Cromwell, ever a bridge between the army and Parliament, was caught up in trying to resolve the incompatible demands of each. In early May 1647 Cromwell, with three others, went down to army headquarters at Saffron Walden to talk with the soldiers about mitigating their grievances.

The accumulation of so many troops at Saffron Walden was leading to a militant atmosphere, akin to that which prevailed among revolutionary soldiers during the early days of the Russian revolution in 1917, with day long debates on grievances, the future political franchise and religious policy. Cromwell was sympathetic to many of the army's concerns but he could not abide those who had signed up to the Levellers radical programme. These radical reformers wanted extensive reforms in society and government and a parliamentary franchise open to all males, except servants. In this heady atmosphere of army disquiet, Charles I was removed from Holdenby by a group of troopers and taken to Newmarket to prevent Parliament negotiating with Charles in London and giving up the freedoms so dearly won by the army. Leveller influence in the army was still growing, as was the army's suspicion that Cromwell and, his son-in-law Henry Ireton, were not representing them forcibly enough.

Between 28th October and 11th November 1647, army regiments sent representatives to Putney church to debate a new Leveller inspired constitution, where the discredited king and parliament would be ignored and replaced by a compact signed by all men who wished to enjoy the rights of citizenship. The Putney debates convinced Cromwell that brokering any kind of settlement with Charles I would not be acceptable to a large part of the army. In Parliament in early 1648 he was beginning to speak as if Charles did not deserve to be restored to his throne, asserting that Parliament '*should not any longer expect safety and government from an obstinate man whose heart God had hardened...'.*

The Scots invasion of England to restore Charles I in the summer of 1648 (the Second Civil War) saw Cromwell's first victory in full command, at the messy three-day Battle of

Preston between 17th and 19th August. It also saw his total conversion to the idea that negotiations with the king must now end and that Charles must be removed from any role in a future government. While Cromwell mopped up resistance in the north, the restless army in London wanted the king brought to trial. Their 'Remonstrance' dated 22nd November 1648 demanded that `the capital and grand author of our troubles, the person of the king ... may be speedily brought to justice for the treason, blood and mischief he is guilty of'. A vote on the 'Remonstrance' in the House of Commons was defeated by 125 votes to 58. At 7 o'clock on the morning of 6th December 1648 the troops of Colonel Thomas Pride were stationed around the House of Commons. Pride was armed with a list of MPs proscribed by the army and he stopped all those so named from entering the chamber. This 'purge' (later known as 'Pride's Purge') left around eighty MPs to form a 'Rump' Parliament. This 'rump' was joined the next day by Lieutenant General Oliver Cromwell who, many contemporaries believed, had contrived to stay away in the north just long enough to avoid being tainted with the drama of purging a Parliament by force.

If this was true perhaps it was because Cromwell was not insensible to the irony that the men who had gone to war with a king because he struck down parliaments that would not do his bidding had now done the same. While the radical preachers of London thundered 'death to the king' Cromwell was not yet set on such a course – he believed that regicide would be counterproductive given the inevitable and extreme backlash, both in England and abroad, that it would provoke. Only when he was convinced that Charles would never agree to abdicate did he see a trial, and the death of the king, as inevitable. As he gazed down at the royal corpse he is said to have murmured 'Cruel necessity'. From the day of Charles' death Cromwell was de facto head of the Parliamentary army. He was first and foremost a soldier, he had always been a reluctant politician, and he had no master plan for the settled future of a kingless Commonwealth. A 'Godly reformation of church and state' was about the extent of his religious and political creed. He saw the 'Rump' Parliament as a necessary expedient until the regime could settle down to hammer out a longer lasting and just settlement.

Military matters would take him away from London for two years from July 1649 until mid September 1651 when he was campaigning in Ireland and Scotland. The campaign in Ireland has stained his name, as it should, for the barbarous way he handled the slaughter of surrendered soldiers, and some civilians, at the sieges of Drogheda and Wexford. At Drogheda his soldiers killed around 3,000 royalist troops including their commander, who was clubbed to death. They also executed 300 soldiers who had surrendered, killed all the Catholic clergy and an unknown number of civilians. At Wexford more than 2,000 people were slain, including a large number of civilians.

The spring of 1650 found Cromwell back from Ireland and being given official command of the New Model Army to take on the Scots. After some strategic errors that left him stranded on the coast at Dunbar, his knack for tactical brilliance returned and he surprised and destroyed the Scots army at the battle of Dunbar on 3rd September 1650. After a year of manoeuvring in Scotland he moved his army north of the main Scottish force, tempting them, and their newly crowned King, Charles II, to invade England, which they did on 9th August 1650. This was a bold move but Cromwell pursued them south, gathering fresh troops as he went. He met the Royalists at Worcester on 3rd September 1651, where his superior numbers crushed them with minimal loss to his own force. Charles II escaped to spend the next nine years in exile in France and elsewhere.

Returning from his Scottish and English triumphs in mid-September 1651, Cromwell was faced with a 'Rump' Parliament whose idea of urgent and fresh elections was to put off its own dissolution until November 1654, and Cromwell wanted an end to it. His patience snapped in April 1653 and he demanded that the 'Rump' now establish a council of forty, drawn from itself and the army, and then abdicate. Faced with this semi-ultimatum, Parliament first agreed to debate his suggestion and then quickly set it aside. On the 20th

April 1653, with troops arranged near the chamber and white with rage, Cromwell took his seat in the commons. When he rose to speak, he started pacing furiously about the chamber, attacking all the members present for being corrupt, self-seeking enemies of the people. *'I will put an end to your prating. You are no Parliament. I say you are no Parliament. I will put an end to your sitting'.* Then with the help of around thirty or so musketeers with 'lighted match' he cleared the chamber and carried off the mace. Once more, force of arms had extinguished a Parliament. The 'Rump' was over!

But what would follow? As usual Cromwell had no master plan, but the army was not slow in coming forward to set up a council of state to run the government on a day-to-day basis. After some debate this council agreed to set up a 'constituent assembly' made up of a 140 'nominated' god-fearing men who had unequivocally supported the parliamentary cause and were committed to religious liberty. This 'assembly' would work over the next eighteen months to set out a new plan for a settled government based on an extended franchise. Whatever they decided it was now clear that little of moment could be achieved without Cromwell's agreement. His ousting of the 'Rump' had brought him immense personal prestige and from this spring of 1653 rumour and counter rumour circulated in London about his future role as an elective king or protector. Surprisingly, after all that had gone before, many people, both high and low, now believed that a return to some kind of monarchical rule was indispensable for the stability and better governance of the country.

Much like the old 'Rump', the 'nominated assembly' soon got bogged down in procedural issues while the reason for their existence, the establishment of a long-term constitutional arrangement for a freely elected parliament, seemed as far away as ever. In December 1653, recognising that they would not meet the agreed deadline for a settlement, a majority of the 'nominees' voted themselves out of existence. Some last ditchers, who remained in their seats, were, once again, forced out of the chamber by musketeers. One of the ex-nominees, a Major-General John Lambert, sensing the mood of the time, now put forward his detailed 'Instrument of Government', which now incorporated an individual as a head of state. Senior members of the army, including Cromwell, had seen an early draft of Lambert's paper and on 15th December 1653 Oliver Cromwell was sworn in as head of state. On 16th December 1653, after a ritual involving the presentation of the great seal, the sword of state and the cap of maintenance, that would have done justice to any medieval king, Cromwell was officially installed as 'His Highness the Lord Protector.'

For the next four years and nine months Cromwell as Lord Protector of the Commonwealth, together with a council of state, would have more power than any king before or after him. Parliaments, based on the army's suggested £200 householder franchise, would be called only every third year and sit for not less than five months, their sitting after that time to depend on the Lord Protector and the council of state. This would mean that there would be long gaps between parliamentary sittings during which Cromwell and his council would rule by decree. Cromwell now took up permanent residence in the palace of Whitehall. But he did not see himself as a king; rather he saw himself as a Moses leading his people out of monarchical slavery to a new Godly and just society.

The first protectorate parliament met on 4th September 1654 but was dissolved by Cromwell without warning on 22nd January 1655. This obviated his being seen to reject the plans for a new constitution that they planned to place before him. In order to improve local security and to stem public disquiet over the taxation necessary to maintain a large peacetime army, Cromwell now embarked on a bold plan to halve both the tax and the army. He proposed replacing regular troops with well-trained militias made up of demobilized veterans and paid for out of a ten percent tax on the income of all convicted or suspected royalists. These militias were to be managed by eleven 'major generals', each responsible for a group of counties and assisted by groups of shire commissioners. This plan was eventually put in place in October 1655, when Cromwell also charged these 'military dictators' to be watchful of the local populace, waging war on vice and promoting the reformation of manners wherever they could. In reality this 'war on vice' meant stopping the performance of plays, forbidding maypoles, restricting ale houses, banning race-meetings, bear baiting, cock-fighting, ancient local ceremonies and processions and ordering shopkeepers to stay open on Christmas day. No other act of Cromwell's was received so badly as the rule of the major generals. That the tax to make all this possible was against all law and custom and smacked of the 'ship money' and other taxes that Charles I had so unlawfully exacted seems to have passed Cromwell by. With the return of Charles II in 1660, memories of these alien impositions among the general population were easy to recall and they soon surfaced to welcome a new lighter, brighter and more convivial regime. Cromwell's second parliament met on 17th September 1656, during which a group of councillors and MPs planned to bring in a draft bill to make Cromwell king. After some soul searching Cromwell rejected the title but accepted a revised constitution under which he could nominate his own successor. Under the terms of the 'Humble Petition and Advice,' passed by this Parliament he could also supervise the establishment of a new House of Lords populated with his own nominees. This new 'upper' house would eventually contain no less than eighteen of Cromwell's near, or distant relations.

He dissolved his third and last parliament in February 1658, after only fourteen days of sitting, after various republican groups had joined together to refuse to cooperate with the new House of Lords. Cromwell's experience with parliaments was not good. Here in the spring of 1658 he was once again an unwilling 'dictator' backed by an army but no representative assembly to recognise or support his actions. To these mounting public cares would soon be added the poignant loss of his daughter, Elizabeth Claypole, his beloved 'Bettie'. Oliver never got over her death, the burden of which, together with his worries over the future settlement of the government, took a serious toll on him physically, leaving him looking old and careworn.

Since the 1630s Cromwell, like many others during his time, had endured bouts of malarial fever, especially during times of stress, and in 1655 he also suffered a series of bladder troubles, including the recurrence of the painful bladder stone that had plagued him for many years. The Royalist surgeon who attended him in 1655, and who affected a temporary cure, would not accept a money payment but drank Cromwell's wine and provocatively toasted Charles II with his glass. It didn't stop Oliver sending him £1,000 the next day that he asked the man to accept *'in the name of King Charles.'* In January 1656 Cromwell also suffered from a painful boil on his breast and was rarely without an attack of gout. On the night of 17th August 1658 he was struck down with severe pains, this time in his back and bowels, and over the next few days he suffered from a series of fits. Whatever was happening to him, Cromwell assured all those around him not to worry for he was convinced that God would not call him yet.

European Malaria rarely caused death but the parasite's destruction of the haemoglobin contained in the red blood cells could cause chronic anaemia that weakened the immune system and rendered the sufferer more susceptible to other diseases. Cromwell had been weakened over many years by the 'tertian' malaria. His bladder stone induced a kidney and bladder infection, leading to a severe case of septicaemia (or blood poisoning) that could be lethal. During Friday 27th August Cromwell suffered severe hot and cold fits, typical of renal failure, which left him semi-conscious. On Monday night, 30th August, the hot dry summer weather gave way to the worst storm in living memory. So keen were later chroniclers and poets to associate Cromwell with either the wrath, or the benevolence, of God that this tempest would often be ascribed to the day of his death. But they were four days premature, and over these four days Cromwell fell into and out of consciousness. Although Cromwell rightly predicted to his doctors on the morning of 3rd September 1658 that *'I shall not die this hour'*, his end did come in the afternoon of that day, the anniversary of his great victories at both Dunbar and Worcester. The malignant bladder stone he had shared his life with for so long now died with him. Dr Bate, in carrying out the post-mortem, noted that Cromwell's spleen was suppurating with infection *'though sound to the eye'*, it was inside *'a mass of disease and filled with matter like the lees of oil'*.

During the later part of his illness the question of who was to succeed the Lord Protector had begun to concern the council and like Elizabeth I, drowsily nodding consent to James I as her heir, the comatose Cromwell is said to have reacted positively when the name of his eldest son Richard was mentioned as his successor. Not the most auspicious beginning for a new dynasty. But first Richard's great father had to be buried. Here the story of the last resting place of Oliver Cromwell turns into a series of competing legends all premised on the idea that the great leader was obsessed with preventing any future insult or desecration to his corpse.

One story has it that Cromwell requested that he be buried secretly somewhere on the battlefield of Naseby and tells of coaches arriving in the dead of night, spades being collected and a field being freshly ploughed over. Yet another one had it that some trusty soldiers and near relations dropped his heavily weighted body at midnight in the deepest part of the river Thames. A third story told how he had commanded that another body be substituted for his in his 'official' grave while he was secretly buried somewhere else, while a fourth story had the living Cromwell opening up tombs in Westminster Abbey so that the bodies could be swapped around leaving it a mystery as to where he would eventually end up. As the prospect of death came on Cromwell suddenly and unexpectedly, it is unlikely that he had time to make detailed plans for his final resting place. The truth, though more prosaic, was not without its dramatic moments.

Dr Bate, one of Cromwell's regular doctors, reported in 1660 that although Cromwell's body was embalmed in the usual manner and then wrapped in two coffins, one of lead, the other of wood, the stench of the rotting spleen could not be eliminated. He said that *'yet the filth broke through them all...'* so it was prudent *'to bury him immediately which was done in as private manner as possible'*. The evidence thus points to Cromwell's body being interred quietly and privately in a vault at the eastern end of Henry VII's chapel in Westminster Abbey sometime in early September 1658. Later, on 20th September, an ornate, but quite empty, coffin was transferred to Somerset House for the official lying in state. If the actual interment was hasty and unceremonious this exhibition, based on the funeral of James I, was to be a splendid reminder of the power and glory of the late Lord Protector. The public were allowed into this solemn theatre of death from 18th October until 10th November. They would pass through three rooms, heavily guarded by Cromwell's old regiments, all covered with black velvet and hung with shields and escutcheons until they reached the fourth room. Here, in the ultimate funereal grotto, they would stand in awe before the bed of state draped in more black velvet but now trimmed with golden fringes and tassels.

On the great catafalque, lit by eight tapers on five foot high silver candlesticks, lay the empty coffin surmounted by a life size image of a regal Cromwell clothed in a rich suit of black velvet, a purple robe trimmed with gold lace and an outer robe of purple velvet, again set with gold trimming. In one hand the effigy clasped a sceptre and in the other a globe. The life-like appearance was given credence by the wax face of the great doll having been carefully crafted from Cromwell's death mask. Just behind the painted head, on a gold-encrusted chair, in full view of all, lay an imperial crown. The Lord Protector may have refused the 'title' of king in his lifetime but with his scruples now lying with him in his vault he was being crowned in melancholy magnificence after his death. Later the effigy was moved from the coffin and stood upright with its glass eyes wide open and the imperial crown now placed on its head.

On 23rd November 1658, nearly three months after his death, the effigy of Oliver Cromwell, now returned to lie on the empty coffin, was solemnly carried in an open chariot, from Somerset House to Westminster Abbey. As was done for the old kings of England, some poor men of Westminster headed up the cortège followed by servants, bargemen, watermen, musicians and then the great and the good of Cromwell's 'court.' It took seven hours to complete the journey through the, largely deserted, streets of London. By the time the procession reached the gloomy abbey, (no one had remembered to arrange for candles or any heating) it was too dark, cold and miserable to do much else but plant the elaborate hearse and its effigy in Henry VII's Chapel and go home. There were no rites, sermons, speeches or orations and the whole grand finale petered out like a damp squib – the spirit of the body in the vault below would surely have expected someone to say something.

It may have come to a gloomy end but things were being said about the extravagance and cost (estimated at c£29,000) of the funeral display. The poet Abraham Cowley noted that *'there had been much more cost bestowed than either the dead man, or even death itself could deserve'*. The Anglican diarist, John Evelyn, enjoyed the end of the tyrant; it was the *'joyfullest funeral that I ever saw; for there was none that cried but dogs, which the soldiers hooted away with a barbarous noise, drinking and taking tobacco in the streets as they went'*.

It is a remarkable testament to the strong hold that Westminster Abbey had on the national feeling that not only did Cromwell and his family end up in Henry VII's chapel but that the other grandees of the Commonwealth also sought to be buried there. Given their 'commonwealth' principles we might think that they would shun the last home of those ancestors of Charles I, to whom the idea of a 'Commonwealth' without a monarch at its head would have been totally repugnant.

As the eldest of Cromwell's sons, Richard Cromwell now found himself as Lord Protector. He had served his father effectively enough as a supporting player, but faced with financial chaos and the growing confrontation between the government and the army he was way out of his depth. Lacking both the charisma and determination of his father, he was forced to dissolve Parliament in April 1659 and he was overthrown in May of the same year. Plagued by debt (the debts of the Protectorate itself seem to have become vested in him), he managed to escape to France in the summer of 1660. Around 1680, using the name of John Clarke, Richard was allowed to return to England. This one-time Lord Protector now sensibly retired quietly into obscurity at Cheshunt in Hertfordshire, *'a little and very neat old man'*, giving no cause for Charles II or his heirs to disturb or molest him. He died aged 86 in 1712 during the reign of Queen Anne and was buried in the chancel of Hursley Church, Hampshire. While hiding in France, Richard Cromwell would have heard that his father's remains were not to rest in peace.

After the restoration of Charles II in 1660, Royalist acts of revenge were mostly confined to those men who had a material hand in the death of Charles I. One effigy of Oliver Cromwell was said to have been burnt on the day of Charles II's entrance into London and another, said to be the very one that graced the funereal 'grotto' at Somerset House, was later hung out of a window in Whitehall. But defiling effigies wasn't quite satisfying enough for the new Royalist Parliament. The living regicides, when found, could be hanged or pardoned but what of those who were already dead? In the House of Commons a Captain Titus suggested that the bodies of Oliver Cromwell, Henry Ireton (died in 1652) and John Bradshaw (died in 1659) be taken up and hanged as traitors at Tyburn.

On 29th January 1661, in what Dr Johnson called *'the mean revenge'* of the Restoration, the corpses of the three chief regicides were taken from their tombs in Westminster Abbey. Other corpses associated with Cromwell, including that of his mother, were also removed at the same time, some being re-buried near St Margaret's Church in Westminster and others placed in a common pit. The body of 'Bettie' Claypole, Cromwell's favourite daughter, was not found and she remains the only member of Cromwell's family to stay buried in Westminster Abbey. The bodies of Cromwell and Ireton were taken to lie overnight at the Red Lion inn in Holborn. Bradshaw's body joined them the next day. At dawn on 30th January the three corpses, still wrapped in their cerecloths, were dragged from Holborn to Tyburn on open hurdles in imitation of the ritual that normally presaged the hanging of live traitors.

Evelyn noted: *'This day – O the stupendous and inscrutable judgements of God! ... were the carcasses of those arch rebels ... dragged out of their superb tombs in Westminster among the Kings, to Tyburn and hanged on the gallows there from nine in the morning until six at night, and then buried under that fatal and ignominious monument in a deep pit, thousands of people who had seen them in their pride being spectators'*. Later in the afternoon the hangman took the corpses down and, with some difficulty given the thick bandaging that surrounded the bodies, hacked off the three heads. It took eight blows to remove Cromwell's head and six for that of Ireton. The headless bodies were then thrown into a deep pit dug beneath the gallows while the heads were later put on poles and stuck on the front of Westminster Hall, where they stayed until around 1684. But was it really Cromwell's headless corpse that was dropped into the pit at Tyburn? His last journey, with that overnight stay at the Red Lion inn, gave rise to the legend that members of his family bribed the soldiers guarding it and substituted another in its place. Given that the head stuck on a pole at Westminster Hall would still have been recognisable to many people and that no one who saw it said that it was other than Oliver Cromwell's head, this theory seems no more than fancy.

A more credible scenario is that after the hanging Cromwell's daughters bribed the soldiers at Tyburn to let them take the headless body away and bury it somewhere else. Newburgh Priory near Coxwold in North Yorkshire, owned by the husband of Cromwell's daughter, Mary Lady Fauconberg, is one location often touted as his last resting place. There is a mysterious kiln-like tomb there which, after re-building work, now lies between two floors. Its fascination is made all the more intriguing by the refusal of successive owners of the Priory to have it examined. The Church of St Nicholas at Chiswick in London is cited as yet another location for Cromwell's body. In the 1670s Mary Fauconberg moved to Sutton Court in Chiswick and this story has it that after saving her father from Tyburn and taking him to Newburgh she then exhumed him again and brought him to London with her to lie in the parish church where both she and her husband were eventually buried.

In the 1880s this church was rebuilt and during the building works the vicar is supposed to have spied three coffins in the Fauconberg vault, one for Mary, one for her husband and one looking like it had been knocked about a bit. He made no detailed examination of the third coffin and, fearing that if it was the body of Cromwell, he might have to suffer crowds of visitors idolizing his tomb, he instructed the builders to seal it up again. The various legends concerning Cromwell's journey around England after his death sit well with a man who was so difficult to read in his lifetime but, without any real proof to the contrary, it seems likely that the headless corpse of Oliver Cromwell lies deep below the ground where the old Tyburn gallows stood. This spot, near the present day Marble Arch, lies at the junction of Connaught Place and Connaught Square in London. In the small RAF Chapel at the eastern end of the Henry VII Chapel in Westminster Abbey, a simple floor plaque set over the site of the original Cromwell vault records *'The Burial Place of Oliver Cromwell 1658-1661'*.

The journey of that lonely head stuck on a pole at Westminster Hall seems to have generated a more reliable provenance. After being blown down during a terrible gale in the 1680s a soldier picked it up, recognised it as Cromwell's, and took it home. His daughter sold it and it later changed hands many times before ending up with one Canon Wilkinson, who on his death left it to Cromwell's old college, Sidney Sussex College, at Cambridge. After various inspections and tests, the skull was buried near the college chapel in 1960.

164

The college has recorded the precise location of the skull but they have no intention of telling any one outside a select few where it is. Old Oliver's skull had, at long last, come to a permanent rest.

Though no king of England, Oliver Cromwell is included here because he rose higher than any other Englishman not of royal birth. In many ways he rose higher than *any* king or queen, for as Lord Protector he was both king and first minister all in one. Cromwell had no originality of view in either politics or economics, and if his dream of an England governed by a parliament acting in the best interests of all the people had succeeded, he would not have had to wrestle with either. The best military leader of his time he was sustained and comforted by a belief that God ordered his victories. For Cromwell, the object of war was to win decisive battles and his strategy was often bold and daring, as before the Battle of Worcester when he tempted his enemy to invade England where, stretching his energy and resources, Cromwell could destroy him more completely. Unlike his military career, his political leadership was marked by humility and self-doubt. In the end his wish to make the world safe for the landowning gentry, alongside his equal desire to transform society by a Godly reformation, proved irreconcilable. His failure to secure the execution of justice in ways that treated the poor on the same terms as the rich was a failure that haunted him during the last years of his life.

CHARLES II (born 1630 reigned 1660-1685)

Charles II was born on 29th May 1630 at St James' Palace. He was the second (but first surviving) son of Charles I and Henrietta Maria, a princess of France. Unlike many previous royal children, Charles seems to have enjoyed a happy childhood, loved and cherished within the bosom of his family. When Charles was six the forty six year old earl of Newcastle was appointed his governor and they got on well together. Newcastle was cynical and despised pedantry and any sort of priggishness or fanaticism. An accomplished horseman he encouraged Charles in athletic pleasures like riding, fencing and dancing. He also lectured Charles on women, prayers, good government and the nature of kingship. Above all he exhorted him to read and to study history, *'that you might so compare the dead with the living; for the same humours is now as was then; there is no alteration but in names'*. Charles had an unusually dark complexion and is often referred to by his contemporaries as the 'black boy'. He was also very tall for his times and with his black eyes, thin moustache and profuse dark hair that he wore to shoulder length, he cut an unusual rather than an obviously attractive figure. Before Charles was eight he was aware of the chaos growing around his father and he started to be moved from house to house for his safety. As civil war threatened Charles moved north with his father and was put in charge of a regiment of cavalry. Later at the age of twelve, his father sent him south to head a new West of England Alliance. After his father's defeat at Marston Moor Charles toured Dorset, Devon and Cornwall trying to drum up support for the royalist cause. With the defeat of the royalist forces at Naseby in 1654 Charles I wrote urging Charles to avoid capture at all costs and to go to his mother in France. She was to have *'the absolute full power of your education in all things, except religion; in that, she is not to meddle at all...'*.

After a failed attack on General Fairfax's parliamentary army, dug in near Truro, Charles left England for the Scilly Isles. He was just short of his sixteenth birthday. After the Scilly Isles he moved on to the island of Jersey where he stayed for a time and was entertained by the ladies until lack of resources and boredom sent him off to France to join his mother. He arrived at St Malo on 26th June 1646 where the eight year old Louis IV took two months before he sent him a note of welcome. The French relatives of his mother, Henrietta Maria, a daughter of King Henry IV of France, were too involved in their own internal strife to help Charles and King Louis IV suggested that Charles marry a rich heiress as soon as possible. Eventually Louis did give Charles a small pension but his mother, always a bully, grabbed it from him to pay her own expenses. It was clear that he was not going to get much help from the French. Help might have come from his sister Mary and her husband William II, the protestant Prince of Orange, but William died prematurely in November 1650 and the possibility of Dutch aid from his brother-in-law died with him.

In July 1648 Charles, who was in Holland at the time, took eleven English ships that had defected to him, and made a crazy foray up the Thames estuary looking for the parliamentary navy. When they met, a storm blew up and drew them apart and Charles had to retreat back to Holland. He had captured several merchantmen along the way and he subsequently sold these to parliament for £12,000. After this he settled down to writing letters to the crowned heads of Europe asking for money and support. Charles learned of his father's execution five days after the event. Apart from his grief which was heartfelt his estate was now desperate. Charles was now Charles II, outside England at least, and parliament condemned him to death in absentia. Lack of food and lack of money to buy food for himself and his servants was condemnation enough at this time. He would have to take drastic action.

In early 1650, Charles turned to the traditional home of The Stuarts, Scotland, for help. This was a tragic episode as Charles soon found himself embroiled in some shameless bargaining with the Scots. In return for their support in restoring him to the throne they wanted nothing less than his total commitment to the Covenanters creed of the presbyterian

Kirk, not just in Scotland, but also in England and Ireland and within his own household. Charles knew that these terms were impossible to deliver in England, let alone in Ireland. But, like his father in 1648, the need to get his throne back overrode all other considerations. He would make promises now and, when restored to his crown, he would choose what promises he would keep. But there would be an immediate victim. The bold Marquess of Montrose, an Anglican Scot, had raised an army for Charles in Scotland but now Charles was forced to renounce him as an enemy of the Scottish people, after which the Covenanters executed him. There were echoes of the betrayal of the earl of Strafford by Charles I here. Charles II had to 'hold a candle to the devil...' and it was very uncomfortable. In April 1650, Charles met representatives of the Covenanters at Breda in Holland, just north of the present day Belgian border. After many days of soul searching he agreed to their terms, but only as far as Scotland was concerned. He set sail for Scotland on 24th May 1650.

While sailing off the coast of Scotland, Charles received news that he must swear to introduce presbyterianism in England, something the Covenanters must have known he could never deliver. On arrival, he was also made to denounce the lives of his father and mother. It must have seemed to him that there was no end to the new conditions to which he had to agree in order to get Scottish soldiers into the field. He confided to an Anglican churchman at the time 'The Scots have dealt very ill with me - very ill'. While Charles was being humiliated by these demands, the Scottish army he was supposed to be getting in return for all his concessions were being torn apart by Oliver Cromwell at the battle of Dunbar on 3rd September 1650. The malice of the Covenanters was not confined to Charles. By a new 'Act of Classes' they set about culling their own armies of any strong lads who did not entirely conform to the Covenanter's creed – a bigoted act of stupidity not dissimilar to Stalin's purge of the Russian army before the Second World War.

Charles was crowned King of Scotland at the Cathedral of Scone on 1st January 1651 and his limited progress around Scotland (Cromwell controlled most of the south east and south west) certainly aroused curiosity and interest. But the people of Scotland had been at war on and off for thirteen years. This disputatious country now wanted peace, not new military adventures, and their bonny king riding amongst them looking regal was no substitute for that. Despite these cravings Charles, at the head of a motley band of 12, 000 Scots, entered England on 5th August 1651 and he was proclaimed King of England at Penrith. The further south he marched the more his soldiers elected to go back home and the parliamentary spies in his legions grew. The hoped-for rising of the Anglican royalists never materialised – he was after all at the head of a band of the hated Scots, who were also radical presbyterians!

Charles persisted and on 22nd August his army, exhausted and dispirited, arrived at the city of Worcester. By 29th August Cromwell was in position with 30,000 soldiers and the stage was set for Charles' first and last military command in the field. On 3rd September the fighting began. Many contemporary observers remarked that Charles fought bravely and valiantly with his men until 2,000 of them, to Cromwell's 200, lay dead in the blood-soaked streets of Worcester. Charles' escape from Worcester is a 'Boys-Own' tale of derring-do. This six-week adventure, probably the most important six weeks of Charles' life, drew out his very best qualities. Surrounded by an ever watchful military presence he emerges from this episode as a bold, decisive and courageous young man, suddenly finding out how the other half lived, and rising to the challenges of disguise, flight, rapid concealment and the failure of many well-laid plans.

His small party first made their way, via Kidderminster and Stourbridge, to White Ladies, which they reached at dawn on 4th September. Thereafter Charles was hidden in various places, including the Boscobel Oak, where he remained for a whole day with his head resting on a certain Major Carlos' lap. Many more hiding places were to follow. During this time, with a bounty of £1,000 on his head and more than sixty people involved in hiding or moving him, it was a miracle that no one claimed the reward, the equivalent of half a lifetime's wages for an ordinary workman. After several setbacks and near misses with parliamentary troops, Charles eventually arrived in France, on the coast near Rouen, just before dawn on Thursday 16th October 1651.

His next nine years would be flat, miserable and mostly unproductive. Indeed, instead of continuing the role of dashing young hero, his councillors found him pleasure-loving, lazy and not attentive enough to his business. While in France, Charles had acquired his first known mistress, the beautiful Lucy Walter, by whom he had a son, James, the future duke of Monmouth. Such pleasures did not put food on the table and Charles was almost penniless, living on handouts, depressed and always disappointed by the failure of his diplomatic efforts to secure support for himself and his little court. He moved about from France to Spa, to Cologne, to Dusseldorf as a well-dressed, itinerant beggar. For most of this time Charles had no idea what was going on in England. What information did come his way was months out of date and not always reliable. The idea that under these conditions he could be the dynamic planner of a successful Royalist rising in England, in what was a tightly controlled police state, was a pipe dream.

All the Royalist risings during this period failed. It would take Oliver Cromwell's death in September 1658 to open the door for Charles' restoration. But it would not happen quickly. After two years of near constant bickering and mounting confusion, General George Monck, backed by his northern garrison, marched south to London and led a successful move to restore Charles II. When Charles arrived in London on his thirtieth birthday to cheering crowds in May 1660, it looked as if the clock had been turned back to 1649. Parliament even backdated his reign to that year. But the outward show was deceptive. Too many changes had occurred in the last eleven years for Charles II to simply take up where his father had left off. Parliament, however welcoming, was now a completely different animal from what it had been in 1649. It had tasted powers that it had not known before and it was not likely to relinquish them easily. Charles II, charming, cynical and raised in the school of calamity, would need all his powers to trim his way through the next twenty-five years.

Five issues would dominate those years: dealing with the 'regicides', religion, the Dutch wars, Charles' personal lifestyle and the succession.

Charles II generally wanted to bury the past and his own Bill of Indemnity and Oblivion was eventually agreed by a reluctant House of Lords in August 1660. This granted a general pardon for all treasons, felonies etc., committed since 1637, and all acts of hostility between king and parliament committed during that time were consigned to perpetual oblivion. The exceptions to all this royal forgiveness were the forty-nine men, still living, who had signed his father's death warrant or been instrumental in bringing about his death. Nineteen of these had already given themselves up and been pardoned, two died in Massachusetts and of the remaining twenty eight put on trial in October 1660 only ten were sentenced to death. As noted above, the corpse of Oliver Cromwell and others were disinterred and hung on the gallows at Tyburn.

The religious issues that bedevilled his father had also not gone away; indeed they were now worse. During the Commonwealth, sectarianism had flourished and a thousand dissenting flowers had bloomed. In his 1650 declaration at Breda setting out his 'manifesto' to parliament, he had promised *'liberty to tender consciences'* and, at this time, he probably meant it. But this toleration of dissenters was not a creed that any parliament, Anglican or presbyterian, would accept, and Charles' dream of a land of religious toleration for all was never going to happen. The 'Cavalier Parliament' returned in the elections of March 1661, paved the way for imposing a strict Anglican religious settlement and some two thousand non-conformist clergy eventually left their parishes. Growing in confidence, this parliament became even less tolerant of dissenters, later passing two 'Test Acts' to prohibit non-Anglicans from holding public office or serving in the House of Commons.

Members of Parliament may have suspected, rightly as it turned out, that Charles' tolerance of dissent was directed towards relieving Catholics more than any other group. His mother, his brother James (who openly proclaimed his conversion to Catholicism) and later his wife were all Catholics, as were a number of his close friends. Charles' tolerance was not really aimed at presbyterians, *'not a religion for gentleman'*, at whose hands he had suffered enough humiliation in Scotland. Charles II never felt as strongly Anglican as his father or this latest Parliament, and his initiative, a 'Declaration of Indulgence' in December 1662, to help curb the latter's Anglican extremism, was simply ruled out of hand.

Charles muddied the waters of his own religious convictions when in 1662 he married the twenty-three year old (and very Catholic) Catherine of Braganza, daughter of John IV of Portugal. A small, frail woman, whose teeth stuck out, distorting her upper lip, she was no great beauty - *'they have brought me a bat'*, Charles had exclaimed on first seeing her. The only children she bore Charles would be still-born, but she brought the useful dowry of half a million pounds in cash, Tangier, the island of Bombay and free trade with Brazil and the East Indies – these latter bringing into England its first sugar and mahogany. She survived Charles, eventually returning to Portugal, where she died in 1705.

If he could not to sire an heir with his wife, Charles certainly made up for it with his mistresses. Such a 'stable' of ladies did he have (he acknowledged at least eight as mothers of his children) that he was popularly called 'Old Rowley' after one of the stallions in the Royal Stud. No one has ever been able to make an accurate count of his mistresses; there were at least thirty-nine, who produced fourteen bastards that Charles acknowledged. The current dukes of Buccleuch, Richmond and St Albans are all descended from Charles' bastards. Barbara Castlemaine alone had five children by Charles, founding the noble houses of Sussex, Cleveland, Grafton, Litchfield and Northumberland. The old British House of Lords was full of the descendants of Charles' bastards until its partial reform in 2004. The loveable Nell Gwyn was one of Charles' mistresses who did not get involved in court intrigue, but Barbara Castlemaine was a most notorious user of her place, weaving a massive web of favour-seeking, including pensions for her friends and cash filched from the king's treasury. Charles himself thought that it was not Barbara's meddling that people objected to but her cost, being thought disproportionate to the service she gave.

The plump Louise de Kéroualle was another intriguer who, as well as being a favourite mistress, also acted as a spy for Louis XIV of France. She bore Charles a son, Charles Lennox, whom he made duke of Richmond. She, too, used her place to advance her own wealth and those friends who took her fancy. Being French, Catholic, grand and bumptious she was the least popular of Charles' mistresses but she gave Charles a level of homely comfort he had not known since he was a boy. Louise was also an instrument in aiding his conversion to Catholicism on his deathbed. She survived him and most of her critics, founded a hospital for nuns and died aged 85 in Paris. Many courtiers wondered how Charles could find the time for the problems of government so time-consuming were some of his ladies and Pepys noted sadly that Charles was *'only governed by lust, and women, and rogues about him'*.

The judgement of God on the indolence of Charles' court and the work of French Papists would be invoked as the cause of two of the great calamities of Charles' reign. In May 1665, forty-three deaths from bubonic plague were reported in parishes in London; by June this had risen to 600 and by July, as the excessively hot weather helped nurture the disease, the deaths were being counted in thousands. In September over 30,000 people perished in London alone. The nobility, gentry and, shamefully, many priests, soon had themselves and their families on the roads out of London and Charles moved his court to Oxford. There was nothing he could do to stop the plague and the death of their king would not have helped his subjects either. Charles did, however, put in place restrictions to halt the exodus from the city; he legislated to have public events banned, he appointed examiners for every parish in London, householders were to sweep up the street before their door and wait for their rubbish to be removed, and stray dogs and cats were to be killed. Over 40,000 stray dogs were killed and five times as many cats. The medical authorities of the time still believed that plague was distributed by bad vapours in the air, so the slaughter of animals that might have helped destroy the infected rats that carried the fleas that brought the disease is knowledge that we have that they did not. According to the bills of mortality in London, around 70,000 people were report killed by the plague, but this is almost certainly an underestimate. London was not alone in its sorrow; Norwich, Southampton, Portsmouth, Sunderland and Newcastle were also ravaged by the disease.

The Great Plague of London was shortly followed by the Great Fire of London, which started in Pudding Lane on 2nd September 1666 and spread with great rapidity from one wooden building to another. On the second day of the fire, Charles and his brother James, duke of York, both involved themselves directly in helping to quell the inferno. James directed the fire fighters while the black-faced king ran about encouraging the soldiers to demolish more buildings to create a firebreak. Old St Paul's went up in flames and a stream of molten lead from its roof poured down Ludgate Hill. Although only nine people died, the fires eventually laid waste an area a mile long and half a mile wide and destroyed 13,000 buildings, including 87 churches. Sir Christopher Wren would later be charged with rebuilding many of the churches, including his masterpiece the new St Paul's, where he would be buried in 1723.

Religious questions remained unstable throughout Charles' reign and his pro-Catholic disposition was given yet more credence by his preference for Catholic France on the international stage. The three major powers of Charles' day were the Dutch, the French and the Spanish. He flirted with all of them, but in April 1662 the French and Dutch concluded a defensive alliance. England had been intermittently at war with Holland, over trading rights and maritime supremacy, for almost fifty years. The Dutch were great ship builders and they had a superior fleet that was generally better manned and better equipped than the English fleet. Wherever England was struggling to develop her trading empire, the Dutch were there or close by. In January 1665, the English Parliament, outraged by the many Dutch obstructions to British trade, declared war on Holland. A brief British victory off Lowestoft in June 1665 was followed by the bloody stalemate of the 'Four Days Battle' off Ostend in 1666. In June 1667, with London barely recovered from the Great Fire, and in a bold move that caught the British navy totally off guard, fifty-one Dutch men-of-war sailed up the Thames estuary to the River Medway, where much of the British fleet lay at anchor, looting, pillaging and burning ships with impunity. This great humiliation sent the city, court and government into a panic and Charles was eventually forced to seek peace, and make concessions to the Dutch, at the treaty of Breda in 1667.

The Dutch wars had wasted the public purse and in 1670, desperate for cash, Charles signed the 'Treaty of Dover' with the French that, in return for regular subsidies from Louis XIV, allied England with France against the Dutch and included a secret clause in which Charles agreed to convert to Catholicism and to promote the cause of Catholicism in England. It is unlikely that he ever intended to carry this out but the shadow of 'popery' continued to dominate domestic affairs. In the summer of 1678 a 'Popish Plot' was discovered and, although Charles suspected it to be a Whig concoction designed to destabilise his relations with his brother James, than a real threat, a number of men were executed. Without a legitimate child to follow him after his death, Charles announced that his brother, James, would be his heir. The years 1679 to 1681 were largely taken up with the struggle between the king and his Tory supporters and the Whigs over James's succession. The Whigs being energetically supported by Charles' first illegitimate son, the protestant duke of Monmouth.

The Whig dominated House of Commons, led by lord Shaftsbury, voted to exclude James twice, and only Charles' pressure on the House of Lords, and later military pressure on the Whigs, averted a new civil war. In 1683 a new plot 'The Rye House Plot', aimed at murdering the king and his brother as they travelled back from Newmarket races to London, supposedly engineered by Monmouth and the Whigs, set the scene for Whig executions and exile and the removal of Whig officials from both local and national office. During the various challenges of his reign, one gets the impression of Charles seeking expedients, always experimenting with this or that strategy just to get past the current crisis. Finding a stable basis for government, when consensus on religious matters, so important at the time, seemed impossible, required improvisation and Charles was a great improviser. He was also very interested in experiments and scientific 'gadgets', being something of an amateur scientist with his own chemistry laboratory. Charles helped establish the Royal Society, giving it a royal charter in 1662. He allowed women to act on the public stage for the first time and instituted Newmarket as a centre for horse racing. He also established the beginnings of a small standing army. His health was generally good and he loved to take brisk walks across St James' park with his spaniels, his entourage trailing behind him. He drank moderately, played tennis and rode out at dawn to go hawking and doted on his children.

This healthy, happy king was not to escape the impact of a sudden, unexpected and serious illness in early 1685. The last, miserable, week of Charles II began on Sunday 1st February 1685. On this day, he reported feeling ill and after his usual hearty supper, its only unusual component being two goose eggs, he toddled off to see Louise in her apartments. The king settled down to lounge with his ladies, the courtiers continued playing for high stakes and a French boy sang love songs. Later, and in high spirits, the king went off to bed. Unusually he had a restless night, even talking in his sleep, something he had never done before. In the morning the normal olive skin of the king 'was as pale as ashes' and his speech became seriously impaired. The etiquette of the court allowed for no enquiry as to the king's health or any change in the king's routine. So no one dared point out what must have seemed very obvious to those present, that the king was very sick.

While having his morning shave at 8am on Monday 2nd February 1685, Charles suddenly let out a piercing shriek such as could not be ignored by the most protocol-bound court servant. Some royal doctors were already on hand to dress a sore that had been irritating the king's heel. The first thing they did was bleed Charles taking sixteen ounces of blood from a vein in his arm. James, duke of York, and as many of the king's privy council as could be rounded up were called for as more doctors flocked to apply their various remedies and be the first to 'recover' the king. They shaved his head, put a blistering agent on him and took a further eight ounces of blood. Despite these ministrations, the king recovered for a while and he was able to talk. He told the duke of York how he had awoken feeling queasy and went giddy on leaving his privy closet. Everyone was relieved to see him recover and the official daily report on the king pronounced him to be out of danger after a brief fit.

Despite Charles' recovery, precautions were taken to hinder any communication to the duke of Monmouth and William Prince of Orange in case they should seek to take advantage of the situation. As had happened after Cromwell's death in 1658, all the ports were closed to both incoming and outgoing vessels and extra troops were posted in Whitehall. Thus ended day two of the king's illness. Some days later, outgoing shipping was approved but the lord Lieutenants in the counties were still asked to be on the alert in case of trouble. On Tuesday 3rd February, the king, now attended by twelve physicians, suffered another convulsion and the doctors embarked on an excited scramble to torture the king with good intentions.

More than fifty potions were applied to Charles over the next four days. Sneezing powder was applied to clear his nose; plasters of spurge and Burgundy pitch and red hot irons were applied to his naked feet along with more plasters and cantharides. The red hot irons were also applied to his shaven head. The fiendish cantharides were composed of chemicals extracted from the dried body and wing cases of a blister beetle (Spanish Fly) and used to raise blisters for medical purposes. What raising blisters were meant to achieve is now lost in the history of medicine, as no doubt is the applying of red-hot irons to a patient's head. The value of the oriental bezoar stone from the stomach of an eastern goat, spirits of a human skull and an antispasmodic julep of black cherry water, all of which were inflicted on the dying Charles II like an 'Indian being tortured at the stake', is probably also now lost. On top of all this, some of the doctors had trouble finding veins to carry out the bleeding and some of the scalding medicines caused the king's mouth and tongue to become painfully inflamed.

On Wednesday 4th February, the king seemed to rally but another convulsion in the afternoon quashed any hopes of a rapid recovery. The king did not suffer alone. Some seventy odd lords, privy councillors, doctors, servants and bishops filled his bedchamber. This lack of privacy was to make the execution of Charles' last secret wish difficult to accomplish. One of the five bishops present, Thomas Ken, once the king's private chaplain and now Bishop of Bath and Wells, pressed Charles to take Holy Communion. Charles replied that there was no need for haste and that he was too weak. He also feigned being unable to answer when Ken asked him to declare himself a member of the Church of England.

During Wednesday night, the king became worse with cold sweats and intermittent bouts of fever. By Thursday afternoon the convulsions were mounting and his body was racked with fever. For all their catalogue of treatments, the doctors still did not know what they were treating and when asked what was causing the king's fever and convulsions turned dumb and looked perplexed. Whatever the root cause of his illness, by Thursday night the king was sinking. During those long four days since Monday he had been purged and blistered, sapping his strength without any evidence of amelioration or cure. Now it was time to prepare for death and his wife, and his mistress Louise, were both certain that this must include his conversion to the Catholic faith. No more dangerous plan could have been imagined. The king had always been a public protestant; he had not asked for a priest and the religion was still proscribed in England with Catholic priests still being jailed and even executed.

James, duke of York, a public Catholic, who had suffered innumerable slights and intrigues because of his religion, knew well the dangers if such a conversion was known. However, pressed by the queen and Louise and convinced that Charles would not have to live to explain his wish, he softly enquired of the king if this was his wish. The danger was heightened by James having to repeat his request several times but eventually Charles whispered to him 'Yes with all my heart'. The challenge now was to find a priest and then smuggle him into the king's bedchamber without anyone knowing. The first part proved difficult. All the queen's priests were Portuguese, a language the king had never mastered, and the duke of York's priests were Italian, well known and disliked. By a stroke of luck the seventy-seven year old Father Huddleston was visiting the queen and he agreed to help. Twenty-five years had passed since he had helped Charles after the battle of Worcester, but the coincidence of his being near the king he had helped save, as Charles' life drew to a close, must have seemed providential. James cleared the sick room of all save two trusted friends and Father Huddleston, disguised in a wig and cassock of an Anglican churchman, was smuggled in via a secret door.

Charles could not believe his eyes, 'You that saved my body are now come to save my soul', and was clearly pleased to see his old friend. Huddleston put a number of questions to Charles about his faith. Charles answered them all positively, albeit in the soft whisper that was all he could now muster. The father then sat and prayed with the king for a short time and then, after just forty-five minutes, he left by the secret door. The head of the Church of

England would now spend his last hours as a Roman Catholic. Charles was conscious for most of Thursday night and apologised to those around his bed for the unpardonable time he was taking to die. The surgeons then returned. Death would steal away their chance for settling the matter to their own satisfaction so it should be put off for as long as possible! Charles, normally so stoic and patient with this pack of blunderers, did say that *'I have suffered very much and more than any of you can imagine'*. The king made his goodbyes to his queen and his brother commending his bastard children, excepting the exiled Monmouth, into James' custody and urged him to *'not let poor Nelly starve'*. At 6am on Friday morning the king asked for the curtains to be drawn back so he could watch the sunrise over the Thames for the last time.

The doctors still took more blood, twelve ounces this time, and gave him a heart stimulant, but by 10am the king had fallen into a coma and he died just before noon on Friday 6th February 1685 in his fifty-fifth year. The official description of his illness was 'apoplexy' a generic term of the time for what we would call a stroke. But Charles was never paralysed down one side as stroke sufferers usually are, he recovered his speech totally after Monday morning's convulsions and later he was fully able to answer father Huddleston's solemn questions. Most historians now agree that Charles was suffering from progressive uraemia (a morbid condition resulting from the presence of urinary constituents in the blood normally eliminated by the kidneys) or chronic renal failure probably aggravated by his physicians.

The king had never been more popular than at the time of his death and ordinary people *'walked about like ghosts'* and *'almost every living soul cried before and at his Decease as for the loss of the best Friend in the World'*. The king's body lay in state in the Painted Chamber at Whitehall. Queen Catherine now took centre stage. She received the condolences of the great and the good that came to pay their respects, and although Charles' mistresses were allowed to wear black, their households were not and they were only allowed to draw muslin from the stores for mourning while the queen's household wore cambric.

As surveyor of the fabric of Westminster Abbey, Sir Christopher Wren was involved in constructing a new vault at the east end of the south aisle of Henry VII's chapel, work on which began on Monday 8th February, to be in readiness for the funeral six days later. The funeral after *'the private manner'* took place on the night of 14th February. The king's body was enclosed in a lead coffin bearing a solid silver plate that dated his accession once again from the year of his father's execution. This was then enclosed in an outer wooden coffin covered in purple velvet with gilt metal fittings. Charles' vault was accidentally opened in 1867 during work to put heating in the chapel. His coffin was seen to be very much corroded and had collapsed; making the king's remains visible. Opened again in 1977, it was seen to be in a similar condition. Although James II and his wife accompanied the procession from Whitehall to Westminster, he did not attend the funeral. By custom the Chief Mourner was not the nearest relative and in this case Charles' nephew-in-law, Prince George of Denmark (married to Anne, later Queen Anne), supported by two dukes and sixteen earls, took on the role.

A night time funeral was not unusual as private funerals were held at night for the duke of Gloucester in 1660 and Prince Rupert in 1682, but the low-key nature of Charles' funeral caused some comment. Evelyn recorded that *'... the King was this night very obscurely buried in a vault under Henry 7th's Chapell in Westminster, without any manner of pomp and soone forgotten after all this vanity, and the face of the whole court changed into a more solemne and moral behaviour; the new king affecting neither Prophanesse, nor buffoonery. All the Great Officers broke their white-Staves over the grave according to form'*. Another commentator noted that *'he did not lie in state: no mournings were given: and the experience of it was not equal to what an ordinary nobleman's funeral will rise to'*. One reason for the lack of lavish ceremonial may have been that Charles had left his brother James II little cash with which to pay for one, but the basic solemnities were observed.

As well as shortage of cash, another reason for the low-key nature of the ceremony may have been the king's last minute conversion to Catholicism. Catholic James II would not have wanted his brother to be buried according to the Anglican rite but could not come out and insist on a Catholic one. In death Charles was thus caught in the middle of a religious schism, albeit a secret one, of a kind he had spent his life trying to avoid. The late king's bishops ensured that his funeral service conformed entirely to the rites of the Anglican Church. A greater breach with precedent, particularly after Cromwell's lavish ceremonial, was the lack of an effigy to accompany the coffin. A fine wax and wooden effigy of Charles standing upright was eventually made some months later. The remarkably lifelike face, its lines twisted and sad reflecting the pain his physicians put him through, was regarded by contemporaries as a very accurate representation and was probably based on a cast made after death. The large nose, rather coarse features, prominent lower lip and thick eyebrows are very close to Pelle's famous bust (1682) at Burghley House. The 6ft tall effigy theatrically dressed in the original garter robes (restored in 1933/34) can be seen in full array at the museum in the Norman Undercroft at Westminster Abbey.

The figure is unusual in that it is depicted as if it has been frozen in an act of movement, confirming its primary role as a portrait memorial figure, not a funeral effigy. It was this figure, positioned inside a glass case, which stood over the king's (otherwise almost anonymous) grave until the 1830s. No other monument was erected to Charles II and he had to wait until the nineteenth century before getting his name cut into the paving of the chapel above his vault, together with those of the other occupants.

JAMES II (born 1633 reigned 1685-1689, died 1701)

James II was born, the third (but second surviving) son of Charles I and his wife Henrietta Maria of France, on 14th October 1633. Both James and his elder brother Charles (later Charles II) were present at the battle of Edgehill, the first major battle of the Civil war in 1642, where they both narrowly escaped capture by parliamentary forces. After Edgehill, James accompanied his father to Oxford where he spent some time being tutored by fellows from the university. James was present at the surrender of Oxford in 1646, after which he was taken as a prisoner to St James' Palace in London, from where he subsequently escaped, dressed as a girl, in April 1648. Taking ship from Tilbury, he made his way to stay with his sister Mary at The Hague in Holland. She was married to William II of Orange. Forty odd years later it would be William and Mary's son, William III of Orange, who would be James' nemesis.

In early 1649, James left The Hague and went to Paris to join his mother. On his way there he spent some time at the Benedictine monastery at St Armand, where he experienced, for the first time, life in a Roman Catholic community. On arrival at his mother's court at St Germain-en-Laye, he heard of his father's execution and it was there in June 1651 where he also learned of his brother's defeat at the battle of Worcester. For all James knew at that time Charles could have been killed and he was already King James II? But Charles successfully evaded capture after the Battle of Worcester and returned to France to begin a long and penurious exile.

In 1652, needing cash, and after borrowing some money to equip himself, James enlisted in the French army under the command of the Huguenot general, the Vicomte de Turenne. He came to admire and respect Turenne and acquitted himself well in various actions having *'behaved himself with extraordinary courage and gallantry'*. In July 1654 Charles had to leave France and move to Bruges as the French government had begun negotiating an alliance with Cromwell, which, to Charles' dismay, they concluded in 1655. Charles called James to join him in Bruges, where in December 1656 their sister, Mary Princess of Orange, visited them accompanied by her maid of honour, Anne, the daughter of Charles' loyal councillor Edward Hyde. This meeting may have sparked a romance for by November 1658 Anne Hyde was pregnant by James and he had promised to marry her.

The news of Cromwell's death in early September 1658 cheered the two exiles up immensely until they both realised that the Royalist risings that they eagerly expected to erupt all over England in 1659 failed to materialise. After a miserable Christmas the year 1660 dawned with little to commend it to the disappointed brothers. How could the 'Commonwealth' have survived for more than a year with Cromwell dead? James was just about to accept the King of Spain's invitation to be high admiral of Spain when the news of General Monck's coup in England reached him. He and Charles would be in England by May. His first exile was over, his brother would be crowned King Charles II and he would become Lord High Admiral, not of Spain, but of England.

Like his brother Charles, James was a notorious libertine. In 1677, Charles II confided to the French ambassador that 'I do not believe there are two men who love women more than you and I do but my brother, devout as he is loves them still more'. James enjoyed several mistresses, including: Arabella Churchill, the sister of the duke of Marlborough, Frances Jennings, the sister of Marlborough's wife Sarah, and Catherine Sedley countess of Dorchester, the daughter of a poet and playwright, who retained his affections longer than any of the others. Pondering on her long-term attraction to James, Catherine Sedley mused 'It cannot be for my beauty, for he must see that I have none, and it cannot be for my wit, for he has not enough to know that I have any'.

James is generally thought to have been a dull but assiduous lover, but eight children with his first wife Anne Hyde, seven with his second wife Mary of Modena, four by Arabella

Churchill and one daughter by Catherine Sedley, certainly attest to his sound fertility. Unlike Charles II, James produced legitimate heirs who survived to adulthood; Mary and Anne by Anne Hyde and James (the Old Pretender) and a daughter Louisa by Mary of Modena. After chasing women, his interests narrowed somewhat to horse riding, horse racing and foxhunting. After these came spending money, extravagance and running up debts. '*The prince applies himself but little to the affairs of the country and attends to nothing but his pleasures*'.

As Lord High Admiral of England James did have to 'apply himself' to managing the 130 warships that he inherited from the Protectorate. He presided over a Navy Board made up of seven men, three commissioners and four other officers, including Samuel Pepys as Clerk of the Acts. Pepys recorded that James was '*concerned to mend things in the navy himself and not leave things to other people*'. It is difficult to know, given his other interests, just how involved James was in the day-to-day running of the navy. He was certainly on board the 'Royal Charles' at the battle of Lowestoft during the Second Dutch War in June 1665 and boldly ordered it to follow the Dutch fleet to their base. Unfortunately one of James' household told the crew to break off and wait for the rest of the British fleet. The Dutch got safely home and the timid servant got the sack. James was on board ship again in May 1672 at the battle of Southwold Bay during the third Dutch war, when his own ship was crippled. He moved over to another ship that was then damaged so badly that he had to move to a third. Whatever people thought of James at this time he was always keen to be where the action was and never lacked courage during the military actions he was involved in. These naval close encounters worried Charles II so much that he eventually banned his brother from further exposures of this kind.

After 1670 it became clear that something about the 'old religion' strongly appealed to James. His wife Anne Hyde, who died in 1671, had secretly converted to Catholicism and during 1672 James stopped taking communion in the Church of England. In 1673 he had to resign his post as Lord High Admiral when the passing of the Test Act made Catholics ineligible to hold government office advertising to the world that he was now a practicing Catholic. In September 1673, at the age of 40, James married the fifteen year old Italian, and devoutly, Catholic, Mary of Modena, a girl who was only four years older than his eldest daughter Mary. After 1676 we find James totally committed to the Catholic faith.

The old adage that there is 'nothing as adamant as a convert' was very true of James as he was to hold rigidly to his new religion come what may. It would be the root and stem of the troubles that afflicted the last years of his brother's reign and of the many tragedies that would befall him in the future. As his brother's heir, the contradiction of a Catholic heading up the Church of England was too great for any future compromise to overcome. James was as immovable on this as his father, Charles I, had been over his belief in the divine right of kings. For Charles II, having an heir only three years younger than himself, not a child who could be tutored, formed and moulded, was a challenge that even tested his close and life-long friendship with his brother. After the 'Popish Plot' of 1678, vigorous attempts to stop James acceding to the throne were made in the three parliaments between 1679 and 1681. The Whigs in Parliament, led by the earl of Shaftesbury and Charles II's eldest bastard son, James duke of Monmouth, were well organised and determined to stop James coming to the throne.

Charles II shared James' autocratic instincts, but usually had neither the energy nor the determination to follow them. But during this 'exclusion' crisis he confounded everyone with the energy, wit and skill with which he tackled his enemies and, just, only just, avoided a new civil war. By dissolving or proroguing parliaments before they could pass an 'exclusionist' Bill, he denied the Whigs the oxygen of publicity they needed to stir up the populace and in early 1679, to help lower the political temperature, he sent James to Brussels. James returned, in disguise, in September 1679 on hearing that Charles was ill, but Charles, none too pleased to see him, sent him off again, this time to Edinburgh, where he was to act virtually as a viceroy until his return to England in 1682. During these three years he seemed to have 'ruled' Scotland well for his brother, seeking to bring some peace to the religious conflicts that raged there in as humane a way as possible.

After Charles' death in 1685, and after all the hysteria of the recent exclusion crisis, it was remarkable that the accession of his Catholic brother went off without public discord. James addressed his first privy council thus: *'I shall make it my endeavour to preserve the government in church and state as it is by law established'.* There was a kind of unwritten assumption that James would now practise his faith discreetly, abide by the Test Acts and not seek to flaunt his Catholicism; that he would reign a Catholic in private devotion but a protestant in all matters pertaining to the government. In this atmosphere of assumed compromise, James' first Parliament voted him the same annual revenue as it had for Charles II and later topped it up to fund the army, needed to face two immediate insurrections.

In Scotland Archibald Campbell, earl of Argyll landed at Campbeltown in May 1685 proclaiming James II a Catholic impostor and James, earl of Monmouth, to be the rightful king. James' earlier, diplomatic successes in Scotland now paid off. Argyll only managed to raise 2,500 men and he was soon defeated and then executed. Monmouth, having been expelled from his exile in Holland on James' accession, then landed at Lyme Regis in Dorset in June 1685 and issued a proclamation asserting his 'protestant' claim to the throne. Armed with the extra funds voted by Parliament, James' superior forces, led by John Churchill (later duke of Marlborough), routed Monmouth's army at the battle of Sedgemoor on 5th July 1685. Monmouth was executed in London ten days later and any other captured rebels were tried at the 'Bloody Assizes' held under the auspices of the notorious Judge Jeffries. Hundreds of them were hanged and quartered and around 850 transported to virtual slavery in the West Indies.

These victories were a mixed blessing for James. Mixed because, like Queen Mary after she had seen off Lady Jane Grey, he now began to see them as providential. God wanted him to be king and a Catholic king at that! He now began to insist on Catholic officers being allowed to enter the army and used his royal dispensing power to grant them immunity from prosecution under the Test Acts. James' court became riddled with conflict as Catholic and protestant councillors battled it out to secure offices and favours. In 1687, having been thwarted by Parliament, James issued a Declaration of Indulgence suspending all penal laws against nonconformists, be they Catholics, Quakers, or any other protestant dissenters. Despite its toleration of all forms of 'peaceable' dissent, this action was widely seen as a device for bringing back Catholicism as an equal, or possibly a replacement, religion for England.

The nightmare of many monarchs is their failure to produce a legitimate male heir but for James II the opposite was true. Having produced two legitimate daughters, Mary and Anne, who had both been brought up as protestants, his curse was then to have married a fertile young Catholic who, on 10th June 1688, gave birth to a son, James Francis Edward Stuart. The expectation, widely held on his accession, that James II would be succeeded by one of his protestant daughters, resulting in a happy end to an unhappy Catholic distraction, was now in tatters. Here was a boy, a Prince of Wales no less, who would take precedence over his half-sisters and who would be brought up a Catholic. For diehard Anglicans it now seemed that their nightmare might never end. Mary of Modena, though fertile, had suffered two miscarriages, seen three infants die within their first year and another child die at the age of four. No one expected her to successfully bear a seventh child, let alone such a bonny and healthy one, so scurrilous pamphlets were soon circulating around London suggesting that the queen's new baby was a substitute child that had been smuggled into St James' Palace in a warming pan.

Later that same month, the Archbishop of Canterbury and six bishops, who had refused to read the Declaration of Indulgence in their churches, were acquitted of seditious libel amid wild rejoicing in the streets of London. If James had had eyes to see it, the writing was now clearly on the wall. In just three years he had frittered away the good will that had accompanied his accession. He had badly miscalculated the English gentry's allegiance to the Anglican settlement and severely underestimated their dislike of arbitrary government. In doing so, he had lost the confidence of parliament, the Church and the people. During the summer of 1688, James continued with his plans for a new general election that would pack the House of Commons with men who would do his bidding. He was also planning to make more peers if necessary in order to 'pack' the House of Lords, and his purging of Anglican militias, commissions of the peace, parliamentary boroughs and Anglican clergy in the shires was ongoing. Unknown to him, a group of six wealthy magnates, including the dukes of Devonshire and Shrewsbury, and one churchman, the Bishop of London had other ideas. They sent word to William of Orange in Holland inviting him to invade England.

Despite all the news of William of Orange's preparation for invasion coming out of Holland, it was only on 24th September 1688 that James really came to believe that it was going to happen. Only then did he start to back-track on the steps he had taken to secure total control over Parliament. He called senior clergymen and others in to see him and promised to dismiss Catholic officials and to remedy the wrongs that he had inflicted on both central and local government. No one believed him. After some delays, William of Orange landed at Torbay, on 5th November 1688, the anniversary of that famous Catholic 'powder' plot of 1605. The same easterly winds that brought William's ships to England kept James' fleet becalmed in the Thames estuary, and so James' first and most important defence, the sea, had been easily breached. William and his army stayed on in the West country awaiting intelligence, resting from their voyage and welcoming the steadily-growing flow of deserters from James' army. James eventually arrived at Salisbury to lead his army on 19th November, only to receive conflicting advice from his commanders over whether to march on William or return to fortify London against the inevitable onslaught.

This confusion, allied with a bout of severe nosebleeds, sent the agitated and worn out king to his bed. James, whose instincts tended towards protecting London and his family ('*Tis my son they aim at ... and 'tis my son I must endeavour to preserve whatever becomes of me'.*) and believing that William was closer to him than he really was, eventually withdrew back to London on 23rd November. This move precipitated mass defections from his army. Now John Churchill (the future duke of Marlborough), who owed everything to James, deserted the king and went over to William, as did many other commanders. Churchill's wife Sarah and the Bishop of London took James' daughter Anne to join with William, and James' cause seemed damaged beyond repair. London was now alive with rumour and counter rumour. The French had landed in Cornwall or Kent! The papists of the city were preparing to burn London and massacre all the inhabitants! James' world was collapsing around him. His doctor reported that '*The king is much out of order, looks yellow and takes no natural rest'*. As before, the fatal mix of protestant and Catholic councillors offered up contradictory advice. In ill health and lacking sleep, James also became a victim of perilous thoughts on the death of those kings, like his father Charles I and Richard II, who had been forced to negotiate with an armed power from a position of weakness.

In the end, his worries about the drastic concessions that he would have to make in any negotiated deal with William, the defections from his army and fearful of what might befall him if he stayed in London, he decided to leave. Just after midnight on 11th December 1688 he left London, dropping the great seal into the Thames as he went. He had already sent his wife and infant son to France three days earlier and he now sought to join them. Unfortunately, he only got as far as the Isle of Sheppey where he was captured by a band of roaming seamen and taken to Faversham. From here he was rescued by some loyal troops, and brought back to London. This merry-go-round could not last. Without an army James was now a virtual prisoner in London, only waiting for William to come and close the cell door completely. William on his part wanted James to leave England but, more than that, he wanted it to look as if James had left on his own account. William had James moved to Rochester on 18th December and 'guarded' there in such a slack way that James could easily escape which he did, vowing not to return until his subjects' eyes had been opened. He took a ship for France on 22nd December and arrived there on Christmas day. The 'Glorious Revolution', as the events of 1688 became known, was beginning.

William now accelerated his march on London and by the end of December was in complete control of the civil and military government. He summoned a 'convention' (the great seal at the bottom of the Thames precluding the issuing of writs for a Parliament) whose members had little choice but to recognise the reality that William, backed by an army, was now acting like a king. This convention declared that by seeking to pervert the laws of England and then deserting his people James had abdicated the crown, which was then offered jointly to William and his wife, James' protestant daughter, Mary on 13th February 1689. In France, James' cousin, Louis XIV, gave James comfortable shelter at the palace of St Germain-en-Laye just west of Paris. There James would have stayed, hunting, entertaining and praying quietly if Louis XIV had not insisted that he should claim back his crown by using Ireland as a springboard. Louis was also interested in tying up William's men and ships in the Irish sea rather than having them available to harass him in the English channel. Thus, on 12th March 1689 James landed in Ireland and convened a Parliament in Dublin. This assembly repealed the hated 1662 Act of Settlement, that gave protestants seventy-five percent of the land in Ireland, thereafter guaranteeing William of Orange the firm allegiance of all the alienated protestants in Ulster.

James found himself in a quagmire of disorganisation in Ireland. He either had more troops than he could afford, but with no weapons, or carts full of weapons rusting in places where there were no troops. The indecision that shrouded those December days in London in 1688 returned to him, and after the expensive siege of Derry ended without taking the town on 22nd July, James found himself surrounded by bickering advisers, less French help than he had been promised and the prospect of William leading a professional army to Ireland in the following year. This was exactly what happened. On 14th June 1690 William landed at Carrickfergus and put together an army of 40,000 men whose equipment, sustenance, wages and morale were far superior to James' army. Moving south towards Dublin, William met James' army at the River Boyne. During the subsequent battle of 1st July 1690, and with remarkably few casualties on either side, William crushed James' army and the last Stuart king of England returned to exile in France. He was fifty six and he would never return.

James' last years were spent ruminating on the loss of his kingdom and contemplating God's displeasure. He became convinced that his failures in England and Ireland were the direct result of God punishing him for his youthful sins. He took to hearing mass twice a day, went on retreat to the severe monastery of La Trappe or to the English Benedictine house in Paris and immersed himself in devotional works, even writing some spiritual meditations of his own. He became obsessed with mortifying the flesh that had committed those youthful transgressions, scourging himself and wearing an iron chain, studded with spikes, around his thighs. He now beheld the pomp and state of kingship he had once enjoyed as empty and sinful and began to long for death, despite anticipating a slow journey through purgatory in order to suffer more. Despite his public declarations to the contrary, he had little interest in trying to reclaim his crown. As each scheme for his restoration was put to him he listened but he brought little energy to bear on putting them into effect, always retiring into the passivity of his regular sigh that 'God's will be done'. He did travel to Normandy in 1692 in order to join a French fleet to attack England, but a decisive Anglo-Dutch victory at La Hogue over the French ships that were supposed to carry his army across the channel, scotched that plan.

A further scheme to invade England in 1696 foundered because the French expected the Jacobites in England to rise first while the Jacobites expected the French to arrive before they made their move. It all confirmed James' belief that '*the good Lord did not wish to restore me*'.

Meanwhile, his little court at St Germain-en-Laye grew poor, ragged and melancholy and was made even more miserable by the contagion of faction and intrigue among his supporters that had bedevilled James throughout his life. In 1697, Louis XIV of France made peace with William III, recognising him as king and promising not to aid anyone who might try to overthrow him. He did not repudiate James' claims to the throne but it was clear that, tired of war, Louis had betrayed James and James would never recover from it. Louis XIV was now moving into a mode where James, despite his being a cousin, was becoming more of an embarrassment than a useful tool against protestant England. The poet Mathew Prior who visited James in 1698 found him '*lean and shrivelled*' and in March 1701 James suffered a stroke that partly paralysed his right arm and leg. He seemed to recover but in August he complained of stomach pains and spitting blood, possibly the result of stomach ulcers. On 22nd August 1701, he fell ill again while at Mass and two days later suffered an internal haemorrhage. He remained stable, and lucid, for a week, pardoning his enemies and giving instructions to his servants and his thirteen-year-old son as to how they should behave after his death.

As an ardent lover of many women, James II, like his brother Charles II, may well have contracted syphilis some time after his wife, Anne Hyde gave birth to their two daughters. The effects of syphilis, and the use of mercury to help cure it, can have an accumulative toxic effect damaging nervous and vascular systems and causing changes in personality. The change in James' character later in life, his indecisiveness, his poor choice of councillors and his inability to compromise in any way over religious matters is sometimes ascribed to the toxic effects of syphilis. On 1st September 1701, his condition worsened and the next day he had a fit, after which he lay motionless for two days until his mouth was forced open causing him to vomit a great quantity of blood. Louis XIV visited him on 2nd September but James was too weak to embrace him. Louis promised him that he would recognise his son as James III of England and the two cousins parted in floods of tears. Now James' physicians, following the precedent set by that motley crew who had experimented so extravagantly on Charles II, intensified their remedies, including the dreadful blistering over several parts of his body '*which gave him much torment*'. Like his brother before him he bore these painful ministrations stoically, perhaps considering it another manifestation of the punishment that he justly deserved. By 4th September James was weakened by continual convulsions and shaking in his hands and he died as the result of a cerebral vascular thrombosis on the afternoon of 5th September 1701, aged 67.

James had ordered that his body should be buried in the church of St Germain-en-Laye with the minimum of pomp and ceremony. Louis XIV, perhaps suffering some pangs of conscience about his recent treatment of James, insisted that James' funeral should be handled with care and some ceremony. Strangely, this care involved embalming James' body, cutting it up and sending the pieces to five different locations. Part of his viscera was buried in the church of St Germain-en-Laye, the other part was sent to the English Jesuit College of St Omers. As James had requested his heart was buried at the nunnery of Chaillot, which his mother had patronised, and where James and his wife had spent many hours in contemplation, and his brain was sent to the Scots College in Paris. The remainder of his corpse was buried in the church of the English Benedictines in Paris.

Those involved in all this 'carving', surgeons, servants and soldiers, also took bits of his body and clothing away with them, while some dipped handkerchiefs in his blood to keep as relics of his saintly latter years. His tomb at the English Benedictines in Paris became a popular praying spot; there were even some miraculous cures attributed to his intercession.

James would have probably been appalled at all this, regarding his later years as no more than a modest recompense for his idler and more wasteful days. He would have been even more amazed when, in 1734, the Archbishop of Paris began to hear evidence in support of the case for his canonisation but, in keeping with so many schemes and ventures associated with James, this came to nothing. The digging up of aristocratic graves and monuments that accompanied the French Revolution saw to it that no traces of James' scattered corpse remain anywhere. There is a monument to him at the church of St Germain-en-Laye, but that is all.

James' daughter Mary died seven years before him in December 1694 and his great enemy, William III was dead one year after him. William was succeeded by James' youngest daughter, the very Anne who had gone over to William the 'invader' in 1688. Although we don't often think of her as such, she would be the last Stuart monarch to reign in England. James' son, James Francis Edward Stuart, known as the 'Old Pretender' in England (James III in France) would live on in France, Madrid and Rome, his very existence fuelling the occasional rumbles of Jacobite rebellion in England. He did land in Scotland once in 1715 to support a Jacobite rising organised by John Erskine, earl of Mar, during the time of George I, but his troops were forced to retreat and he fled back to France. He died in Rome in 1766. His son Charles Edward Stuart, the 'Bonny Prince Charlie' of legend, would invade England from Scotland in 1745 and reach as far south as Derby before disagreements among his commanders forced him to turn back to Scotland. He was eventually defeated at the battle of Culloden on 16th April 1746, after which he spent five months roaming the highlands as a fugitive before escaping back to France with the help of Flora Macdonald. He died in Rome in January 1788, a notorious drunk and wife abuser.

James II is not a popular king with biographers. Both he and his brother Charles II are often seen as something of a distraction between the Commonwealth and the real business of setting up a constitutional monarchy after the 'Glorious Revolution'. But at least Charles II had trimmed, whereas James II had stayed stubborn. Charles knew more about the fears of his countrymen with respect to Catholicism than James ever did. Generally honourable in his conduct towards friends and enemies alike, James' lack of political skill in appointing councillors, his inability to comprehend the suspicion his fellow subjects had of Catholics, and his autocratic resistance to any check on monarchical power, lost him supporters even amongst those who welcomed his broader ideas of religious toleration. In the end a kind of fanatical belief in the rightness of his own views stopped him understanding, or even considering, the views of others. It was a fatal flaw.

WILLIAM III (born 1650 reigned 1689- 1702)
AND MARY II (born 1662 reigned 1689-1694)

William of Orange was born on 4th November 1650 at The Hague in Holland, the son of William II of Orange and Mary Stuart, the eldest daughter of Charles I. Mary was born on 30th April 1662 at St James' Palace, the first daughter of James II and Anne Hyde. Thus, Mary's father and William's mother were brother and sister and they both shared Charles I as their grandfather. William's father died of smallpox eight days before William was born and his mother, Mary Stuart, died when he was 10 years old. The Dutch United Provinces were governed by federal states general that drew representatives from the governing assemblies of each individual state. Each state also elected a stadholder and William's great grandfather, William the Silent, who led the Dutch struggle for independence from Spain, had occupied this position in many of the states. This gave the House of Orange a unique position in Dutch politics, wielding almost monarchical power in an outwardly republican system. Unfortunately, William's father, Prince William II of Orange, had quarrelled with the governing classes of the United Provinces, prompting a strong anti-Orange and pro-republican movement that sought to limit the family's influence. Thus little William, instead of looking forward to 'inheriting' his father's honours, spent his childhood amid a series of power struggles within the United Provinces.

At a great assembly of all provinces in 1651, the states of Holland and Zeeland persuaded the other states to leave their posts of stadholder vacant, so that the positions that William would normally have inherited were, for all intents and purposes, abolished. These acts were compounded in 1654, when, during the peace negotiations to end the First Anglo-Dutch war, Oliver Cromwell insisted on a clause excluding William from ever being appointed to his family's traditional offices. After 1660 when William's uncle, Charles II, was restored to the English crown, and the Dutch perceived that trading opportunities might flow from treating his nephew better, this 'exclusion' act was repealed but William's future status continued to fluctuate wildly. Losing a father before he was born and a mother when he was still a child, William's youth was spent isolated from family affection. Lonely and surrounded by a maelstrom of intrigue, there was little time for him to develop the charm and sociability of a Charles II. Instead he grew to be cold, taciturn, aloof, practical and industrious and with little time to suffer fools gladly. None of these is an endearing quality and William would rarely endear himself to his subjects, either as a stadholder or a king.

From the late 1660s it became clear that Louis XIV of France was intent on expanding his realm into the Spanish Netherlands (today's Belgium). In 1672, when he was twenty two, all of the Dutch provinces agreed to make William of Orange admiral and captain general of the United Provinces and William's great life work, of opposing Louis XIV of France whenever and wherever he could, was about to begin. William, though a bold and industrious commander, made an unpromising start. He found the Dutch army under-equipped and under-strength at just 8,000 troops. Against such odds, Louis's army found it easy to cross the Rhine and leave the United Provinces holding just Friesland, Holland and Zeeland. Despite this setback, people in the states did not blame William but revolted against the republicans who had let their defences decline, and state assemblies everywhere were clamouring for William to be made stadholder. On 9th July 1672 amid great ceremony he accepted.

William now became the standard bearer for all those nations who sought to be independent of Louis XIV and he aimed to contain Louis by forging as many alliances against him as possible. By mid 1674, William was at the height of his powers, having achieved considerable successes against the French, but the restless republicans within the states, particularly in Amsterdam, whose merchant citizens provided most of the taxes needed for war, began to fear the scope of his ambition. In 1684, the United Provinces accepted a twenty-year truce with the French, bringing William back to where he was six years earlier. Across the channel in England, William's first cousins, Charles II and James II, both pursued a policy of trying to moderate William's stance towards Louis XIV, who supported them financially, without alienating their majority protestant population, whose sympathies generally lay with the Dutch. However, the treaty of Dover in 1670, that secretly pledged Charles II to become a Catholic and the English to join the French in attacking the Dutch, destroyed whatever was left of this balancing act. In the summer of 1673, a weak Dutch fleet managed a series of brilliant defensive actions in their home waters to prevent an Anglo-French force gaining a decisive victory, and in 1674 the English concluded a separate peace with the United Provinces at the Treaty of Westminster. Family harmony might have been expected to improve after William married James' eldest daughter Mary in London in November 1677, but both sides continued to expect changes in policy that neither could deliver. William's lavish entertainment in 1684 of the duke of Monmouth, Charles II's bastard son, whom Charles believed to have been part of a plot to assassinate him, certainly did nothing to heal past wounds.

When James II's began bullying the English parliament to try and repeal the Test Acts, and to use of his royal prerogative to overrule them, it looked to William as if England could dissolve into internal chaos. An England preoccupied with internal feuds would hardly be inclined to join William in his wars against Louis XIV. William had been in touch with Whig 'exclusionists' since 1671 and now, in 1687, his emissaries to England sought to establish a more effective network of informers and correspondents. By the end of 1687, an embryonic pro-Williamite party had begun to emerge, and in June 1688 the 'immortal seven' secretly invited William to intervene and he landed at Torbay, on 5th November 1688.

His skilfully compiled 'manifesto', published at the end of October 1688, stressed that his sole aim in invading England was *'to have a free and lawful parliament assembled as soon as possible'*. There was no mention of deposing James. William's original objective was to stop James exceeding his prerogative, force him to allow the election of a free Parliament, and thereafter get a united Stuart England firmly committed to war with France. James' unexpected panic and then flight took William by surprise and it changed the dynamics of the expedition. A forcible seizure of the English crown could backfire. Many Englishmen might resent interference from the representative of a country whose navy had been in conflict with England three times during William's lifetime, and yet the way was now open for what could be a peaceful usurpation. The corporation of the City of London, concerned that a power was now needed to maintain law and order in the city, made the first move and invited William into the capital on 11th December. It is probably at around this time that William definitely decided to take the throne, garrisoning London with his own elite Dutch troops and sending all armed Englishmen 50 miles away.

William was an early user of the printed word for propaganda, but his printers now had to change tack. His message now moved from his original declaration seeking a 'free' Parliament, to his personal role as the providential deliverer of England from a devastating constitutional crisis. He made no effort to intervene in the arrangements for electing the 'convention' that met in January 1689, but while they dithered over whether to offer him the crown, he did make it clear that if they didn't offer it to him he would return to the Netherlands, taking all the guardians of law and order with him. Faced with a choice between King William and anarchy, the 'convention' voted to offer him the crown. However, they laid down four conditions, which, while remodelling the English monarchy a little, did not seem to interfere with William's principal ambition of mobilising his new kingdom against France.

Firstly, while conferring actual executive power on William, he did have to share the throne with his wife Mary, ensuring some continuity with the Stuart line. Secondly, William

183

had to accept new oaths of loyalty, which implied that he was only a *de facto*, rather than a *de jure* monarch. Thirdly, William would have to accept a 'declaration of rights' setting out new limits to the royal prerogative before accepting the crown. Fourthly, in order to prevent the importation of a wholly foreign dynasty, William had to acknowledge the right of his sister-in-law Anne (James II's younger daughter) and her children to succeed before any children he might have by a wife after Mary. Just fifteen weeks after landing at Torbay, William had succeeded to the English throne with no bloodshed and most of the Stuart prerogatives intact. No wonder it was soon being called the 'Glorious Revolution'.

England may have fallen into William's lap easily, but Ireland would be another matter. After defeating James II at the Battle of the Boyne in 1690, William had to leave a large force in Ireland before some peace could be restored in 1691. In Scotland, with its separate parliament and Jacobite sympathies, William found himself facing a Jacobite uprising and some hard bargaining. He had to accept the end of the rule by bishops and the end of the royal supremacy over the Church in Scotland before he could secure the Scottish parliament's acceptance of his and Mary's joint rule there. These were much greater compromises than he had had to make in England. William, now straddled two quite different states and began a lifelong juggling act to direct their joint resources to his great matter – the curtailment of Louis XIV's territorial ambitions. William had already learnt to rein in his autocratic tendencies in his battles with the republican United Provinces. They did not want to see their Stadholder acting like a king, and the English Parliament did not want to see an English king behaving like Charles I. William would spend much of the next 13 years, when not on a battlefield, wrestling with an English Parliament that still continued its old traditions of Whig and Tory factionalism. In May 1690, England, horrified by the French support of the Jacobite rising in Ireland, declared war on France. England would later be joined, in a 'Grand Alliance', by Scotland, the Austrian empire, Spain, Savoy and many German states. William's dream was coming to pass and in 1691 he crossed back over to the Netherlands for the first time since 1688, leaving his wife Mary in England.

Mary had joined William from the Netherlands in February 1689 and after their joint coronation in April, she took up the role of dutiful wife and consort. She had no wish to take up any kind of executive role. She had been brought up a protestant and her marriage to William had begun, as so many royal marriages had before, as a matter of diplomatic alliance. Her father, James II, wanted her to marry the Catholic French Dauphin but her uncle, Charles II, bullied James into accepting William of Orange, and they were duly married in November 1677. It is said that when the match was announced to her in October before the wedding, she wept for two days. She was fifteen; she was musical, tall, attractive, passionate, lively and loved dancing, while William was twenty-seven, a foreigner, short, cold, dour and humourless with blackened teeth, a slightly hunched back and a hooked nose. Mary's sister Anne called him 'Caliban'. Mary miscarried in the spring of 1678 and again in 1679, and never conceived again. That her sister Anne also miscarried after a number of pregnancies suggests that the two sisters may have inherited some kind of genetic problem from either their father, the notorious libertine James II, or their mother, Anne Hyde. William took a mistress, Mary's friend Elizabeth Villiers, before two years had elapsed and, while making no move to counteract it, Mary did take it very badly. She had now come to love William much more than she ever thought she would and when he left Holland to invade England in 1688 she said that *'it was as if one had torn out my heart'*.

When some, at the 1689 English 'convention' urged Mary to become Queen Regnant in her own right, she replied *'that she was the prince's wife, and never meant to be other than in subjection to him, and that she did not thank anyone for setting up for her an interest divided from that of her husband'*. This declaration would have been highly gratifying to William, who had made it clear that he had not come to England to be *'his wife's gentleman usher'* and that *'he could not think of holding any thing by apron strings'*. Mary's

184

unequivocal stance on this certainly speeded up the process by which Parliament offered William the crown. However, if he was to pursue his policy against Louis, William was going to be absent from England on a number of occasions. Though he was reluctant at first to involve the needle-working and home-loving Mary in government affairs, he was persuaded that she should act as queen when he was away. It was a necessary step as William would be out of England for over two and a half years between 1690 and 1694; more than any monarch since the 15th century.

Thus, on the cusp of William leaving for Ireland in 1690, the Regency Act was passed which charged Mary *'to exercise and administer the regal power and government of the kingdom'*. It would be the first in a series of instances when Mary would have to act in this way, though William always made sure that she was advised by a council of the principal ministers of state. They in their turn would often be frustrated by Mary's tendency to delay non-urgent matters until she knew William's opinion. Mary's poor relations with her sister Anne began when, in 1690, Anne managed to get the House of Commons to vote her an annual allowance of £50,000, which Mary thought unnecessary and excessive. Later, William's indifference to Anne's husband, the docile George Prince of Denmark, when they were campaigning in Ireland, and his later order preventing George from joining the navy, caused a further rift. The main quarrel between the two sisters, though, took place in October 1691 when William accused Anne's favourite, John Churchill, earl of Marlborough, of corresponding with James II and of conspiring with his wife, Sarah Churchill, to alienate Anne from Mary and himself. John Churchill, an experienced turncoat, had indeed been in correspondence with James II and William cashiered him from all his offices and in January 1692 banned him and his wife from attending the court. In an act designed to provoke, Anne then turned up at Kensington Palace, one month after William's ban, accompanied by Sarah Churchill. The next day, Mary asked Anne to dismiss Sarah from her company and when she refused Mary evicted Anne from her residence in Whitehall. On 17th April, Mary ordered that no one who had visited Anne could now appear at court. The sisters would never meet again.

Mary helped smooth the way for William in ways which we may not find printed sources for today. Her very presence at the court, her example of piety and devotion, her geniality, enthusiasm and gentleness affected all who met or knew her. She provided a backdrop against which William could pursue his great objective and, via her Stuart blood, gave him a credibility that could not be ignored. How much her devotion and love had sustained the taciturn William in managing his complex affairs would only emerge during her final illness. During the latter half of 1694 London was beset by a virulent strain of smallpox that soon reached epidemic proportions. Smallpox was transferred from person to person, though victims of the disease were infectious to others for only a short time. It is characterised by initial symptoms that resemble influenza and then a rash that spreads over the body, eventually developing into pus-filled blisters. During November and December 1694, the weather was also very cold so that many London citizens, their immune systems weakened by head colds, were more easily infected. Mary had had a cold in the autumn and her friends were concerned that she might fall prey to smallpox, as, unlike William, she had never caught the less virulent form of the disease, which reduces the risk of a second infection.

On 24th November 1694, Mary was present at a service conducted by her friend Archbishop Tillotson, during which the Archbishop collapsed with a stroke and died a few days later. This clearly upset Mary and it was from this time onwards that she started to feel unwell. On 19th December, she became ill but told no one and called for no doctors. Instead, she shut herself away in her closet at Kensington Palace and started putting her papers in order including burning some that she did not want found should she die. Even at this early stage, she must have believed that she did have smallpox, as she also wrote out instructions concerning her funeral, insisting that no great expense should be incurred, and that her body should not be opened to test for poisoning. She also left a letter, locked in a bedside desk, which touched vaguely, but firmly, on the hurt she had received from William's relationship with Elizabeth Villiers.

Only after putting her affairs in order did she tell William about her illness. He became instantly pessimistic and gloomy. His mother, Mary Stuart, had died of *'the inexorable and pitiless distemper'* and his father had also died from it. He perceived that, whatever was now done, there would be no hope for the queen and in despair he fell to sobbing and exclaiming *'from being the happiest, he was now going to be the miserablest creature upon earth'* and that he had never known a fault in her: *'there was a worth in her that nobody knew beside himself'*. For a time Mary looked like she might recover, when, early on Christmas day, the rash subsided, but this was a 'false friend'. As so often with smallpox, there can seem a time of improvement, when in fact the disappearance of the rash really signifies that the disease has turned inwards, 'sinking' into the patients system. By the evening of Christmas day, it was clear that she was very ill. William now had his camp bed moved into Mary's room and controlled his asthmatic coughing so well that Mary thought he had left the room; but he could not control his weeping. Mary now had blood in her urine, was spitting blood and the doctors could not control the bleeding in her throat. As her physicians struggled against the odds, Archbishop Tenison felt it his duty to tell her she was dying, for which she heartily thanked him and said that now, having put all her affairs in order, *'she had nothing then to do, but to look up to God and submit to his will'*.

On 27th December, she slipped into unconsciousness and died at Kensington Palace at just before 1am on the morning of 28th December 1694; she was just thirty-two years old. William was so distraught that he had to be carried out of her room. He then lay on his bed, motionless, refusing to speak to those around him who, in turn, feared that the shock of Mary's death might kill him. He was inconsolable for weeks after and it became impossible for any group to conduct business with him. The loud lamentations of the warrior king, who normally displayed so little emotion, amazed all those who saw it. William's deep grief had let slip the mask of indifference and shown his true feelings for Mary. Perhaps the cold and dour Dutchman had loved the passionate and easygoing Mary after all? Jacobite pamphleteers saw Mary's death at such a young age as a judgement on a wicked child who had helped to depose her own father, but Mary's admirers saw her early death as God's judgement on a sinful nation, taking away a pious and dutiful queen whom they did not deserve; she was *'a glass by which the crooked age might have rectified itself'*. At St Germain-en-laye, her father, the exiled James II showed no visible signs of sorrow over Mary's death and ordered that there should be no mourning for his eldest daughter.

Mary's body was embalmed the day she died in order to mitigate the well-known putrescent effects of smallpox, but, for some reason, it took almost two months from the day of her death to get her ready for her lying in state at the Banqueting House in Whitehall. This started on 21st February 1695 when the public were admitted to see her lying with her hands crossed over her breast, a crown and sword at her head and at her feet a sword and shield. Four ladies of honour in mourning clothes, each one relieved every half hour, stood at each corner of the corpse, which lay in state from noon until five o'clock every day until 5th March.On that raw, cold day and powdered with snow, Mary's coffin was taken to Westminster Abbey to be buried, Sir Christopher Wren having supervised the construction of a walkway, bounded by rails covered in black cloth, all the way from the Banqueting House in Whitehall to the abbey. Her coffin was followed, for the first time in history, by members of both houses of parliament. Normally, parliament was dissolved by the death of a king or a queen regnant, but King William surviving Mary had created a unique situation, and so her procession was one of the largest, and one of the most expensive, at £50,000, ever held for an English monarch. Her coffin entered the abbey to Purcell's especially composed funeral anthem and after the casket was laid under a black velvet canopy the Archbishop of

Canterbury preached a sermon. It was then lowered into the Stuart vault in the south aisle of Henry VII's Chapel, alongside Charles II. A wax effigy of Mary II was later placed on display in the abbey.

William III had mixed success in dealing with the Whig and Tory factions in his Parliament. His solution was to employ members from both groups in his administration, changing from one group to another depending on how they performed. He chose his councillors for their talent and if they failed him he switched to others who might do better. Thus, neither Whig nor Tory could depend on his patronage as he refused to become the prisoner of one faction. The way was always open for the opposition to come back into office if they could offer a more effective solution. William's mission to secure resources to pursue his war with Louis XIV meant that he was willing to accept changes to his status in England that earlier kings would not have accepted. Although he often stood up to Parliamentary demands that he felt encroached on his royal prerogative, he was just as often forced to give in or compromise to save his war effort.

This almost-enforced cooperation with Parliament would result in a number of significant constitutional changes. A new Civil List Act gave the commons unprecedented control over the king's expenditure; a Triennial Act was passed requiring a new Parliament to be summoned every three years rather than as and when the monarch decided; a Mutiny Act prevented the employment of a standing army in times of peace without the consent of the commons; and an Act of Indulgence permitted Christian non-conformists (but not Roman Catholics) to worship freely subject to specific conditions. The establishment of the Bank of England in 1694 to support the public debt during William's expensive wars was an important step in preparation for it becoming the head of the nation's financial structure.

Finally, one year before William's death, the Act of Settlement in 1701 provided for the succession of a protestant to the throne. If William or Anne died without a child surviving (now a virtual certainty after the death of Anne's only surviving child in July 1700) the crown would pass to Sophia, Electress of Hanover, (a granddaughter of James I) and her heirs. This ensured a Hanoverian succession by passing over the superior hereditary rights of the exiled Stuarts. The religious question that had dominated English politics since Henry VIII was now also made crystal clear. Gone forever was Henry VIII's prescription that the kingdom must follow the religion of its king. Now English monarchs would have to follow the established religion of their people, as Parliament declared it to be *'inconsistent with the welfare of this protestant kingdom for the monarch to be a papist catholic or to be married to a papist'*. No English monarch has been a Catholic or married to a Catholic since. Other clauses, that Judges could not be dismissed without the approval of both Houses of Parliament and that royal pardons were powerless to bar impeachment, were also important.

William's health seems to have broken down to debilitating levels after his return to England from a visit to the Netherlands in November 1700. A lifelong asthmatic, he was now very weak. His doctors could find no particular reason to account for it, but by May 1701 his condition was obviously grave. One doctor diagnosed anaemia for which he prescribed a harmless infusion of herbs and wine. Though worn out, sick and disillusioned William could not succumb yet: there was still work to be done, and in June 1701 he was in the Netherlands again to garner further allies against Louis. This time, he was accompanied by his old enemy Marlborough, whom he now planned to make his successor on the battlefield. William saw the Second Grand Alliance between England, the Empire and the United Provinces signed in September 1701. Most of the German princes would join later. William would not live to see these great forces set in motion; ironically it would be the old turncoat Marlborough who would complete William's dream.

While still involved in the frantic diplomacy of alliance building at The Hague, William suffered severe attacks of asthma, headaches and digestive disorders; and, with both his legs now badly swollen, he could not walk easily without support. Early in November, he returned to England with his old doctor Bidloo attending him. On 21st February 1702, William went out riding at Hampton Court and as he took his new mare Sorrel into a gallop, it stumbled on a molehill and he was thrown, breaking the collarbone in his right shoulder. The bone was quickly reset but was displaced again during an uncomfortable coach journey back to Kensington Palace. Over the next two weeks, the shock of the fall, his swelling legs, his languor and his laboured breathing persuaded all those around him that William was dying. On 4th March he walked in the gallery at Kensington Palace and then sat alone at an open window, enjoying the sun and looking out on the park. He fell asleep and when he awoke the sun had gone and he was cold and shivering.

The next day he developed a fever that caused him such severe sickness that he was unable to retain either food or medicine. During the early morning of 8th March, his doctor, Bidloo, found William gasping for breath and held him in his arms so the king could sleep. Others took turns at holding William up, as he struggled for breath, and at around 5am the king asked to receive the last sacrament. The doors of his bedroom were now opened so that his courtiers, many on their knees and in tears, could witness the ritual. Just before 8am on the morning of 8th March 1702, pressing the hand of his lifelong friend Bentinck to his heart, King William III died. Fastened to his left arm by a black ribbon was a ring containing a lock of Mary's hair.

Two days later the post-mortem revealed that William was badly emaciated, and both his legs were badly swollen, as was his right hand and arm. His left lung was badly inflamed and infected: *'Tis very rare to find a body with so little blood as was seen in this; there being more found in his lungs than in all the parts beside put together'*. It is most likely that William died from a blood clot that became detached, reached his heart and pushed into the vessels going into his lungs. The trauma from his fractured collarbone probably complicated a pre-existing heart condition, causing a terminal pulmonary embolism. The Jacobite toast to *'the wee gentleman in black velvet'*, paying tribute to the molehill that caused the fall that precipitated William's last illness, while not totally accurate, did have an element of truth in it.

As the courtiers left Kensington Palace and trooped off to St James' Palace to salute their new Queen Anne, preparations were made for William's funeral. It was a very quiet affair. William's body was taken at midnight on 12th April to Westminster Abbey, to lie in the same vault as his late wife Mary. The abbey, again hung in black and lit by candlelight, was filled with the voices of the choir who met his coffin at the door and led it into Henry VII's chapel. Politics even followed William to the grave, for in order to placate the English weavers, mourning was in English silk rather than Italian crepe. Queen Anne, still in mourning for her father James II, who had died in 1701, wore black for him and just some purple trimmings in honour of William. Although William had put their quarrels behind them and befriended Anne after Mary died, Anne did no more than she had to do as far as his obsequies were concerned. All was correct, decent and simple but mourning ceased altogether after the coronation on 23rd April. The resolution made by the Privy Council to erect a monument to William in Westminster Abbey was never carried out. In 1705 Daniel Defoe, shocked at the lack of attention given to William's memory, launched an angry attack on English ingratitude. He believed that in return for saving the English from popish despotism William had been treated with suspicion and dislike that *'ate into his very soul, tired it with serving an unthankful nation, and absolutely broke his heart'*.

No effigy was made of William at the time of his funeral but the account books kept by the Chanter of Westminster Abbey show that two figures, one of William and one of Mary, were put on show on Monday March 1st 1725. They had cost £187 13s 2d and had been commissioned by the abbey as a way of generating income. For an extra fee visitors were shown these elaborately dressed, and very realistic, representations of these two monarchs who now stood alongside those effigies of their ancestors that had been set in stone and copper gilt.

The constitutional changes that took place during the reign of William III had huge consequences for the future government of England and Scotland. They laid the foundations for the Act of Union in 1707, for a central banking system that would help fund Britain's growing empire, freedom of the press (which had been granted in 1695) and for Parliamentary scrutiny of the accounts of all the monarchs that followed him. The English never loved 'Dutch William' and they made little celebration of his life and work, but his legacy was one which all Englishmen would cherish and fight to keep.

ANNE (born 1665 reigned 1702-1714)

The younger daughter of James II (duke of York as he was then) and Anne Hyde, Anne was born at St James' Palace on 6th February 1665, just five years after her uncle Charles II had been restored to his throne. She lost her mother when she was six, and when she was eight her father married Mary of Modena, an Italian Roman Catholic who, as the potential mother of male heirs, could block Anne and her elder sister Mary from the crown. In order to shield them from their father's unpopularity as a convert to Catholicism, Charles II insisted that Anne and Mary be brought up as strict protestants. Both daughters thus had an uneasy relationship with their father and stepmother, although for Mary, who in 1677 married William of Orange, it was easier, as she lived in the Netherlands.

Anne's education, like that of her sister Mary was limited to domestic skills such as sewing and embroidery, although she did become very proficient in French. Anne's religious mentor, Bishop Henry Compton, encouraged her in a profound devotion to the Church of England as the one true church and this formed the main focus of her future religious and political life. Between December 1680 and March 1681 George Ludwig, prince of Hanover (the future George I), visited England to consider marriage to Anne. After what is thought to have been a veto on the idea by both Charles II and Anne's father, George left without any formal proposal being made on either side.

Two years later, in 1683, when she was eighteen and he was thirty, Anne was married to another George, this time a handsome Prince of Denmark, who, like his new wife, was no intellectual but he did enjoy eating and drinking and, like Anne, he grew very stout. George was a Lutheran who was born in Copenhagen and who, like William III, was a lifelong asthmatic. George never quite grasped the mechanics of the English language and, although covered in various honorific titles, was generally rated by his contemporaries as an amiable nonentity. Charles II said, *'I have tried him drunk and tried him sober, and either way there is nothing in him'.* William III did not rate him either and kept him out of the military advancement that Anne constantly sought for him.

After her marriage, Charles II allowed Anne and her husband to live in the 'Cockpit' a royal residence located near the site of present day Downing Street. Here, against her father's wishes, she made Sarah Churchill one of her ladies of the bedchamber. Sarah Churchill (nee Jennings) had been a maid of honour to Mary of Modena and in that role became an intimate friend of Anne, who was five years younger. Sarah was strong minded, assertive and sharp tongued, and in late 1677 or early 1678 she married John Churchill, a soldier from a Dorset landed family. This partnership would later have a huge effect on Anne's reign, John in politics and on the battlefield, and Sarah in the chambers and cabinets of Anne's royal household.

Prince George and Anne cultivated a separate little court at the 'Cockpit' where George proved himself to be a faithful and loving husband. Their love would be tested many times in that one arena where love and pain is most tested: that of their children. From 1683 until 1710 Anne had no fewer than seventeen pregnancies with repeated miscarriages. In 1687 a smallpox epidemic took the lives of Anne's two infant daughters and in October of the same year, just as rumours of Mary of Modena's pregnancy began to circulate, Anne suffered her third miscarriage. Only five of Anne's children were born alive and only one child, William duke of Gloucester, lived past infancy. Sadly, William suffered from hydrocephalus, an excess of cerebrospinal fluid that collected, usually under increased pressure, within the skull. This caused the back of his head to swell badly, and he died aged 11 in 1700. His mother and father, already mourning so many dead children, were heartbroken. All of Anne's children were buried in the tomb of Mary Queen of Scots, Anne's great-great-grandmother, in the south aisle of the Henry VII Chapel at Westminster Abbey.

By the end of July 1688 Anne undoubtedly knew of the invitation by the 'immortal seven' asking William of Orange, to come to England to restore the rule of law under the guidance of a 'free parliament'. After William landed in England on 5th November 1688, John Churchill and Prince George deserted James II and went over to William, while Anne, aided by Sarah and Bishop Compton, left London and went north to Nottingham. Not long after her father's departure from London, she was back at the 'Cockpit' with all her women dressed in orange! Anne had long suspected that Mary of Modena's new baby was a substitute child (indeed, she may have been the prime source for the story) and she had become convinced that her father was in favour of restoring Roman Catholicism as the national religion.

For a time Anne wanted to press her claim that she should follow her sister Mary as queen when Mary died, thus dislocating William whose claim rested on Parliamentary invitation rather than on a direct line from Charles I. The Churchills, more in touch with the *real politick* of the situation, advised Anne against pursuing this and in February 1689 the 'convention' called to discuss William's claim received Anne's message that she would give up her right in favour of William. Anne's husband Prince George, now became duke of Cumberland and John Churchill was made earl of Marlborough. The £50,000 per year that Anne received from Parliament in December 1689, against the wishes of William and Mary, but encouraged by Sarah, gave Anne some financial security, and in thanks for her help in securing it Anne gave Sarah a pension of £1,000 a year. From this time onwards Anne and Sarah agreed to write their, often intimate, letters to each other under the names of 'Mrs Morley' (Anne) and 'Mrs Freeman' (Sarah).

In early 1692, William III dismissed Marlborough from all his offices after discovering that he was in secret correspondence with James II. He also banned him, and by implication his wife Sarah, from attending the court. In February 1692, Anne, clearly in defiant mood, came to a formal gathering at Kensington palace with Sarah and this was too much for Mary, who, the next day demanded that Anne dismiss Sarah from her household. Anne stubbornly refused, after which Mary ordered her, and her husband, to leave the 'Cockpit. Mary and Anne met once more, after Anne had given birth to a son who only lived for a few minutes. At this sad moment Mary repeated her demand. Anne refused again and immediately leased Berkeley House in Piccadilly as her new residence. Mary then issued instructions that anyone who visited Anne would not be welcome at court and Mary died in 1694, never having seen her sister again. After Mary's death, William III knew that he must be reconciled with Anne, who was now the heir apparent. He gave Anne most of Mary's jewels and let her have St James' Palace but these signs of reconciliation was at best superficial. Anne's intense dislike of William never abated, while her ties to Sarah and John Churchill grew more intense.

Anne suffered severe bouts of rheumatism during the summers of 1692 and 1693 and by 1700, aged just thirty-five, she was, for all intents and purposes, an invalid. She had great difficulty walking any distance and had to be carried around in specially made chairs. In June 1701, William, correctly assuming that Marlborough would be his sister-in-law's chief advisor when she was queen, brought him out of disgrace. He appointed him ambassador-extraordinary to the Dutch republic and gave him plenipotentiary powers to negotiate a new European alliance against Louis XIV of France and his grandson Philip V of Spain. The new 'Grand Alliance' was signed in September 1701 and Marlborough's career as a victorious commander of the alliance's armies was about to begin. William III died on 8th March 1702 and Anne celebrated the *'sunshine day'* that made her a queen by telling her first Parliament that *'I know my own heart to be entirely English'*. Her accession was celebrated throughout England and she was to remain highly popular throughout her reign.

Although she would never have admitted it, Anne was a beneficiary of William's legacy as the first English monarch to experience the new constitutional settlement forged in

1689. By attempting to rule through men of experience and skill rather than promoting one faction over another, William had, just about, managed to keep the country united and, most importantly, his war aims intact. Anne would attempt a similar approach to combating factionalism in parliament and government and she would find it just as frustrating as William had done. She was crowned on St George's day 1702 and later made it very clear that she would pursue William's domestic and international policies without alteration.

Both Sarah and John Churchill now reaped the reward for their intimacy with Anne. John was made captain general of the army, master general of the ordnance, ambassador-extraordinary to Dutch Republic; and, in 1702, he was raised in the peerage to be duke of Marlborough. Sarah became groom of the stole, mistress of the robes and keeper of the Privy Purse. At the height of their powers, the Churchills enjoyed a joint income of around £60,000 per annum. The high Tories hailed Anne as a firm supporter of Anglican protestantism and urged her to purge Whig influence at every level of the government.

The Tories, however, did not hail the rise of the Marlboroughs and they stopped Anne handing over an annual Post Office pension of £5,000 to them, earning the lifelong hatred of Sarah Churchill for their pains. But Anne ignored Tory advice when she appointed her friend Sidney lord Godolphin as Lord Treasurer. Godolphin, a reliable and gifted administrator, had served both Charles II and William III at the treasury but his continued correspondence with James II in exile forced him to resign in 1696. As Lord Treasurer, Godolphin would be able to ensure that his friend Marlborough had all the resources he needed to support his military operations on the continent. Throughout the war, Marlborough and Godolphin would rely on the support of the moderate Tories and Whigs for voting the heavy taxes that were needed to prosecute the war of The Spanish Succession against France.

On her accession, Anne kept Robert Harley, a moderate Tory, as Speaker of the commons and in 1704 made him Secretary of State. Elected as an MP in 1689, Harley had helped secure the Triennial Act of 1694 and he maintained a formidable intelligence network that helped him secure support for the Anglo-Scottish Union in 1707. The writer Daniel Defoe was Harley's chief agent in Scotland during the negotiations for the union of the English and Scottish Parliaments. Harley was also a key figure in piloting the Act of Settlement through Parliament in 1701, and in 1710 he became Chancellor of the Exchequer. In 1711, and after an assassination attempt on his life, Anne made him 1st earl of Oxford and Mortimer.

Marlborough, Godolphin, Harley and, not least, Sarah Churchill would form the principal grouping who, sometimes pulling together, sometimes pulling in opposite directions and sometimes plotting against each other, would guide Queen Anne through her twelve year reign. Sarah, now virtually a party manager for the Whigs in parliament, constantly bombarded Anne with her prejudices against the Tories believing that, at heart, most of them were secret Jacobites intent on restoring Anne's half-brother, the 'Old Pretender'. Anne steadfastly rejected this stance but was careful, during the sometimes-stormy, correspondence between them, to find words to appease Sarah in order to keep her husband, Marlborough, from resigning his various military positions. For Anne, Harley was the voice of the moderation that she saw as her way through the strident factionalism that surrounded her, and he was often successful in taking the sting out of opposition to Anne's government.

A typical battle was that over the second Occasional Conformity Bill, introduced by the Tories late in 1703. This sought to punish dissenters financially who 'occasionally' conformed to the Church of England if it would help them secure office. Anne was opposed to this Bill and after it failed to pass the House of Lords by twelve votes, the Tories set up the cry of 'The Church in Danger', which Anne saw as a particularly hurtful insult. The crafty Harley counteracted this by putting forward a plan for the financial relief of clergy who lived in the poorest parishes on pitiful stipends. Taken from the Crown's entitlement to its traditional 'first fruits' income from the church, this 'relief' became known as Queen Anne's bounty and, as might be expected, proved very popular among the clergy and easily counteracted the Tory slight against Anne.

Another challenge was regular Whig support for the idea that the Electress Sophia, the mother of the future George I, or a member of her family, should come and reside in England to show solidarity with the protestant succession. Throughout her reign Anne opposed this. She had, herself, been the centre of a 'court in waiting' during William III's reign and she was adamant that she should not have to deal with one. Given her lack of an heir, the question of the succession rarely left the thoughts of both English and Scottish politicians and was always enlivened by continuing Jacobite support for the 'Old Pretender' living in exile at St Germain-en-Laye. It was a question that also gained added urgency as the queen's physical condition deteriorated. The restless Scots were also active in the matter of the succession to 'their' crown. In 1704 they passed the Act of Security. This basically called for a protestant successor to Anne in Scotland but stipulated that it should *not* be the person who inherited the English throne. The English Parliament's passing of the 'Aliens Act' in 1705, designating all Scots not living in England as aliens, and banning all trade with Scotland, was a skilful repost to this, aiming to hit the Scots where it hurt, in their pockets.

In August 1704, Marlborough and Prince Eugene of Savoy inflicted a major defeat on the armies of Louis XIV near a small village on the Danube called Blenheim. In December of that same year, Anne granted Marlborough the royal estate of Woodstock, near Oxford, where he could build a palace to celebrate his great victory. Blenheim Palace was constructed, with public money, between 1705 and 1722. Sarah Churchill never liked it. She considered it to be absurdly expensive and was constantly quarrelling with its principal architect, Vanbrugh.

Like James I and William III before her Anne was keen for the union of Scotland and England. One result of this would be that only the assent of one Parliament, in London, would be needed to guarantee the protestant succession. On 27th February 1706, Anne appointed two groups of 31 commissioners, one Scottish and one English, to sit down and hammer out the terms of 'union'. Within nine weeks they had agreed the terms of a 'treaty' and this was presented to Anne on 23rd July 1706. On 16th January 1707 the Scottish Parliament, amid riots and confusion in Edinburgh, passed the Act that would result in their own extinction. The payment of just over £398,000, to compensate the Scots for taking on part of the English national debt, free access to trade with England and, more importantly, to the very profitable trade with the English plantations overseas, helped sweeten the bitter pill. The union finally took place on 1st May 1707 and was marked by a great thanksgiving service at St Paul's in London, during which Anne wore the combined orders of the Garter and the Thistle.

Anne's husband, George, died on 28th October 1708, aged just 55. Anne had lost her closest friend, confidante and the principal object of her care and devotion. He *'had been throughout the whole of her married life a pattern of domestic affection'*. Anne's grief was said to be unsupportable. She went on kissing George's lifeless body until Sarah Churchill persuaded her to stop. Prince George was buried in Westminster Abbey on 13th November 1708 *'after the same manner of King Charles II, which was privately, at 12 at night'*. His coffin was one of the largest that anyone had ever seen. Like Queen Victoria, 150 years later, but for much less time, Anne sank into a stupor of mourning. She kept George's rooms just as he had left them and often sat there alone with his carpentry tools and books around her. For the next six months she lived in complete seclusion except to visit her chapel, shrouded in black and purple.

Anne's court had never been a very lively place but after the death of her husband it became even duller and more boring than before. Jonathan Swift noted that at one palace function about twenty people stood about in Anne's bedroom hardly saying a word until the queen retired to dinner. lord Chesterfield wrote that *'Her drawing rooms ... had more the air of solemn places of worship, than the gayety of a court'.* Anne had very little conversation that wasn't gossip or tittle-tattle and seemed oblivious to the achievements in the arts, literature and architecture that were going on around her. This was the time of Wren, Defoe, Swift, Addison, Steele and Pope but Anne showed little or no interest in them. She liked to drink spirits, hence her nickname of 'Brandy Nan', and, almost to the end of her life, she loved hurtling across the countryside in a reinforced chariot to go hunting.

Sarah Churchill's relationship with Anne as queen was basically one where Sarah bullied and pestered Anne to support her various causes while Anne invariably replied by doing what she thought best, which was often not what Sarah wanted. This sometimes prompted Sarah to darkly hint that she '*possessed a thousand letters written by the queen*' and allude to '*the stuff not fit to be mentioned, of passions between women*'. This, less than subtle threat to publish letters that could be deeply embarrassing to the queen is the principal foundation for the story of Sarah and Anne's physical intimacy. Anne's cultivation of Sarah's first cousin, Abigail Lady Masham, from 1705 onwards, as her intimate confidante also fuelled Sarah's wrath, prompting further letters hinting at Anne's lesbian tendencies. Anne and Sarah's friendship came to an end, after yet another quarrel in December 1708, and in January 1711 Sarah was finally dismissed from the offices she held at court. Both she and Marlborough went into voluntarily exile on the continent from 1712 to 1714. Marlborough was an exceptional military commander and diplomat who was recognised as such throughout Europe during his lifetime. His victories at Blenheim (1704), Ramillies (1706) and Oudenarde (1708), put England in the forefront of European power and made it a major force in continental politics.

Anne was the last sovereign to 'touch for the king's evil' in accordance with the supposition that the royal touch could cure scrofula and one of those she touched was the infant Samuel Johnson. Unfortunately, a queen's 'touch' could not help Anne herself. From an early age Anne had suffered from short sight and she was unable to read or use her eyes intently for any length of time. When queen she never read state papers but had to have the key points explained to her by her ministers. Anne obviously became pregnant without difficulty but she would have suffered from the inevitable anaemia that followed from so many full term pregnancies. When she was thirty-three Anne developed polyarthritis, a peripatetic arthritis, which caused unpredictable multiple joint pains in her feet, hands, arms and knees.

Throughout her life Anne suffered from a variety of painful ailments which, as well as her hearty appetite, may have contributed to her almost disabling obesity. From the descriptions of these various illnesses we can guess that Anne had an antibody in her blood that, as well as causing miscarriages, produced a cocktail of other effects including fatigue, fever, nausea, joint pain, anaemia, neurological problems, kidney failure and arthritis. This chronic condition, known today as, systemic lupus erythematosus (SLE), is an autoimmune disorder in which the body's immune system, for unknown reasons, attacks the connective tissue, as if it were foreign, causing very painful inflammation. Some versions of this disorder can affect various systems of the body, particularly the joints and kidneys, and these symptoms can periodically subside and recur with varying degrees of severity. One characteristic is the emergence of a red, blotchy, almost butterfly shaped rash over the cheeks and bridge of the nose.

In 1707 Sir John Clerk described a queen crippled with gout: '*Her Majesty was labouring under a fit of the gout in extreme pain and agony ... Her face, which was red and spotted, was rendered something frightful by her negligent dress, and the foot affected was tied up with a poultice and some nasty bandages ... Nature seems inverted when a poor infirm woman becomes one of the rulers of the world'.* In December 1713, Anne became very ill with fever and suffered a loss of consciousness which lasted for several hours. Over the next seven months the queen also appeared to be suffering from an abscess on her thigh but, as only Dr Arbuthnot was allowed to examine this, a second opinion on this was never possible.

On Tuesday 27th June 1714, Anne attended an acrimonious cabinet meeting at Kensington Palace, which dragged on well passed midnight without producing any result. Distraught over the constant bickering among her ministers Anne left the meeting and spent the night weeping in her bedchamber. The next day she attended yet another cabinet meeting to appoint Treasury Commissioners where, in low spirits, silent and withdrawn, she was clearly showing signs of emotional strain. On Thursday morning 29th August, Anne suffered trembling in her hands, a pain and heat in her head and some nose bleeding. Later that day, as was usual when a sovereign was seriously ill, the members of the Privy Council were called for. On Friday morning the queen suffered two violent convulsions which lasted for two hours after which '*she was speechless, motionless and unsensible*'. On rallying briefly, the queen was asked to hand the Lord Treasurer's staff of office to the duke of Shrewsbury, which she did. She could now hardly speak beyond answering 'yes' or 'no'.

The Privy Council, now operating as a 'Privy Council for the Defence of the Realm', moved to alert the chief officers responsible for security in the country. The Governor of the Tower, the Lord Mayor of London, judges, mayors, and garrisons, were notified that the queen was likely to die quite soon and that they should take steps to keep their towns and counties quiet. Orders were issued to lord's lieutenants of the counties authorising them to seize the arms and horses of all Roman Catholics and to keep a watch on all suspected persons. Regiments were moved closer to London, all the ports were closed and arrangements were made to transport British troops back from Flanders in case of need. All of this was to prevent the 'Pretender' gaining any kind of foothold during the vulnerable period between the queen dying and George, the Elector of Hanover, arriving to claim the crown. A message was also sent to Hanover to warn the Elector that the queen could not possibly live and urging him to come to England as soon as possible.

Anne was attended on by no less than seven doctors who, after shaving her head and administering blistering and other painful remedies, could not stop the queen falling into a coma for several hours before dying at around 7.30 on the morning of 1st August 1714. Dr Arbuthnot, one of Anne's doctors, wrote to Swift, 'I *believe sleep was never more welcome to a weary traveller than death was to her*'. Anne's body lay at Kensington Palace for three weeks and on the night of 23rd August her vast, almost square, coffin was conveyed, by means of a specially constructed wooden bridge, from Palace Yard to the prince's chamber in the Palace of Westminster. Her funeral took place the next night. Although it was to be a private interment, she was accorded a noble send off. Her coffin, escorted by three dukes on either side, was carried under its sumptuous canopy by fourteen carpenters, just in case any repairs might be needed, all wearing loose black coats and caps. The Duchess of Somerset, wearing a veil of thirty yards of crepe, was chief mourner, supported by two more dukes. Fourteen countesses, each also trailing twenty-five yard long crepe veils, followed behind. She was buried in the vault before the altar in the south aisle of the Henry VII Chapel alongside her husband, William and Mary and Charles II.

Accounts, dated 1714-15, have been found relating to a payment of £13 14s 3d '*for the head and hands of Queen Anne*', the implication being that a wax portrait head of the queen was made shortly after her death, possibly from a death mask, all in the expectation that an effigy would be set up and displayed near her tomb. But no money was spent on buying the robes and other materials to complete the effigy until 1740. When the effigy was completed the face was an accurate portrait of the queen as she was towards the end of her life and when the whole image was completed it was displayed, as she often needed to be, seated. The significant time gap between the commissioning of the hands and face and the setting up of a full image suggests that these realistic images now had more of a 'memorial' function than the more transient role of an image solely for the day of a funeral. As with the effigies of William III and Mary II, these images developed a 'tourist' value, supplementing the wages of the vergers and minor cannons who showed them to abbey visitors. The effigies of all three monarchs clothed in full royal regalia can be seen in the museum in the Norman Undercroft at Westminster Abbey.

Sarah Churchill's memoirs provided the most immediate source of material for historians examining the reign of Queen Anne, but this was mostly propaganda on behalf of the Churchills. Sarah's image of Anne as a weak and irresolute woman, making every decision on the basis of likes and dislikes, is not born out by the stubborn way Anne resisted both Whigs and Tories during the various crises that beset her reign. The boundaries between the monarchy and Parliament, established after 1688, were still tentative when Anne became queen in 1702. She was the first Queen Regnant since Elizabeth I, she was an invalid, and her country was immersed in a long and expensive war for most of her reign. It had been a struggle for her. She had not been educated or trained to rule, but she was a canny observer and the men who served her always sought her approval. Anne's active support during the war with France enabled Marlborough to achieve his great victories just as her interventions in support of peace after 1710 helped bring the war to an end in 1713. Despite her poor health, Anne was a most active and industrious monarch, presiding regularly over cabinet meetings, holding daily sessions with her ministers and regularly attending the House of Lords, usually incognito. Dull she may have been, but she was never a puppet queen.

GEORGE I (born 1660 reigned 1714-1727)

Although we associate the family of George I with Hanover and German blood through his mother, Sophia, Electress of Hanover, whom Queen Anne was so keen to keep away from England, he was a Stuart, being the great-grandson of James I. His grandmother was Elizabeth Stuart, daughter of James I, who married that Fredrick V, the Elector Palatine, who was intemperate enough to take the offered crown of Bohemia against the will of the Habsburgs, and was soon driven out of both Bohemia and his Palatinate. Their daughter Sophia was more fortunate in marrying a duller, but more stable, man in Ernst August of Brunswick-Lüneburg in 1658, and George Ludwig, their eldest son (later George I), was born at Osnabruck in Hanover on 28th May 1660.

Sophia, as a grand-daughter of James I, would have been Queen of England, after the death of Princess Anne's only surviving child in 1700, had she lived two months longer. Ernest August became duke of Hanover in 1679, when George was nineteen. The destiny of the future George I was uncertain in the whirlwind that was European politics after the thirty years war, and he learned German, French, Latin and some Dutch and Italian but no English, despite his connections to the English royal family. First and foremost, George was a military man. He fought his first campaign when he was fifteen, supporting the Dutch against the French, and was commended for his bravery at the battle of Conzbrücke. He was involved in three more campaigns in that war and later he helped raise the siege of Vienna in 1683. In 1684 and 1685 George and his brothers campaigned against the Turks in Hungary and George later commanded armies in three more continental wars, all of which added to his military lustre. His interest and skill in all things military occupied him for the rest of his life, equaled only by a love of horsemanship and hunting, the latter becoming his greatest passion.

In November 1692, George married the beautiful sixteen year old, Sophia Dorothea, a daughter of his uncle, George Wilhelm duke of Celle. This match was important to George's family as it would secure the future union of the two duchies and improve Hanover's claim to be an imperial electorate. Their first child, George Augustus (later George II), was born in November 1683 and not long after this George and Sophia began to drift apart. Since 1691 George had taken Melusine von der Schulenburg, who was seven years his junior, as his mistress, but when Sophia Dorothea took the dashing Swedish count Philip von Königsmarck, a colonel in the Hanoverian army, as a lover and refused to be discreet about it, or their plans to elope together, her fate was sealed.

George played no part in the murder of the dashing count on 1st July 1694, which was probably carried out by Hanoverian courtiers supported by Ernst Augustus. One story has the unfortunate count being given a false assignation with Sophia from which he never returned. Twenty years later his bones were said to have been found under the floorboards of Sophia's dressing room. George divorced Sophia in 1694 and, after making reasonable financial arrangements for her, confined her to the castle of Ahlden, near Celle, for the rest of her life, ostensibly to prevent her being used as a pawn in European politics. Sophia's son, George Augustus (later George II), was eleven when all this happened and, as his later behaviour towards his father suggests, he may have been badly affected by it. Sophia died in 1726, aged forty-nine, after a 32 years of confinement. In 1698, Ernst Augustus died and George succeeded him as duke of Hanover. After many years of negotiation with the Emperor and after promises of Hanoverian military aid, Hanover eventually became an imperial electorate in 1708. This elector's 'cap' was very important to George's family and was the culmination of his father's dream. The military and political interests of Hanover would thus never be far from George's thoughts whatever else might happen to him.

Contemporary commentators visiting Hanover found George to be a brave and experienced soldier, popular among his people, calm, reserved, not given to losing his temper, frugal in his habits, punctual in paying his debts, courageous, passionate about hunting and his mistress, to the exclusion of other diversions, and zealous in his belief that the French project to dominate Europe should be contained. This was, of course, a description of a man comfortable in his home environment, where he spoke the same language as his councillors and his subjects, a world in which he had been brought up and where he was supported by a network of well-established family ties. Contemporary descriptions of him as King of Great Britain would rarely be as complimentary and, along with other issues, this may partly be due to the huge differences he faced between the show and 'majesty' expected of a king compared to the homely formalities involved in running a small electorate.

The death of Queen Anne's only son, the duke of Gloucester, in 1700 made George's succession to the English throne a real prospect, despite the continued presence of the 'Old Pretender' still loitering at St Germaine-en-Laye. The Act of Settlement of 1701 named George's mother, the Electress, and then him as the nearest protestant heirs to the English throne, and from this time onwards George kept in close contact with English ministers and the Whig faction in Parliament. His mother's death in June 1714 was closely followed by Queen Anne's two months later. Anne died early on the morning of 1st August 1714 and George Ludwig was proclaimed King George I of Great Britain and Ireland at 4pm the same afternoon.

Confident of overwhelming Whig support for his accession, George made his way casually to England, stopping off to enjoy congratulatory festivities held in his honour in Holland. So fearful of death was Queen Anne that she never got round to signing her will and so died intestate. Her only specific bequest was that £2,000 should be distributed in her memory to the poor and, on his arrival, George I agreed to carry this out. Otherwise, all of her estate reverted to the crown. George I ordered that Queen Anne be buried before he came to England and this was done well before he arrived at Greenwich on 18th September, shrouded in swirling fog. George I spent his first night on British soil in the Queen's House in Greenwich park before entering London on 20th September with his son and his mistress, Melusine. She, seeking to ingratiate herself with the London mob as they passed into the city, is reported to have shouted, *'You mistake, my friends. We come here for your goods'.* Melusine bore George I three daughters, none of whom George acknowledged. They were officially described as Melusine's nieces. Made Duchess of Kendal, Melusine was very tall and very thin and in England was given the nickname 'The Maypole'. She acted as an intermediary for government ministers who were reluctant to approach the king directly with their ideas, and later she was heavily criticised for receiving free stock during the scandal of the South Sea Bubble.

George I was crowned king in Westminster Abbey on 20th October 1714, aged fifty four, at that time the oldest person to succeed to the English crown. Though professing to appoint ministers on their merits, he in fact appointed mostly those Whigs who had been constant in support of a Hanoverian succession. He had never forgiven the Tories for signing the separate peace of Utrecht with Louis XIV in 1713 while he had to continue fighting France until Louis made peace with the empire in 1714, and he still suspected some of them as harbouring Jacobite sympathies. The coronation was not entirely without disturbance as some riots were reported on that day in various towns and villages, some of which continued for several months afterwards. The trouble was mostly being fomented by high church Anglicans, who, fearing a rise in protestant dissenter preference under a 'Lutheran' king, began attacking dissenting meeting houses. George reacted decisively by impeaching the leading Tories, arresting some MPs and purging the army of colonels with Jacobite leanings. In 1715, the Riot Act was passed, making it a felony for members of a crowd of 12 people or more to refuse to disburse within an hour of being ordered to do so by a magistrate. These measures were a clear signal of George's intent to use strong measures to protect his succession.

The high Anglicans had some cause for concern as George was eager to assist non-Catholic dissenters and strongly supported the repeal of the Occasional Conformity and Schism Acts in 1719. This Act forced all dissenter teachers to have to get a licence from a bishop before they could teach. After the dominance of the moderate Tories in Queen Anne's later years, the Whigs now insisted on consolidating their power by pressing for the impeachment of former Tory ministers. This was just the kind of violent factionalism that both William III and Anne had strived to avoid, but with the non-English-speaking George in their power they wanted blood. Many of the excluded Tories fled to France and later supported the 'Old Pretender's' abortive attempt at a rising in Scotland in 1715. George I had reinstated Marlborough as captain general of his forces and he oversaw, though Marlborough did not actively command, the forces which put down the Jacobite rebellion of 1715. The fallout from the 1715 rising completely destroyed Toryism as a major political force for the next 40 years. In 1716, the great warrior, Marlborough, suffered a disabling stroke and he died in 1722. His wife Sarah lived on, still meddling in politics whenever she could, until 1744. Their descendent, Winston Churchill, would also, though not on the field of battle, live to be a great war leader.

William III had to operate within the Bill of Rights passed by Parliament after the 'Glorious Revolution' of 1688, but George I had this and the Act of Settlement of 1701 to 'guide' his exercise of monarchical prerogatives. A principal clause of the latter prevented a British monarch from giving hereditary peerages, public offices or land to any Hanoverian not naturalized before the accession of George I. Although an understandable limitation, probably in response to William III's occasional ennoblement of his Dutch intimates, it had the unintended consequence of pushing George's Hanoverian friends into novel ways of making the kind of money that all followers of all courts in the early 18th century expected as a norm. Some of them, set themselves up as intermediaries who, for a fee, would ease the way for petitioners to gain access to the king, and for the London pamphleteers, though much exaggerated, this foreign lust for British gold was a regular front page story. British ministers also felt that they should exercise British patronage, as an essential tool of political power, and so eventually the Hanoverians were squeezed out. Contrary to popular opinion, once he had settled down as king, George I did not surround himself with large numbers of Hanoverian servants. However, he did retain, and even increase, the number of Hanoverian cooks he kept to prepare his favourite Hanoverian food and satisfy his huge appetite.

Another clause in the Act of Settlement of 1701 required a future monarch to obtain the consent of Parliament before leaving the British Isles. Although he had a dedicated Hanoverian office in London to help him deal with his affairs there, George had responsibilities in Hanover that often needed his attention on the ground and this restrictive clause, intolerable to George I and embarrassing to Parliament, was repealed in 1716. In July of that year, George made the first of the six visits he made to Hanover during his reign. Some of these lasted 28 or 30 weeks and were the cause of much criticism at the time. Although some contemporaries and later historians often complained that George I was an absentee king, he only spent a total of two and three-quarter years of his nearly 13 year reign abroad, about half the time that William III was absent during his 13 years.

Like William III, George I was not comfortable with the 'majesty' required of the public face of a British monarch and, like William III, he preferred small intimate gatherings of close friends, mainly German speaking, where he could relax and be more comfortable. These gatherings rarely included his son. George I had never given his son much in the way of real responsibility, either in Hanover or Britain, and, perhaps as a rival in soldiering, he took pleasure in denigrating his son's military success at the battle of Oudenarde, in 1708, where George Augustus had been commended for his bravery by Marlborough. George Augustus was also said to have never forgiven his father for the way he treated his mother and, as a boy, was rumoured to have tried to swim the moat around castle Ahlden to try and see her. In the early years of George I's reign in Britain, it seemed that father and son complemented one another. George Augustus and his wife, the coquettish Caroline of Anspach, gave a friendlier, more open and lighter face to the royal family. They were both well liked, they held dances, card games, they spoke English and cultivated English visitors to their soirées, and life around them was just so much more fun than at the stiff and dour court of George I.

The issue of the Prince of Wales' role in government came to a head in 1716, when George I had to decide what kind of arrangements to put in place while he was away in Hanover. Rather than let him act as regent, George I designated the Prince of Wales as 'guardian of the realm,' an almost empty title with no executive responsibilities. After this the prince declined to attend cabinet meetings and began cultivating those Whig politicians who opposed his father. The intensity of party conflict in England probably surprised George. With the Tories out of office, the Whigs had no political enemies to fight other than those they constructed among themselves. This they did in April 1717, when Robert Walpole and a number of other ministers resigned over what was perceived as George's Hanoverian ambitions in the Baltic and his concerns for Hanoverian interests during negotiations for a post-war alliance with France and the Dutch.

George I's split with his son was confirmed during a scene of family farce at a christening. Later in 1717, Caroline of Anspach gave birth to a son, George William, who was to die in infancy. The king insisted that precedent required the duke of Newcastle, as Lord Chamberlain, to be a godfather to the child. The Prince of Wales, wanting to make a point, objected strongly to this interference in his personal affairs. After the ceremony he publicly abused Newcastle telling him that, *'You are a rascal, but I will find you'*. The confused and fearful Newcastle left the church, mishearing the *'find you'* as *'fight you'* and thinking that the prince had challenged him to a duel. On hearing this George I banned the Prince of Wales from attending court at St James' Palace and ordered him to leave his children in the king's care. In early 1718, like Anne in William and Mary's time, George Augustus and Caroline set up a rival London household at Leicester House (where Leicester Square is now) and welcomed there anyone in opposition to the king, including Robert Walpole when he was out of office. They were to stay there until George I died in 1727.

Neither of the two Georges who followed George I as king enjoyed good relations with their eldest sons, indeed George Augustus, when George II, would confide to his friends his absolute hatred for his heir. Perhaps these Hanoverian kings couldn't cope with the intimations of mortality that came with a visible heir 'in waiting', but this had always been the case. All monarchs had to face the fact that, as they got older, the question of the succession became a regular, and very public, talking point. Henry IV had been filled with fear and trepidation that his wayward son would succeed him, Henry VIII had broken with Rome to ensure a male heir, Queen Elizabeth would not have the question of succession mentioned in her presence and Charles II had risked another civil war to ensure that his brother, James II, succeeded him. William III took sensible steps to ensure that Anne's accession would go smoothly despite his bad relations with her. During the reign of Anne herself, and given her state of health and the two potential heirs (her Stuart half-brother, the Old Pretender and George Ludwig), waiting impatiently across the sea, it became an almost daily talking point.

George I's break with his son initiated something of a popularity contest between the two courts, forcing a reluctant George I to come out of his comfortable seclusion and attempt a more visible, convivial and sociable court. He now sometimes dined in public, took to visiting the homes of Whig grandees near London, took visitors walking in his gardens and even held balls and concerts at Hampton Court during the summer. Improving his 'visibility' by hunting more often near Hampton Court was probably the happiest and easiest of these 'chores' for him. In 1717, as part of his new programme of meeting more people, George I made a carefully planned journey to meet scholars and dons at the 'loyalist' Cambridge University. That this was regarded as such a big event underscored the reality that George hardly knew the country he ruled over and never ventured out of the south of England before he died.

George I did enjoy the theatre, although his attendance during his estrangement from the Prince of Wales was curtailed somewhat by the fear of bumping into his son. George's greatest contribution to the culture of British life was his patronage of George Frederick Handel. Handel had been made Kapellmeister at the court of Hanover in 1710 and he continued to produce music for George I in Hanover and England, where he soon became a national institution. In 1717 he composed his 'Water Music' to accompany a royal progress along the Thames. It was played by musicians in the barge immediately following the king's, and George I was said to be absolutely delighted with it. In 1742 he produced his oratorio the 'Messiah', and in 1749 his 'Music for the Royal Fireworks'. Along with William Hogarth, he was a major benefactor of the Foundling Hospital in London, staging annual concerts there for its benefit. He left the hospital the rights to the 'Messiah'.

The king and his son were formally, if coolly, reconciled in 1720 and Walpole returned to the government just in time to bail the king, his mistresses, much of the British nobility and other courtiers out of the scandal caused by the South Sea Bubble. The South Sea Company had been chartered in 1711 to trade with South America and in 1713, under the terms of the treaty of Utrecht, it was awarded the very profitable Asiento contract to supply slaves to Spanish colonies. The Tory ministers who founded it also saw it as an alternative source of credit to the Whig Bank of England. In 1719, a complicated scheme for the company to assume more of the national debt encouraged holders of government stock to trade it in for the company's stock. The company had agreed to charge the government a lower rate of interest than that which it had had to pay under wartime conditions. The company gained its subscribers, against competition from the Bank of England, by giving bribes, of notional stock holdings, to prominent politicians, courtiers and George's mistresses.

The bubble 'burst' in September 1720 after some big investors perceived that a ceiling had been reached and sold their shares, causing a rapid collapse in confidence. For many savers, large and small, this was a catastrophic result. Many had sold substantial assets, including land and other forms of property, to buy shares at grossly inflated prices. George I, his mistresses and many others lost heavily, some investors lost so much that they had to flee abroad and some committed suicide. Walpole came back, took control and pushed a solution to the Bubble crisis through the commons, which would protect the national debt and save the face of the court and many MPs of all political colours. This success earned him an enduring reputation as a man for 'screening' corruption and fraud in high places. In April 1721, Walpole was made Chancellor of the Exchequer and First Lord of the Treasury with absolute control over patronage. It was his great spring board to an era of Walpolian supremacy, or, as his opponents would later call it, 'Robinocracy'.

Sophia Dorothea had remained unburied for seven months after her death in 1726 and in early June 1727 George I started out on his way to Hanover to sort out her burial. He was apparently in good health and good humour and looking forward to meeting his brother, Ernest Augustus, the sole surviving relative of his own generation, at the bishop's Palace at Osnabruck. He arrived at Delden in the Netherlands at around 8pm on the evening of 8th June where one story has him receiving a letter, written by his wife before her death, prophesying that he would die within a year of her. If he did receive such a letter it did not seem to bother him too much as he happily entertained five or six Dutch ladies who wanted to meet him. The next day George and his convoy of friends and servants set off early, at around 7am. The king revealed that he had been kept awake all night by stomach pains, which he put down to an excess of strawberries and oranges at supper the previous evening. Though urged to return to Delden to rest, George insisted that he now felt fit to travel and that the journey should continue. He did stop on the road to answer a call of nature, and on returning to the coach his face was distorted and he seemed to have lost the use of his right hand. Within minutes he grew very pale and fainted.

As luck would have it, a surgeon was travelling in one of the following coaches and he was able to diagnose that the king had suffered a stroke. George was then lifted out of his carriage and placed on the ground, where he was bled. When he recovered consciousness he signalled for the journey to continue. After being put back into his coach, he fell into a deep sleep, accompanied by heavy and very noisy snoring and the doctor began to fear the worst. The cortège stopped again while various remedies (drawing plasters on his right hand and neck and strong spirits) were tried on the king while he lay in another open field.

The doctor reassured everyone that they could continue and that the movement of the carriage would not worsen the king's condition. Messengers were sent on to Osnabruck to warn Ernst Augustus of the situation and to disperse the people waiting to greet George, so that he could be carried up some back stairs in the palace without being seen. On his arrival at Osnabruck, between 10pm and 11pm, having been on the road for nearly fifteen hours, George was alert enough to use his left hand to remove his cap in a limp greeting to his childhood home. Once in bed, he sank into unconsciousness again and, despite more blood-letting during the night, he died sometime after midnight on 22nd June 1727. He was sixty seven and had reigned for nearly 13 years. George had often said that he wanted a sudden death. The, still fresh, reports of the desperate and painful work done by doctors on Charles II, William III and Queen Anne may have been in his mind when he spoke. He almost got his wish, as his last illness was sudden and unexpected, but no monarch could escape the affliction of royal doctors completely. However, luckily for George, they could minister only for hours, rather than days, before he died.

George had left no instructions for his funeral, other than that his body should not be opened or embalmed. His son, now George II, decided that his father's body should not be brought back to Britain but should be buried next to his mother, the Electress Sophia, in the church at Leineschloss in Hanover. This area was heavily damaged during the Second World War and so George's body was later re-interred in the church at the Palace of Herrenhausen.

The suddenness of George's death turned out to be a service to his kingdom as it took the Jacobites in England and in France totally by surprise, allowing his son, George II, to ascend the throne easily and without any disturbance. Interestingly when told of his father's death, the Prince of Wales did not believe it, thinking it a trick to prompt him into an outburst of joy and celebration that would then be held against him on his father's return. George I's long-time mistress, Melusine, 'The Maypole', retired to Twickenham, where her departed lover was said to call on her in the guise of a raven.

On his accession, George I faced a kingdom that was completely different from any of the other monarchies in Europe, or even his electorate of Hanover. There was no room for absolutist tendencies in a nation where successive acts of parliament had limited the kind of royal prerogatives that continental monarchs took for granted, where Parliament controlled the money, the succession and the protestant religious settlement. Yet he adapted well to the role of a constitutional monarch, rarely stepping outside the boundaries so recently established. His love of horses and hunting paralleled that of his old enemy James II, but he also became patron of The Royal Society, though Isaac Newton kept the invitation 'hidden' from the king for more than ten years before George realised he had been asked. He patronised the theatre, the Italian opera and Handel, and he knighted the painter Thornhill, the first English painter to be so honoured. George built no palaces, although he laid out Kensington gardens and made some improvements to Hampton Court, and his reputation as a stiff, dull, reclusive and awkward buffoon has dominated the pages of his story. But we should remember that in 1714 the Hanoverian succession was precarious. There were enemies, both within and without Britain who were poised to destabilize it. But by the time of his death, George's prudent, and often skilful, handling of his councillors had firmly secured the revolutionary settlement of 1688 for his son. He had made Britain a force to be reckoned with in European politics and, most importantly, had continued the enlargement of the Royal Navy, started by Oliver Cromwell, which would eventually make it the most powerful force on the world's oceans.

GEORGE II (born 1683 reigned 1727-1760)

The last British monarch to be born abroad, George Augustus (later George II) was the only son of George I and his wife Sophia Dorothea. He was born on 10th November 1683, at the Palace of Herenhausen in Hanover, a year after his parent's marriage. His only sister, born in 1687, later became Queen of Prussia. When he was eleven, George's mother was imprisoned in Castle Ahlden and he was largely brought up by his Stuart grandmother, Sophia, the dowager Electress of Hanover. He was educated as a German prince and given a grounding in European history and languages, though his principal interest was military tactics and strategy.

In 1705, George Augustus married Caroline of Anspach, daughter of the Margrave of Brandenburg-Anspach. Caroline was attractive, flirtatious and intelligent and, despite his often being unfaithful, George became devoted to her. They had seven children who survived past infancy, including Frederick Louis and William Augustus. The perspicacious Caroline had achieved some fame, and credit in England, when she refused to marry the future Holy Roman Emperor because it would have meant her becoming a Catholic. After the French Catholic wife of Charles I, the Portuguese Catholic wife of Charles II and James II's wife, Anne Hyde, who converted to Catholicism before she died, Caroline's undiluted protestantism was seen as a breath of fresh air, and was an important factor in George's early popularity in Britain.

His eldest son, Frederick (later Prince of Wales), was born in 1707 and a year later, with an heir in the bag, George I allowed George Augustus to fight as a cavalry officer under Marlborough at the great victory over the French at Oudenarde. He acquitted himself well, having had a horse killed under him at the height of the battle. In later years, as George II, he would bore his dinner guests, time after time, with his report of this battle. George Augustus accompanied his father to England on 18th September 1714 and was created Prince of Wales four days later. He was thirty one short, but not ugly, less reserved than George I and he spoke English, albeit with a heavy German accent. Before leaving Hanover, he is reported to have exclaimed *'that he had no drop of blood that was not English'*. A 'slight' exaggeration, certainly, but he did seem enchanted with his new country and made a good impression on his father's subjects. A page at the court noted that *'I find all backward in speaking to the king but ready enough to speak to the prince'*, and Lady Cowper thought that he danced *'better than anybody'*. George Augustus's ability to speak English clearly set him far above his father as far as social chit-chat was concerned. George I conducted his cabinets in French other than when he talked to Walpole, when he spoke Latin as his Chancellor did not speak French. The Prince of Wales took his seat in the House of Lords and attended the king's council but he was given no formal role in government.

After the 'Guardian of the Realm' debacle in 1716 and the farcical hissings at the royal christening in 1717, George Augustus and Caroline moved to Leicester House, where they set up their rival court. The estrangement was a public and painful business for both sides, but in one respect it helped George Augustus. In 1715, the South Sea Company had elected the prince as a governor of the company but after the quarrel with his father, the king took the prince's place. When the 'Bubble' burst in 1720, although the prince had invested heavily, he was not as exposed as his father. After the public reconciliation with his father in 1720, George Augustus kept a low profile as far as political alliances were concerned. While he kept in touch with both Whig and Tory politicians he stayed on the margins of party politics.

After his father's death at Hanover in June 1727, George Augustus ascended the throne without any show of opposition and was crowned in Westminster Abbey on 4th October 1727, aged forty-three. The new king was still smarting from his, one-time friend, Robert Walpole's accommodation with George I in 1720, and with this memory in mind

George II started off his reign hoping to form an administration without Walpole. He quickly learned that few men wanted to face an opposition led by the master of parliament and Walpole's navigation of a generous Civil List settlement through the commons cannot have harmed his cause. While the opposition sought to cultivate George's mistresses, Walpole had always cultivated Caroline. She was to be the most influential of all the Hanoverian queen consorts and, in private, Walpole summed up his successful policy somewhat crudely when he proclaimed that *'he had the right sow by the ear'*. Although Caroline found the twenty-stone Walpole physically repulsive, she identified with his tolerant, worldly and cynical outlook, which was very close to her own. It was an alliance that paid off handsomely for Walpole and he was soon back as the king's chief minister. Although not yet accorded the title, Horace Walpole is regarded as Britain's first 'prime' minister.

One early ripple disturbing the calm waters of George II's accession came when the Archbishop of Canterbury produced George I's will. George II instantly took it, hid it and it was never seen again. The king also took steps to obtain the other two copies held by the emperor and another German prince. Walpole assumed that the ungenerous George II wanted it so that he could avoid paying some of the legacies that the late king had stipulated. However, research has shown that the will outlined George I's wish to separate the crown of England from the Electorship of Hanover a desire he had nurtured well before he died. His wish was that after the death of his grandson, Frederick, the crown of Britain would go to the elder son and Hanover to a younger son. The latter would have to be a 'son' as only a male could inherit in Hanover. In making this wish, George I was pushing at the constitutional boundaries, as only Parliament could change the terms of the accession as set out in the Act of Settlement. Whatever the merits of George I's wish, and it had some merit, George II, if he were going to separate out the family honours, might not have wanted Britain to go to Frederick or his heirs.

George II's difficulties with his own father were replicated in his relations with his eldest son, Frederick. George II was no intellectual or lover of the arts and always had an explosive temper and a tendency to bluster. The more refined Frederick, who was fond of art, botany, gambling, games and women was only allowed to come to England a year after his father's accession, and he was made Prince of Wales the year after. He was twenty-one and was warmly welcomed by the court, if not by his father. Frederick's one-time wish to marry a Prussian princess, whose father George II detested, had already put father and son on bad terms well before Frederick arrived in England. When he became king, George II called off the match saying that, *'I do not think that ingrafting my half-witted coxcomb upon a mad woman would improve the breed'*.

The animosity that continued to fester between them became even more virulent than that that had existed between George II and his father. Both George II and Caroline openly stated their preference for their youngest son, the corpulent bully, William duke of Cumberland, over Frederick, and harboured ill-concealed dreams that he might one day become king. George II once exclaimed that, *'Our first born is the greatest ass, the greatest liar, the greatest canaille and the greatest beast in the whole world and we heartily wish he was out of it'*. If anything, Queen Caroline detested Frederick more than her husband and once remarked that, *'I wish the ground would open this minute and sink the monster into the lowest hole in hell'*. As soon as the prince was settled in England, George II left to visit Hanover, making his wife Caroline, not the prince, regent in his absence. The situation had all the hallmarks of the way George I had snubbed George II when he was Prince of Wales. No wonder one wag commented that *'the Hanoverians were like pigs, they trampled their young'*.

Once installed in St James' Palace, the royal court soon adopted the kind of dull routines that George II had so pilloried his father for. The king's two mistresses, Henrietta Howard, countess of Suffolk, and Mary Scott, countess of Deloraine, settled down into a kind of domestic harmony, sometimes even having to be protected from George's unpredictable whims and tempers by Queen Caroline. George could never understand Caroline's joy in reading and the arts or her need to converse with men of learning. He regularly complained about her 'schoolmistress' obsessions and made a point of regularly criticising and snubbing her in public. A hectic game of cards was about as much excitement as the court could rise to. The king insisted on strict court etiquette and absolute punctuality. This latter became an awkward obsession even in his pursuit of carnal pleasure. Walpole wrote that '... *his time of going down to Lady Suffolk was seven in the evening; he would frequently walk up and down the Gallery looking at his watch for a quarter of an hour before seven, but would not go till the clock struck'*. If, in the twentieth century, George V inherited his obsession with clocks and timekeeping from this ancestor it was certainly not to time his arrival at a mistress's bedchamber at precisely seven o'clock.

In April 1736, Prince Frederick married Augusta of Saxe-Gotha and embarked on a campaign in the House of Commons to improve his financial allowance, which, although he lost, soured relations with the king even further. When Augusta announced that she was pregnant, Caroline was so taken aback that she suspected that it was a trick and that a substitute baby would be produced in order to stop the succession of the duke of Cumberland. How the intelligent and normally sensible Caroline could believe that Frederick and Augusta would not have had children, if for no other reason that to prevent that, is a mystery. It underscored the deep and irrational hatred that Caroline had for her eldest son and now, it seemed, for his wife. Frederick was so worried that something might happen to the mother or the child under his parents' roof that when Augusta went into labour at Hampton Court, where his parents were also resident, he quickly bundled her into a coach and drove rapidly to St James' Palace, where she gave birth to a girl. This was all too much for George II, who, after shouting abuse at his wife and declaring that it was all her fault, turned the prince, his wife and the new baby out of St James' Palace. The new female heir to the throne was then moved into Leicester House. This was once the home of the rebel George, before he became George II. Here the child's mother and father would preside over a second court, one even more mischievous and troublesome than the one her grandfather had formed.

Queen Caroline would not have to put up with the 'burden' of Frederick's child, or George II's unpredictable tempers, for very long as she died, aged fifty four, on 20th November 1737 after a painful and protracted illness. During her illness George II had been beside himself with grief and hovered round her bed, alternating between cursing her for being ill, offering advice and weeping profusely at the thought of her death. He faithfully attended on her during her last days, urging her to lie still, protesting his undying devotion and even sleeping on the floor of her room. As she was dying, Caroline urged the king to marry again but he assured her that he never would, he would just make do with mistresses.

George II never did marry again and for some time afterwards, as he could not bear to see the 'Queen' in a pack of cards, his courtiers removed them before they were put on a card table. George was heart-broken at her loss and although he had known many women he declared that *'I never saw one fit to buckle her shoe'*. Caroline was buried in a new vault constructed right in the centre of Henry VII's Chapel, between the stalls for the Order of the Bath, on the night of 17th December 1737 to the strains of an anthem specially composed by Handel for the occasion. Unusually for royal burials in Britain, George II had ordered that Caroline's coffin should rest inside a large stone sarcophagus within the vault. It was large so that it would also accommodate George's body when the time came. As custom dictated, George II did not attend Caroline's funeral but for some time after her death he suffered from morbid dreams about her. One story, recorded in a letter from lord Wentworth to his father, told of how on *'Saturday night, between one and two o'clock, the king waked out of a dream very uneasy, and ordered the vault, where the Queen is to be broken open immediately, and have the coffin also opened; and went in a hackney chair through the Horse Guards to Westminster Abbey, and then back again to bed. I think it is the strangest thing that could be'.*

George and Caroline's relationship was a complex one, with George admiring and respecting her for the brightness and verve that she brought to his court, but never being able to understand her wide range of interests or why she was more popular than he was. Caroline's strong character, friendship with Walpole and influence over the king was well known to her contemporaries. Despite, in his heart of hearts, knowing how much he had relied on her it still irritated George that everyone else knew too, causing him to snub and bluster against her at the mere hint of it. A popular rhyme, chanted behind the king's back, summed up just the kind of sentiment that George feared many people felt. *'You may strut, dapper George, but 'twill all be in vain, We know 'tis Queen Caroline, not you, that reign'.*

There was some truth in the rhyme's sentiment as Caroline, the much brighter and faster thinking of the duo, often did manipulate George into following her (often Walpole's) advice, but the king did attend to his papers, he did comment, sometimes strongly, on what his ministers were doing and he was not a total prisoner of their opinions or preferences. One of the issues that caused George I to distrust his son so much was that George Augustus's first reaction to any problem or issue was to bluster fiercely about it without giving it due consideration. In his latter years, as George II, he retained this reputation, but on important issues he more often than not returned to discuss something he had exploded at earlier in a calmer, more considered way.

After twenty years at the head of ministries for both George I and George II, Walpole tendered his resignation in February 1742. Walpole saw it as his time to go. He had always been against war, as war taxes alienated too many interests, but the Prince of Wales's party wanted it and got it: first with Spain in 1739 and then against France. Having sought it for so long Walpole's enemies would be disappointed by the result. In the event George II retained most of Walpole's old ministers and he filled other places with some of Frederick's friends. They were only too happy to drop the prince to grasp a 'bird in the hand', leaving Frederick isolated again.

The way constitutional government had been evolving under Walpole meant that the only arena where the monarch could be really influential was in foreign affairs. George II's continental motives, like those of his father, were often seen as giving preference to the interest of Hanover over those of Great Britain. This was highlighted when Britain intervened in the War of the Austrian Succession (1740-48). This war involved a complex web of central European rivalries and interests, including Hanover, Prussia and France. Maria Theresa of Austria was fighting to reclaim Silesia, which had been seized by George's nephew, Frederick the Great of Prussia, in alliance with France. Such an annexation by Prussia would leave Hanover vulnerable to both Prussia and France and, in his sixtieth year, George crossed the channel to go down in history as the last reigning king of Great Britain to lead an army into battle. At the battle of Dettingen in June 1743, George showed considerable personal courage in leading an infantry counter-attack against Prussia's French allies who then withdrew to Alsace to begin peace negotiations.

Just two years later, George II faced a different kind of military adventure when the son of the 'Old Pretender', Charles Edward Stuart (Bonnie Prince Charlie), sailed from France to Scotland and landed in the Hebrides in July 1745 with just seven men. Seeking to retake the British throne for the Stuarts, Charles raised his standard at Glenfinnan at the head of Loch Shiel and, supported by the Camerons and the MacDonalds, he began his famous rebellion of the '45'. He reached Edinburgh in September, defeated government forces at the battle of Prestonpans (East Lothian) and, after taking Carlisle, he advanced southwards reaching as far as Derby. The expected Jacobite risings in England to support Charles did not materialise, and, with his army losing men to desertion by the hour, his advisors urged him to turn back to Scotland. Faced with a larger, better equipped and more disciplined army, led by

George II's younger son, the duke of Cumberland, Bonnie Prince Charlie, was defeated at Culloden on 16th April 1746. This defeat and 'Butcher' Cumberland's ruthless tactics after the battle, which approximated to what today we would call ethnic cleansing, destroyed the clan system in Scotland and put paid to any further chance of a Stuart resurgence coming out of that country or anywhere else for that matter. Bonnie Prince Charlie spent five months as a fugitive in the Highlands before escaping to France with the help of Flora Macdonald. He made a secret visit to London in 1750 and converted to Anglicanism, but plans for another rising in 1752 came to nothing. His father 'The Old Pretender' died in 1766 and jaded, broke and drunken Bonnie Prince Charlie died in 1788.

During 1750, with Walpole safely neutralized, Frederick, Prince of Wales began to anticipate his father's death, preparing plans to take up the reins of power and put his friends into office. Instead, a year later, Frederick was dead. During March 1751, he went for a walk at Kew on a bitter cold day and then returned home to lie down on a couch in a very cold room for three hours. He seemed to be all right, but later that night he was seized with a violent fit of coughing and, after clutching his stomach and crying out that he was dying, he died. The Gentleman's Magazine reported that the prince had *'complained of a sudden pain, and an offensive smell, and immediately threw himself backwards and expired'.* Rumours that Frederick's death was due to him having been hit by a cricket ball may have stemmed from the post-mortem. This suggested that he had been hit by something, albeit many years before, and that it could have contributed to his death.

George II seemed truly shocked by the suddenness of Frederick's death and sent kind messages to Princess Augusta. Yet to another correspondent he wrote, *'I have lost my eldest son, but was glad of it'.* His 'gladness' did not run to giving his son much of a royal send-off as Frederick's funeral service, on the night of Saturday 13th April 1751, was a paltry and brief affair with just *'two drums beating a dead march during the service'.* Frederick was laid in the vault next to the mother who couldn't bear to be near him in life. This may have been the first occasion that an undertaker was commissioned to handle a royal funeral, as a bill for £43 9s. 6d. was paid to a Mr Harcourt for various services, including providing a coffin, six men to carry it and a winding sheet. Prince Frederick's death had been quite sudden, giving little time for the royal physicians to prolong his agony, and his father's death would be even quicker. Walpole described the scene in a letter to a friend:

'He went to bed well last night; rose at six this morning as usual, looked
I suppose, if all his money was in his purse, and called for his chocolate.
A little after seven, he went into his water closet – the German
valet de chamber heard a noise louder than royal wind, listened,
heard something like a groan, ran in, and found the hero of Oudenarde
and Dettingen on the floor, with a gash on his right temple, by falling
against a bureau – he tried to speak, could not, and expired'.

No blistering, cupping and leaching for George II, then. He was dead before even his unmarried daughter, Princess Emily, could be summoned from her rooms nearby. Walpole, noting the result of the post-mortem, continued: *'the great ventricle of the heart had burst. What an enviable death'.* It was the morning of 25th October 1760 at Kensington Palace and the king was aged seventy-six.

King George II was little mourned. He had become more and more bad tempered, pompous and irascible as he got older and people around him were beginning to look forward to the personable Englishness of his young grandson, the hated Frederick's boy, George III. George II's funeral was held only 15 days after his death, on the night of Tuesday 11th November 1760. His body was conveyed from Kensington to the Prince's Chamber near the House of Peers at Westminster, where it rested the night before the burial. The king was to be buried in the same vault as his wife in the Henry VII Chapel of Westminster Abbey.

Walpole attended the funeral and wrote a detailed and witty account of what he saw:

'It is absolutely a noble sight. The Prince's Chamber, hung with purple, and a quantity of silver lamps, the coffin under a canopy of purple velvet, and six vast chandeliers of silver on high stands, had a very good effect. ... The procession through a line of foot guards, every seventh man bearing a torch, the horse-guards lining the outside, their officers with drawn sabres and crape sashes on horseback, the drums muffled, the fifes, bells tolling, and minute guns, all this was very solemn. But the charm was the entrance of the Abbey, where we were received by the Dean and Chapter in rich copes, the choir and almsmen all bearing torches; the whole Abbey so illuminated, that one saw it to greater advantage than by day; the tombs, long aisles, and fretted roof, all appearing distinctly, and with the happiest chiaroscuro'.

After all the grave decorum of the journey to the abbey and the solemn greeting by the senior clerics, the order of the funeral then seemed to dissolve into a melee:

'... no order was observed, people sat or stood where they could or would, the yeoman of the guard were crying out for help, oppressed by the immense weight of the coffin, the Bishop read sadly, and blundered in the prayers, the fine chapter, 'Man that is born of woman' was chanted not read, and the anthem, besides being unmeasurably tedious, would have served as well for a nuptial. The real serious part was the figure of the Duke of Cumberland, heightened by a thousand melancholy circumstances. His leg extremely bad, yet forced to stand upon it for nearly two hours, his face bloated and distorted with his late paralytic stroke, which has affected too one of his eyes, and placed over the mouth of the vault, into which, in all probability, he must himself so soon descend – think how unpleasant a situation! He bore it all with a firm and unaffected countenance. This grave scene was fully contrasted by the burlesque Duke of Newcastle. He fell into a fit of crying the moment he came into the chapel, and flung himself back in a stall, the Archbishop hovering over him with a smelling-bottle – but in two minutes his curiosity got the better of his hypocrisy, and he ran about the chapel with his glass to spy who was or was not there, spying with one hand, and mopping his eyes with t'other. Then returned the fear of catching cold, and the Duke of Cumberland, who was sinking with heat, felt himself weighed down, and turning round, found it was the Duke of Newcastle standing upon his train to avoid the chill of the marble. It was very theatric to look down into the vault where the coffin lay, attended by mourners with lights'.

What Walpole, and most of the other mourners there that day, didn't know was that George II had left strict instructions that his coffin was to be placed in that great stone sarcophagus that had been made for Queen Caroline, and that a side board of each coffin was to be removed so that their bones might lie together as they had in married life. When the vault was opened in 1837, the two boards were still there, propped up against the wall of the vault. A touching gesture, underscoring yet again George's devotion to the woman he could never properly understand. George and Caroline were the last king and queen of Great Britain to be buried in Westminster Abbey. As Walpole anticipated, the duke of Cumberland, who had stood sweating over the vault in 1760, was indeed lowered into it in 1765, followed by Frederick's widow (and George III's mother), Augusta, in 1772.

Although, like his father, he never travelled out of southern England, George II had more opportunity than his father to get to know the English and understand the way in which government and monarch operated, but he was never comfortable with it. He once cried out in frustration: *'I am sick to death of all this foolish stuff and wish with all my heart that the devil may take all your bishops, and the devil take your Minister, and the devil take your Parliament and the devil take the whole island, provided I can get out of it and go to Hanover'.* Back in Hanover there was less consultation, less politics and less need to argue with ministers; in Hanover everyone knew their place!

George's last years saw the slow rise of William Pitt, whom he did not like very much at all. In the military sphere, things now seemed to be going right. 1759 and 1760 turned out to be years of great military triumph: Britain's complete command of the sea, the seizure of Quebec from the French, foreshadowing the British acquisition of Canada, and important conquests in India and the Caribbean. Though deaf and blind in one eye, George would have basked in the glory that these reports brought him but the greatness never quite stuck to him. That hint of the ridiculous that dogged all the Hanoverians dogged him more than any of them. Too bluff to be a dissembler, the best that might be said of George was, as lord Charlemont, observed *'he was always what he appeared to be. He might offend but he never deceived'.*

GEORGE III (born 1738 reigned 1760-1820)

The future George III was born at Norfolk House, St James' Square, on 4th June 1738, the son of Frederick Prince of Wales and Princess Augusta of Saxe-Gotha. He was the first of the Hanoverian heirs to be born in England and to speak English without a foreign accent. He spent most of his youth at the 'alternative court' set up by his father and mother at Leicester House in London, and at Kew, where his mother had developed a botanic garden that would eventually mature into Kew Gardens. He was twelve years old when his father died and he succeeded him as Prince of Wales.

His widowed mother, who had expected to be queen one day, was possessive and dominated his adolescence, along with her principal councillor (some said also her lover) John Stuart, earl of Bute. George III was a poor student, indolent and sullen with a *'kind of unhappiness of temper'*. He was thought young for his years and was described as *'silent, modest and easily abashed'*. In later life, George III would exchange indolence for restlessness, and inattentiveness for an obsessive meticulousness. He could speak French and German, he was a great book collector and he loved music, playing both the flute and the harpsichord. After his death, his extensive 'King's Library' became a major part of the British Museum's book and manuscript collection.

On George II's death in 1760, his grandson was twenty two years old and he was crowned King George III on 22nd September 1761. Bute had taught the young George III that his grandfather was a despicable cipher in the hands of corrupt ministers and that he, when king, should avoid these pitfalls at all cost. Bute, the teacher, was angling to become Bute the first minister. That he lacked any experience in practical politics never seemed to have crossed his mind. That great observer of the court, Horace Walpole, noted that the young George III was blessed with many advantages: *'His person is tall and full of dignity, his countenance florid and obliging'*. In his youth, George III is said to have fallen in love with a Quaker girl, one Hannah Lightfoot, the daughter of a cobbler from Wapping, who, it was rumoured, had borne him three children. Later, in 1759, just before he became king, he fell for the stunningly beautiful Lady Sarah Lennox, who was descended from Charles II and his mistress, Louise de Kerouaille. George was badly smitten and he really thought that she could become his consort.

Sadly, for a Hanoverian king there could be no marriage with one's own subjects and he was steered well away from her. Instead, he was pledged to the plain, Lutheran, German Princess, Charlotte of Mecklenburg-Strelitz, who was seventeen to his twenty three. It was a whirlwind marriage, if not a whirlwind romance. The two met for the first time at 3pm on the afternoon of 8th September 1761 and they were married six hours later. As luck would have it, they fell in love and remained devoted to each other until the years of George's final illness. They enjoyed a quiet and unexciting home life, almost Victorian in its domesticity, calling each other Mr and Mrs King when they were together in private. The middle classes who, hitherto, had sought to ape the aristocracy now found a king who behaved just like them – no aping was needed. Their first son George (later George IV) was born one year after their marriage.

Charlotte did not take on the role of a Caroline of Anspach; instead she would spend the first 23 years of her married life bearing 15 children. Unlike his father, grandfather and great-grandfather, George III never took a mistress and his court, to the despair of those who looked forward to jollier times after dull old George II, became a model of piety and frugal living. No book-reading intellectual, George III made up for his lack of knowledge by effort. He was conscientious, intensely hard-working, punctual, an early riser and, unusual for a Hanoverian, deeply religious.

Always conscious of his duty to his God and his people, he proclaimed that steps had to be taken to reverse the disreputable moral tone of his grandfather's court and within months of his accession he issued a royal edict encouraging piety and virtue. The accession of George III also introduced a new London base for the court. Two weeks after his coronation, on 22nd September 1761, George bought Buckingham House, then a much smaller residence than Buckingham Palace is today, and in 1775 he settled it on the queen. With the exception of George Prince of Wales, all their children were born there. George disliked St James' Palace in London, disliked Kensington, and, despite its country location, he also disliked Hampton Court. For country air, he preferred Kew or Windsor. Always happy when visiting the farms at Windsor and talking with the farmers there about the latest developments in farming techniques, George III gained the nickname 'Farmer George' in his lifetime. He wrote, '*I certainly see as little of London as I possibly can and I am never a volunteer there*'.

When nervous, George III tended to speak rapidly and he would fill gaps in any conversation with meaningless words like '*what, what*'. This nervousness has often been misread as early signs of the illness that affected him so badly in his later years, but there is no evidence for this. George had been inoculated by Bute to be a 'patriot king', pledged to rule only in the national interest, to override party faction and to do away with jobbery and corruption. The first step in such a programme was to bring an end to the 40-year-old Whig ascendancy that had dominated the reigns of his two predecessors. This would mean bringing the Tories into government and would inevitably prompt the hostility of the Whigs who, seeing their pensions and patronage dwindling, were bound to cry 'despotism' and 'royal tyranny'. George had no plans to become a despot but he believed that whatever power the crown had reserved to itself under the 'Glorious Revolution' of 1688 had been slowly slipping away under his two predecessors and he was determined to stop the rot.

George's problem was that the constitutional settlement of 1688, reinforced by the Act of Settlement of 1701, was at heart ambiguous. There were some fixed points, e.g. that monarchs could not be Catholic or marry a Catholic, and they could not maintain a standing army in peacetime without parliamentary approval, but many crucial everyday matters, such as how the crown used its right to choose ministers, were left open to interpretation. These 'guidelines' were akin to the Ten Commandments in their 'thou shalt not' emphasis. There was nothing much in them to guide a monarch as to what he or she could do. George III's conscientious and active interest in government, and his very reasonable exercise of the royal prerogative, was always going to look intrusive in comparison with the 'hands off' indifference of George I and George II.

Parliamentary government was at heart adversarial; it thrived on disputation, and its task, at bottom, was to resolve serious conflict without recourse to civil unrest or even civil war. The growing role of the 'first minister', after Walpole put yet another powerful agent in play that could, and often did, see issues quite differently from the monarch. In a still fluid parliamentary system, the parties were by no means fixed; they split, re-formed and split again as the great issues changed. A first minister brought in to shore up a ministry with the monarch's, and, ostensibly, parliamentary, support could soon find himself facing new issues, his own view of which might be seriously at odds with both the monarch and the parliamentary majority that had so recently called him to office. Active government was in the hands of a committee of the Privy Council known as the cabinet. George III's reign is noted for its ministerial re-shuffles and to that extent, from our modern perspective, his reign has come to be regarded as one of the most unstable of the century. If a monarch wanted to break the monopoly of the old Whig corps there was bound to be more instability. His grandfather, George II, was damned for being a prisoner of the Whigs but being a prisoner was a much more stable, and possibly comfortable, condition than breaking out and embracing wider sections of opinion.

When George III became king, the Seven Years War (1756-63) had been raging for four years. Undertaken in pursuit of ambitions left unfulfilled by the War of the Austrian Succession, it was preceded by the escalation of conflict between France and Britain in North

America. After Britain lost Minorca to the French in 1756, the outcry brought the unfortunate Admiral Byng to execution on the quarterdeck of his ship and William Pitt 'the Elder' to office in December of the same year. Pitt was always suspicious of the fast-moving roundabout of continental allegiances and advocated more reliance on British naval force to protect British interests and achieve military dominance.

In India, Britain successfully faced both the French and Indian forces, culminating in Robert Clive becoming Governor of Bengal in 1757. One setback on the continent was when George II's son, 'Butcher' Cumberland, was defeated by the French and forced to sign the convention of Klosterzeven, which his father, George II, promptly repudiated. The year 1759, however, proved to be one of many victories for British arms. British and German troops defeated the French at Minden and the British took Guadeloupe and Quebec from the French. In November 1759, Hawke's victory over the French fleet at Quiberon Bay gave the British complete command of the sea, and in January 1760 the British decisively defeated the French in Southern India.

George III came to the throne just after these great victories but, tutored by Bute that a king should avoid onerous military adventures, he planned, at his first opening of Parliament, to refer to '*the bloody and expensive war*', but Pitt's anger got him to change it to '*just and necessary*'. George was certainly correct on the 'expensive' angle. It was the most successful war of the century for Britain, being the only one to bring substantial gains and it made Britain the leading world power. But all this came at a huge cost, nearly doubling the size of the national debt. Waged on a more global scale than ever before, the many victories at sea were a vindication of Pitt's maritime strategy. Pitt himself resigned in October 1761 after he lost support for his policy of making war with Spain, who had formed a new alliance with France. The earl of Bute, the one-time tutor of George III, now achieved his ambition and became First Lord of the Treasury in 1762, but the uproar over the widely unpopular terms of the Treaty of Paris in 1763, ending the Seven Years War, upset him so much that he resigned. The attacks on Bute had been led by John Wilkes, the great radical pamphleteer, whose weekly publication 'The North Briton', lampooned Bute as a bumbling royal favourite. Out of sight, but not out of mind, Bute assumed the role of the 'advisor on the back stairs', to the discomfort of George Grenville, Bute's successor at the Treasury.

In an attempt to recoup some of the costs of the Seven Year War, Grenville initiated the, as it turned out, disastrous policy of trying to raise new tax revenues in the West Indies and America with the Stamp Act of 1763. The war had made defending the British colonies expensive and in order to help defray the costs of their defence, all official and legal papers, newspapers, pamphlets, playing cards and dice were to carry duties similar to those already charged in Britain. Such a tax was expected to raise £40,000 to £100,000 per year. This move met unexpected and determined resistance from the American colonists who, although used to being charged customs duties, found the idea of an internal tax unconstitutional, prompting the famous cry of '*no taxation without representation*'. George III dismissed Grenville from office in July 1765, and, after holding back as long as he could, he called on Pitt once again in 1766. It was the fifth government of George's six year reign and it was a disaster. Within four months of taking office, Pitt suffered a nervous breakdown. He took to hiding in darkened rooms and more or less gave up attending to public business while, outside in the daylight, John Wilkes, the energetic pamphleteer, kept up his venomous attacks on the king. In October 1768, Pitt resigned.

The stamp tax was repealed in 1766, but relations with the colonies had suffered beyond repair. The American war began in 1775 and would continue until 1782. From 1770, Frederick, lord North took over the government and he spent much of his energy, and the nation's treasure, fighting the Americans in their war of Independence. It escalated into a 'world war' when the French also declared war on Britain in 1778, followed by the Spanish in 1779 and the Dutch in 1780. North's ministry would last twelve years, longer than all of

George III's previous ministries put together. After the War of the Spanish Succession, The War of the Austrian Succession, and The Seven Years War, the American 'world' war caused an enormous strain on Britain's resources. The effort of supplying and supporting a navy and an entire army across the Atlantic whilst fighting all the other major European naval powers was, in the end, just too much. Strangely for a king who had come to the throne opposing war, the successes of the Seven Years War had fostered a bellicose nationalism in George III and his subjects. Used to reports of serial victories, the loss of the American colonies seemed all the more shocking. It badly dented British confidence for a time but, in the end, due to the buoyancy of British manufacturing industry, it had no effect on the booming North Atlantic trade, and trade was what eighteenth century Britain was all about.

The war's longer-term effect on political reform in Britain (for instance the gaining of Irish legislative independence resulted indirectly from the war), is difficult to judge. The calls of pamphleteers like Tom Paine for liberty and 'The Rights of Man' raised questions about the way Britain was governed that would simmer slowly until emerging in the guise of agitation for the First Reform Act of 1832 and the Peoples Charter of 1838. Whatever its later impacts, the defeat of his armies by the American colonists certainly did nothing for the health and temper of the king. George finally acknowledged that the colonists had won their independence in September 1783, and in June 1785 he managed to pen a welcome to John Adams, the new ambassador to the independent United States of America: *'I will be free with you. I was the last one to consent to separation; but the separation having been made and having become inevitable, as I have always said, as I say now, that I would be the first to meet the friendship of the United States as an independent power'.*

Lord North's ministry fell in early 1782, and in 1783 George III, almost in despair, called on the son of his old wartime prime minister, William Pitt 'the younger,' to form an administration. Pitt, an MP for only three years, had come to prominence in the House of Commons as an eloquent speaker in support of parliamentary reform. Not the likeliest of bedfellows, Pitt, the young reformer who had criticised the management of the American war, was twenty four, and George, by now a sovereign severely jaundiced by what he perceived to be the shallowness of personal loyalty, was forty five. Pitt's obvious integrity helped gain him the confidence of the king and, because, like his father, he was seen as an independent-minded man of principle, he retained strong support in the House of Commons. Rather than party affiliation, Pitt's main interest was to promote good fiscal management and sound government.

Pitt's mastery of government and Parliament was, temporarily, put in jeopardy by George III's first serious illness in 1788. The king became ill in the summer of 1788 when he complained of stomach pains and in October he had an alarming attack of convulsions after a day spent riding in the rain. George was fifty and his behaviour was becoming extremely erratic. One story, probably apocryphal, had the king talking to a tree in Windsor Great Park believing it to be the King of Prussia. George did begin babbling unstoppably, and sometimes obscenely, and certainly announced that he lusted after the countess of Pembroke, one of Queen Charlotte's ladies. He developed blood-shot eyes and sometimes frothed at the mouth. It is not surprising that this behaviour worried and disturbed those around him.

On 5th November 1788, George began to show the first signs of violent derangement. At a dinner in Windsor castle, talking non-stop gibberish, with foam coming from his mouth and his eyes 'red as the devil', the king attacked George, Prince of Wales, and tried to smash his head against a wall. After this episode the king was moved from Windsor and taken to Kew, where various doctors were called. Their diagnosis was that the king was 'mad' and had to be restrained. He was strapped to a specially made iron chair that George ironically referred to as his 'coronation chair'. The king now had his dignity systematically stripped away by these unthinking 'quacks'. He was abused, lectured, splashed with cold water and had his body covered in poultices of Spanish Fly and mustard in the belief that the terrible blisters thus created would draw out the evil humours that afflicted him.

Alan Bennett's film 'The Madness of King George' (1994), as well as providing a different interpretation of George III from the tyrant of many histories, probably captured the essence of the cruel treatment that was meted out to the king. There was almost universal relief when George's recovery was announced, just three days before his son, George, Prince of Wales, was to be declared Prince Regent. To the chagrin of the Prince and his supporters in the commons, the king was well enough to attend a service of thanksgiving for his recovery in St Paul's on 23rd April 1789, after which he spent some days bathing in the sea at Weymouth.

The cataclysm of the French Revolution, beginning in 1789 (just as the British were celebrating the centenary of their own bloodless 'Glorious Revolution'), sent shivers through the thrones of Europe. George III, despite denouncing the murder of the French king as the work of savages and welcoming a war against *'that unprincipled country whose aim at present is to destroy the foundations of every civilised state'*, seemed less affected by the news from France than many of his court. Remembering the French support of the American Colonists, he saw it more in terms of a divine retribution on the Bourbon monarchy for aiding another country's subjects in a war against their king. Yet another costly war with France, albeit as just one partner in a mosaic of shifting European alliances, began in 1793 and would continue until Wellington's defeat of Napoleon at Waterloo in 1815.

The French Revolution was bound to inflame the radicals of all colours in Britain, many of whom, initially at least, took the opportunity to oppose George III and Pitt in the name of a 'new world' devoid of royal tyranny. An unexpected consequence of the French Revolution was its impact on events in Ireland. Stability there was important on a number of counts, not least because it had always been a major recruiting ground for some of the fiercest fighters in the British army, and that its largely Catholic population might be used by the French as a 'back-door' to an invasion of England. The emergence of radical disturbance there was something that both George III and Pitt would want to avoid at all costs.

Catholics in Britain had received some help in the Relief Act of 1778, which repealed some of the harsher anti-Catholic laws of the late 17th century, but many protestants saw in this a wicked betrayal. In 1780, an angry mob, led by lord George Gordon, marched on parliament to present a petition for the repeal of the Relief Act. Some Catholic chapels were attacked on the same day and, after clashes between crowds and the authorities, London entered a spiral of violence that lasted for ten days. Public buildings were destroyed and the houses of known Catholic sympathisers were attacked, prompting George III to summon 12,000 troops to quell the rioters. They fired on the unruly crowds and some 700 people were killed and 450 were arrested, 160 of whom were later indicted and 25 of them were executed. Gordon was tried for high treason but was acquitted and later converted to Judaism.

The Irish Parliament had enjoyed legislative independence since 1782, and in 1793 an Irish Act was passed that allowed Catholics to vote, to hold certain restricted and defined public offices and to attend Trinity College Dublin. In 1795 lord Fitzwilliam became Lord Lieutenant of Ireland and he favoured and foolishly promoted (given George III's known proclivities) complete Catholic emancipation so that Irish Catholics, as well as voting in their parliament's elections, could also sit as MPs. George III was horrified when he heard this and quickly reminded everyone that his family had been invited to assume the British crown specifically to protect the protestant settlement and that such a break with the principles behind that invitation could not be contemplated. Lord Fitzwilliam came home after only seven weeks in Dublin.

For some time Pitt had believed that a union of the Parliaments of Britain and Ireland, as had been achieved with Scotland in 1707, was very desirable. Catholic emancipation could then be granted to the Westminster Parliament in the full knowledge that Catholic MPs in the

United Kingdom would always be a small minority. George III possibly sensed that Pitt, the one time reformer, might seek to bring in Catholic emancipation throughout his realm and warned him that *'though a strong friend to the Union of the two kingdoms, I should become an enemy to the measure if I thought a change in the situation of the Roman Catholics would attend this measure'*. Pitt had touched on a raw nerve. George believed that Catholic emancipation would be a dire breach of his coronation oath and he would have none of it. Pitt wrote to George saying that he was *'unalterably fixed'* on the move.

George, though loath to lose Pitt, moved quickly to invite the Speaker of the House of Commons to form a new government. Parting from the king amid expressions of mutual esteem, Pitt resigned in 1801 after serving as prime minister for eighteen uninterrupted years. He did return to office briefly in 1804, but his health worsened and he died in January 1806. No great war leader, as his father had been, Pitt's creativity lay in the arena of finance (he levied the first 'temporary' income tax), overseas trade and colonial government, and in these he initiated a secure foundation for his successors. In his person he came to represent the national will to resist tyranny: *'England has saved herself by her exertions, and will, I trust, save Europe by her example'*. He was the greatest prime minister since Walpole and no leader comparable to him would emerge until Robert Peel forty years later.

George III added Ireland to his title of King of Great Britain on 1st January 1801 and, with Napoleon now firmly ensconced as Emperor of the French, he abandoned England's ancient claim to the crown of France. In February of the same year, the king again suffered from his old illness. He became over-excited, talkative, hoarse and delirious but luckily this particular bout lasted for only four weeks. However, with Queen Charlotte's support, his doctors kept him almost a prisoner until the following May. These months of semi-captivity left George thin, tired and less robust and his eyesight was getting worse. The queen, fearful of a return to violence, supported the doctor's inhumane restraining of her husband and began locking her bedroom door against him. Her daughters bore the brunt of her temper and lord Hobart noted how sad it was *'to see a family that had lived so well together, for such a number of years, completely broken up'*.

George's sons, following the now well established pattern in Hanoverian families, did nothing to contribute to the king's sanity. Two of George III's sons secretly married non-royal widows, one of whom was illegitimate. George III was furious and caused Parliament to pass the Royal Marriages Act of 1772. Henceforward no member of the royal family, under the age of twenty-five, who was a British subject, could marry without the monarch's consent in council under the great seal. The Act remains in force today. Undeterred by such formalities, Prince August Frederick, George III's sixth son, dressed himself *'like a common shopkeeper'* in December 1793 to be privately married to an eight month pregnant Lady Augusta Murray. The marriage was declared null and void in July 1794. George III's third son, William, (later King William IV) avoided the pitfall of clandestine marriage vows and instead made himself comfortable with a popular actress named Mrs Jordan and produced a large family of children who were given the surname Fitzclarence.

As if genetically ordained, George III's relationship with his eldest son soon replicated that of his two royal ancestors. Aided by a priest, recently released from the debtors' jail, the Prince of Wales also went through a marriage ceremony with a Mrs Fitzherbert, which, since she was a Catholic, was in breach of both the Marriages Act and the Act of Settlement of 1701. Alongside his illegal marriage, the Prince of Wales also accumulated serious debts. By 1795 these totalled around £630,000 and were spiralling out of control with no immediate remedy in sight. He could only escape bankruptcy by a marriage, that would bring in a new parliamentary grant, to a royal princess, and so in 1795 he agreed to marry his cousin, Caroline of Brunswick. In 1810, George's old illness, of 1788 and 1801, came over him again and he became hopelessly ill and the brutal physicians who had attended him then were called back to 'help.' In November of the same year, George's youngest, and favourite daughter, Amelia died and the king was distraught. George was soon confined to a set of Spartan room overlooking the North Terrace at Windsor Castle, and in February 1811 the Regency Act was brought into play. The Prince of Wales, now the Prince Regent, and his followers rejoiced in their access to the royal chequebook. Despite the reputation George III has gained as the 'mad king' he had only suffered a total of six months of illness in the whole of his first seventy years. It was only in 1810 that permanent insanity set in. The last decade of his life was very sad.

Shut away from the society of any but the 'mad' doctors who abused him, he settled into a twilight world of make believe, the occasional lucid intervals of the early years evaporating into a prison of anxiety and delirium. His wife grew increasingly exasperated and uneasy about seeing him and after a brief visit in June 1812, Charlotte never saw him again. She retreated to her *'little paradise'* at Frogmore in Windsor Home Park where she lost herself in gardening. George III was now a blind and deaf old man with a long white beard, shambling around an isolated set of rooms at Windsor, wearing a violet dressing gown and an ermine nightcap, hammering away at the keys of his harpsichord to try and hear the notes. He often burst into tears and spent hours tying and untying his handkerchief and buttoning and unbuttoning his waistcoat. Occasionally he wore mourning clothes *'in memory of George III, for he was a good man'*. He sometimes wore uniforms and the star of the Order of the Garter pinned to his chest and his mind found some release in the past. He talked with men long dead, addressed Parliaments long dissolved and inspected parades long gone. He died, in terminal dementia, on 29th January 1820, aged nearly 82.

Ironically, in 1814, George had been declared king of Hanover at the Congress of Vienna after a decade of having been occupied by France, but he never knew of the promotion. Queen Charlotte, who had been given the care of the king by parliament, died, unhappy and unloved, in November 1818 and George's second son, Frederick duke of York, took on the oversight of the king, happy no doubt of the £6,000 per year which went with the job. One of the doctors who attended George III excused the ghastly treatment that he meted out to the king by saying *'Sir our Saviour himself went about healing the sick'*. The king replied, *'yes, yes, but He had not £700 a year for it'*. After George's death it was calculated that the doctors who had attended him had racked up nearly £272,000 in fees since January 1812, a fantastic sum for the times.

Modern analysis of George's illness (the rapid pulse, an angry rash, yellow or bloodshot eyes, swollen feet and purple coloured urine) point to him suffering from a rare, hereditary disease known now as porphyria. The disease disturbs the porphyrin metabolism, the process which creates red pigment in the blood. When too much is produced, the urine becomes discoloured and the whole nervous system, including the brain, is poisoned. To the physicians of 1810, these exotic symptoms all pointed to madness and this was how the poor king was treated.

For some reason George III's body was not embalmed. After the post-mortem it was wrapped in a waxen linen cerecloth and then sealed up in a lead lined coffin. The king's body lay in state in the King's Audience Chamber (hung with purple cloth from the ceiling to the floor) at Windsor. Despite having been hidden away for nearly ten years, his people had not forgotten him. His blameless domestic life, his promise to stand against any invasion by Napoleon and his down to earth interests in science and agriculture made him, for many, a true father of his people. Having observed what awaited them with the Prince Regent, many saw in his death the passing of an era. The lying in state of previous monarchs had usually only been open to those who could call themselves nobility or at least 'gentry' but, on this occasion, in keeping with the general feeling of losing a 'father,' anyone who could appear in respectable mourning was allowed to attend. Viewing by the public was allowed from Tuesday 15th February until Wednesday 16th February and the roads to and around Windsor were choked with carriages coming to pay their respects. No less than 30,000 people walked past the lines of yeomen of the Guard to view his bier on the first day. At 4.30pm, after the public had left, the Eton Scholars and their masters, all in deep mourning (black crepe around their hats), were allowed in. At 9pm on the Wednesday, George III's body was taken on the short journey, within the precincts of Windsor Castle, to its funeral at St. George's Chapel. Ironically, and too late to help the king now, the cortège included two surgeons and two apothecaries to his majesty. The king's second son, Frederick, duke of York, for whom the lines of 'The Grand old duke of York' were composed, was the chief mourner and the long procession of courtiers and officers of state made its solemn way to St George's Chapel. On each side of the nave were ranged the Foot-Guards, every second man holding a wax light, and behind these stood around 500 Eton scholars. Boys from Eton College would, from now on, become a regular feature of royal funerals at Windsor. The king's coffin was lowered into the tunnel leading to the vault he had so carefully planned some sixteen years before and where his wife, two young sons and his beloved Amelia already lay. The ceremony lasted for two hours and was all over by 11pm.

Business throughout London was suspended for the day; Minute Guns were fired in Windsor Great Park and at the Tower of London, and bells were tolled in churches all over the country. Soon after the funeral, the duke of Wellington's friend, Mrs Arbuthnot, wrote, *'And thus has sunk into an honoured grave the best man and the best king that ever adorned humanity and it is consoling that such a sovereign was followed to his last home by countless thousands of affectionate subjects drawn to the spot ... to pay a last tribute of respect to him ... who, for sixty long years, had been a father to his people.'.* Sir Nathaniel Wraxall in his memoirs noted that, *'confined as he was to his apartments at Windsor, unseen except by his medical attendants ... yet his people have clung to his memory with a sort of superstitious reverence; as if, while he still continued an inhabitant of the earth, his existence suspended or averted national calamities'.*

Before his illness, George III had reigned with stubborn dignity and was the only Hanoverian king who could honestly be called a genuinely decent and good man. At his death, loyalty to the old Stuart dynasty, always a potential threat to his predecessors, had become an affair of sentiment rather than practical politics. But like his two predecessors, the kingdom of George III, in terms of what he heard and what he saw, was confined to the south of England. He never visited Wales, Scotland, Ireland or the north of England. Unlike his predecessors he never, even once, visited his Electorate (later Kingdom) of Hanover, though he protested that it was very dear to him. His sober habits, restrained domestic life and frugal diet made him the butt of the graphic satirists but he had been loved by the people. George's example of prudence and dedication to his people put clear water between him and his contemporary, the Bourbon king in France, who paid for his rather different diet and lifestyle with a terminal visit to the guillotine.

The Royal Vault at St George's Chapel Windsor

The birth of George III's fifteen children raised the spectre of multiple marriages and an extended family that could run into hundreds. As it happened, George III's sons and daughters produced few legitimate children but one consequential challenge of their potential fecundity was the disposal of them, and their children, when they when they died. The vaults of Westminster Abbey, including the one built for Caroline of Anspach and George II in 1737, were now full to overflowing, a new location and new thinking was called for.

The last king to have been buried in Edward IV's St George's Chapel Windsor had been Charles I and he had been quietly dropped in the old Henry VIII vault for which, as yet, there was no plaque or monument. George III spent many of his leisure hours at Windsor, and St George's Chapel Windsor had almost become the family church. It seemed appropriate then to develop his new 'Royal Vault' somewhere in that chapel. Between the years 1802-

1810, George instituted a huge excavation of the disused Wolsey Chapel just to the east of St George's Chapel to create a deep vault, high and wide, that would serve as his family's mausoleum. One record notes that it had space for 81 bodies. The vault was linked by a wide corridor which ran, under the main altar, to a space below a removable ledger stone in the centre of the choir of St George's Chapel. When the ledger stone in the choir is lifted, a coffin could be lowered into the corridor below, from where it could be trundled into the main vault. For the first time, during the funeral of Edward VII in 1910, a mechanical winch was installed which operated a lift that could carry both a coffin and catafalque to the corridor below, and this system was still in use at the royal funerals of George V and George VI. A small, discreet, stairway just visible behind the altar of St George's Chapel, allows court officers and servants to get to the corridor to carry out their duties below.

In George III's time the coffins stood on a stone table that ran down the centre of the vault, but in the last years of her reign Queen Victoria had some alterations made and the coffins were set on shelves on each side of the vault. The Illustrated London news of February 23rd 1952, covering the story of George VI's funeral, carried an artist's impression of the vault as it was then. There was a small altar at the eastern end and each of the shelf areas were enclosed by wooden screens that closed up the space between the stone pillars holding up the roof of the vault. George III's forward planning was fortuitous as at least eight of his family were buried in this vault before his own death in 1820, including his youngest daughter, Amelia. George III, his two sons, King George IV and King William IV, and many more of the Hanoverian royal family lie there undisturbed. Many others, including Prince Albert, Queen Victoria's mother the Duchess of Kent, Edward VII, George V, George VI and George duke of Kent rested in the centre of the vault for a time before being moved to other, permanent, locations. Many of the tourists today, walking around the monuments in the Albert Memorial Chapel, have little inkling that they are walking above one of the largest royal tomb houses in Europe.

GEORGE IV (born 1762, Prince Regent from 1811, reigned 1820-1830)

George Augustus Frederick (later George IV) was born on 12th August 1762 at St James' Palace, the eldest of the fifteen children that would be born to George III and his wife Queen Charlotte. As an infant, George was provided with his own establishment of two rockers, wet nurses, dry nurse, seamstress and even a 'necessary woman'. At five years old he was bright and precocious and could write in a neat round hand, and at six, although occasionally hot tempered and lacking in determination, he seemed to be making good progress. George III had strict rules on how his children should be brought up and George and his brother Frederick (later duke of York) were installed in the Dutch House at Kew to live under a harsh regime of lessons and close supervision from early in the morning until 8pm at night.

The sober and practical George III was determined that his sons should be shielded from the vile temptations of the outside world. He wanted them taught the virtues of hard work, honesty, punctuality and the simple life that he valued and aspired for them to value. If found to be lax, lazy, or dishonest their tutors were instructed not to spare the rod. One of their sisters recalled how she had seen one of the tutors hold them *'to be flogged like dogs with a long whip'*. History is full of fathers subjecting their sons to harsh regimes in the hope of forming a decent, godly, and worthy adult, only to see their aspirations broken on the wheel of a fierce reaction. And the reaction of George IV against his father and all he stood for, was to be total.

As a young man he was tall and dignified, handsome and charming. In 1779, after watching her play the part of Perdita, in Shakespeare's A Winter's Tale, he fell in love with the beautiful actress, Mary Robinson. She gave up the stage to become his mistress and he promised her £20,000 when he came of age. He wrote incautious letters to her under the name of 'Florizel' and when he tired of her, 'Perdita' decided that, to compensate, she would raise a little cash by publishing them. To avoid the inevitable scandal George III had to buy the letters from her. As she walked away with £5,000 in cash and an annuity of £500 Mary recalled the charms of her lost love: *'the grace of his person, the irresistible sweetness of his smile, the tenderness of his melodious yet manly voice'*. More mistresses followed and the prince gained notoriety for his scandalous private life, made public in print and picture by enthusiastic satirists, including James Gillray. George III was disturbed and hurt to see his son falling in with rakes, wastrels and various members of the Whig opposition, including Charles James Fox.

Charles Fox, who had held various offices under George III, had once resigned, in support of the Prince of Wales, over the Royal Marriages Act, which gave the king power to control the marriages of his adult children. George III believed that Fox, a well-known rake and gamester, at the track as well as the tables, was largely responsible for leading the prince into dissolute ways. Profound disgust with George III was the leading theme of Fox's later politics, and George III saw Fox's friendship with the prince as a malicious faction constantly working against him. The more the king opposed Fox the more he, unwittingly, fuelled the allegiance between Fox and the prince. It was a strange alliance. Fox the radical, who supported repeal of the Test and Corporation Acts, the abolition of the slave trade and, at its inception, the French Revolution, bosom friends with a preening, pompous prince of the royal house! The Bishop of Llandaff believed that part of the problem was of the king's own making and that the prince: *'was a man occupied in trifles, because he had no opportunity of displaying his talents in the conduct of great concerns'*.

In 1784, the prince embarked on a *'great concern'* that would shock his father, most bishops and the court when he fell desperately in love with a Catholic widow, the curly haired, full-figured, charming and respectable, Mrs Maria Fitzherbert. Born to a Roman Catholic family in Shropshire, she had been widowed twice by the time she met Prince

George and, being 'respectable', she resisted his advances and fled to France. George sent passionate letter after passionate letter across the channel, pleading for her to return. Maria still resisted, and so, to draw more attention to his broken heart, George then stabbed himself, not too deeply, and Maria returned to England and consented to marry him. An Anglican clergyman, the Reverend Robert Butt, was sprung from the debtors' jail in the Fleet and the wedding took place in 1785, secretly, in the bride's Mayfair drawing room. The Reverend Butt's condition for conducting the marriage was that he should be given a bishopric when George became king. This secret conjunction was doubly illegal, being against the Royal Marriages Act of 1772 and the Act of Settlement of 1701 that excluded those married to a Roman Catholic from the succession. Undeterred by these considerations, the impact of which he would have known only too well, the prince must have been moved by a deep, perhaps even noble, love for Mrs Fitzherbert, which, at that brief moment at least, bestowed some honour on a man whose later life would know little of it. After 26 years of being in and out of his affections Maria Fitzherbert would finally break with George in 1811. She died in 1837, outliving him by seven years.

After settling down with his amiable widow, George's concerns shifted to dealing with his huge debts, which by the 1780's were nearly £270,000. To show the world the penury that his father's meanness had brought him to, he closed down his palatial, and half-finished, home at Carlton House and moved down to Brighton to live modestly with Maria. He hoped that Parliament might help him but his 'secret' marriage was now quite well known and so any mention of his financial problems, in either house, would certainly prompt questions about his marital status. On the prince's behalf, his friend Charles Fox denied the rumours of an illicit marriage and publicly branded them a scandalous lie. Poor Maria was so distressed to hear of Fox's denial, and the stain that it put on her reputation, that she threatened to leave the prince, and for some time after Fox's announcement she refused to see George. On finding out the truth, Fox was greatly embarrassed. After the first of many parliamentary financial settlements, Maria relented and she and the prince were reconciled.

By George's late thirties, 'Perdita' would not have recognised her 'Florizel'. His taste for gargantuan meals and heavy drinking had turned him into a mountain of flesh very close to the image depicted by Gillray in his *'A Voluptuary under the horrors of Digestion'*. This showed George reclining after an enormous meal, picking his teeth with a fork, his belly bursting from his breeches, his red face on the verge of apoplexy. From now on he would always be presented as the 'fat regent' or the 'fat king', his grossness always a metaphor for his debauched and lazy life. The prince and his friends could not contain their joy when George III suffered his first serious illness of 1788. The prince went about telling everyone that his father had spent most of his life insane, giving out intimate details of his condition and mimicking his ravings to his servile followers. The king's recovery was a dreadful blow to him and to those who were salivating at the chance of office and patronage. The old anti-monarchist radical, Charles Fox, no doubt eager for office, found himself arguing that the prince (no radical he) should assume all the royal powers that would accrue to him as if the king were dead. All this damaged an already dubious reputation and harmed the prince's relationship with his mother who held him responsible for her husband's condition.

It was not long before the prince's debts had him again appealing to parliament for more money. They agreed to find him some funds, but many MPs, no doubt enjoying the spectacle of forcing him into bigamy, insisted that, before getting his hands on any cash, he must marry a royal princess in order to produce a legitimate heir. By 1794, his debts had spiralled to around £39 million at today's values. In 1795, after declaring that *'one damned German frau was as good as another'*, George agreed to marry his cousin, Caroline of Brunswick. Many royal marriages had been a mistake but this one was to surpass all others in its calamity. To show his contempt for the duty that parliament had insisted on, he sent his mistress Lady Jersey to greet Caroline on her arrival in England. Caroline was twenty six to

George's thirty two and she was probably the worst possible choice that could be found for the witty and sophisticated George.

Caroline was cheerful, tactless, boisterous, coarse and unconventional. Generally good-natured, she was talkative, swore like a trooper and was disinclined to wash. As a stranger to soap and water, her personal hygiene was somewhat wanting and on first embracing her an appalled George jumped away quickly, retired to the far corner of the room, and called out: *'I am not well, pray get me a glass of brandy'*. The wedding took place in the Chapel Royal on 8th April 1795 and George spent their wedding night hopelessly drunk and passed out in the fireplace. He did manage to get into bed with her in the morning and nine months later, to the day, their daughter Princess Charlotte was born, but by then her parents were separated, Caroline living at Blackheath and George ensconced back at Carlton House. Princess Charlotte was now heir to the throne and, although popular with the press and public, she was too much like her mother for George's taste. Three days after his daughter's birth, George made a will in which he bequeathed Caroline one shilling and declared that Mrs Fitzherbert was *'the wife of my heart and soul'*. By the summer of 1800, George, after again threatening suicide if she did not return, was back with his 'other wife', Maria Fitzherbert. She cultivated a quiet domestic life for them at Brighton, curbed his drinking and nursed him when he suffered from a painful inflammation of the stomach.

Charlotte was to be George's only legitimate daughter. The number of his illegitimate children has been difficult to determine, although he did accept the parentage of three illegitimate sons. If there were children by Maria Fitzherbert, she kept them well hidden or disguised them as children of relatives – a common ruse in the eighteenth century. Caroline's little court at Blackheath attracted politicians who were hostile to her husband, including George Canning, whom the prince believed to be her lover. During 1805, Caroline was branded as a dissolute adulteress after rumours of her having given birth to an illegitimate child began circulating in London. The prince authorised a commission to investigate the 'delicate matter' of the princess' behaviour, and, although the commissioners found her to be indiscreet and careless of her person and reproved her for her *'levity of conduct'*, they could find no positive proof of adultery.

No doubt disappointed that he could not shake off Caroline by a divorce due to adultery, George took up with a new mistress, the Marchioness of Hertford, a rich, stately and very formal woman who answered well his need to be dominated by an authoritarian older woman. All George's diversions were cut short by the start of his father's final illness in October 1810. It was soon apparent that this time George III was unlikely to recover and the prince was formally sworn in as regent on 5th February 1811. This was the moment his Whig friends had been waiting for. They had already planned who would be doing what in their new administration, but they were to be badly disappointed. George's mistress, Lady Hertford and his two brothers, the duke of York and the arch-conservative, duke of Cumberland, all urged him to keep the status quo. So despite his many promises to his Whig friends, George was too lazy to change the Tory administration that was already in place. His Whiggism had really been just another way to annoy his father and oppose William Pitt, who was his father's man. Like his father, George believed that Catholic emancipation would be a denial of his coronation oath and was firmly against it, opposing the many Whigs who wanted it brought in. George's old friend and gaming companion, Charles James Fox, did not live to see his prince's betrayal as he had died four years earlier.

Making new enemies from betraying old friends was just one of the challenges George faced as he contemplated his role as head of the government. George now had to cope with something completely new in his life: a 'work load'. Overwhelmed by the quantity of papers that he was expected to read and sign, George sighed that *'Playing at King is no sinecure'*. The MP George Tierney noted that *'The prince is very nervous, as well he might be at the prospect before him, and frequent in the course of the day in his applications to the liquor chest. I much doubt however, whether all the alcohol in the world will be able to brace his nerves up to the mark of facing the difficulties he will soon have to encounter'.* The Whigs were up in arms at being betrayed, Caroline left the country to live in Italy and George's daughter Charlotte, having inherited some of her mother's boisterous coarseness, was becoming difficult to handle. On the prince's fiftieth birthday, in 1812, Leigh Hunt named and shamed him: *'A libertine over head and ears in debt and disgrace, a despiser of domestic ties, the companion of demi-reps, a man who has just closed half a century without a single claim on the gratitude of his country or the respect of posterity'.*

The air of Brighton was more invigorating than the official papers and satirical jibes of London and soon, Carlton House having been completed at horrendous cost, the prince turned his attention to the Marine Pavilion at Brighton that he planned to have re-built in the most extravagant style. From 1815, the architect John Nash, who had designed Carlton House Terrace, would help the prince squander another fortune on a fabulously elaborate, dome-and-minaret encrusted pavilion for Mrs Fitzherbert that would become known as the Royal Pavilion at Brighton. Nash, a particular favourite of the prince, also planned London's Regent Street, Regent's Park, Trafalgar Square, St James' Park, Marble Arch and the transformation of Buckingham House into Buckingham Palace. Such projects engaged the prince in a way that no other part of acting as regent could and his ministers came to despair his lack of application to government affairs.

In 1817 George's daughter Charlotte died after giving birth to a stillborn son. Although deeply distressed at her death, George's reputation ran before him and he was accused of not being distressed enough and of not sharing the widespread general grief over a young woman who had been so much more popular than himself. Charlotte's husband Prince Leopold of Saxe-Coburg was distraught at her death. He was the brother of that Victoria who would marry George IV's brother, the duke of Kent, and give birth to a new female, replacement, heir to the throne, Princess Victoria. There had been no monument to a British king or queen, or a prince or princess, since the small one, built for two of James I's children, had been placed in Westminster Abbey but Princess Charlotte was to get one. Although an early resident of George III's huge family vault Charlotte's extravagant monument, in white marble, showing the princess, rising from her draped corpse, and, carried by angels, rising heavenward with her infant, stands in the Urswick Chantry at the west end of St George's Chapel, Windsor.

George's father, George III, followed soon after Charlotte, dying on 29th January 1820. This moment, which the fifty seven George had waited so long for, was now unexpectedly marred by his becoming gravely ill and there were legitimate fears for his life. To lose a new king so soon after losing an old one would look careless even for early 18th century physicians and, as badly as George IV was regarded, many believed that it would be a greater calamity if the crown was to fall in stages to his equally childless and dissolute brothers.

It was at this moment also that Caroline decided to return from her continental adventures keen to take her legitimate place as queen beside her husband. The courts of Europe had been much entertained by colourful stories of her personal life, including the well publicised allegation that she had been sleeping with her major-domo, Bartolomeo Bergami. George had had agents following her about in Italy to gather evidence for adultery and he had these vivid reports sent to Parliament in the hope that it would not only find her guilty of adultery but also try her for high treason. But it was not to be. Bergami, being an Italian citizen was not subject to English law, the events reported on had taken place outside England and key witnesses refused to come forward. Though the House of Lords voted by a slim majority that the queen was guilty, such a majority would not be repeated in the House of Commons, where the queen had many more supporters, and so the bill was withdrawn. George was devastated and even talked of giving over the British crown to his brother, the duke of York while he retired to the quieter political waters of Hanover. George's discomfort was made worse by the populace of London taking Caroline to their hearts as the much-maligned consort of a debauched king, and large, often hostile, crowds gathered in the streets to insult George and shout their support for Caroline.

George soon recovered enough to immerse himself in preparations for his coronation, which Parliament had voted the extraordinary sum of £243,000 to facilitate. This was just the kind of event that he loved to work on. Throwing off his natural indolence and his many ailments, he became the master of every detail; he would oversee the shine on every candlestick, the colour of every robe and carpet and the placing of every notable guest. It was probably the most elaborate coronation ever seen, the ultimate festival of regal splendour with the new king looking like *'some gorgeous bird of paradise'*. Queen Caroline, forbidden by George from attending Westminster Abbey, defiantly turned up and ran madly from door to door being denied entrance at each. Now, the London crowds, intoxicated with the splendour of the occasion and showing that partiality to inconsistency that all crowds can muster, heartily booed and jeered Caroline as her coach drove her away. Pleased to have regained some popularity in England, George now did what his ancestors had never done and visited Dublin and, in 1822, Edinburgh, where he paraded down Princes Street, wearing the Tartan of the Stuarts. He made a good impression in both capitals and returned believing that he was popular and liked in some quarters of his kingdom at least.

But dressing up and striding about in parades did not address government, ministers or great issues and George was about to face a great issue that even he had strong views about. In 1828, George had reluctantly agreed to the repeal of the Test and Corporation Acts, which freed Roman Catholics from many restrictions, including those that prevented them entering Oxford and Cambridge or sitting as MPs. But in 1829, George's, ironically ultra-Tory, prime minister, the duke of Wellington, urged George to accept the Catholic Relief Act. This 'betrayal' of all his family had stood for caused George immense agitation and on one occasion he talked to Wellington for over five hours about it, only stopping to top up with copious glasses of brandy. On 29th January 1829, Wellington craftily managed to get George to sign the minute committing the cabinet to an emancipation bill that would allow all qualified Roman Catholics freedom of worship and full civil rights. George's brother, the duke of Cumberland, was an arch-protestant and Catholic hater, having been Irish Grand Master of the Orange order since 1817. Although George had little regard for him, Cumberland, in the guise of a fanatically protestant Iago, was daily hanging on George's ear never missing a chance to tell him that he was being duped by his ministers. All of this had its effect on the weak and vacillating George. Having given in to Wellington, he could feel the power of the crown slipping away and he grew peevish and resentful, threatening to sack his ministers and change his mind on the Catholic issue.

When George refused yet again to confirm his original agreement to Catholic Relief, the cabinet resigned en-bloc on 4th March 1829. A frightened George relented the next day and he reluctantly signed the Act into being in April. George's foot-stamping petulance on this issue was the last throw of a dying man. The last two years of his life were spent in gross self-indulgence, eating and drinking to such an immoderate degree that men normally unfazed by gluttony were minded to comment on it. The duke of Wellington observed one breakfast to be made up of *'a pigeon and beef-steak pie of which he ate two pigeons and three beef-steaks, three parts of a bottle of Mozelle, a glass of champagne, two glasses of port and a glass of brandy! He had taken laudanum the night before [and] again before this breakfast.'* And this was just at the start of the day!

After dinner, it was not unknown for George to call a servant over and ask him to bring a piece of beef up from the servants' table. Such gluttony was bound to take its toll and those who saw George during 1829 and 1830, now literally held together by corsets, ointments and greasepaint, knew that they were looking at a man who, was eating and drinking himself to death. The artist Wilkie, engaged to paint George during what would turn out to be the last month of George's life, said that at close quarters George looked frightful and that it took three hours to dress him *'to lace up all the bulgings and excrescences'*. The king was addicted to laudanum to the extent that his body had now adjusted to it. George could, just about, stay standing after having imbibed 250 drops of the drug (often taken with a brandy or cherry wine) over a 36-hour period. By now, as his father had been before him, George was nearly blind. A rubber stamp had to be made with his signature on it. When he could be bothered to attend to state papers this stamp could be used as long as three witnesses were present.

George, desperate to conceal himself from view, now had soldiers posted to exclude the public from the normally open paths and avenues in Windsor Great Park so that curious passers by could not catch sight of their gross king. This act, and his hiding behind the thick hedges of the Royal Lodge, at Windsor, made him now nothing more than an expensive recluse, increasingly irrelevant to his subjects. Inside the damp and humid rooms of the Royal Lodge George was increasingly plagued by gout, arteriosclerosis, breathlessness, inflammation of the bladder, terrible coughing fits and cirrhosis of the liver. He was regularly 'leeched' to quell his bladder pains and occasionally, despite his doctors' disapproval, he opened a vein or two himself. It became painful for him to lie down and he spent more and more of his time propped up in bed wearing exotic dressing gowns and turbans and sipping laudanum. George's cries of pain as his diseased organs began to fail him were so loud that the sentries in the quadrangle below his windows at Windsor had to be moved to avoid hearing his distress. Contrary to what might be expected of such an obese and ailing man, George was constitutionally very strong. One courtier wrote that, *'In constitution and in mind he is certainly a wonderful man: he behaved in the face of death as a man would on a field of battle'*.

In the early hours of 26th June 1830, George was sleeping, as he now did most nights, in a chair slumped over a table in front of him. After emptying his bowels, *'a large evacuation mix'd with blood'* at 3am, and feeling faint, he asked for a window to be opened. He soon became very breathless and, holding tightly on to his companion's hand he suddenly declared *'My boy this is death'* and fell back in his chair, dying at 3.15 am *'without any apparent pain or struggle...'*. His post-mortem revealed that all those organs prone to gather fat were *'excessively loaded with it'*, including the surface of the heart. The valves at the beginning of the aorta *'were ossified throughout their substance'* as well as the inner coat of the aorta. Part of the large intestine *'had formed unnatural adhesions to the bladder, accompanied by a solid inflammatory deposit the size of an orange'* and *'in the stomach was found a clot of pure blood weighing six ounces ... The immediate cause of his Majesties' dissolution was the rupture of a blood vessel in the stomach'*. The long list of elements that made up George's pathology would be no surprise to those who knew him. George's final gastric haemorrhage may have resulted from the violent coughing that his doctors often reported, rupturing one or more of the varicose veins that lined the upper part of his stomach, causing massive internal bleeding.

George had named the duke of Wellington as one of his executors and instructed him to bury him in whatever night clothing he was wearing at the time of his death, and with any ornaments that he might have about him. The duke tenderly explored a black ribbon around the king's neck and found it to hold a diamond-encrusted locket containing a miniature of Mrs Fitzherbert. One report of the king's will noted that, like his grandfather George II, he had asked that his coffin be made in such a way that a side panel could be removed so that when Maria Fitzherbert was buried beside him her panel could be removed so that they might forever co-mingle.

The king could have made such a romantic gesture but it is unlikely that he would could ever have believed that, after his death, the new king and his councillors would agree to the body of his illegal Catholic wife being placed in the royal vault at Windsor.

On the evening of 26th June, George's body was simply wrapped in cerecloth (it was not embalmed) and then soldered up in its lead coffin and his funeral set for 15th July. Large quantities of George IV's outsize clothes and other stuff were sold off at public auction (probably to help pay some of his debts). George's old flame, Mrs Fitzherbert, had her £6,000 a year pension raised to £10,000 to compensate her for the loss of her one great love. In keeping with the old traditions of robbing kings after their death, George's last mistress, Lady Conyngham, was seen loading wagons with piles of presents that George had given her, and other valuables which he had not, that she then trundled out of Windsor in a great hurry. Well before George's death, Sir William Knighton, George's former physician and now his Private Secretary, admitted to his wife that he had been gathering up one or two souvenirs from the kings apartments, and on 23rd June Knighton's coachman was fined £60 for carrying furniture away from Windsor castle, while everyone slept, at 5am. Given his status as a servant it would seem that the fine was levied on the wrong man.

On Sunday 12th July, Londoners had the opportunity to view the king's huge and sumptuously velvet-covered coffin when it was displayed with pride in the Haymarket showrooms of Banting and France, the royal upholsterers. The next day, on Monday 13th July, some of the residents and tradesmen of Windsor were allowed into Windsor Castle for two hours in the morning for a private view as the king's body lay in state. This may well have been the last contact with the king or their unpaid bills that many of the local tradesmen would have. On the following two days, gentry and nobility were admitted to the crimson and gold splendour of the drawing room where George lay. The room now looked as George had wished it to be, less sombre with brilliant gold and purple accoutrements surrounding the king's coffin. The Morning Chronicle reported that some of the vehicles dragged into service to get to Windsor might otherwise have been *'consigned to a corner of a barn or a stable till times hammer should knock them to pieces'*. And that before the day was over *'there was a fine a promenade of beauty and fashion in all the most noted rambles round Windsor, as Kensington Gardens can show in its most favoured hours'*. George IV would have been delighted!

The same newspaper did complain that the solemnity of the occasion was spoiled somewhat by the noisy preparations still being made by carpenters, bricklayers and others to build the walkways and barriers ready for the coffin to pass into St George's Chapel. They felt that the sound of workmen barking orders and hammering and jumping over barriers in their dirty 'working clothes' was not in keeping but that the public who were queuing to pay their last respects rose above all this and behaved *'in a manner not only decorous in itself, but well suited to the solemnity of the occasion'*. Interestingly, other newspapers reported that the visitors, as they queued, made just as much noise as the workmen and that overall the scene was more that of jolly day out rather than a solemn day of mourning.

The actual funeral, which began at 9pm on 15th July, also had mixed reviews. In a break with the usual protocol, that the new monarch did not attend the funeral of the old, the dead king's brother, now William IV decided to attend as chief mourner and chose purple for his cloak rather than black. As he followed George's coffin into the Chapel, William stopped to talk loudly, animatedly, and some said frivolously, to those on each side of him and chatted noisily to those around him throughout the ceremony. The waiting mourners and soldiers, who had been assembled for two hours previous to William's arrival, joined in, giving the whole assembly the look of *'some raree-show than to the chamber of death ... there seemed to be a predominant feeling not to mourn at all...'*.

After two hours of the service, William IV left the Chapel before it had ended and before his brother was lowered into the passage below to join his father and his brother, the duke of York, who had died in 1827. On the day of George's funeral, William Cobbett described London and its surroundings as a place of festive merrymaking and the absence of grief, pity or remorse seems to have been the tone of reports from all over the country. The Times newspaper took the opportunity to rage against the memory of such a gross *'Leviathan'* reporting that *'there never was an individual less regretted by his fellow creatures than this deceased King'*, deploring his *'most reckless, unceasing and unbound prodigality'* and his *'indifference to the feelings of others'*. In the House of Lords the ever-loyal duke of Wellington praised George for *'a degree of knowledge and talent much beyond that which could reasonably be expected of an individual holding his high station'*. Sir Walter Scott also praised George's *'exalted and good breeding'*, but such warm words were few and far between. The painters, planners, architects and skilled artisans who had worked on George's great projects at Windsor, Buckingham Palace and elsewhere were the true mourners of a monarch who had lavished his patronage on them like no other Hanoverian king. No king since Charles I had commissioned so much art and filled his palace with so many paintings as George IV had, and this embellishment of the cultural life of Britain, not really enjoyed by large numbers until the next century, is really his only positive legacy.

George IV, as Prince Regent from 1811 to 1820 and king from 1820 until his death in 1830, exercised all the powers of a sovereign for nineteen years, and while he was enjoying the range of pleasures that he raised to an art form, Britain was in the grip of an industrial and social revolution that was beyond George's comprehension. From our distant perspective we can see that the fierce antagonism that arose between George and his father weakened and demoralised the prince. George III had tried to squeeze his son into a moral mould that he would never fit and in consequence they both denied the other the very affection that each so desperately craved. Some of his youthful experience may have contributed to his aversion to unconvivial work, but as an adult he could have taken the time to remedy this. Instead as he grew older he remained untrustworthy, weak and vacillating. He could not handle robust disagreement and because he was too lazy to see through the thoughtful resolution of problems he always sought the easy way out.

His intelligent conversation and patronage of art and architecture apart, George was an abject failure at being a king. Perhaps he would have been better if George III had brought him into the business of government, given him some responsibility and offered him a leadership role in an area suited to his talents. George did tell a good story. In later years he used to like winding up the duke of Wellington by pretending that, in disguise he had served, unknown to the duke, with him in the Peninsular Wars, and had won one battle by leading a successful cavalry charge. He also swore that he had been present at the battle of Waterloo. 'No king he, but a good story teller' should perhaps have been his epitaph.

WILLIAM IV (born 1765 reigned 1830-1837)

William Henry, duke of Clarence, was born on 21st August 1765, at Buckingham House, the third child and third son of George III and Queen Charlotte. With two older brothers in front of him there was no reason to expect that William would ever be king. For a time he was educated with his two elder brothers under the stern eye of various tutors, where he gained a reputation as a boy of boisterous high spirits, though he does not seem to have been alone in this appellation. One who attended on the three princes noted that *'there was something in the violence of their animal spirits that would make him accept no post to live with them'*. In 1772, William's two elder brothers were moved to their own establishment while William and his younger brother were supervised at Kew by a Swiss General from the Hanoverian army, who knew a great deal about the flavour of tobacco, and the grave-faced Dr John Majendie. As a young man, William was burly, blue-eyed, with cropped red hair. As a sixty five year old king he was red-nosed and weather beaten with an ungraceful air and carriage. His head, shaped a bit like a pineapple, would give plenty of scope for satirical illustrators.

George III knew that Parliament would not stand for funding all his sons out of the public purse. Some of them would have to earn their own living, and so at thirteen William was sent to sea as a midshipman. The king was also conscious that his eldest son, George, Prince of Wales, was showing signs of the dissipation and self-indulgence that would later become his badge as heir, regent and king, and he did not want his impressionable third son being tainted by George's influence. Thus, on 15th June 1779 William joined His Majesty's Ship Prince George, where, in 1780, he was present when the English fleet captured twenty-two Spanish ships, one of which was re-christened the 'Prince William' in his honour. During the next three years William visited Gibraltar, New York, Dominica, Cuba, Jamaica and many of the brothels in between. It was during his Caribbean cruise that William met the young Captain Horatio Nelson. Nelson wrote to a friend that William would be *'... an ornament to our service'*. Nelson's opinion, probably not a little influenced by an eye on promotion, was not shared by George III, who thought it time to remove his third son from the rough company and uncouth manners of the quarterdeck. William would be sent to Hanover to learn more of the social graces befitting a gentleman, an officer and a king's son. Like all of George III's schemes for his sons, it failed. Bored and irritated by those who supervised him and longing for the *'pretty girls of Westminster'*, William now gave vent to his romantic and sexual appetites. He fell in love with one of his cousins and after her, the daughter of an army officer. Later he fathered a son with another woman who eventually turned up in England, accompanied by his mother.

From his elder brother Frederick, who was already in Hanover, William acquired a taste for gambling, but without anything like the deep pockets necessary to sustain it against the skilled aficionados that flocked to his table. The inevitable consequence was that an unhappy George III had to liquidate his gambling debts. In the end it was Frederick, now duke of York, who urged his father to recall William to the navy to prevent his brother falling further into the pit of dissipation. George III reluctantly agreed but insisted that William return home in disgrace and face a full board of the Admiralty to decide his fate. In the event, on 17th June 1785, as a reward for his bad behaviour, the Admiralty agreed to make William a Lieutenant.

Later, while based in Portsmouth, William fell in love with a Sarah Martin and, being refused marriage to her by the king and queen, who quickly had him removed to Plymouth, he fell into a deep depression. William seems to have fallen in love easily and, just as easily, the pain of a forbidden love was soon forgotten. He recovered from this setback and in April 1786 he was appointed Captain of the frigate Pegasus and sailed off to spend the summer of that year on the rugged shores of Newfoundland. The party for his twenty first birthday was celebrated by an orgy of drunkenness there, before he sailed again for the West Indies and a renewed acquaintance with Captain Nelson. Nelson liked William and wrote that, '*He has his foibles, as well as private men but they are far overbalanced by his virtues. In his professional line he is superior to two thirds, I am sure, of the list*'. In fact, William's rumbustious appetites, while in the Caribbean, exhausted Nelson as well as everyone else. William only slowed down in 1787 when the revenge of the West Indian brothels caught up with him. This inconvenience was probably syphilis but he seems to have recovered, and probably retained only a mild form of it throughout his life, as none of his children by Mrs Jordan showed any signs of it.

One incident, with one of his Lieutenants in 1786, betrayed the impetuous, and perhaps something of the imperious, nature of William as a ship's commander. This man had the temerity to offer William advice on the use of stern discipline for trifling offences. Their quarrel grew until each man could not stand the other and eventually a variety of senior officers had to intervene to settle the matter, which at one point involved placing the unfortunate Lieutenant in jail. This foolishness did not enamour William to the Admiralty, who rightly divined that William's obduracy in not accepting the compromise of a fellow officer's tendered apology illuminated his unfitness for high command. All this sourness receded somewhat when, in 1787, William found himself in Halifax, Nova Scotia, where he '*would go into any house where he saw a pretty girl, and was perfectly acquainted with every house of a certain description in the town*'. He also became 'acquainted' with the wife of the Surveyor General at Halifax and was sad to leave her for home waters, and the prospect of more admonishments from his father, towards the end of 1787. To avoid the latter, William did not venture out of Plymouth but did enjoy a two day drinking party with his two elder brothers.

In early 1788, William again fell in love, this time with the beautiful Miss Winne, a Plymouth merchant's daughter. When the king found out he responded in his usual brisk manner: '*Aye, what! What! What! William playing the fool again! Send him off to America and forbid the return of the ship to Plymouth*'. Thus, in August 1788, William found himself once again among the delights of Halifax, Nova Scotia, where he is said to have fathered another son. Clearly George III was never going to win! It was towards the end of 1788, while cruising in the West Indies, that William received the news of his father's attack of insanity. He promptly wrote to his brother supporting him in his quest to secure full powers as regent, no doubt hoping to benefit from the bounty of a loving brother to help him out of his usual round of indebtedness. '*I only hope to be admitted to the party*'.

The Prince of Wales called William home but, by the time he arrived in England, George III had recovered and the hoped-for bounty had evaporated. Not long after George III's recovery he made William duke of Clarence, sighing as he did so that, '*I well know that is another vote added to the opposition*'. Now William wanted the cash to go with his new status and, moaning that the £12,000 a year voted by parliament for him was insufficient, he foolishly wrote to his father asking for more. The aggressive response from George III frightened William into a speedy apology, but his relations with his father would never really improve. At least William could now set up an establishment of his own, and he eventually bought a house which he renamed Clarence Lodge.

In May 1790, William reluctantly returned to active service but found the ladies of Plymouth less entertaining than before, '*Not a woman fit to be touched with the tongs, not a house to put your head in after dark*'. In December 1790 the prospect of war with Spain receded and William was able to return to Clarence Lodge to concentrate on finding a mate to share his bed and board. This last, six month, posting in a home port would mark the end of his ten-year naval career. His first attempt at 'home-making', installing the notorious courtesan Polly Finch, failed after she, having put up with his incessant readings from 'Lives of the Admirals', discovered that there was more than one volume. Like his brothers, William was constrained as to whom he might marry by the Royal Marriages Act of 1772, promoted by George III after two of his sons, the dukes of Gloucester and Cumberland, married women he did not approve of. The Act sought to ensure appropriate, non-Catholic, marriages for his other sons, whose behaviour was anything but appropriate. In reality it achieved exactly the opposite effect. Not being able to marry the women they fell in love with, George's sons chose to live with them in 'sin', rather than marry the dour and boring German princesses that their father would have found for them.

Thus it was to be with William. Dorothy Jordan was the foremost comic actress of her day. She was no great beauty but her personality and bubbling vitality charmed all who saw her and she had unusually neat legs. In 1790 William saw her in a farce called 'The Spoil'd Child' and he fell instantly in love with her. Dorothy already had three children by two previous lovers and, after some coy refusals, she moved in with William in October 1791. For the next twenty years the couple lived together and produced ten children, five boys and five girls. They were all given the surname 'Fitzclarence' and William loved them all.

The writer Hazlitt declared that Dorothy's *'smile had the effect of sunshine and her laugh did one good to hear it'*. She certainly made William happy and he settled into a quiet domestic life with her and his growing family. In 1797, George III, though aware of William's unusual domestic circumstances, showed a rare toleration of his need for more space for his illegitimate family. He made William ranger of Bushy Park, near Hampton Court. This appointment came with a spacious 'William and Mary' residence, Bushy House, and William and his new family moved in. After the outbreak of war with France in 1793, William offered his services to the fleet but his loose tongue, personal hostility to the war, and overt dislike of William Pitt, kept him from command of a ship, let alone the squadron that he felt he deserved.

Instead of war, William took to farming and, while he did enjoy entertaining at home, Mrs Jordan noted that their life was generally so quiet that they might be *'dead and buried without our friends knowing even that we had been ill'*. Mrs Jordan could not afford to stay 'dead and buried' for too long. Although William gave her an allowance of £1,000 a year, she needed more money to support her children from previous liaisons, and so she regularly returned to the stage to supplement the family finances. The satirists had a wonderful time with William's domestic arrangements and often pilloried him for living off the wages of an actress. In October 1792, he told his bankers, Thomas Coutts, that *'Mrs Jordan is getting both fame and money: to her I owe very much'*. The cartoonists could also make use of the happy coincidence that 'Jordan' was the popular name for a chamber pot. Although castigated by both his father and his eldest brother about his vociferous opposition to the war with France, William still turned up at the House of Lords, where he was quite active in defence of the slave trade. He believed that his experiences in the West Indies gave him a unique insight into the working of the plantations and that the abolition of slavery would lead to chaos and disorder for both the masters and the slaves.

When his brother was made Prince Regent in early 1811, after George III's descent into senile dementia, William's expectations of greater involvement in government were quashed when his brother left him out of any political consideration. His financial affairs were still bothersome; his expenditure always running well ahead of his income and, despite Mrs Jordan's fees for performing, William was still besieged by anxious creditors. He began to consider setting Mrs Jordan aside in favour of a wealthy heiress and in October 1811, while acting in Cheltenham, she received a letter from William urging her to meet him at Maidenhead to discuss the terms of separation. The shock of this proposal must have been deeply hurtful to the loyal actress and yet she still confided to a friend that, *'Money, money, my good friend, or the want of it, has, I am convinced, made HIM at this moment the most wretched of men'*.

In January 1812 Mrs Jordan agreed to a financial settlement that included the very harsh clause that the £1,500 a year allowed for the maintenance of her youngest daughters, was conditional on her not returning to the stage. If she did, she would lose both the cash and the custody of her daughters. Given that she had helped support William from her acting fees, and that no word had been said about her suitability to look after her children then, this seems particularly hypocritical of William, the bluff, honest 'Jack Tar'. In 1815, defrauded by one of her daughter's husbands and heavily in debt after helping another daughter, Mrs Jordan fled to France, hoping for financial help from William's officers, but none came. She died, in France, penniless in 1816. Meanwhile her erstwhile partner enthusiastically took up the hunt for a wealthy heiress. William proposed to no less than six possible candidates before giving up the chase, after March 1814, when the Duchess of Oldenburgh, the widowed sister of Tsar Alexander, rejected him on the grounds of his vulgar familiarity describing him as 'awkward, not without wit, but definitely unpleasant'.

For a time William settled into a comfortable bachelordom until November 1817, when he received the news that Charlotte, the Prince Regent's only daughter, and heir, had died after giving birth to a stillborn child. Now only his two elder brothers stood between William and the throne. The need for a wife to help ensure the future of the Hanoverian line was now more urgent. After further rejections and, with some reluctance (he was £56,000 in debt and worried that some foreign princess might not take kindly to a household full of Fitzclarences), William accepted that he should marry Princess Adelaide of Saxe-Meiningen. This amiable, religious, graceful, but plain young woman was married to William on 11th July 1818. Adelaide was twenty six to William's fifty three but, despite her being of German stock, they seemed to get on well together right from the start.

Kind, affectionate, loyal and unassuming, Adelaide proved that a German princess could accept, and warm to, William's children by Mrs Jordan, and her good nature soon won him over. They spent the first year of their marriage in Germany, largely to avoid William's creditors, but later they were comfortably ensconced at Bushy Park, where Adelaide worked on both William's finances and his rough manners. William was certainly fond of his new wife, but his love for her deepened as they faced the failure of a number of her pregnancies. Adelaide's first child was born prematurely, possibly as a result of excessive bleeding by her doctors and she miscarried again at Calais in September 1818. In December 1820 things looked better when Adelaide presented William with what seemed to be a healthy girl but the baby died, of inflammation of the bowels, three months later. The year 1822 saw a further miscarriage of twins and it is not hard to imagine the anguish that they both endured. Yet again a royal prince had fathered a brood of healthy illegitimate children, while his legal wife was denied even one child of her own. William was not insensible to his wife's suffering: 'I want words to express my feelings at these repeated misfortunes to this beloved and superior woman' he wrote to his eldest brother, 'I am quite broken hearted'.

Their loss was all the more galling, as William's younger brother, Edward duke of Kent, had managed to father a bouncing baby daughter, Victoria (later Queen Victoria), before dying himself in 1820. That year also saw the death of George III, and William's elder brother proclaimed as King George IV. William supported his brother in his highly public attempt to set aside his wife Queen Caroline and was rewarded with a sinecure post of general of marines at £4,000 a year. This was fortuitously supplemented by an extra £3,000 a year, as heir presumptive, when his elder brother, Frederick duke of York died in January 1827. The latter's funeral at St George's Chapel, Windsor, was held in temperatures so cold that a number of the older mourners followed the duke of York soon after.

William now saw what had been an unlikely prospect come to pass; he was next in line to the throne. He had no heirs himself but his normally robust health should see him live past his raddled brother and the prospect appealed to him, if to no one else. As a result of a political resignation in spring 1827, William was made Lord High Admiral, a largely symbolic post last held by Queen Anne's husband. Not to be held back by mere 'symbols', William threw himself into a commission on the poor state of naval gunnery, adopting terms of reference that the Admiralty, and the prime minister, the duke of Wellington, disapproved of. Despite William being the innovator here, his ideas on the future of naval gunnery were very sound and hardly radical; his brother the king had to force him to desist from further interference. Not to be disheartened, William continued his tour of inspection of British ports, and, on 31st July 1828, he found a small squadron of ships at Plymouth, hoisted his flag, and took them out to sea for ten days. No one was sure where they were, and on their return his brother, under pressure from Wellington again, reluctantly enforced William's resignation as Lord High Admiral. William was famous for not bearing grudges and he bore none to the duke of Wellington, whose measure on Catholic emancipation he, surprisingly, strongly supported in 1829.

At 6 o'clock in the morning of 26th June 1830, William was awoken at his house in Bushy to be told that his brother was dead and that he was now King William IV. He was excited, he had been expecting it, and he took off in his carriage to Windsor grinning and waving to bystanders as he bowled on past them. This beginning would have confirmed the worst fears of many courtiers that it was only a matter of time before William, like his father, was declared insane. They were wrong. In place of insanity they would get an amiable eccentric. He would also be popular. He opened up the walks around Windsor that George IV had closed off and he cleared the way between Regent Street and Regents Park. He took every opportunity to let the people of London see him, once even being mobbed while strolling in St James' Street and having to be rescued by the members of White's Club. As king, William lived mainly at St James' Palace, Windsor and the Royal Pavilion at Brighton. He disliked the remodelled Buckingham palace and even offered it to parliament after their chambers burnt down in 1834. They politely refused. William was crowned on 8th September 1831, aged sixty six, at a scaled-down coronation that had none of the extravagant splendour lavished on the coronation of his late brother.

Like George V, his great-great-nephew, William IV was happy following the life of a country squire, but he was fastidious in carrying out his royal duties. His first task was to sign the 48,000 state papers that his brother had been too lazy to attend to. Queen Adelaide sat by him with a bowl of warm water to bathe his fingers as he tackled a huge pile every night until they were done. His greatest challenge was the growing movement in the country to reform the parliamentary electoral system. The Duke of Wellington's government was defeated in November 1830 on a technical vote and William called on the sixty six year old Whig, lord Grey, to form a government. Grey wanted to bring in a modest measure of electoral reform and soon presented William with proposals for abolishing the worst of the rotten boroughs, removing one member from others, and providing every constituency with a minimum number of resident voters. Although a drastic measure by William's standards, the king's main worry was the agitation that was going on in the country to secure reform, and the further agitation that could be expected as a hostile House of Lords, inevitably, rejected it, causing an election. William distrusted all elections as periods *'of disorder, of general relaxation, and more or less of outrage'.*

William's fears were well founded as the next eighteen months proved to be a roller coaster ride of agitation and unrest. Grey's first bill was defeated in March 1831 and he persuaded William to dissolve parliament and call an election. Grey's government was re-elected, and in early July 1831 Grey managed to get his bill through the House of Commons with a majority of 136, but the House of Lords defeated it in October 1831. Grey waited for a time and then introduced a revised reform bill that was passed by the House of Commons in March 1832 but was again thrown out, via a crippling amendment, in the Lords on 7th May. The government resigned on 9th May, in protest, but William had to call Grey back on 15th May, as the duke of Wellington could not form a government. On 18th May 1832, Grey received a written assurance that William would create as many new peers as was necessary to pass the bill in the House of Lords, and this threat (much as it would in the reign of George V) prompted enough peers to absent themselves from the chamber to allow a majority of 84 for the bill, and the First Reform Act passed into law on 7th June 1832, being assented to by the king's commission, rather than by the king in person.

The act conferred the right to vote on propertied adult males, paying an annual rent of £10, while in the counties the forty-shilling freeholders retained their franchise. The net effect of the Act was to release 143 seats out of a total of 658 that could be redistributed to more populace cities and towns. 65 were given to the counties, 44 were given to large towns such as Birmingham, Manchester, Leeds and Sheffield, and 21 were given to smaller towns, each receiving one MP, 8 were given to Scotland and 5 to Ireland. It was a start; it mitigated some of the grievances of the growing middle classes, but it was a small start. The nobility and gentry would still dominate parliament and many more reform acts would have to follow the 1832 act, over the next 100 years, before there was anything like a fair electoral franchise in Britain. William may have found the push for electoral reform difficult to stomach but he would have to face more changes yet, particularly in that graveyard of 19th century politics, Ireland.

At this time Irish peasants were obliged to contribute to an alien church through the payment of church tithes, and in 1834 the great question of the day was lord John Russell's desire to divert some of the revenues raised for the Church of England to lay purposes such as education. Rather than endure lord John Russell, a *'dangerous radical'*, as Leader of the House of Commons, William foolishly dismissed Melbourne's government and in December 1834 appointed the Tory, Robert Peel, as prime minister. Peel called an election in early 1835, but still failed to command a majority in the House of Commons. He resigned in April 1835, forcing William to summon lord Melbourne again and suffer the humiliation of Melbourne's stringent conditions of *'unequivocal support'* for the government. A king of Britain could no longer whistle up a majority for a politician simply by making him his prime minister and no British monarch has attempted such a move since.

During May 1836 the king was noted as showing less than his usual vitality and was noted as being *'somewhat shrunk both in mind and body ... After his dinner naps he wakes shaking and he is not so strong on his legs ... The medical men about him consider the decay of age is fast coming upon him'*. Notwithstanding these concerns, the year 1837 began with fears about the health of Queen Adelaide, who had returned from Germany feeling unwell. Then in April 1837 William's favourite daughter, Sophia died unexpectedly, two weeks after giving birth to a child, and a depressed William was taken ill in May 1837. He had suffered from asthma for many years and, at seventy one, his heart and his general constitution were beginning to fail, and by the middle of May he began to suffer fainting fits. Realising that he might die, he resolved to call up all his reserves of energy to stay alive until his niece, the Princess Victoria, reached her majority, when she became eighteen on the 24th May. This would ensure that her mother, the Dowager Duchess of Kent, whom William loathed, could never assume regency. Once he cleared this hurdle, the next target he set himself was to live for one more anniversary of the Battle of Waterloo on Monday 18th June. He appealed to his doctor, *'Doctor, I know that I am going but I should like to see another anniversary of the battle of Waterloo. Try if you cannot tinker me up to last out that day'*. The duke of Wellington enquired if the famous anniversary dinner should be cancelled, but the king would not hear of it *' Tell the Duke of Wellington I hope the dinner may take place tomorrow. I hope it will be an agreeable one'*. The young Benjamin Disraeli noted that, *'The King dies like an old lion'*.

Queen Adelaide was with William constantly, reading prayers and passages from hymnbooks to him that, for a man who had never seemed very religious, seemed to comfort him greatly. But by now both his energy, and the need for further 'targets' were, ebbing away. Bluff and hearty to the end, he tried to jolly his weeping queen along (she had not been to bed for ten days) by exalting her to *Bear up! Bear up!* At twelve minutes past two on the morning of 20th June 1837, King William IV died at Windsor, in the room where his brother George IV had also died. *'His majesty expired without a struggle and without a groan, the Queen kneeling at his bedside and still holding his hand, the comfortable warmth of which rendered her unwilling to believe the reality of the sad event'.* William was in his seventy second year. Later that day a post-mortem revealed that the valves of William's heart had ossified, his lungs were full of blood and his liver and spleen were much enlarged. The cirrhosis of the liver and the granular structure of one of his kidneys indicated a longstanding condition. His grossly enlarged heart, the valvular disease and the thickened lining of the aorta may well have been of old syphilitic origin. The immediate cause of William's death was the state of his lungs, which exhibited basal pneumonia developed as a result of cardiac failure.

Unlike his father and brother, William's body was then embalmed and sealed up in a leaden coffin before the sun had set on his last day. His coffin then lay in state in The Waterloo chamber in Windsor Castle from Friday 7th July until 3pm on Saturday 8th July, during which time the public were allowed in to pay their last respects. The Times had received the news of William's death in time to print an extra edition, edged with black, and letters had been sent to all theatres ordering them to close on the evening of the day of the king's death and on the day of the funeral. All this seemed justly reverent but, Charles Greville asserted that the funeral itself was *'... a wretched mockery'.* He went on to declare that a variety of people, of all ranks, were *'chattering and laughing, and with nothing of woe about them but the garb. I saw two men in an animated conversation, and one laughing heartily at the very foot of the coffin as it was lying in state. The chamber of death in which the body lay, all hung with black and adorned with scutcheons and every sort of funeral finery, was like the scene in a play, and as we passed through it and looked at the scaffolding and rough work behind, it was just like going behind the scenes of a theatre'.*

At 8pm on 8th July, the king's brother, the duke of Sussex, now a seasoned attendee at funerals of his family, took up his position as chief mourner at the head of the coffin and at 9pm the funeral procession, including a number of William's Fitzclarence sons, began making its way down to St George's Chapel. The route from the Waterloo Chamber to the entrance of the Chapel was lined by dismounted cavalry of the Household Brigade, all holding torches, while men of the Foot Guards lined the south aisle of the chapel. At the end of the service William's coffin was lowered into the opening opposite the altar and was then wheeled through the passage into the royal vault to join his father and two brothers. As had been customary, from the days of the middle ages, officers of the king's household knelt by the side of the vault, broke their staves and cast them in. Since George III began the habit of burying the royal family at Windsor, the trades' people of that town always looked forward to a royal funeral. There was always money to be made from hiring carriages, renting hotel rooms and selling food and drink, and so it was at William's funeral.

William, the 'unexpected' king, unlike his brother George IV, was universally mourned by his people, if not by the proud and busy aristocrats who made up his court. He had been too much of the unsophisticated, bluff sailor for them but these were the very attributes that endeared him to his people. Miss Wynne, a contemporary diarist, noted the contrast between the genuine sorrow that greeted the death of William IV, compared with the indifference that met George IV's demise. *'Then few, very few, thought it necessary to assume the mask of grief; now one feeling seems to actuate the nation! Party is forgotten and all mourn'.* The Times, vitriolic in its condemnations after the death of George IV waxed lyrical about William calling him *'the good, the kind, the affable, the companion and commander of his people'.*

William had made some mistakes, particularly over his dismissal of Melbourne in 1834. He also sometimes came across as a bit of a buffoon but he was good hearted and dutiful. His great achievement was that, after just seven years, he had turned a monarchy that was in disrepute and decline, sick and unloved, into one that was well-respected and thriving. This was due, in the main, to his lack of ostentation, his desire to mediate between conflicting political passions and his, generally, affable and open demeanour. As a third son, it seemed unlikely that he would ever accede to the throne so he was given little by way of training for royal duties He was inexperienced in public affairs and much less intelligent than the politicians with whom he had to deal. Despite being the monarch who presided over the passing of the First Reform Act of 1832, William was still more a man of the eighteenth than the nineteenth century. Queen Victoria would have to spend many more years coping with parliaments bent on momentous social and political change, but William's legacy at least left her with some positive feelings towards the monarchy, something she would not have inherited had she become queen seven years earlier.

After William's death in 1837 his queen, the gentle Adelaide, suffered from a variety of illnesses that sent her travelling to Mediterranean climates for some relief. During the time of the Reform Act agitation, her conservative nature was regarded as a reactionary influence on William IV, and her carriage was once attacked in the streets by an angry mob. Though strongly opposed to political change there is no evidence that Adelaide was ever actively engaged in political influence over the king. She died from the rupture of a blood vessel in her chest at Bentley Priory near Stanmore, Middlesex, on 2nd December 1849. She was fifty seven and she was buried next to William, in the Royal Vault in St George's Chapel, Windsor. Her diligent, pious and regular philanthropy, extending quietly over many years, had played its part in reviving the status of the monarchy after the decadent years of George IV. The Australian city of Adelaide was named after her.

QUEEN VICTORIA (born 1819 reigned 1837-1901)

Alexandrina Victoria was born on 24th May 1819 at Kensington Palace, London, the only legitimate daughter of George III's fourth son, Edward duke of Kent and his new wife, Princess Victoria of Saxe-Coburg-Saalfeld. This Victoria, was the sister of Leopold, the widower of Princess Charlotte. He would become Leopold I, King of the Belgians in 1830 and, until his death in 1865, would be a close and valued advisor to Queen Victoria. After the death of Princess Charlotte in 1817, the duke of Kent abandoned his comfortable French mistress of 28 years to find a wife who would bring him a Parliamentary annuity and, hopefully, an heir with the legitimate genes needed for the, so-far, threadbare House of Hanover. The duke and Princess Victoria were thus married in Germany in May 1818. They were to enjoy only 20 months of married life before Edward died, after catching a chill, in January 1820, while staying with his wife and daughter at Sidmouth on the Devon coast.

The duke's daughter, Alexandrina Victoria, was only eight months old at her father's death and her adult life would be spent seeking out strong male influences to give her the masculine guidance and support that she felt had died with her father. Her first name, Alexandrina, was the result of a fit of pique by the then - Prince Regent (he did not much like his brother Edward), who withheld his approval of the child's name until the exact moment of her christening. He then insisted on Alexandrina in tribute to the Czar of Russia. Victoria's memory of her childhood is that of a lonely little girl wandering around Kensington Palace surrounded only by adults. To some extent this was true, but occasionally she did have some children 'bussed' in to play with her, and she did visit George IV at Windsor. Her tutors gave her an excellent grounding in the non-classical subjects and her education was intense and comprehensive. She also learned to draw and later showed herself to be an accomplished artist when making sketches of her family and politicians.

Victoria's biggest challenge was Sir John Conroy, the controller of her mother's household. He was supremely ambitious and, after George IV's death in 1830, he saw the princess, as the heir apparent, as his ladder to future power and influence. Under his 'system', Victoria would be kept away from the court and the chance of infection by other, unwelcome, advisors. She would be isolated from any ideas other than those put forward by him and her mother. She would depend on them alone and, when the time was right, he would secure her agreement to make him her private secretary when she was queen. His mistake was to bully and cajole Victoria. He showed her little respect, no affection and no kindness and her memory of his arrogant behaviour would ensure that his dreams would never come true. The Duchess would also feel the pain of her daughter's revenge. She had not been the simple tool of Conroy; she was his co-conspirator, and Victoria knew it!

When William IV became king in 1830 the duchess of Kent, urged on by Conroy, boycotted William's court, snubbing both the King and Queen Adelaide in a variety of ways. The duchess kept Victoria from visiting them on the grounds that she should have no contact with the illegitimate Fitzclarences. Both William and Adelaide were known to be fond of children and the duchess's behaviour was clearly intended to hurt as well as to snub. In 1832, when William IV was wrestling with the difficulties of the 1832 Reform Act, the duchess took Victoria on a stately progress through England where they received loyal addresses from groups campaigning for the Act. The duchess continued taking Victoria on these popularity processions around the country for the next three years, embarrassing William at every opportunity as she went.

After a number of further slights William IV, who now detested the duchess and Sir John Conroy, rose to speak at his own birthday banquet, in August 1836, in front of a hundred guests. He declared that he hoped he would live long enough for Princess Victoria to accede to the throne in her own right so that power was not *'in the hands of a person now near me, who is surrounded by evil advisors and is herself incompetent to act with propriety in the situation in which she would be placed'.* During this tirade the Duchess kept her composure, but Victoria burst into tears. After this relations between the two courts remained quietly hostile.

Victoria was given the news of King William's death, and her accession, at 6 o'clock on the morning of Tuesday 20th June 1837. She received the messengers alone, signalling the immediate end to her mother's and Conroy's control. With regard to William IV, she confided to her journal: *'Poor man, he was always very kind to me and he meant it well I know I am grateful for it and shall ever remember his kindness with gratitude. He was odd, very odd, and singular, but his intentions were often ill-interpreted'.* Victoria would not accede to the crown of Hanover, as under its Salic law no woman could inherit its crown. That privilege fell to William IV's younger brother, the bad old duke of Cumberland, breaking forever the Hanoverian link with the crown of England. Victoria was, of course, a 'Hanoverian' but when she married she would take the family name of her husband. Victoria soon quit Kensington Palace, where she had always slept in her mother's room, for Buckingham Palace. She banished her mother to rooms well away from her own and dismissed Conroy from her household, but not from her mother's.

After her uncle, King Leopold of Belgium, who she saw only infrequently, Victoria's next father-substitute was her first prime minister, the Whig lord Melbourne. This urbane, avuncular, charmer of fifty eight completely entranced Victoria with his knowledge of the world, his quick wit and wide experience of courts and politics. Melbourne's skilful flattery gained him a virtual monopoly of the young queen that some saw as unhealthy. Lord Aberdeen likened Melbourne's position to that of the Protector Somerset in the reign of Edward VI: *'He has a young and inexperienced infant in his hands, whose whole conduct and opinions must necessarily be in complete subservience to his views'.* Melbourne was a man of few political views. Stable government was probably his only political objective, but his inborn scepticism did incline him to the virtue of tolerance. No social reformer, he urged the queen to avoid worrying about the condition of the poor, highlighted by authors such as Charles Dickens. A Whig of the old school, his usual repost when any kind of reform was suggested was: *'Why not leave it alone?'.*

Victoria's inexperience, lack of judgement and overt Whig sympathies became manifest at the beginning of 1839. The unmarried Lady Flora Hastings, a Tory lady- in-waiting to the Duchess of Kent, was, with only a sighting of her in a carriage with Sir John Conroy, suspected of being pregnant by him. In fact, the poor woman was suffering from a cancerous growth on the liver, which made her seem pregnant. The double link of a Tory connection and the hated Conroy led Victoria to believe the worst and Lady Flora was more or less forced to subject herself to a medical examination that proved that she was a virgin. She died in agony on 5th July 1839 and, not surprisingly, public opinion turned against Victoria. She was hissed at when visiting the races at Ascot and greeted with shouts of *'Mrs Melbourne'.* Victoria's infatuation with Melbourne and the Whigs caused further problems when the Tory, Sir Robert Peel, formed a government in 1839 and, as was the norm, expected to replace the Whig ladies of the queen's bedchamber with Tory supporters. The queen resisted and Peel resigned, leaving Melbourne to hang on for two more years. The earnest, reserved and business-like Peel would be back in 1841 and by then he would be embraced by the equally earnest and business-like Prince Albert: the third, and most important, masculine figure in Victoria's life.

Victoria met her cousin, Albert of Saxe-Coburg Gotha, for the second time in October 1839. She fell madly in love with him and quickly proposed (it was not his place to propose to a queen) in the same month. They were married on 10th February 1840. Albert's father, King Leopold's brother, was duke of a German state about the size of Worcestershire and Albert's elder brother would inherit this on his father's death. Albert's marriage to a Queen of England was not a bad consolation prize for a second son. Albert was never as deeply in love with Victoria as she was with him but he did have a strong affection for her. Parliament, and public opinion, certainly did not like, or love him and regularly upset Victoria by quibbling about questions of precedence and a suitable allowance for him. Albert was very much seen as a 'pauper Prince' arriving in England with a begging bowl!

The marriage was a happy one, though peppered with fierce quarrels that were passionate on Victoria's side and steely cold on Albert's, mainly about the upbringing and medical treatment of their children. Early on, Victoria made it plain to her new husband that she, alone, handled the politics of being queen and that Albert could confine himself to sorting out the chaotic and wasteful household they had inherited from Victoria's two royal uncles. This he did, but aided by his vast reserves of patience and his wife's nine pregnancies, he was soon master not only of his wife, but of the queen as well, putting forward strong opinions and often composing her replies to ministers. His dominance over Victoria became total and, although his chilly rationality often resulted in Victoria responding more thoughtfully to the issues of the day, it was achieved by nothing less than breaking her will.

From 1840 onwards, Victoria settled into family life with Albert, who encouraged her to get on with Peel and to take more of an interest in social issues. He became interested in projects for workers' housing and the relief of poverty as well as projects for the encouragement of trade and industry, culminating in the Great International Exhibition of 1851, which Victoria saw as a great triumph for her beloved Albert. The proceeds from the exhibition went to help fund the great museum complex at Kensington and Imperial College London. The statue of Albert opposite the Albert Memorial Hall has him holding a copy of the exhibition's catalogue. No monarch or consort had taken such an interest in the education, training and well-being of the people as Albert, and the Schools of Arts and Science that opened as a result of his various initiatives, although now largely forgotten, made a serious contribution to the health of British art, trade and industry.

Victoria's court reflected middle-class virtue rather than the finesse and false manners of the landed aristocracy. When he was prime minister, lord Salisbury was confident that in gauging the view of Victoria he was also gauging the view of the middle classes. Such a family, happier with the quiet and prosaic routines of domestic, rather than ceremonial, life needed a home of their own. Buckingham Palace, Windsor and the Brighton Pavilion were owned by the state and all had disadvantages with regard to absolute privacy. So Albert and Victoria bought the Osborne estate on the Isle of Wight in 1845 and, in September 1846, the royal family moved into Osborne's Italianate Palace, most of which was designed by Albert. Their next 'private' purchase was Balmoral, on Deeside, on the east coast of Scotland. Highland pursuits drew the family north of the border every autumn and unwilling ministers, usually less enamoured with tartan, mountains, porridge and rain, followed as government business dictated.

The revolutions that broke out over much of Europe during the late 1840s touched Victoria and Albert through their vast network of royal connections. Some of the revolutionary aggression was directed against their friends and relatives, and Victoria and Albert wanted to find ways of showing solidarity with them rather than with the radicals who wanted to bring them down. This put them in direct opposition to Palmerston, the Foreign Secretary at the time, who, although deeply conservative and imperialist, was keen to give moral support to continental liberal movements in order to embarrass other European rulers and perhaps curry some favour with radicals in England. Led by Albert, Victoria insisted that she should see all of Palmeston's despatches to foreign governments before they were sent, and this was done, or rather it was done most of the time.

In the summer of 1850, Victoria and Albert asked the prime minister, lord John Russell, to dismiss the maverick Palmerston, which he refused to do. As it happened, Palmerston was dismissed a year later only to return as Home Secretary in the next government. Albert's clumsy interference in foreign policy was highlighted in 1854 during the run up to the Crimean War when Albert drafted a plan for peace, which was leaked and, in the middle of the great public clamour for war against Russia, got himself branded as a Russian spy. Palmerston returned to haunt Victoria as prime minister in 1855, but this time he earned her respect by his hard line with Russia at the Peace Conference after the Crimean War. He also supported her long-desired wish to make Albert Prince Consort. She had hoped that parliament would have approved this by now but, tired of waiting, she did it by letters patent in 1857.

Victoria's mother the duchess of Kent, who with Albert's encouragement had been reconciled to her daughter, died in March 1861. Victoria became hysterical with grief. Such was the depth of her grief and breakdown that rumours spread around the courts of Europe suggesting that she was mentally ill. Later, in November of the same year, Albert's health was not good. He was possibly suffering from cancer of the stomach or bowel but Victoria, so wrapped up in her own grief, found his illness a tiresome distraction. Albert had never been a robust person and perhaps Victoria just saw this latest bout as more of the same. After three days of hopes rising and falling, Albert died of typhoid fever on 14th December 1861. As well as his physical ailments, Albert had been suffering from anxiety and insomnia over the news that Edward, Prince of Wales (known as Bertie), had had a brief fling with an actress, Nellie Clifden, while with the army in Ireland. Just before his death, Albert had returned from Cambridge, where, on a cold, wet day, he had remonstrated with his son about the ills of sexual licence. For some time afterwards Victoria blamed Bertie for his father's death, declaring *'much as I pity I never can or shall look at him without a shudder'*.

The devastation that Albert's death caused Victoria stemmed from his almost total control of her life and character. She hardly chose a bonnet without his approval; how would she continue as head of a rapidly changing, industrialised state without him by her side? Her answer was to make widowhood, mourning and tears a full time occupation. *'I do not want to feel better… the relief of tears is great … they come again and again every day and are soothing to the bruised heart and soul'.* Victoria did attend dutifully to her ministerial papers but she hid herself away from the public at Balmoral, Windsor or Osborne, communicating with her ministers mainly through the post. But she was not alone. Albert was *with her*. Now the queen would draw his high moral spirit from pictures, busts and mementoes, always trying to imagine how he *'the purest and best of human beings'* would act. If politicians thought they had seen the last of Albert they were mistaken, his ghost would haunt their despatch boxes for the next forty years.

Victoria's behaviour in the years after Albert's death provoked suspicions that she may have inherited the 'madness' of George III. Parts of Windsor, Osborne, Balmoral and Buckingham Palace were now given over as shrines to Albert. Victoria had the Blue Room at Windsor photographed the day after Albert's death so that it could be preserved just as it was at ten minutes to eleven on the fatal night. She ordered that Albert's dressing gown and fresh clothes should be laid out each evening. The glass from which he had taken his last dose of medicine was kept on a bedside table and stayed there for more than forty years. She filled the Blue Room with pictures and a bust of Albert and had fresh flowers strewn about his bed. It was much the same at Osborne. After a visit there, Lord Clarendon said that he expected Albert to arrive at any minute, so carefully were his things arranged. Notices sprang up on the doors of any rooms that Albert had arranged reminding people that they must not disturb anything. The crushing solemnity of all this, executed with a Prussian attention to detail, must have been oppressive to the poor servants when upstairs and the butt of much ribaldry when they were downstairs. Victoria's court was now even duller than before with little by way of diversion for those expected to attend on her. Dinners, in particular, were painful affairs conducted in whispers and long periods of silence. In addition two or three of Victoria's numerous relatives died every year and prescriptive court mourning, with its stifling conventions and different degrees of black and gloom, added yet another layer of melancholy to the royal household.

Victoria now needed a man close to her whom she could trust and, more to the point, one whom Albert would have trusted. Enter the fourth man whom she was to lean on, domestically at least, for the next twenty-two years. John Brown had attended on the royal couple when they were at Balmoral and thus came with Albert's seal of approval. Brown, a countryman who was a bit rough round the edges, impressed Victoria by his total lack of affection. By just being himself, by giving her sympathy and understanding, by caring, and by not being afraid to speak his mind: *'Hoots, then wumman. Can ye no hold yerr head up',* he became the chief focus of her emotional life. He ordered Victoria about, in ways that no one else would dare but his most valuable contribution was to get her outside into the fresh air, riding and taking some exercise. His influence was deeply resented by Victoria's children, who hated to see a servant rise so high in the queen's favour. We will never know the extent of their intimacy, despite the rumours and press reports about 'Mrs Brown' during Victoria's life, and after her death. Brown died in 1883 and Victoria erected a large obelisk at Balmoral and a granite seat at Osborne to his memory but, on her own death, her son, Edward VII, had everything associated with John Brown quickly removed from all his mother's rooms.

During her long reign Victoria worked with, or against, ten prime ministers. After Melbourne, Peel and Palmerston the most important, to her at any rate, were Disraeli, Gladstone and, for all but three of her last fourteen years, Robert Cecil, lord Salisbury. Disraeli first became prime minister (briefly) in 1868 and enchanted Victoria with his author's flair for romance and chivalry and, in 1874, pleased her even more by becoming the first Tory leader since Peel to win a parliamentary majority. Now he flirted with Victoria; he flattered her, he sought her opinion and guidance and always seemed to value her many years of experience. Victoria lapped it up and Disraeli admitted to his friends that with the queen, *'you should lay it on with a trowel'.* When he lay dying in 1880 Disraeli was asked if he would like the queen to visit him. He replied, *'No it is better not. She would only ask me to take a message to Albert'.*

After all this swish and swill, William Gladstone's election in 1868 was a deep disappointment. Despite his leadership of the greatest reforming administration of the nineteenth century, Victoria thought Gladstone a humbug and a hypocrite and his chilly intellectualism left her cold. To her he was a dangerous radical, he was not safe and, perhaps recognising a kindred spirit, she accused him of being obstinate. After the great Liberal success in the election of 1880, and fuelled by an 'anyone but Gladstone' emotion, she invited other Liberal leaders to form a government. Her failure just served to strengthen Gladstone's position, as their weakness, and Gladstone's obvious superiority, was even more exposed. Unlike Disraeli, Gladstone was somewhat in awe of Victoria as his sovereign and despite his own wife urging him to 'treat her as a woman'; he could not find ways of making himself agreeable to her. Of course, his high church instincts and his policies, Home Rule for Ireland, the Disestablishment of the Church of Ireland and his radical reform of the career structures of the civil service, the army and local government, cast him in the role of interfering demon.

Seizing another opportunity to harass Gladstone in 1885, Victoria blamed him for the death of General Gordon at Khartoum. *'We were just too late as we always are – it is I, who, have as the Head of the Nation, to bear the humiliation'.* Worse than all of his policies however, was Gladstone's attempt to draw Victoria out of her self-imposed seclusion. This issue was now getting serious. By the late 1860s many voices, both inside and outside Parliament, were being raised about the queen's isolation. These focussed on her hoarding of royal revenues while refusing to open Parliament or carry out the other public duties expected of a constitutional monarch. Republicans now had a clear target: an absent queen who was squirreling away money, while refusing to work. Other radicals joined in and a number of newspaper articles and pamphlets appeared that were highly critical of Victoria. Simon Schama noted that all this served, *'to nourish the most sustained British flirtation with republicanism since the Civil war of the 17th century'*.

Despite these criticisms, of which she was obviously aware, Victoria remained adamant that she would not go about in public to be stared at by curious crowds. As time went on, of course, her non-appearance just served to make the public, the newspapers and the cartoonists, even more curious about the recluse of Osborne. The queen, if she cared about this at all, was unwittingly helped by Bertie, who went down with typhoid in 1871, and teetered on the verge of death. Bertie recovered fully during early 1872 and, instead of moans about the 'hidden' queen, a grateful nation now celebrated the safe deliverance of the heir to the throne. Five years later Disraeli persuaded a reluctant Parliament to proclaim Victoria Empress of India. She was delighted and from this time onwards Victoria did, very slowly, start to emerge from her reclusive shell. By the time the nation celebrated her Golden Jubilee in 1887 she had dispensed with some of the trappings of gloom and signs of the feisty, stubborn, assertive girl who had dismissed Conroy so abruptly in 1837 began to resurface. Suppressed over 25 years ago by Albert's lectures and hectoring, her true character was now springing back. Her heated struggles with Gladstone during the 1880s reflect a queen who seemed almost re-born, breaking with the rigid self- control that Albert had carefully layered over her more passionate nature.

Robert Cecil, lord Salisbury, was prime minister between 1886 and 1892 supported by those Liberal Unionists who had defected from Gladstone over Irish Home Rule. His third government, of 1895-1902, would see out Victoria's reign. A man of many paradoxes, Salisbury was often gloomy; he was a pessimistic, anti-democrat despite being the principal beneficiary of the extension of the franchise in 1884. He was, electorally, the most successful Tory leader until Margaret Thatcher. More a Gladstone than a 'Dizzy' in his personal relations with Victoria, he 'worked' for her because they largely agreed on the big issues of the day, particularly Ireland. As with the 'Bedchamber Crisis' of 1839, Victoria's weakness for conflating the personal with the political while convincing herself that all her actions transcended politics, was a recurrent theme throughout her reign. When Melbourne had given way to Peel in the 1840s Victoria had, for a time, continued an unconstitutional correspondence with Melbourne, seeking his advice and allowing him to comment on her new prime minister. She did the same when Disraeli was out of office, corresponding with him about Gladstone, and later she passed government papers to lord Salisbury when he was briefly out of office. While Albert was alive these habits of keeping a line open with those opposition politicians of whom Victoria approved was mostly kept in check but its occasional resurgence, throughout her reign, shows a queen often acting on the edge of constitutional propriety.

Victoria did not read Walter Bagehot's 'The English Constitution' published in 1867, which urged that a constitutional monarch only had the right to be consulted, to encourage and to warn. Nor would she have approved of it. Unwittingly she would later become a convert to Bagehot's *'theatrical* show' of society as part of an aristocracy that enjoyed the display of power, while the middle classes got on with exercising *'despotic power'* and the *'masses'* were just kept in check. It would not be so easy for Victoria's successor to interfere, although he tried, and Victoria herself found it more difficult towards the end of her reign. The infant constitutional monarchy that had begun with William III in 1689 was coming of age two hundred years later as the widening of the electoral franchise put the people, not the monarch, in the driving seat. Party lines and party differences were also hardening. The Liberals had emerged as a butterfly from the larvae of the factious Whigs and the Tories had the new foundations of 'Unionism' and 'Empire' to bind them more tightly together. The British governing elites had come through the dangerous 1840s and avoided 'revolution' by trimming and by being willing to compromise and regroup around gradual reforms, guided by enlightened self-interest. They had not accommodated all this to hand over extended personal prerogatives to any monarch. By the time of her Diamond Jubilee in 1897, Victoria's popularity had returned to a high level. Too lame to leave her carriage, Victoria presided over a brief open air Service of Thanksgiving, outside St Paul's Cathedral on 22nd June 1897, triumphant in her survival of a sixty year reign. Ironically, given her reticence towards public show, it was she who inaugurated the large scale royal processions and ceremonial that would become the principal role of the British monarchy in the future.

Victoria's health had been declining since 1900. It had not been a good year for her family. Her second son, Alfred, had died from throat cancer in July 1900 and her grandson, Prince Christian, had died of enteric fever on his way home from South Africa. Lady Churchill, the last of her ladies-in-waiting from Albert's time, died on Christmas day 1900. Victoria now had trouble sleeping at night and she tended to fall asleep during the day. She was old and frail, her eyesight was failing, her rheumatism was troublesome and she had lost her once hearty appetite. Victoria began her first diary entry for 1901 with *'Another year begun & I am feeling so weak and unwell that I enter upon it sadly'*. The Boer War was still raging and, although the news from there was now more positive, she believed that the early defeats of her army in South Africa had contributed significantly to her declining health. She dictated her final diary entry on 13th January 1901, ending the daily record that she had started in 1832, a unique account of her days, as she saw them, covering nearly 69 years.

The public became aware of the queen's ill health when the first bulletin was telegraphed from Osborne on 18th January. The various bulletins issued on the 22nd January prepared them for the worst. Osborne, 8am: *'The Queen this morning shows signs of diminishing strength and her majesty's condition again assumes a more serious aspect'*. Osborne, 12 o'clock: *'No change for the worse in the Queen's condition since this morning's bulletin. Her Majesty has recognised the several members of the Royal Family that are here. The Queen is now asleep'*. Osborn, 4pm: *'the Queen is slowly sinking'*. Osborne (untimed): *'Her majesty breathed her last at 6.30pm surrounded by her children and grandchildren'*. With her eldest grandson, the German Kaiser, Wilhelm, supporting her on one side of her bed, and her doctor Sir James Reid supporting her on the other, Queen Victoria moved in and out of consciousness and eventually passed peacefully away. She died of senile decay or, as we might say today, simply of old age, she was eighty one.

Ever alert to the ceremony surrounding other people's funerals and always attentive to the burial of her favourite dogs, it was not surprising that Victoria had carefully planned her own funeral. As head of the armed forces she wanted a military funeral. She was not to be embalmed; she hated 'black' funerals so she was to be dressed in white, wearing her white wedding veil. Her coffin, covered in a white pall, was to be pulled by white horses. A key component of her plan was the items that she wanted placed in her coffin. These included one of Albert's dressing gowns, a plaster cast of his hand, numerous photographs, various rings, chains and little mementoes from nearly all of her large extended family. Two items that Victoria requested, which her relatives did not see added to her coffin, were a photograph of John Brown and a lock of his hair, which were to be placed in her left hand, discreetly covered by a posy of flowers. She also wore Brown's mother's wedding ring that he had given to Victoria just before his own death in 1883.

The funerals of both George IV and William IV had been regarded by many commentators as less than dignified and this would not do for the 'grandmother' of Europe. The problem was that three organs of royal ceremony needed to be involved: the Lord Chamberlain's Office (a practical, experienced and well staffed operation), The duke of Norfolk, who as Earl Martial of England, was in overall charge of state ceremonies (but who had no staff and little experience) and the College of Heralds (who, since Edward IV's time, had had some hand in royal funerals, particularly the finicky bits associated with orders of precedence, shields and coats of arms). The Comptroller (a senior official working in the Lord Chamberlain's Office) at the time of Victoria's funeral was the Hon Sir Spencer Ponsonby-Fane (PF). It had been sixty-four years since the last royal funeral and the once well-oiled State Funeral machine had perhaps got a little rusty.

PF indicated in the various notes he made at the time (now held by the Royal Archives at Windsor) the frustration he felt at the shambles going on behind the scenes. *'The preparations for the Queen's funeral were carried in and carried out in the most extraordinary hurly burly of confusion'*. PF could not believe that the duke of Norfolk insisted on his right to organise things. *'He had no staff ready for such a purpose, and the heralds he collected together were as ignorant and inefficient as can be [expletive]'*. Victoria's coffin had to travel, by sea, from the Isle of Wight to Portsmouth. It would then go by rail to Victoria Station in London, and then in procession through London to Paddington station. From there it would travel by train, again to Windsor, before yet another procession. Clearly a lot of things could go wrong!

In the end, the arrangements were divided into four parts: part one covering the journey from Osborne, part two covering the procession in London, part three the procession through Windsor and part four the final small procession from Windsor to the Royal Mausoleum at Frogmore. A committee, made up of representatives from the three offices concerned, was set up to consider the multiplicity of issues that Victoria's last journey would involve. The meetings became bogged down in disputes over who should do what and for PF *'... it was the most trying 10 days I have ever gone through from the uncertainty of what was done and what the theory wished, and the utter imbecility of the heralds'*. In the end, although it looked to the public that all went without a hitch, *'It was to my mind a disgrace when connected with so helpless a body as the Heralds College in a ceremony of this kind.'*

The queen's body lay at Osborne House from 22nd January until 1st February 1901, where members of her household, tenants, local gentry and intimates of the queen were allowed to visit and pay their respects. On Friday 1st February the queen's triple coffin, of oak, lead and more oak, and weighing half a ton, was born from the house by a party of sailors from the Royal Yachts and then escorted to Trinity Pier by the Queen's Company, Grenadier Guards where it was loaded on to HMY Alberta for the trip across the Solent to Gosport. On the journey across the Solent, the Alberta passed between a line of 30 British and 8 foreign warships assembled between Cowes and Spithead, each ship firing a 'minute' gun as the stern of the Alberta passed by. At Gosport the queen's body remained on the yacht overnight and on Saturday 2nd February it was put on a train, destined for Victoria Station in London, where it arrived at 11am. There, while a guard of honour stood in a bitterly cold wind under a grey sky, brushing flakes of snow from their greatcoats, her coffin was put on a gun carriage. It was drawn by eight cream-coloured horses and after a long procession through London to Paddington station she was loaded on yet another Royal train, this time bound for Windsor.

At Windsor station a naval guard of honour, 100 strong, who had disdained to wear their greatcoats, stood to attention as the coffin emerged, to be loaded on to a gun carriage drawn by horses of the Royal Horse artillery. It was at this moment that one of those accidents that no amount of planning can predict took place. The Royal Train was about half an hour late and everyone at the station, including the horses, had been in place for about one and a half hours before the train arrived. The gun-carriage horses had not been able to move or exercise during this time. After the coffin was placed on the carriage and the officer in charge gave the order to advance, the horses nearest the wheels started to rear up and kick about. This then spread to the horses at the front, who severed the traces linking them to the carriage, and left the royal coffin looking as if it would topple off.

A whispered discussion with King Edward VII soon resolved that the horses should be taken away. The naval guard of honour was then formed up into fours and attached to drag ropes made up of the trappings from the horses, bits of the communication chord from the train and sundry bits of rope. After about five minutes the naval ratings stepped off at the slow march to drag the queen's remains up the steep hill to Windsor Castle. So impressed was Edward VII by the navy's prompt action during this crisis that he instructed that, from this time on, naval ratings would always draw the gun carriage carrying the royal coffin at Windsor. From the time of George V, a loyal navy man, this order was extended so that naval ratings would draw the monarch's coffin at state funerals through London as well. As in George III's time, the boys and masters of Eton College, and the Eton volunteers, lined the hill from the Long Walk Gates up to Windsor castle, where some 3,000 wreaths carpeted the Chapel precincts. After the funeral service in St. George's Chapel, the coffin was taken to lie in the Albert Memorial Chapel, where it stayed from Saturday 2nd February to Monday 4th February.

After Albert's death, Victoria decided to modify the royal tradition of being buried in ancient churches with royal associations. Her mother, the Duchess of Kent, had asked Albert to build her a mausoleum in the grounds of Frogmore House. It was almost completed when she died in 1861 and on 14th December of that same year Albert also died. Within four days Victoria had decided that her husband, and later she, would also lie in a similar mausoleum at Frogmore. It would cost £200,000 (more than the total cost of building Osborne House) and it would be based on one she had seen at Coburg in Germany. While it was being built, Albert's body rested in a temporary sarcophagus at Windsor. Although the internal decoration of the building was not completed until 1871, the body of Albert was moved there in 1868 and placed in the huge sarcophagus, (resting on a base of Belgian black marble), made from a single block of grey Aberdeen granite, said to be the largest block of flawless wrought granite in existence. After Albert's death, this became a place of pilgrimage and solace for Victoria. She would retreat here to contemplate 'his beloved features' and, in the early years after his death, to pray that she would join him soon.

That day came at 3pm on Monday 4th February 1901 when her coffin was, this time successfully, put on another gun carriage and she was taken down the Long Walk to Frogmore. There, in a private ceremony, Queen Victoria was laid to rest beside her husband. The long wait was over! For safety, Victoria's effigy, carved at the same time as Albert's, by the Italian sculptor, Carlo Marochetti, had been stored away somewhere. After a frantic hunt, an old workman said he remembered it being walled up in the stores at Windsor around 1862. After demolishing a brick wall in a storeroom it was found and then lowered over her tomb to lie next to Albert's. The white marble effigies, of Albert facing upwards to the mosaics in the dome, and a very young looking Victoria, her face slightly inclined in adoration of her husband, are both lit by a flood of light that falls in romantic shafts from the dome above. Marochetti was asked to portray Victoria as she was at the moment of Albert's death but her face looks much younger than forty two, more like the girl of nineteen who married Albert in 1840. Victoria's was the first Royal funeral at which photographs were taken and newspapers and journals were keen to make the most of this new technology. On 30th January the Illustrated London news devoted 48 pages to a special pictorial edition chronicling Victoria's life, and on 7th February it produced another special edition under the banner of 'The Funeral Procession of Queen Victoria'.

Victoria was the longest-serving monarch in British history and all her nine children survived to adulthood, a situation only matched by the children of George III, and unusual even among rich Victorians. Since the end of the First World War all but seven of Europe's kingdoms have become republics. Yet, through the elaborate network of intermarriage between Victoria's nine children and the royal families of Europe during the nineteenth century, in six of those seven kingdoms, Britain, Norway, Denmark, Sweden, Belgium and Spain, descendants of Victoria and Albert still reign as Head of State. The Netherlands is the exception, but their present queen is descended from Britain's King George II.

EDWARD VII   (born 1841 reigned 1901-1910)

Albert Edward, the first son and second child of Queen Victoria and Prince Albert was born at Buckingham Palace on 9th November 1841. Although named Albert after his father, he was always known as 'Bertie' in the family. He was the first heir to be born to a reigning sovereign since 1762, and the last to be verified as such (to confirm no fraud or trickery) by the presence of privy councillors at his birth. After this only the Home Secretary needed to be present to testify to an heir's legitimacy!

From an early age it became apparent that Bertie was a slow learner. Ignoring this evidence Prince Albert framed a detailed syllabus him which, for a boy who was obviously not bookish or intellectual, was not going to work. The dire parallels with George III that he was following by insisting on such a programme for his eldest son eluded Albert, whose ideas on education were fixed and immoveable. Victoria reported that *'Bertie had a small, empty brain'* while Albert wrote *'I never in my life met with such a thorough and cunning lazybones'*. As Bertie continued to fail most of the milestones that his father had set, his parents' added vinegar to his woes by regularly reminding him of how much brighter, his elder sister 'Vicky' was. Victoria had dreams of 'Bertie' becoming the mirror image of his upright and dutiful father engaging on equal terms with politicians, artists and scientists. She was surprised when Hanoverian history repeated itself and Bertie swapped austere morality and rote learning for the pleasures of hunting, smoking, gambling, food and women. It really was looking like George IV all over again!

A visit to Paris in 1855 with his parents, as part of a state visit to Napoleon III, impressed the sixteen year old prince, who fell in love with the life and energy of the city. He would visit it again, many times, when he was older. Further attempts to get him engaged in academic study, by keeping him isolated at the White Lodge in Richmond Park, accompanied only by his tutors and three hand-picked companions, yielded no better results than before. Although he did become fluent in French and German, always speaking English with a slight German accent, Albert and Victoria eventually gave up trying to turn Bertie into his father. The journey was going to take too long! A short period at Oxford was followed, between July and November 1860, by a successful trip to Canada and the USA, the first by an heir to the British throne. Released from the strait-jacket of Buckingham Palace and 3,000 miles from home, Bertie's charm and natural bonhomie, avoidance of politics and easy manner with everyone he met, showed that he had the makings of a good royal ambassador.

On his return to England Bertie spent the summer of 1861 at an army camp at the Curragh near Dublin, where his fellow officers smuggled the actress Nellie Clifden into his tent. While Bertie was being initiated into one of the pleasures that would dominate his life, his mother and father were busy arranging for him to marry Princess Alexandra of Schleswig-Holstein-Sonderburg-Glücksburg. Bertie then spent some time at Cambridge University, where his father caught up with him towards the end of 1861. Although not well Albert felt that he had to tackle his son about the now simmering Nellie Clifden affair. He was anxious about the behaviour of his son and its possible impact on the family, particularly its impact on Bertie's forthcoming marriage to Alexandra. Shortly after returning from this trip to see his son, Prince Albert died of typhoid Fever at Windsor.

Bertie and Princess Alexandra were married on 10th March 1863 in St George's Chapel, Windsor. Queen Victoria, covered in black, looked on from high up, hidden behind the oriel window once used by Catherine of Aragon to watch the garter ceremonies. Disraeli was flattered to be invited to the wedding and noted *'... the magnificent music, the Queen in her widowed garments in her Gothic cabinet, all deeply interesting or effective'*. Alexandra was tall, very beautiful, slim, elegant and rather deaf. She was every inch a princess. Sensitive and loyal, she became a popular consort through her unpretentious kindness and her devotion to good causes, particularly the Red Cross. Her deafness got much worse as she grew older, adding to the isolation she often felt as Edward spent time away from her with a variety of upper-and lower-class mistresses. After their marriage she and Bertie set up home at Marlborough House, in Pall Mall, in London. In 1861 Albert had acquired Sandringham House estate in Norfolk as a country home for Bertie, in the vain hope that the plump pheasants that prospered there, which Bertie loved to shoot, would pull him away from the fleshpots of London. His London base secure at Marlborough House, Bertie did indeed take to Sandringham, holding lavish hunting and shooting parties there on a regular basis. Sadly for Albert, London had no monopoly on fleshpots; the country was just as awash with them, and Bertie moved around the grand houses of England enjoying them all. Town or country, Bertie and Alexandra set about providing a lively and bright alternative to the gloom of the widow's habitat, and much of London's society flocked to their door.

Victoria, still immersed in the fiction that Albert was alive and well and governing her every move, could see no need for Bertie to make it a triumvirate. She resisted every prime minister's attempt to find the Prince something useful to do and then, just like George III, complained about his racy companions and his indolent life. For many years Bertie was not allowed to sit on commissions or public bodies of any kind. Despite her almost total, and much resented, seclusion, she even forbade him from representing her at public events. This level of exclusion was all the more galling for Bertie as Victoria allowed Prince Leopold, her fourth and youngest son, to act as her confidential secretary and gave him access to her minister's despatch boxes. Bertie was given a précis of some official documents but Victoria's clear message to him was that he couldn't really be trusted with anything very important.

Bertie was thus to spend sixty years as a Prince of Wales doing nothing much of importance. Without a formal role his predilections ran to pleasure. He enjoyed the races, the music hall, hunting, shooting, country house parties, travelling to Biarritz, and visiting the spa of Marienbad in Bohemia. All these coalesced in a social round that filled Edward's time and, a rule, they didn't coincide with the more austere seasonal routine of his mother. The Prince's greatest pleasure was women, and he cultivated a range of mistresses, including the actress Lily Langtry, Daisy Brooke Lady Warwick, Mrs Alice Keppel, Agnes Keyser and others. Nellie Clifden, who prompted Albert's tortuous visit to the Prince in 1861, was an early but brief affair. Edward's later female companions tended to be attractive, intelligent and capable of interesting conversation, although Daisy Brooke's flirtation with socialism was probably a 'conversation' too far for Edward's taste. The Prince *'preferred men to books and women to either'*.

Confining his attention mainly to married women with accommodating husbands, Bertie generally did not seek to hide his female companions and often took them with him on his visits to Europe. But some wives were not so easy to handle. In early 1871 the prince was involved in a divorce case in which Sir Charles Mordaunt had wanted to cite the prince as one of his wife's lovers. Mordaunt's twenty one year old wife, in convulsions of guilt over the blindness of one of her children, had confessed that Sir Charles was not the father and that she had *'done wrong'* with *'the Prince of Wales and others, often and in open day'*. That 'open day' admission must have sent shock waves through the Victorian middle-classes. In the end, after some pressure from ministers, Mordaunt cited two of the Prince's close friends as co-respondents but Bertie was subpoenaed to appear as a witness. He boldly denied any suggestion of adultery despite clear evidence that he had often called on the lady during afternoons, when she was alone. In 'open day', no less! As poor Lady Mordaunt had been sent to an asylum for the insane before the trial started, the court dismissed her husband's petition on the grounds that as she had been deranged when she made her confession and she could not be party to the suit. She was not the first woman to be punished while the men who preyed on her walked free, but her story is no less poignant for that.

This scandal erupted during a period when Victoria was being attacked by republicans and others for her refusal to carry out her proper duties or to appear in public. The exposure of Bertie as one of a fast set who cared nothing for the social conventions that bound ordinary people added fuel to this fire and ministers became alarmed lest more skeletons should appear from the closet of their idle prince. Before the Mordaunt trial, Gladstone had put forward the radical plan that Bertie should become Viceroy of Ireland, living there in a royal residence and acting almost as a constitutional monarch. Two years of argument with the queen failed to gain her agreement and this plan was dropped.

Typhoid, the disease that had taken her beloved Albert, now came to aid both the queen and the prince. In November 1871, while visiting a country house near Scarborough, Bertie caught typhoid and his condition became critical. The queen hastened to the prince's bedside at Sandringham and as time went on without any sign of recovery, she became fearful that Bertie would die, on the anniversary of Albert's death, taken by the same disease. After a month or so of life and death struggle, and on the very day, the 14th December, that the queen had so feared, Bertie's doctors announced that he was past the critical point. A sense of general relief swept the country. Outrage and republicanism were now replaced by warm feelings of gratitude that the Prince of Wales had survived. Prime minister Gladstone, keen to capitalise on emotions that had long been dormant in the public psyche, persuaded a reluctant Victoria to ride with her son, in an open carriage, to St Paul's Cathedral for a service of thanksgiving in February 1872. The royal party were cheered enthusiastically through the streets. The happy crowd, the banners, flags and church bells echoed a universal feeling of goodwill towards the widow and her stout son. The cries of the republicans were drowned out by the celebrations, and they would never recover.

The 1870s saw Bertie being given more ceremonial roles, and perhaps less time to get into trouble. In October 1875, he set off to India, where for five months he murdered tigers and impressed everyone with his easy manner. While there, he was strongly critical of the 'rude and rough' manner used by British officers towards native Indians. Back at home, the prince also sat on a number of royal commissions, including one on the housing of the working classes and another on the aged poor. Nothing about Edward's subsequent behaviour suggests that his time listening to the appalling evidence on these issues, and visiting poor housing in the east end of London, had any impact whatsoever on the social conscience of the future king. At home in their palaces, Princess Alexandra provided Bertie with six children. The first, Albert Victor (prince Eddie), was born prematurely, but safely, in January 1864. He was soon followed by Prince George, Princess Louise, Princess Victoria and Princess Maud. Another son was also born but died shortly after his birth. Alexandra was devoted to her children, to the extent that it was feared that her daughters might never leave their 'darling mother dear' to get married. In the end, only her second daughter, Victoria, died as a spinster. Bertie also loved his children and was painfully aware of how his own education had failed him. He thus took steps to ensure that his sons avoided the terrible isolation that he felt had held him back. Both Albert Victor and George were sent as naval cadets to the training ship Britannia, but the early signs of Albert Victor's poor attention span and weakness of mind turned, as he came of age, to hopeless dissipation (see below). His early death in 1892 may have been a blessing as far as the safety of the crown was concerned leaving his brother, George (later George V), as next in line to the throne.

Scandal can emerge from unexpected circumstances and in 1890 Bertie was in the news again. During a house party, one of the guests, a Sir William Gordon Cummings, had been accused of cheating at baccarat, a game that was illegal in England, but was still a regular diversion among Bertie's set. The affair would normally have remained one of those private disputes between 'gentlemen' that rarely impinged on the public consciousness. But rumours of cheating began to circulate and Cummings, to protect his name, decided to bring an action against his accusers and subpoenaed the prince as a witness during the public trial.

In 1891, Bertie testified to the quality and trustworthiness of those who had accused Cummings and, by doing so, branded himself as an illegal gambler. Some newspapers, and nonconformist preachers, enjoyed taking the high moral ground and the prince was censured for his lack of wisdom in mixing with such dissipated company. Despite this, Bertie generally fared well with newspapers. They rarely pursued such exposures with vigour and had no stomach for seeing their future king dragged through the mud. In 1898, Bertie formed intimate friendships with two women that would last until the end of his life. One was the attractive and discreet Sister Agnes Keyser, a matron of a nursing home for army officers, who became the prince's mistress and often entertained him with very plain dinners. The other, who also became his mistress, was the beautiful, clever and vivacious, Alice Frederica Keppel. These two women formed an important part of the prince's non-palace life during his later years and clearly meant much more to him than his earlier liaisons.

In 1901, Queen Victoria died and Bertie's long wait was over. On becoming king, Albert Edward, dropped his first name and with it the long remembered burden of his parents' impossible expectations. Instead, he would be known as King Edward VII. His official reason for this was that there could be only one 'Albert the Good' and it would be churlish for him to take on such a sainted and valued name. Having waited for so long to become king, Edward wasted no time in making his mark on the physical legacy left by his mother. Never fond of Osborne, he gave it over as a training centre for naval cadets, retaining just a few rooms as a monument to Victoria. He modernised Buckingham Palace, which had been deserted by his mother, replacing the plumbing and gutting the funereal apartments that had been left dedicated to Albert. It would be his main London residence. During Victoria's last years it was common knowledge that many of her servants at Balmoral were often drunk while serving at dinner, breaking plates and scattering food around the floor. To the amazement of her guests the old queen seemed to tolerate this behaviour while other, more minor, indiscretions of protocol were still frowned upon. No drunkard himself Edward soon rooted out this behaviour even sacking a man of thirty years service when he found him drunk.

Edward resumed the practice of opening parliament in person; Victoria had not done so since 1886. Edward's love of processions, ceremonial state visits and royal progresses gave the king a visibility that contrasted starkly with the dull days of the withdrawn widow. The newspapers loved following his movements and reported on them in graphic detail – truly the 'bread and circuses' of royal pageantry was back and the public lapped it up. 'Edward the Ostentatious' would not have been a bad nickname for their new king. The fun and games of the country house parties continued, but Edward maintained a rigid formality on all public occasions.

Almost sixty, stout, bedevilled by ailments that stemmed from his lifestyle (five meals, twenty cigarettes and half a dozen huge cigars a day), he was, remarkably, not short of energy. He created the Order of Merit, limited to 24 British members who had distinguished themselves in the arts, sciences and literature, he initiated a major fund to support hospitals in London and helped to popularise the motor car. His remarkable success with his racehorses made him a popular son of the turf with the general public, who often wagered, and won, on his horses. Despite his nickname of 'Tum Tum', he was also a man of fashion. His, necessary, habit of leaving the lower button of his waistcoat undone was taken up by those who had nothing better to do and he popularised the modern dinner jacket with black tie. His wearing of a Homburg hat became popular but his habit of creasing his trousers at the side never caught on. He would pass on his obsession with correct dress, arrangement of military decorations and punctuality to his son George V. He was constantly frustrated by Queen Alexandra's poor timekeeping.

Edward believed that Britain had become dangerously isolated during the Boer war and that it was now time for him, as king, to play that much desired role in foreign affairs that had been denied him as Prince of Wales. Working, initially, in secret, he planned a state visit to various European countries. Edward was well travelled and he believed that his extensive reservoir of European connections put him in an unrivalled position to bring Britain and the old enemy, France, closer together. In the spring of 1903, Edward first visited Portugal, Gibraltar, Malta and then, unofficially, as his cabinet disapproved, the pope in Rome. This was the first visit that a British sovereign had ever made to a pope, and his Catholic subjects in Ireland were quick to applaud his initiative. He returned home via Paris, the main reason behind his tour.

Initially, the old suspicions surfaced and he was received coolly by French society but then Edward initiated a moment of spontaneous charm that set the city alight. During an interval at a theatre, the king noticed a famed French actress. He approached her, and addressing her in French said, '*Mademoiselle, I remember applauding you in London where you represented all the grace and spirit of France'*. News of this incident spread around the city like wildfire and from that point on his visit became a great success. Following on from his trip to France Edward hosted a successful visit by the French President and his Foreign Minister to England in 1904. The evolution of Anglo-French relations into the Entente Cordiale of April 1904 was not due only to Edward VII's initiatives, but it owed much to an objective secretly formulated by the king and to his tact and perseverance in following it through.

From 1906 onwards, the king's bronchitis and gout worsened and despite suffering from excess weight and nights of coughing, he still defied his doctors, continuing to eat vast quantities of food and smoking his immense cigars. He had suffered a number of minor injuries during his life including an accident to his knee-cap and a trip over a rabbit hole in Windsor Park, but his main problem was the increasing number of bronchial attacks. In February 1909 a reluctant Edward was urged by his government make a State Visit to Germany. He was ill, melancholic and had little affection for his nephew Kaiser Wilhelm. While there, Edward collapsed in a spasm of coughing after a lunch at the British Embassy, and had to be revived by his doctor. On his return home, his wheezing got much worse. He began falling asleep over lunch and dinner as well as snoring soundly through performances at the opera and the theatre.

Edward would need all his reserves of strength to stay awake, for although weak and tired, the king would soon face a constitutional dilemma that would require all of his attention. The Liberal Party had won an overwhelming victory at the General Election of 1906 and was bent on serious reform of the fiscal system. Early in 1909, David Lloyd George, Chancellor of the Exchequer, had put together his momentous 1909 budget. Money was needed to fund old-age pensions and pay for the new dreadnought battle ships that the Unionist opposition had supported. He intended to get the cash from new taxes, mainly on the rich: '*I shall have to rob somebody's hen roost and I must consider where I can get the most eggs and where I can get them easiest and where I shall be least punished'*. His 'Peoples Budget' was duly introduced in April 1909 '*to raise money to wage implacable warfare against poverty and squalor'*.

The budget included taxes on motor cars and petrol: a new graduated income tax, a new 'Super Tax' on all incomes over £3,000 per year: increased charges for liquor licences and, most provocatively, a measure on land valuation that would pave the way for new taxes on land. As expected, the great landowners represented, in the main by the House of Lords, went into a frenzy of opposition. Lloyd George toured the country enjoying every moment of the drama he had set running. '*The question will be asked 'Should 500 men, ordinary men, chosen accidentally from among the unemployed, override the judgement – the deliberate judgement – of millions of people, who are engaged in industry which makes the wealth of this country?'*.

On 30th November 1909, the Lords rejected the budget by 350 votes to 75, the first time in 250 years that they had rejected a finance bill. The Unionist leader Arthur Balfour had only 147 Unionists in the House of Commons but he was supported by five hundred Unionist peers in the House of Lords, all bent on exercising power by opposing the Liberal majority in the House of Commons.

On 10th December 1909 the prime minister, Herbert Asquith, announced that the Liberal Cabinet would not again suffer the humiliations dished out by the Lords over the previous four years. *'We shall not assume office and we will not hold office, unless we can secure the safeguards necessary for the legislative utility and honour of the party'*. After a rather uninspiring General Election, in January 1910, the Liberals gained 275 seats, considerably down on the 377 they had gained four years earlier. The Unionists came back to Westminster with 273 seats, but still remained a minority. The Liberals could rely on the 82 Irish Nationalists and 40 Labour members to vote with the government but, without them, they now had only had a two seat majority over the Unionists. The support of the Irish MP's would be critical for securing a credible majority for the budget in the commons. But Irish support came at the price of Home Rule for Ireland and a total break with the crown and parliament of Britain. The only chance that such a great reform could ever be passed by parliament was to destroy the centuries-old veto of the House of Lords.

When the new Parliament assembled in February 1910, the Unionist leaders in the House of Lords bowed to the inevitable and passed the budget on 28th April 1910. Now, in return for the support of the Irish MPs, Asquith announced that he intended to eliminate the veto power of the House of Lords. This news was received by the king and the peers with undiluted horror! Although Asquith told Parliament that he had not requested, or received, a pledge from the king to create five hundred new peers, the very mention of this option, in public, was deeply worrying to Edward VII. The king knew that the House of Lords would have to face change but the thought of being asked, by a legally elected government, to sign into being five hundred new peers left him distinctly queasy. Some reports have Edward even discussing with his secretaries the possibility of him abdicating should he be pressed too hard on this issue.

In March 1910, the king left London, and its politics, for Biarritz, seeking sun and solace with his mistress Mrs Keppel. On the way there he suffered a bad attack of indigestion, shortness of breath and pains near his heart. His time at Biarritz was no better. It rained for much of the time and, after six weeks, still struggling with bronchitis, he returned to London on 26th April, right in the middle of the Lord's debates on Lloyd George's budget. One great debate was ending but another, on the Lords veto, was just beginning. Although he had little sympathy with the 'backwoodsmen' among the peers, Edward's role as head of the aristocracy gave him an instinctive rapport with the ancient privileges of the House of Lords. It was all part of the England he had inherited from his mother, and the Liberal agenda, and the kind of action that it might involve, looked dangerously like socialism!

But neither bronchitis nor politics was going to stop Edward enjoying himself. He went to see *Rigoletto* at Covent Garden in the evening of his arrival back in London and a few days later he went to see *Siegfried*. On Saturday 30th April, the king went to Sandringham for the weekend, and on Sunday, in cold wind and rain, he made his usual rounds to inspect improvements to the estate and visit his pedigree animals. Edward was back at Buckingham Palace on Monday 2nd May, when his heart began to fail and he could only breathe with difficulty. In order to avoid complicating the king's holiday with Mrs Keppel, Queen Alexandra had been vacationing in Corfu and, on hearing of the king's illness, thought it was probably just one of his regular attacks and so she dawdled home, stopping off at Venice. Edward revived enough to continue working on state business, saying of his health, *'I must fight this'*. And when urged to rest, *'No I shall not give in. I shall go on. I shall work to the end'*. Queen Alexandra arrived back in London on Thursday 5th May and the next day

Edward insisted on being dressed in his formal frock coat to receive his closest friend, the banker Sir Ernest Cassel who had done so much to organise and improve his finances. He told him that, '*I am very seedy but I wanted to meet you*'.

Shortly after this meeting with Cassel, the king collapsed but resisted attempts to put him to bed. Instead, he sat hunched in his armchair as a series of heart attacks thumped away at his failing body. His doctors declared that there was now no hope of the king recovering and gave him morphine to dull the pain. Later in the afternoon, Edward was persuaded to go to bed, where, in a gesture of remarkable generosity by Queen Alexandra, Mrs Keppel was invited to see him to make her farewells. As the day wore on, Edward grew weaker but was lively enough to take in the news that his two year old horse, 'Witch of Air', had won the 4.15 race at Kempton. When his son George, Prince of Wales, repeated this news to him the king replied, '*Yes I have heard of it. I am very glad*'.

Appropriately enough for a sporting monarch these were his last coherent words. Edward died just before midnight on Friday 6th May 1910. Randall Davidson, the Archbishop of Canterbury, who had been praying by the king at the last, said that, '*... he simply ceased to breathe. I have seldom or never seen a quieter passing of the river*'. Various bulletins, issued by the king's doctors during the day, had begun preparing the nation for the worst and crowds gathered outside Buckingham Palace throughout the evening as the news spread that the king was dying. Alexandra declared that she '*... felt as if she had been turned to stone, unable to cry, unable to grasp the meaning of it all, and incapable of doing anything*'. Yet she did manage to write a letter to the nation, published in all the morning papers, thanking the people for their sympathy '*... in my overwhelming sorrow and unspeakable anguish*'.

The prime minister, Herbert Asquith, was on board the admiralty yacht 'Enchantress' on his way to Gibralter when, on Saturday 7th May, he was handed a wireless message announcing the king's death. As the yacht turned round to return home, Asquith saw the long tail of Haley's comet blaze above the predawn sky and ruminated on this irregular, but constant visitor, and the omens that it might portend. The great battle with the Lords was about to begin and he had lost an experienced king who, although daunted by the prospect before him, knew well the history of the situation and, Asquith felt, would act as advised by his ministers. Now he had a king who had little experience of politics, let alone the fierce passions that would be aroused over the next year. Only the monarch could create enough new peers to swamp the House of Lords to ensure the passage of the Parliament Bill into law. George V, within months of his accession, would face a crisis almost without example in the constitutional history of the nation.

Buckingham palace received and dealt with 12,297 telegrams after King Edward VII's death. The king's body remained in his bedroom at Buckingham Palace for over a week. An amazingly calm and serene Queen Alexandra invited members of the royal household, with their wives and children, some old friends of the king, some diplomats and some journalists to come to his room and make their farewells. Dismayed at the lack of planning that preceded his mother's funeral, Edward VII had insisted that plans for his own funeral were made well in advance. On 17th May, in accordance with his own wishes, Edward's body was taken from Buckingham Palace to Westminster Hall, the first British monarch to lie in state on this ancient site. Four Gentlemen at arms were on duty at the head of the coffin, and four Yeoman of the guard stood at the four corners of the catafalque. For three days the Hall was open to the public and more than 250,000 people took the trouble to shuffle silently past the monarch whom they had only known through newspaper stories, pictures and royal processions. The scandals of his youth were forgotten; it was his genial bonhomie and rotund splendour that they remembered now. Despite ruling for less than ten years, the nation had taken him to their hearts and his loss was truly felt by '*all sorts and conditions of men*'.

On Friday 20th May, 14 days after he had died, the king's body was taken by gun carriage from Westminster Hall, through London, to Paddington station. This state funeral procession was accompanied by nine kings, including Kaiser Wilhelm of Germany. The king's coffin was also followed by a man in highland uniform leading Edward's favourite rough-haired terrier, Caesar. From Paddington station the royal train took the kings body, as it had for his mother, to Windsor. There, following the order made by Edward VII at Queen Victoria's funeral, naval ratings pulled the gun carriage up the hill to the castle, where the coffin was taken to St George's Chapel for the burial service. After the ceremonies, a luncheon was held in the Waterloo Chamber of Windsor Castle while men from Garrard the jeweller silently took the regalia from the king's coffin to store in their vaults for safe keeping. Later Caesar the terrier became famous for 'producing' a memoir entitled 'Where's Master?' that filled the stockings of many a child at Christmas 1910.

Although Edward VII was lowered into the royal vault his body rested there for only a few years. It was later buried in a sarcophagus on the south side of the altar of St George's Chapel. After her death in 1925, the body of Queen Alexandra was also laid there and they lie together beneath white marble effigies opposite Catherine of Aragon's wooden oriel window. Caesar, the terrier, sits at his masters feet, immortalised in marble. Edward and Alexandra's last child, an infant son who died soon after being born, is buried in the cemetery of the estate church at Sandringham, as is Prince John, the fifth son of George V, the young, 'lost' prince, who suffered from epilepsy and was kept from public view. Queen Alexandra lived on at Sandringham after her husband's death. Her son, George V, often stayed at York Cottage, in the grounds of Sandringham, only moving into the main house on his mother's death.

Edward's genial demeanour and high public profile meant that, although there were great political issues raised towards the end of his reign, there were none of the complaints about the monarchy and clamour for a republic that had characterised a decade or so of Victoria's reign. His sunny, smiling rotundness endeared him to a population keen to move on from the mourning weeds of Victoria. That he was at heart, a thorough autocrat, and was protected from the worst of his inclinations by his canny secretaries, was well shielded from the public and, most of the time, from his ministers. Edward VII had been Prince of Wales for 60 years and was king for less than 10. Despite his age and ill health his geniality, good humour and common touch aided him in proclaiming something of a new era.

Prince Eddy

Albert Victor, the first son of Edward VII, has generally had a bad press despite a recent television documentary seeking to rescue him from a conspiracy of malevolent biographers. His twenty eight years were characterised variously as idle, lethargic, mentally backward, dissipated, dissolute, and brainless. In the army he resented the rigours of military discipline and his commander-in-chief found him `an inveterate and incurable dawdler'. Queen Victoria, and his father, seriously began to doubt his suitability for the throne. His dissipated lifestyle of heavy drinking and promiscuity (possibly resulting in venereal disease) had undermined his health and the family needed him to be married, preferably to a woman with sufficient strength of character to compensate for his many inadequacies. Victoria Mary of Teck (later Queen Mary) was chosen and the wedding was set for 27th February 1892. By a merciful act of providence, Princess Mary, and the nation, were saved from an unpredictable future by Eddy's death from double pneumonia, after a bout of influenza, at Sandringham on 14th January 1892.

Despite his lack of any redeeming features, his family's love for him is evident by the construction of one of the largest tombs in the history of royal monuments, bang in the centre of the Albert Memorial Chapel at Windsor. Indeed, his grotesque Art Nouveau assemblage dominates the space, ostensibly dedicated to Prince Albert, whose modest monument is dwarfed by the huge tomb for Eddy. The Mexican onyx sarcophagus is too high for visitors to view the effigy, which is dominated by a huge angel holding aloft a crown of eternal glory over the white marble head of the prince.

Many visitors to the chapel are unsure who this monumental tomb is for, Prince Albert Victor not featuring much in the history of the British monarchy. The tomb was created by Sir Alfred Gilbert (better known for his statue of Eros in Piccadilly Circus), who is supposed to have drawn on the tomb of Henry VII in Westminster Abbey for inspiration. The unfinished work brought him near to bankruptcy and he fled to Belgium in 1901 to escape his creditors. Eventually, George V persuaded him to return to Windsor in 1926 to complete the five saints that were still missing from the ornate grill that surrounds the tomb, and the whole elaborate confection was finished by 1928. Many of the monuments noted in this book may not do justice to their recipients, but in this case the recipient hardly justified such a massive tomb, even one as ugly as this.

GEORGE V (born 1865 reigned 1910-1936)

George, later George V, was never meant to be king. Born at Marlborough House in London on 3rd June 1865, he was the second son of Edward Prince of Wales (Later Edward VII) and Princess Alexandra. His elder brother, Prince Albert Victor, later duke of Clarence (known as Prince Eddy), was second in line to the throne after his father. George trained, alongside Eddy, as a navy cadet at Dartmouth and they spent three years on the training ship Bacchante. They visited the West Indies (1879), Spain and Ireland (1880) and voyaged round the world (1880-82). George, though the youngest, was the more dominant of the two brothers and the family kept them together as it was clear that Eddy couldn't really do without him. Placing both male heirs to the throne on one ship at large on the world's oceans was risky; and on a voyage between South Africa and Australia the Bacchante drifted about rudderless for several days and some members of the crew were killed. Despite its harshness, this experience captivated George, who thereafter remained enthusiastic about all things naval, particularly naval uniform, which he loved wearing. When his elder brother moved on into the army to prepare for kingship, George looked set for a happy career as a naval officer.

George had no interest in intellectual pursuits, (he once declared that *'people who write books ought to be shut up'*) but this was no obstacle to progress in the navy and in 1891 he was promoted to naval commander. This achievement was overshadowed by him suffering a bad attack of typhoid and the news in 1892 that his brother, Prince Eddy, had died of double pneumonia. George was devastated. He wrote to his grandmother, Queen Victoria that *'No two brothers could have loved each other more than we did'*. He was twenty-seven and was now second in line to the throne. He gave up the navy in favour of reading Bagehot on the English constitution, and the study of German. He found Bagehot interesting but German both difficult and unattractive: *'a rotten language'*.

George's changed circumstances raised the question of his marriage; he would need a wife to carry on the line and he soon found himself at the centre of discussions to find him one. As usual, Queen Victoria had strong views on the matter. Just before he died, Prince Eddy had been engaged to the impoverished but respectable Princess Mary of Teck, who had been brought up in England. She had been Queen Victoria's choice to help curb the dissipated Eddy. George needed no such curbing but Mary, as a bereaved bride-to-be who was already accepted within the royal circle, was too convenient to let go. She and George were married in July 1893 and between 1894 and 1905 they produced five boys and one girl – the succession was ensured! Mary brought George an enduring rather than effusive love. Like George, she was stiff and formal and found it hard to transmit affection either to her husband or her children. She saw her role as one of duty above all else, but she did have a slightly lighter touch than her husband and this helped her calm the irritability that so often followed his bafflement at the rapidly changing world in which he found himself.

George was of medium height with a fresh complexion, brilliant blue eyes, short brown hair and a high forehead. Always bearded, he cut a trim figure in the formal dress and uniforms that he loved to wear. Although he had a notoriously loud speaking voice, and an occasional fiery temper, he was a shy, private man with simple tastes. Unlike his father, Edward VII, he disliked what passed for fashionable society. Despite these differences, George enjoyed an easy, happy and affectionate relationship with his father.

Edward VII had been frozen out by his mother, Queen Victoria, during the long years he had spent as Prince of Wales and he was determined that George should not suffer the same fate. After Victoria's death in 1901, he shared information with the new Prince of Wales by passing on despatches, daily telegrams and cabinet papers to him and he had their desks placed side by side at Windsor. In the spring of 1901, George and his wife made tours of Australia, New Zealand, Ireland, Canada and India getting to know better what was then called the Empire, and learning what it was like to shake hands with over 25,000 people. On the death of his father in 1910 George wrote in his diary: '*I have lost my best friend and the best of fathers. I never had a [bad] word with him in my life. I am heartbroken and overwhelmed with grief...*'. He would get no such testimony from his own children. The new king ascended the throne having travelled more widely outside Europe and more thoroughly prepared for the task than any of his recent predecessors.

George lacked the intellectual sharpness of his father and had less interest in Europe than him, partly due to not being fluent in either French or German. Sandringham, where he and Mary made their early home, was his domain. It was the orbit of a hunting and shooting country squire and the wide, flat spaces of Norfolk were to him what the sophisticated salons of France had been to his father. He was never happier than when shooting on his estates in Norfolk, and in December 1913 the king and his guests shot 3,937 pheasants in one day. He was recognised as a crack shot and he organised his game book with the same fastidiousness as he did his huge stamp collection. He usually spent three afternoons a week on the latter, leaving a collection of over a quarter of a million stamps at the time of his death. With no interest in cerebral matters to occupy his thoughts, George V became obsessed about details of etiquette and dress code, writing stern rebukes to any of his sons photographed in newspapers with a slight defect or wrinkle in their uniform or formal dress.

He was also obsessed with punctuality and he kept all the clocks at Sandringham half an hour fast. After the restless gaiety of his father's reign, George cut a more cautious figure of solid marital fidelity, dedicated, responsible and hardworking. But he did not find kingship easy. He had none of his father's charm and easiness with people and often came over as stiff, hard and dour. Eventually his bluff, no-nonsense, ship-shape, straightforwardness began to endear him to his subjects, although he never saw his own popularity as being part of his job description. As a young man, George had witnessed the defects of the British Army during the Boar War in South Africa, the rise of German militarism, the growth of trade unionism and the rise of the infant Labour Party. He could see that society was changing and handling change was never something he was comfortable with. Nonetheless, he was to face, and handle effectively, many great changes including one that almost immediately impinged on him, and the constitutional role of the monarchy directly.

After a battle with the House of Lords, and a General Election in early 1910, the Liberal Budget, formulated by Lloyd George, had been passed by the peers. The Liberals then brought in a Parliament Bill that would stop the Lords being able to veto future Commons legislation. The Liberals had promised their Irish supporters during the budget crisis that they would put a Parliament Act in place so as to be able to pass the Government of Ireland Bill. Again the Lords fought this bill strongly and looked to the king as their natural ally. George V found himself between a Liberal government that wanted him to guarantee that he would support their policy if they won another election and the House of Lords who expected him to resist. The Liberals won, yet another, General Election in December 1910 and reluctantly George V made known that he would create more Liberal peers if the Parliament Bill were defeated in the House of Lords.

On 10th August 1911, on the hottest day recorded in England for over seventy years, the peers reluctantly passed the Parliament Act by seventeen votes. It was a momentous decision, ending their age-old privilege to halt and hinder the will of the House of Commons. In February 2005 it was this Parliament Act (amended in 1949) that the Speaker of the House of Commons invoked to pass the ban on foxhunting in England and Wales. In November 1911, George V was no doubt pleased to put all this behind him when he sailed to India. There, on the 12th December, he presided over a 'Coronation Durbar', at Delhi during which he was crowned Emperor of India in a spectacular ceremony before 100,000 people. In his diary George noted that it was '*the most beautiful and wonderful sight I ever saw*'. It was the ceremonial zenith of the old Empire and it was followed by an elaborate shooting party in Nepal where George shot twenty one tigers.

In 1912, as promised to their Irish supporters, the Liberals brought forward their Government of Ireland Bill. The Unionists in the House of Commons, led by Bonar Law, believed that, as the Lords had now lost their veto, the king should use his veto to prevent this measure. Such a power had not been exercised by a monarch since the time of Queen Anne. Bonar Law still seemed to believe that the Unionists ruled whether they had a majority in the commons or not! The few powers that the crown has within the British constitution inevitably surface during times of crisis, when each side calls up different precedents to aid its cause. That George V manoeuvred his way through this maze so well so soon after becoming king proved that his assiduous reading of Bagehot had not been in vain.

George V had felt pressured by the Liberal cabinet in 1911 over the Parliament Act and now he felt pressured by the Unionists over Ireland, and he did not like it. In July 1913 he took a step, unprecedented since the reign of George III, by instigating and chairing a conference of government and opposition leaders on the question of 'Ireland'. Although ending inconclusively, this initiative began the long process of separating the counties of Ulster from those of southern Ireland culminating in the establishment of the Irish Free State in 1921. George V saw early on that losing most of Ireland was inevitable, but he did not feel the same way about votes for women. The suffragette Emily Davison brought this issue right to his door when she died after throwing herself in front of George's horse, Anmerin, during the 1913 Derby.

At the start of the First World War in August 1914, George V found himself in direct conflict with his German relatives, (the Kaiser was his first cousin). He noted in his diary of 4th August 1914 *'Warm, showers and windy ... I held a Council at 10.45 to declare war on Germany, it is a terrible catastrophe but it is not our fault'*. Those last five words *'it is not our fault'* give a clue to George's simple, almost childlike, approach to such a momentous issue. During the war George V was rarely out of uniform, lived even more frugally than usual, visited hundreds of shipyards, hospitals, munitions factories, and of course he visited the troops fighting in France. During one such visit to the front in December 1914, he was thrown from his horse, fracturing his pelvis, causing him severe pain and shock.

George V was the first monarch since 1830 to speak English without a foreign accent, but this did not protect him from the anti-German xenophobia sweeping the country. The question of withdrawing the honour of Knight of the Garter and any other given titles from members of the enemy arose in the press, as did the question of the George's German ancestry. No one could have been more patriotic than George V; he actually disliked many of his German relatives, and so these slights left him bemused and upset. But, again gauging the public mood correctly, George V approved a royal proclamation in July 1917 announcing that in future all descendants of Queen Victoria would bear the family name of 'Windsor' rather than Saxe-Coburg Gotha. This same facility for sensing the national mood lay behind George's attitude to his Cousin the Tsar of Russia and his family after the Russian revolution in 1917. Initially, George supported the idea of them being brought to safety in Britain, but later he changed his mind, fearing a rise of republican sentiment if an old-fashioned feudal dictator was given shelter in democratic Britain. The Tsar, his wife and their five children were executed in 1917 and there is no indication that George V ever regretted his decision to leave them to their fate.

The war, and its aftermath of crippled and unemployed ex-soldiers, seriously affected George V; his accident at the front, the daily reports of mass slaughter and his round of visits to disabled soldiers took their toll, and he was seen to age rapidly by its end. At least he was still there! While slightly consolidating the monarchy in Great Britain, the First World War exploded the system almost everywhere else. The nation celebrated the victory over the Germans with days of rejoicing that had the king and queen at their centre. Hostilities now over, George V returned to the turmoil of domestic politics. Lloyd George selling peerages, post-war austerity, the frustrations of the long post-war depression and the arrival of the first

Labour government under Ramsey MacDonald in 1924 all tested his role as a constitutional monarch. Surprisingly, given his natural proclivities, he was able to distinguish between his own conservative views on society and social behaviour and the political reality of the electorate's wishes, even when the latter were not always very clear. During the General Strike of May 1926, he criticised Churchill's British Gazette for its aggressive stance against the strikers and when the strike was over he urged prime minister Baldwin to beware the hotheads in his cabinet who might seek punitive legislation.

During November 1928, George V fell ill with a severe chest infection. During December his heart grew weaker and it was thought that he might not live. Luckily, his doctor, lord Dawson, managed to find the offending abscess with a needle and drew off the poison. More drainage and the removal of a rib took the king away from the brink. It was during the king's convalescence at Bognor, after a visiting deputation of Bognor citizens had asked if the town might now style itself 'Bognor Regis' that George is supposed to have replied to his personal secretary, *'Bugger Bognor'*. The secretary returned to the citizens to explain that the king was happy to accede to their request. George's illness kept him an invalid for the best part of 1929. In that year, the king had to deal with yet another political crisis involving the formation of a National Government with the Labour leader Ramsay MacDonald as prime minister.

In 1924, an estimated 10 million people had heard George V on the radio as he opened the British Empire Exhibition at Wembley, and in 1932 he again made use of this 'new' medium when he instituted the first Christmas broadcast by a reigning sovereign. Just 251 words long (all written by Rudyard Kipling), many of his subjects heard the king's voice for the first time and the impact was remarkable. The king's Jubilee celebrations, which began in May 1935 with banquets and processions, built on this foundation of enlarged communication, and an almost tearful king confided to his wife, *'I had no idea they felt like that about me. I'm beginning to think they really like me for myself'*.

This discovery, though gratifying, came as the end drew near. George's health had been deteriorating for some time; his chest was still weak, he had always been a heavy smoker and the restless international situation, particularly the Italian invasion of Abyssinia (now Ethiopia) and the sabre rattling of Germany, was causing him great distress. During the autumn of 1935, it seemed to Stanley Baldwin, the new head of the National Government, that he was *'already packing up his luggage and getting ready to depart'*. The king spent Christmas 1935 at Sandringham, engaged in his usual family pastimes, but he was not well. The narrowing of his arteries now caused him to fall asleep during the day but he did not sleep so well at night, often having to take oxygen in the early hours of the morning to relieve his restlessness. On 12th January 1936, his faithful nurse, Sister Black, became concerned enough to call for the king's doctor. Dawson found him feeling unwell with no energy but did not stay. On Wednesday 15th January, the king retired early and the next day decided to stay in his room.

Dawson returned on Friday 17th January to find the king lapsing into a twilight world of only vague recognition of those around him. Dawson issued the first of six bulletins concerning the king's health: *'The bronchial catarrh from which his Majesty the King is suffering is not severe, but there have appeared signs of cardiac weakness which must be regarded with some disquiet'*. Over the weekend, his heart growing weaker, the king drifted in and out of consciousness. On the morning of Monday 20th January, members of the Privy Council gathered by the door of the king's bedroom at Sandringham while, with some difficulty, he signed a document initiating a Council of State that could act on his behalf. All through that day, the king's strength diminished until just before midnight, when he died naturally in his sleep.

Or so the world believed. In 1986, when George V's immediate family were no longer around to read it, Francis Watson, the biographer of the king's doctor lord Dawson, felt able to reveal some of Dawson's clinical notes in an article for the journal 'History Today'. It is a tale of times and timing appropriate for a king for whom clocks and punctuality were so important. At 9.25pm on 20th January 1936, having issued his famous '*The King's life is moving peacefully towards its close'*, Dawson returned to his patient, who had moved from sleep to stupor to shallow coma. He was aware that this last stage of the king's life could last for many hours. Although the king was in no pain, he was, after all, dying from cardiac weakness rather than, say, an agonising cancer Dawson felt that '*Hours of waiting just for the mechanical end, when all that is really life had departed, only exhausts the onlookers and keeps them so strained that they cannot avail themselves of the solace of thought, communion or prayer'.*

This was a strange concern, given that the 'onlookers' were busy having dinner and the king would probably just drift into death peacefully with his family nearby, without pain. But in his diary, written later that night, Dawson gives a better clue to his real concern: '*The determination of the time of death of the King's body had another object in view, viz the importance of the death receiving its first announcement in the morning papers rather than the less appropriate field of the evening journals. The papers knew that the end might come before their going to press and I told my wife on the telephone to advise The Times to hold back on publication'.*

At around 11pm, to achieve this desired end, Dawson injected between five and ten times the palliative doses of morphine and cocaine into the king's distended jugular vein, witnessed only by Sister Black, who had refused to administer the dose. After about fifteen minutes he noted '*breathing quieter – appearance more placid – physical struggle gone'.* So smoothly had Dawson's dose worked that it was difficult to say at exactly what time the king actually died, but it was given out as 11.55pm and announced by the BBC at 12.15a.m. The Times, which had a deadline of 11pm, had already printed 30,000 copies before the news came through but they were able to change their front page quickly to carry the story in the next 300,000 copies. The 'less appropriate' evening papers, who might have been the first to carry the story had the king lingered on until 21st January, would now only be able to report the story second-hand! This little act of euthanasia against a reigning monarch seems to have been tacitly approved by Edward Prince of Wales and as his mother kissed his hand in homage, in the dead king's bedroom, he was no doubt impatient to start doing things his way. He had already ordered the clocks at Sandringham to be put back to Greenwich Mean Time. Edward VIII had many things he wanted to change!

Disliking the long obsequies that had followed the death of King Edward VII, Queen Mary requested that the body of her husband should be buried no longer than a week after his death. The ceremonies began in a quiet way later the next day when, guided by torchlight and a piper playing a lament, the king's coffin was wheeled across a windy, rainy park to lie for thirty-six hours in the little Sandringham church, guarded by gamekeepers and gardeners. The coffin, made of oak cut from the Sandringham estate, was then taken by gun carriage to Wolferton station, escorted by his white shooting pony 'Jock' and a host of Norfolk neighbours and tenants. The train took the king and his close family to King's Cross station, from where another gun carriage, followed by the king's four sons on foot, took the coffin to Westminster Hall for it to lie in state.

The Imperial Crown was secured to the lid of the coffin over the folds of the Royal Standard, but, as the carriage swung into New Palace yard, King Edward VIII saw a flash of light on the pavement as the jewelled Maltese cross that sat on top of the crown, shaken loose by the journey, now lay in the gutter. Not a good omen! Edward VIII had requested that there be no service at Westminster Hall. But Archbishop Lang of Canterbury, wearing a purple cope worn at the funeral of Charles II, insisted on at least one hymn being sung. Nearly one million people came to pay their respects to George V, probably not recognizing the king's four sons, who, after midnight on 27th January, stood guard over his body for twenty minutes.

Edward VIII later wrote that '*We stood there for twenty minutes in the dim candlelight and the great silence. ... I felt very close to my father and all he stood for*'.

On 28th January, as had been the tradition since the funeral of Queen Victoria, George V's coffin was drawn from Westminster, through London, to Paddington by naval ratings and then on to Windsor by train. The procession from Windsor station was hindered by the vast crowds who came to bid the king farewell, making the fastidious timekeeper about one hour late for his own funeral. This was the last time that the royal families of Europe, already much reduced since the First World War, would gather in such numbers for a royal funeral in England. All five of the European kings who attended would see their countries occupied by the Nazis during the new world war that George V went to his grave dreading.

After a service in St George's Chapel, George V's coffin was lowered into the vault in front of the altar as the new king sprinkled earth over it from a silver bowl. The coffin was then wheeled along underground to George III's royal vault at the eastern end of St George's Chapel. It waited there until the spring of 1939 when it was moved again and placed within a new tomb in the nave, between two north aisle pillars, with George's effigy on it. Queen Mary would join him after her death in 1953. Both effigies were sculpted by Sir William Reid Dick who was responsible for Queen Victoria's great statue outside Buckingham palace at the top of the Mall in London.

The arrangements for royal funerals were mostly the concern of the Lord Chamberlain, who at this time was lord Cromer, and involved a plethora of detail that could easily be forgotten. One detail that had been overlooked was that no had thought to arrange any proper security for those bits of the crown jewels that had been used in the ceremony. The regalia that had rested on the king's coffin had to be taken safely back to the jewel house in the Tower of London. With everyone else having their very specific duties to attend to and no vehicle having been allocated a car had to be borrowed and an 'efficient driver' found. A plain-clothes police officer then sat beside him and four more plain-clothes officers followed in a police car. However, no one had the keys to the jewel house and so the little convoy had to stop off at the Lord Chamberlain's Office in London to pick them up.

Another issue occupying the governing elite was the definition of 'full' and 'half' mourning. The new king, Edward VIII, had stipulated that full mourning should continue until 21st July 1936, after which there would be a period of 'half' mourning. The latter was not very well defined and left lord Cromer being bombarded with letters from all over the world about the etiquette of 'half' mourning. The Governor of Newfoundland wanted to know: '*Can official dinner parties, garden parties, receptions and other dances be given. Also as regards dress, is it in order to wear ordinary suits with a mourning band and a black tie and can one wear coloured shirts and socks?*' Lord Cromer replied that dances should not be given and '*With regard to dress bright colours should not be worn, but I really do not think it matters what colour of socks the Governor wears, as no one is likely to see them*'.

The Governor of Ceylon was equally occupied. Could he attend race meetings, football, cricket and hockey matches? Yes he could, but again '*no dancing*'. The Governor of Nigeria was in the middle of touring the country and he needed to entertain his various guests '*even if only simply*', while the Governor of New Zealand was concerned about his entertaining at planned agricultural shows as '*they were a matter of great importance in New Zealand*'. Around the 'colonies' the challenge of ladies who had bought coloured dresses, before the king died, in preparation for a function at Government House also arose. Faced with this huge barrage lord Cromer generally simplified the rules around a '*no dancing, no bright colours*' edict.

George V spent his first 35 years in the nineteenth century and his last 35 years in the twentieth century. He was born at a time of deference, when unearned respect, esteem and veneration were taken for granted by the landed classes, as were the privileges of the House of Lords, and he lived through a period when all these old values were being questioned. For a shy, conservative man he coped well with the picking apart of these old assumptions and some of the fiercest political storms faced by any monarch of modern times. He understood more about the lot of common men than seems evident from his stiffness and reserve and he handled a cauldron of political and constitutional change deftly, leaving the monarchy stronger than he had found it. In a gesture harking back to his love of the sea, he asked that his beloved racing yacht Britannia, left to him by his father, be scuttled after his death and in July 1936 she was duly sunk off the Isle of Wight.

One little story linking George V with the funerals of his father and grandmother involved an old horse called 'Bruiser'. This horse that had helped draw gun carriages at the funerals of both Queen Victoria and Edward VII had then been sent on active service with the army to France in 1914. In 1918, when he was twenty years old, Bruiser was returning home and George V received a letter asking him if he would provide a place for him at Windsor. The king did take him and Bruiser spent his last days dining off the lush pastures of Windsor Great Park. He died in 1928 and was described as '*old and worn out*'. As he neared his own death in 1936 George V would have known exactly how he felt.

George V and the Prince of Wales (later Edward VIII)

While convalescing after his illness in 1929, and possibly ruminating on mortality more than usual, George V had confided to members of his family that he didn't believe Edward would ever succeed to the throne. Six years on, in 1935, he was heard to say that '*I pray to God that my eldest son will never marry and have children, and that nothing will come between Bertie and Lilibet and the throne*'. To Baldwin, at around the same time, he confided '*after I am dead, the boy will ruin himself in twelve months*'.

His concerns about Edward and his affair with Wallis Simpson were based on more than just prejudice against a divorced woman. In early 1935, George V ordered the Metropolitan Police to investigate Mrs. Simpson. His plan was to hold on to any information discovered so that he could use it later to prevent Wallis ever marrying Edward. Their first discovery was that while Wallis was seducing Edward she was also having a passionate affair with one Guy Trundle, a Ford company sales executive. In 1935, MI6 also prepared a dossier for George V and Queen Mary about Wallis' behaviour in China during 1924 when she was married to her first husband, a US naval officer. This is the famous 'China Dossier' that seems to have been seen by a great many people but has now disappeared from public view. Its main findings were that Wallis slept with various naval officers that she learnt 'devious sexual practices' in various Hong Kong brothels and that she was involved in drug dealing and illegal gambling. Needless to say, all this horrified George V and Queen Mary and it is probably from this point on that Queen Mary decided that Wallis would never be Queen of England and later, after the abdication, would never be accorded the title Her Royal Highness. George V may have been old fashioned, stuffy and unbearably pompous but he had seen the future and he didn't like it.

EDWARD VIII (born 1894 reigned 10 months during 1936)

On the death of George V the prime minister Stanley Baldwin broadcast to the nation. He noted how the new king Edward VIII '... *is now summoned to face responsibilities more onerous, more exacting, more continuous, than any he has hitherto been asked to discharge. ... He inherits an example of kingly conduct, of virtue, of wisdom, and endurance'*. He went on to say that George V passes the crown on to his son '... *with its foundations strengthened, its moral authority, its honour, and its dignity enhanced. It is an incomparable and awesome inheritance'*.

The future Edward VIII was the first son of George (then) duke of York and Princess Mary of Teck. He was born on 23rd June 1894 amid the usual parliamentary congratulations that greeted the birth of a royal prince, Keir Hardie, the founder of the Independent Labour Party, risked the abuse of his fellow MPs with this uncanny prediction:

'From his childhood onward this boy will be surrounded by sycophants and flatterers by the score and will be taught to believe himself as a superior creation. A line will be drawn between him and the people he is called upon some day to reign over. In due course, following the precedent which has already been set, he will be sent on a tour round the world, and probably rumours of a morganatic alliance will follow and the end of it all will be the country will be called on to pay the bill'.

This 'superior creation' would be seven years old when his great-grandmother, Queen Victoria, died in 1901 and sixteen years old when his grandfather, King Edward VII died, in 1910. Edward (he was always called David in the family) would thus seem to have his feet firmly in the Victorian and Edwardian age. But this chronology belied the new world that he had grown along with. It was his father who battled against the grain of the modern world to retain the values and protocols of Victoria's time. Edward would struggle in the opposite direction to escape the claustrophobic limits of behaviour and ceremony that were still so sacred to his father.

George V seems to have been a father who enjoyed babies but not teenagers. Babies did what they were told, teenagers did not. In reply to a courtier who implied that he may be a little hard on his growing children George V is said to have replied that *'My father was frightened of his mother; I was frightened of my father; and I am damned well going to see to it that my children are frightened of me'*. This is a somewhat distorted picture of family life under Edward VII. As a child George V had enjoyed the spontaneous love and warmth of a gregarious pleasure seeker and the quite normal affection of his mother, Queen Alexandra. The truth is that George V, lacking much by way of natural warmth and spontaneity, defaulted to fear as the best way to control the normal, but unpredictable, ebullience of his children. For him, visible demonstrations of love and affection were impossible; much better to concentrate on the minutiae of duty and ceremonial, than to worry about what constituted a happy and healthy childhood. It is no surprise then that Edward, Albert (later George VI), George, duke of Kent and Henry duke of Gloucester all suffered various problems coping with adulthood. His youngest child, Prince John, died aged fifteen in 1919 after having been hidden away at Sandringham because of his epilepsy.

Edward was shy, nervous, slight and short, with striking yellow hair that marked him out from his duller brothers. Though generally of a solitary disposition, as he grew he cultivated a charm that captivated onlookers during his various trips to Canada, the USA, Australia, New Zealand and India as an 'ambassador' for his father who preferred not to go 'abroad'. Despite the generally good impression that Edward made on these trips (there were some blips involving late arrivals and a cavalier attitude to ceremony), his father gave him nothing more useful to do. He did not involve him in his relations with government and he did not share any of the day-to-day routine of royal administration with him. The history of Princes of Wales since the middle ages seems to have been 'don't let them get too close'.

Above all, George V wanted him married to a woman that he and Queen Mary approved of. This was a pipe dream. Edward was never interested in the kind of women that his younger brothers would settle down with. He preferred experienced women who had been separated or divorced; a nightmare for George V! He had a long affair with Mrs Dudley Ward whose company, understanding and opinions he valued. She boosted his confidence and supported him in his belief that he possessed skills, energy and talents that everybody but his father recognised. He never quite grasped that much of the admiration lavished on him by the public was due to his status as Prince of Wales and heir to the throne rather than to a catalogue of unrecognised personal talents. Allied with an elevated view of his own gifts, Edward was impatient with the tedious operation of state affairs and the ceremony and protocol that accompanied them. The aimless round of public duties and the incessant spotlight of publicity that royal duties generated irritated him and this irritation became more and more apparent. To escape from the public gaze, including the gaze of his father, he retired to his semi-castellated folly of Fort Belvedere near Sunningdale in Hertfordshire. It is here, just south of Royal Windsor, that one of the world's great love stories would incubate.

Edward first met Wallis Simpson, when she was married to her second husband, Ernest Simpson, in January 1931; almost five years before he would abdicate to marry her. In January 1932 the Simpson's spent a weekend with Edward at Fort Belvedere. From this time onwards his affair with Wallis progressed via holidays, parties and weekends with various friends and aristocrats. The timid British newspapers kept all this from the gaze of the great British public, who remained unaware of the powder keg ready to explode at the heart of the monarchy. On 20th January 1936 George V died and 'David' his eldest son succeeded him as Edward VIII.

At this time there is no evidence in her letters to suggest that Wallis loved Edward. She certainly loved the spotlight, the power she had over a king and the entrée to the highest circles that his friendship facilitated. She was still involved in her affair with Guy Trundle and later, from around November 1936, she began an affair with the bisexual William Bullit, the very wealthy Nazi sympathiser who was US Ambassador to France. All this she kept from Edward while dominating him in private and public amid scenes that both shocked and embarrassed the onlookers. In August 1936 Edward took Wallis and others on a cruise in the eastern Mediterranean. The continental newspapers were full of romantic pictures of them together. On another occasion Edward declared that he was unavailable to attend a public function due to his still being in official mourning. In reality he was meeting Wallis off a train. A photographer caught the deceit in glorious black and white. His brother, the duke of York, had deputised for him and all this publicity did nothing to quell the fears of those in the know. Later in October 1936, a bemused and uncomfortable Stanley Baldwin asked the king to apply a little more discretion to his affair and pleaded with him to get Wallis to abandon her divorce proceedings. The divorce went ahead and in November 1936 the king met Baldwin again and proposed a morganatic marriage to Wallis. Under this arrangement Edward would remain king but Wallis would never be styled 'queen' just 'consort'.

Sixty odd years later Charles Prince of Wales and his 'consort' Camilla declared a similar solution to deal with the 'queen' question. In 1936 the British Cabinet rejected the idea of a morganatic marriage, possibly suspecting that the new king would not stick to any agreement he made and that he would keep pushing to make Wallis his queen. On 3rd December 1936 the hitherto slavishly silent British press were prompted into action after the Daily Mirror broke the story of the king's affair. The flood of pent up disapproval they unleashed sent Wallis scurrying to France to escape the furore. After Baldwin refused him permission to broadcast to the people to put his case (this really would have caused a crisis), Edward declared his intention to abdicate on 9th December and on the 10th December he signed the instrument of abdication. The next day he made his famous broadcast to the nation, explaining his decision. His brother, the duke of York, was declared King George VI on 12th December and Edward, later to be styled 'duke of Windsor', left England for Austria. In May 1937 Wallis' decree absolute came through and she married Edward at an old Chateau near Tours on 3rd June 1937. Edward refused Louis Mountbatten's offer to be his best man as he expected one of his brothers, the duke of Kent or the duke of Gloucester, to turn up; but no one from the royal family came. It was an ominous sign of the things to come.

Initially, Edward's brother, King George VI, and Queen Elizabeth had sent him friendly letters of support as he took up his new station in life but this sentiment soon changed, perhaps under the influence of Queen Mary, to undiluted hostility. In 1938, just two years after the abdication, George VI wrote to the prime minister, Neville Chamberlain, insisting that it be made clear to Edward that he could not visit England if Wallis accompanied him. As with Princess Diana after her divorce, the new royal family also insisted that Wallis should never be accorded the title of 'Her Royal Highness', normally given to the wife of a royal prince. This, and the ban on their travelling to England together was probably the result of pressure from Queen Elizabeth, who never forgave Edward for dropping the crown on poor George's head, and Queen Mary, who hated the scandal of the abdication and whose knowledge of Wallis' early life had so appalled her. Throughout the next sixteen years, the motives conditioning Edward and George's responses to each other would often be ascribed to their wives as if neither of them could act without the goading of their spouses. To some extent this was true, especially in Edward's case, but George VI certainly held strong views about Edward's behaviour after the abdication. He needed no goading to act against his brother to limit the emergence of a second court 'across the sea.'

Of course Edward was not entirely blameless in provoking their anger. He was notoriously greedy and obsessed with money. He saw a bank account with just a couple of million pounds in it as staring into the abyss of poverty and was greatly upset when he learnt that he would not be entitled to the income from the duchy of Lancaster. He still believed that his brother and the government would (somehow) include him (now a private citizen) in the civil list. One complication arose from the normal protocol of kings leaving their heirs various royal houses and estates. George V had left Edward a lifetime interest in Sandringham and Balmoral and he was unwilling to give this up. During the long, and often angry, discussions about his future financing, Edward proclaimed that he only had £90,000 to his name when in reality, as Prince of Wales, he had been stashing his revenues away to the tune of nearly one million pounds. The government and George VI were outraged by this deception and although George made an allowance to Edward of c£25,000 per year (ostensibly in lieu of Balmoral and Sandringham) he made it clear that '*the continuation of this voluntary allowance must depend on your not returning to this country without my approval*'.

The Windsor's' visit to see Hitler in Berlin in 1937, where they seemed comfortably at home among the fascist glitterati, was a big mistake. The British and American intelligence services had had Wallis under surveillance for some time and many documented reports exist that suggest that Wallis was sending information of variable value to Germany via friends and lovers. Hitler was fond of the Windsors. He saw them as people he could 'deal' with to bring Britain to its senses, and the duke believed that Germany was the only hope for Europe. Later, rumours that Hitler, contemplating victory over England, had also contemplated putting Edward on the throne as a 'puppet' king gained credence as Edward's character plumbed the depths of frivolity and shallowness. In 1940, in order to get him away from the intrigues of Europe, Edward and Wallis were sent to govern the Bahamas, but even here their pro-Nazi sympathies shone though via the pro-Nazi friends they cultivated and from speeches that Edward (to Churchill's disgust) gave during trips to the USA.

From the end of the Second World War until their deaths, Edward and Wallis lived in France. Here they maintained an ostentatious and extravagant household with separate chauffeurs to drive them around, a large kitchen staff and several liveried footmen to greet and escort visitors. It was a fantasy house where Wallis was addressed as 'Her Royal Highness' and Edward enjoyed everything that a pampered and wealthy aristocrat might want. At this stage of a brief essay it would be reasonable to identify some redeeming features about them both, but, however we look at it, their lives as socialites and partygoers looked trivial, shallow and frivolous because it was. True, whatever they did, their lifestyle would always be contrasted with the dedicated, sober, service ethic of the new royal family. George VI and Queen Elizabeth were on a mission to reclaim the dignity of the monarchy from the abdication crisis and the British establishment soon circled the wagons around them. There was no place for Edward inside the covers. He was on his own and unfortunately, left to his own devices, nothing much of solid or worthwhile character emerged. On 17th November 1971 a biopsy confirmed that Edward had a deep-seated cancerous tumour of the larynx that was inoperable and in March 1972, Edward was operated on for a double hernia. The duke was now very ill, he weighed less than seven stone and it was clear that he might die at any time. Queen Elizabeth II was advised that she should visit her uncle soon, before it was too late. The British ambassador to France, Christopher Soames, informed the king's doctor that the duke must die `before or after the royal visit but not during'. On 18th May 1972 the queen (in France for the UK's European accession celebrations), although initially reluctant, changed her schedule and visited her uncle. Many hours of preparation preceded her visit and all Edward's tubes, except one hidden intravenous drip, were removed so that he could meet her while keeping some dignity intact. They talked for some time together while Wallis joined Prince Philip and Prince Charles in another room.

Edward drifted into a coma during the evening of 27th May, dying in the early hours of 28th May 1972, just ten days after the queen's visit. Christopher Soames must have been heartened that a royal edict could have such an impact. But controversy is not bounded by the grave. The editors of a tabloid press, quite different from their curtseying and subservient ancestors of thirty-five years ago, would record, in microscopic detail, how the royal family now treated Edward's death and funeral. The 'great love story' would be related all over again, 'Edward the lost king' would dominate their pages, and yet somehow the queen had to bury him with dignity - but not too much dignity. After all the years of vindictiveness, on both sides, some way had to be found to avoid hypocrisy without appearing too callous – a cautious magnanimity would be the order of the day. A number of issues occupied palace officials. How to deal with the duchess of Windsor, whom they had more or less exiled from England? What to do about the annual Trooping of the Colour, due to take place just two days before Edward's funeral? How to handle the sensitivities of the Queen Mother, who was still very much alive, and who's loathing for Wallis had not diminished?

In the event, the queen arranged for Edward's body to be flown to England to lie in the centre of the nave of St George's Chapel Windsor. Wallis was too distraught to accompany it. Eventually, some 58,000 people made the trip to file past his coffin, sometimes queuing as far down Castle Hill as Windsor railway station. When Wallis did arrive, lord Mountbatten met her plane and escorted her to Buckingham Palace, where she was accommodated in a stateroom overlooking the Mall. It was comfortable, but the queen and the Royal family, stiff and awkward, left her alone as much as possible, keeping everything very formal and avoiding anything as personal as engaging with her grief. With Wallis under sedation, the queen went ahead with the Trooping of the Colour on 3rd June (Wallis' and Edward's thirty fifth wedding anniversary), during which it was arranged for the Scotch Guards to play a lament with pipes and drums as a tribute to the late duke. Later that day, accompanied by Mountbatten and Prince Charles, Wallis went to visit Edward's coffin in St George's Chapel. It was strange for Wallis, and she became very distressed. Here they both were, in the tomb house of Edward's ancestors, under the only circumstances that they were allowed to be here together.

The funeral, on 5th June 1972, lasted about thirty minutes, after which Wallis accompanied the Royal Family to lunch before Edward's coffin was taken to the royal burial grounds at Frogmore to be laid near his brother, George, duke of Kent. The grave was near a small hedge that ran along the path to Queen Victoria's great mausoleum, and Wallis observed to the Archbishop of Canterbury that *'I know I am a very thin, small woman, but I do not think that even I could fit into that miserable little narrow piece of ground'*. The archbishop fobbed her off with *'I'm sure you will fit in all right'*, but Wallis would not let this 'space issue' die! Later she contacted her solicitors in London about it and received reassurances from them that there was now around nine yards between the duke's grave and the aforementioned hedge. They also enclosed a sketch to put her mind at rest.

No one from the Royal Family accompanied Wallis to Heathrow before she flew back to France. The television cameras followed her as she entered the plane and many wondered how this frail, slight figure could have terrified the Royal establishment for so long. The duke left Wallis his entire fortune of around $3 million and she retained all the fabulously expensive jewellery that had furnished the physical manifestation of his love for her. The French government obligingly did not charge her death duties and declared that she could live free of income tax for the rest of her life. Nothing in this great bounty could halt her steady decline. She became very ill after 1978, losing the use of her hands and feet, and having to be fed intravenously. Enfeebled, disorientated and almost blind, it was a long decline with brief moments of cruel awareness and understanding. She had become a very sad, sick person and she never left her house on the edge of the Bois de Boulogne after 1981. She died of heart failure on 24th April 1986, aged ninety, fourteen years after the man she had taken from the British throne and whom she claimed to have loved. The Lord Chamberlain flew to Paris to escort her body to RAF Benson, where it was met by Edward's nephew, the duke of Gloucester. Her coffin lay in the same spot in St George's Chapel, Windsor where Edward's had stood, a wreath of yellow and white lilies from the queen lying on top of it. After a twenty-eight minute service attended by 175 people, during which Wallis' name was never mentioned, the Constable of Windsor Castle led the small procession down through the west door and her coffin was driven to Frogmore to lie next to Edward. There was enough space for a 'thin' woman after all!

The sale of Wallis' remaining jewellery at Sotheby's in Geneva in April 1987 caused a great stir and realised $50,281,887, around seven times what the auctioneers had expected. All the money from this sale went to the Louis Pasteur Institute in Paris to support research into AIDS. At the very end, Edward's extravagant decorating of his wife with jewels to make up for the slights she had endured at the hands of his family, was converted from gold to a good cause; probably the best thing that either of them ever did.

Frogmore

The private cemetery at Frogmore in Windsor Home Park lies in the grounds of the house where George III's wife Queen Charlotte would go to escape the trauma of her husband's illness and where Queen Victoria's mother, the Duchess of Kent, used to live. Located near the south arm of the Italianate mausoleum that Victoria had built for Albert and herself it was consecrated in 1928, although some members of the royal family who died before that date were subsequently moved there. Edward, duke of Windsor, is the only ex-king of England to be buried there. His brothers, George duke of Kent (d 1942) and Henry duke of Gloucester (d 1974) are also buried there, as are a growing number of 'royals' whom the wider public have hardly heard of. This cemetery at Frogmore may or may not become the burial place of future kings and queens but it is certainly the most likely future-resting place for minor members of the Royal Family.

GEORGE VI (born 1895 reigned 1936-1952)

The second son of George V and Queen Mary, George VI was born five years before his great-grandmother Queen Victoria died. Known as Bertie within the royal family, he was one of those princes of the royal blood who was never meant to be king, and this suited him down to the ground. Born on the 14th December 1895, (the anniversary of the death of Albert the Prince Consort), Queen Victoria at first believed it to be an inauspicious birth, but later mellowed into believing that this young prince *'had broken the spell of this most unlucky date'*.

Bertie had an appalling stammer from the age of eight that made public speaking an ordeal. This caused a melancholy shyness in him that, in conjunction with a chronic gastric problem, led to occasional outbursts of frustrated rage. As a child he was naturally left-handed but was forced to write with his right hand and, because he was knock-kneed, he had to have his legs encased in splints to try to straighten them out. Like his father, George V, he served in the Royal Navy, between 1909 and 1917, being a midshipman in the battleship HMS Collingwood at the Battle of Jutland in 1916, after which he spent a year in the Royal Air Force. He had a wretched time in the navy, suffering from depression and a painful, undiagnosed stomach ulcer. He was in and out of hospital and, in the winter of 1915, spent some time with his father at York Cottage, in Windsor Great Park, observing how he coped with being a king at war.

He was created duke of York in 1920, and after at least two failed proposals to Elizabeth Bowes-Lyon, the youngest daughter of the 14th earl of Strathmore, he married her in 1923. Her charm, outgoing personality and unflinching loyalty to her husband would be of vital importance to him later. Conscientious, reserved and deeply religious, Bertie was happy to walk in the shadow of his noisy and more gregarious elder brother David, who was destined to become King Edward VIII in 1936. Bertie had no interest in the arts and rarely read a book except for 'The Empty Tomb', a history of the resurrection. He avoided the limelight, concentrating on public duties that attracted less glitz and glitter. While duke of York, he became president of the Boys' Welfare Association and instigated summer camps where working class boys joined with public school boys in outdoor pursuits and campfire singing. In 1925, it fell to Bertie, as President of the British Empire Exhibition, to make the closing speech before a crowd of 100,000 and millions across the empire listening at their wireless sets. It was a disaster for him, but a young Australian speech therapist called Lionel Logue, who was in the audience, contacted Bertie later and encouraged him to stand at an open window intoning vowels and to follow a regime of breathing exercises. It did not cure his stammer but it overcame its worst effects.

In December 1936 this nervous, shy, family man was suddenly thrust unexpectedly into the limelight as King George VI on the abdication of his brother. It was a shock that brought him to near breakdown. In a kind of regression to childhood, he is reported to have sobbed on his mother's lap for a full hour. Queen Mary would have been terribly embarrassed at this close physical contact but she must have seen how this unwanted burden filled her second son with gravest of fears. George's wife, Queen Elizabeth, never forgave the duke of Windsor for bringing this about but she was crucial to George in helping him grapple with the weight of it all.

Emerging from the abdication crisis, the new king strove hard to adapt to his new role. Storm clouds were gathering over Europe as Hitler began his policy of expansion by force of arms. There were only three years to go before the next war with Germany and the king and queen, adopting the mantle of ambassadors during these uncertain days, paid a state visit to France in 1938 and to Canada and the USA in 1939. This latter visit made him the first king of England to enter the land of George III's lost colonies. Sometime during 1939, Queen Elizabeth decided that it was time to do some image building to compete with the chic images of the duke and duchess of Windsor that were regularly featured in the society magazines. She called on Cecil Beaton, who at the time was regarded a somewhat avant-garde society photographer, to photograph her. These photographs, including a series of the queen in a long lace dress with a parasol on the steps and lawns behind Buckingham Palace, were an instant success. Thus began the unpredictable but necessary marriage between the camera and the royal family that grew to such a fever pitch during the time of Princess Diana.

The onset of the Second World War brought the king new challenges. First he had to adapt to dealing with the new 'war' prime minister Winston Churchill, who had been such an active supporter of his elder brother during the abdication crisis. Churchill's spirit and indefatigable patriotism eventually won the king over and, despite their obvious personality differences they grew very fond of each other.

A second challenge was the question of where the royal family should go during the blitz on London. One of the locations explored was Madresfield Court near Upton-on-Severn in Worcestershire. Its owner, the eighth earl Beauchamp, made preparations to receive the royal family including two bedrooms, one each for Elizabeth and Margaret. As long as the possibility of evacuating them to Worcestershire remained, he left a new book, appropriate to their age, at the vacant bedsides during each year of the war. Perhaps it was propitious that the family never moved there. The room chosen for the princesses to shelter in during any bombing was a tiny storeroom partially below the level of the moat with only two narrow and barred windows. It would have been almost impossible to escape from in the event of a fire. The books remained unread but Lady Beauchamp is said to have dined off the stores of tinned Spam laid up for the royal guests for many years afterwards. Monty Python would have approved!

In the event, the king and queen decided to stay on in London. During the early days of the blitz they toured the shattered East End of the city and were booed and jeered by the people standing among the wreckage of their homes and businesses. One east-end housewife complained to a Mass Observation Unit reporter that *'It's all very well for them to go traipsing around saying how their hearts bleed for us and they share our suffering and then going home to a roaring fire in one of their six houses'*. But later, after Buckingham Palace was bombed a number of times and the king still refused to move away, the public mood changed, giving the royal family a chance to shine and overwrite the shadows caused by the abdication crisis. After the bombing of Buckingham Palace Queen Elizabeth is supposed to have said: *'Now we can look the east-end in the eye'*.

At the start of the war Hitler had dismissed George VI as 'a simpleton' yet it was Hitler who gave the king the chance to shine. The rigours of the Second World War actually increased George's stature and brought the shy king the love and admiration of his country. His public appearances all over London, his steadfastness in the face of the blitz and his obvious dedication to his people increased his popularity and saved the royal family from sinking deeper into the messy irrelevance that it had seemed in 1936. But victory, when it finally came in 1945, left the king physically and mentally exhausted. During the war Churchill had kept the king informed on every detail of its progress, much of which, before 1942, had been perilous and frightening and the king had difficulty dealing with it. He smoked and drank more and his uncontrollable rages became more frequent. He had always been a frail, nervous man and the vicissitudes of the war following on so soon after the trauma of the abdication had worn him out. After a visit to South Africa in 1947, he was suffering from nervous exhaustion and was diagnosed with thickening of the arteries as a result of his heavy smoking. He would often tap his leg against a desk or the side of a chair to get his blood circulating and at one time it was even thought that his legs might have to be amputated.

During 1951 a newspaper photographer caught the king leaving a London clinic. He had been diagnosed with lung cancer, but was not been told at that time exactly what his illness was. In September 1951, the king left Balmoral for the last time before undergoing an operation to remove part of his left lung. The operation left him weak and a special heated waistcoat, fuelled by batteries, was made to help keep him warm. Four months after the operation, on 31st January 1952, he went to Heathrow to see his daughter Elizabeth and her husband off on their official visit to Kenya. George stayed out on the tarmac in a bitter wind until her plane was well out of sight – it was almost as if he knew that he wouldn't see her again. He looked cold and frail and was clearly unwell.

In the end it would not be the cancer that would claim him but a coronary thrombosis. On 6th February 1952, less than a week after saying goodbye to his daughter, George VI died peacefully in his sleep at Sandringham in Norfolk after a good day shooting hares on the estate. He had reigned for fifteen years. Despite his various ailments, his death, at just fifty-six, took everyone by surprise. George was a heavy smoker and, at that time, the medical understanding of the link between smoking, cancer and heart disease was in its infancy. A coded message, `Hyde Park Corner', was sent to royal officials announcing the king's death and as the news spread, the House of Commons was suspended as a mark of respect, as was the US Senate and the House of Representatives. Flags in every town in Britain flew at half-mast, sports fixtures were cancelled, all cinemas and theatres were closed and the BBC stopped all programmes except news bulletins. By 9pm on the night of the announcement the police had to press the growing number of mourners back from the gates of Buckingham Palace. The weeping crowds waited in the bitter cold and rain of that February night until long after dark.

Princess Elizabeth, who was at Treetops hunting lodge in Kenya, immediately became Queen Elizabeth II at the age of twenty five. The king's body was put on a special Royal Train to bring it from Sandringham to London and all along the 110-mile route people gathered by the side of the railway track to pay their respects. Then, after being met by his wife and his two daughters in heavy black veils at Kings Cross station, George's draped coffin was taken to lie in state in William Rufus' Westminster Hall. Over the next three days 300,000 people queued in silence to walk past it. The prime minister Winston Churchill (who would lie in state in that same hall thirteen years later) laid a wreath by the coffin inscribed with the two-word motto of the Victoria Cross, 'For Valour'. The quiet, unexpected king had forged a deep bond with his people that no one could have imagined at his accession fifteen years ago. Perhaps it is true that dull men make the best kings and that under our particular constitutional arrangements the last thing we want is a brilliant, glamorous or extravagant personality who's going to rock the boat. After a state funeral through the streets of London, the king's body was taken to St George's Chapel at Windsor for a private burial in the chapel on 15th February 1952.

However, all was not finished. Ten years later, shortly before taking up his appointment as Dean of Windsor and Principal Domestic Chaplain to Queen Elizabeth II, the Venerable Robin Woods received a puzzling, and no doubt surprising, handwritten letter from the queen's private secretary, advising him that he must immediately set in motion plans to bury the late King George VI. Because of George VI's untimely death, no preparations had been made for a permanent resting place, and at the funeral in 1952 his coffin, draped with the sovereign's standard, had been lowered into what was really the aisle of George III's Royal Vault alongside that of his brother, George, duke of Kent. Behind wooden screens, just a few feet on either side, but leaving no space for their erstwhile descendent, lay the dusty coffins of George III, his sons George IV and William IV and many other descendants of the House of Hanover. A beloved king just left in an aisle; something needed to be done!

Queen Elizabeth II did not want another table-top tomb, surmounted by a life-size effigy, in mimic of medieval monuments, preferring, more in keeping with the times, a simple slab of stone laid into the floor. Despite the seeming urgency of the request made to the new Dean in 1962, finding an appropriate space proved difficult. There was no suitable area in the confines of the existing chapel for a new vault to be built and a further seven years were to elapse before an appropriate space could be found. The queen eventually decided to construct a small addition to St George's Chapel. A new George VI chapel would be built with a burial vault beneath it. This would be the first structure to be added to St George's Chapel since 1504.

The first design for the new chapel was rejected by the Fine Arts Commission but a second design by the architects Paul Paget and George Pace was accepted. It would occupy the space between the angles of the north choir and the Rutland Chapel, and the queen paid £25,000 in 1968 for the work to be done. Its design continues the perpendicular Gothic idiom with some twentieth century touches and includes symbols taken from some of the earliest monuments in St George's. The Belgian black marble ledger stone over the vault inscribed, at that time, simply 'George VI' recalls the simplicity of the slab set over Henry VI's tomb and the design of the entrance gates and railings recall the beautiful Tresilian gates built for Edward IV's tomb. The re-interment of the king took place (seventeen years after his death) at 5.30pm on 26th March 1969 after Evensong. No members of the royal family were present, just a small party of churchmen, architects and builders. The Lord Chamberlain and the Dean of Windsor descended the steps to the vault to supervise the raising of the king's coffin on a lift up to the choir. From here it was carried to the new chapel and lowered into the vault beneath it by straps. The black marble slab was then lowered over the vault and the Dean of Windsor placed a spray of flowers from Queen Elizabeth, the Queen Mother over it.

Five days later on 31st March the Dean of Windsor, accompanied by many of the royal family, dedicated the new Chapel. Earl Mountbatten was not present as he was away attending the funeral of President Eisenhower in the USA and the duke of Windsor (the king's elder brother) was not invited. The new chapel is enclosed by wrought iron gates into which have been worked the words of the little known poet Minnie L. Haskins that the king had used in his Christmas Broadcast of 1939. The poem begins: *'I said to the man who stood at the gate of the year: 'Give me light that I may tread safely into the unknown'.* With its four short steps down to the black ledger stone this small chapel has a feeling of snugness about it entirely in keeping with the homely nature of its main occupant. Later the body of the late king's brother George, duke of Kent, was also removed from the 'aisle' of the George III vault on the death of his wife Princess Marina of Kent. They were both buried in the Royal Burial Ground at Frogmore.

The queen, with an eye to the future, instructed the architect to allow a space for four coffins in the new vault: two for King George VI and Queen Elizabeth and two for herself and the duke of Edinburgh. In February 2002, and in a major break from royal tradition, the body of Princess Margaret was taken for cremation to Slough Crematorium. The casket containing the ashes of the much-adored younger daughter of George VI was then placed in the George III vault where her father had rested for so long. The unusual step of cremation for a senior member of the royal family had to be taken as Margaret had insisted on being placed near her father but there was no room for a fifth coffin. Princess Louise, a daughter of Queen Victoria was the only precedent, she was cremated in 1939. For the time being there was no room for her ashes either, as the queen had earlier decreed that George VI's vault should not be opened again until after the Queen Mother's death. Elizabeth, the Queen Mother, died later in 2002 and after lying in state in Westminster Hall and a ceremonial funeral through the streets of London, she was interred beside her husband, accompanied by the ashes of Princess Margaret.

Given Queen Elizabeth II's limiting the George VI vault to four 'placings', King Charles III and King William V, if all goes to plan, will need to sort out a new vault somewhere for themselves. Like Henry VII, George III and Queen Elizabeth II before them, they will have to find a new space for a new group of royal bones. Of course they may decide, following the precedents set by the funerals of Princess Louise and Princess Margaret that in future cremation should be the order of an English monarch's funeral. In which case they will not need a brace of royal navy ratings to tow them through the streets of London just a taxi and an appropriate space for a succession of colourful urns.

A Note on Porphyria

Since Alan Bennett's play, and then 1994 film, about the 'Madness of George III', some interest has been aroused about the uncommon disease porphyria, which is thought to have afflicted King George III. There has also been some debate about who might have been the original carrier of the gene that may have affected members of the British royal family, both before and after George III.

Nature of Porphyria

Porphyria is a complex disease, best described as a group of different disorders that are still not completely understood. It is genetic, but not linked to a sex chromosome, like haemophilia, so either parent can pass (or not pass) the disease on to any child. The chance of an individual within an affected family contracting the disease or transmitting it is quite different from one family to another and it is this unpredictability that makes it so difficult to identify. Modern medicine has identified a group of inherited metabolic defects that lead to an alteration in blood chemistry as toxic substances accumulate, damaging the nervous system. Porphyria is one of these and is caused by abnormalities in the chemical steps leading to the production of 'heme', a component of haemoglobin (the oxygen carrying pigment in the blood). Heme is also found in bone marrow, the liver and other tissues. The genes for all the enzymes in the heme pathway have now been identified. Multiple enzymes are needed for the body to produce heme. If any one of the enzymes is abnormal, the process cannot continue and the intermediate products, porphyrin or its precursors, may build up and be excreted in the urine and stool. The porphyria disorders can be grouped by symptoms – whether they affect the skin or the nervous system.

Cutaneous porphyrias affect the skin, causing blisters, itching, and swelling of the skin when it is exposed to sunlight.

Acute porphyrias affect the nervous system. It causing symptoms of pain in the chest and abdomen, limbs or back; muscle numbness, rashes, tingling, paralysis, or cramping; severe weakness in the limbs; insomnia and breathing problems, vomiting; constipation, memory loss and confusion; mood swings, delirium and personality change.

Diagnosing porphyria is difficult because, as noted above, the range of symptoms is common to many disorders and it can only be adequately diagnosed through, blood, urine and stool tests, the interpretation of which is complex. Attacks of porphyria may develop over hours or days and last for days or weeks, and today can be triggered by many things including barbiturates, tranquillisers, fasting, smoking, alcohol, emotional and physical stress, and exposure to the sun. Treatment may involve treating with heme, giving medicines to relieve the symptoms, or drawing blood. People who suffer severe attacks may need to be hospitalised. The disease may remain dormant throughout the life of a particular carrier or it may cause attacks of various degrees of intensity with remissions and exacerbations. It is rare in children or young people, being mainly confined to adults and, among adults women generally suffer more aggressive attacks than men. There is still no cure for porphyria.

The Original Carrier

The catalogue of complaints involved in porphyria, so disparate, vague, and difficult to diagnose when the patient is present, is so much more difficult to identify when the patient has been dead for two hundred years or more. The only real, telltale, sign of porphyria is purple or wine-coloured urine. The only other way historians have been able to pinpoint the symptoms of porphyria among British monarchs, before the affliction of King George III, is by the reports of the doctors who attended them. Their reports of delirium, irrational behaviour, and mood swings may be the only clue we have as to whether a particular patient was affected by it.

As porphyria was unknown to them, they tended to associate symptoms with ailments and diseases that they were familiar with. As with George III, monarchs, other than queens who were giving birth, were rarely physically examined by their doctors. A strict protocol that precluded any touching of the monarch's body meant that they were restricted to taking a pulse, asking vague questions about symptoms and examining the result of bodily functions. The doctor who attended Queen Victoria for twenty years only discovered that she had a ventral hernia and a prolapse of the uterus as he began to prepare her body after her death. He had treated her *'purely through verbal communication'*. Such diagnosis at a distance, hedged about by protocol, generally leaves a poor footprint as far as the notes or reports made by royal doctors are concerned.

Those searching for a source for porphyria as far back as the late medieval period have seized on Charles V, King of France, who died in 1416. He suffered from well-recorded mental problems and his daughter Catherine of Valois married England's King Henry V. Their son Henry VI suffered intermittent bouts of madness or dementia and so some attention has been paid to Charles V as a source. As Henry VI's son, Prince Edward, was killed at the Battle of Tewkesbury in 1471, and thus Charles V's link died with him, it seems unlikely that he was the source for the English monarchs who followed Henry VI.

One of the sources most often mooted is Margaret Tudor, the sister of Henry VIII. She married James IV of Scotland in 1503 and their son, James V of Scotland, married Mary of Guise in 1538. Their daughter was Mary Queen of Scots whose son, James I of England (James VI of Scotland), is really the father of the present royal family. During her time as a prisoner in England, Mary Queen of Scots, was certainly recorded as enduring bouts of hysterical suffering, irrational behaviour and mood swings, which came and went, much as would be the case for a sufferer of acute and intermittent porphyria. The problem here is differentiating between symptoms caused by porphyria and symptoms resulting from her distress at being incarcerated in various castles for so long. If she had porphyria the trials of incarceration would certainly aggravate it and the pains in her arms and legs, which she often reported in her letters, correspond to the painful paresis of the extremities often experienced by porphyria sufferers. These reports are really all we have to suggest that Mary might have had the disease.

We get something of a breakthrough with the physician who attended Mary's son, James I. This Dr Myerne, kept detailed notes on James' condition, and at one point describes James' urine as *'being purple as Alicante wine'*. James was also reported as having a very fragile skin that was easily injured and very sensitive to sunlight. Such a report suggests that James I may have inherited porphyria from either his mother or his father (Henry Stuart lord Darnley) or both. They were both descended from Margaret Tudor, hence the often voiced belief that she may have been the original 'source', though there is next to nothing known about her state of health. James' father, lord Darnley, was also descended from Mary, the sister of the Scottish king, James III, who was also grandfather to Mary Queen of Scots. If porphyria was lurking in the genes of the Scottish kings of the fifteenth century it is not surprising that it turned up later in their sixteenth century descendants as it often skips a generation or two. James I's eldest son Henry Stuart, Prince of Wales, who died suddenly in 1612 aged only eighteen, from an illness similar to that which afflicted his father, may also have had porphyria. Henry's brother Charles I did not seem to evince the same symptoms, nor did Charles I's sons, Charles II and James II. Queen Mary, the daughter of James II, did not show any signs but her sister, Queen Anne, endured almost constant ill health. The reported blotches on her skin and erratic mood swings may have indicated porphyria. The Hanoverian kings, being descended from a daughter of James I (Sophia, the Electress of Hanover), may have carried the gene from the Stuart branch of their ancestry, materialising at its worst in George III. George IV, whose catalogue of ailments was Babylonian in its compass, is also thought to have shown some of the signs of porphyria. His daughter Charlotte, who died in childbirth, is often described as having many of the symptoms of the disease.

George III did not have any of the attacks caused by porphyria until his 50s. In 2003 a scrap of paper containing a few strands of George III's hair was found in the vaults of a London museum and a Professor Martin Warrene was keen to analyse these to see if it gave any clues to George III's illness. After testing, the king's hair was found to contain over 300 times the toxic level of arsenic. Given that it is rare for men to suffer the severity of the attacks that George III endured, Warrene wondered if the arsenic found in the hair held any clue as to what might have triggered this severity. Professor Tim Cox, an expert on extreme cases of porphyria at Addenbrookes Hospital in Cambridge, confirmed that arsenic can be a trigger for porphyria and that the massive levels found in King George's hair suggested that the king had been liberally ingesting arsenic in one form or another over a long period of time. One of the most common medicines administered to George III, several times a day during his illness, was James' powder, a medicine composed mostly of antimony, which, even when purified, contains significant traces of arsenic. Thus, the very medication being given to the king not only triggered more attacks but made them much more severe and prolonged.

Apart from those mentioned above, other sufferers may have included: Henrietta Anne, Duchess of Orleans, a daughter of Charles I; Frederick Wilhelm I of Prussia, Caroline Matilda, Queen of Denmark, Frederick II, 'the Great' of Germany and Wilhelm I of Hess-Kessel. DNA testing of Charles I's blood-stained execution shroud proved negative, but DNA tests on the exhumed remains of Princess Charlotte, a sister of Kaiser Wilhelm II of Prussia, were positive. Some commentators believe that Queen Victoria's complaints of unspecified illnesses and intense emotions may indicate that she suffered from a mild form of porphyria and passed it on to some of her six hundred or more descendants.

In more recent times, Prince William of Gloucester, the current duke of Gloucester's elder brother, who died in a plane crash in 1972, was said to have been diagnosed with porphyria and this would suggest that Edward VII, George V, and his son Henry duke of Gloucester, were also carriers, if not sufferers, of the disease. George V's wife, Queen Mary, was also descended from George III, and Prince William of Gloucester's mother was descended from Charles II so the royal family's tendency to 'inbreed' may have contributed to doubling-up the pathways available to the gene. The search for the definitive source for porphyria within the history of the British royal family will no doubt continue. For now, our best guess is that a gene for porphyria, possibly starting as a new mutation with Mary Queen of Scots, was transmitted via her son James I through the Stuart line onwards down through to the Hanoverian family.

Sources: Libraries and Archives

I would like to acknowledge the help and support I have received from: the Library of Westminster Abbey, The Society of Antiquaries, London, the Royal Archives at Windsor, the Archives of the Dean and Canons at St George's Chapel Windsor and the Library and Archives of Canterbury Cathedral.

Printed Primary Sources: All available in English translation editions:

The Ecclesiastical History of England and Normandy by Oderic Vitalis, translated by T. Forrester (2 vols) Bohn, 1905
Chronicle of Matthew Paris: monastic life in the 13th century translated and edited by Richard Vaughan, Sutton Publishing, 1984
Robert Fabyan New Chronicles of England and France, 2nd ed. by Sir H Ellis, 1811
Jean Froisart's Chronicle translated and edited by Geoffrey Bererton, London, Penguin, 1968
Edward Hall's The Union of the two Noble and Illustrious Families of Lancaster and York ed. by Sir H Ellis, 1809
Holinshed's Chronicles of England, Scotland and Ireland, 1578
Polydor Virgil's Books on English History comprising the reigns of Henry VI, Edward IV and Richard III, translated by Sir H Ellis, Camden Society, 1844
The Crowland Chronicle Continuation 1459-86 ed. by N. Pronay and J. Cox, London, Richard III and Yorkist History Trust, 1986
William Camden's The Annals of Elizabeth, 1615

Sources : General

Historical Memorials of Westminster Abbey by Arthur Penrhyn Stanley, Dean of Westminster, London, John Murray, 1st ed. 1868, 5th ed. 1882, 7th ed. with author's final revisions 1890, reprinted in 1896, 1911, and 1924. *This is the famous Dean Stanley, a friend of Queen Victoria, who officiated at many of the tomb openings in Westminster Abbey. This work is full of anecdotes about the monarchs of England and descriptions of their tombs and burials. Invaluable, if a tad romantic at times.*
Supplement to the 1st and 2nd editions of Historical Memorials of Westminster Abbey by Arthur Penrhyn Stanley, Dean of Westminster, London, John Murray, 1869. *Valuable additional information to the above.*
A Historical Guide to Westminster Abbey: The Kingdom Power and the Glory by John Field, London, James and James (publishers) Limited, 3rd ed. 2000.
The Funeral Effigies of Westminster Abbey, ed. by Anthony Harvey and Richard Mortimer, Woodbridge, The Boydell Press, 1994 (paperback 2003).
Kings, Queens, Bones and Bastards: Who's who in the English monarchy from Egbert to Elizabeth II, revised by David Hilliam, Sutton Publishing, paperback edition 2004. *Useful for those wishing to start out on this quest. Lots of interesting anecdotes and stories but not always accurate as far as supporting facts are concerned.*
The Oxford DNB Available online via the membership number of a borrower registered with a subscribing library. Most UK public libraries are subscribers. Scholarly, accurate and up-to-date biographies of over 85,000 British persons. An invaluable starting point for the lives of British monarchs.

The Death of Kings: a medical history of the Kings and Queens of England by Clifford Brewer, London, Abson Books, 2000, fifth impression 2005.
An invaluable source for the terminal sicknesses of the monarchs of England. I would like to acknowledge that much of the information on the illnesses that caused or contributed to the deaths of English monarchs in this work is taken from Clifford Brewer's book.
The Monuments of St George's Chapel Windsor Castle, edited by Shelagh M. Bond, Windsor, Dean and Canons of Windsor, 1958, (reprinted 1999). *A highly detailed annotated list of just about every stone, slab and tomb and their inscriptions in St George's Chapel Windsor.* ⚬
The Romance of St George's Chapel Windsor Castle by Peter J. Begent, Windsor, 2001
The Royal Way of Death by Olivia Bland, London, Constable, 1986. *Valuable chapters on the death and funeral arrangements from Elizabeth I to Edward Duke of Windsor and Earl Mountbatten in 1979.*
Battles in Britain 1066-1547 by William Seymour, London, Sidgwick and Jackson, 1975. *A valuable guide to the battle of Bosworth and the death of Richard III.*
Battlefields of England by Colonel A. H. Burne, London, Methuen 1952
I have reported the popular version of Richard III's last charge but Colonel Burne (just as credibly) believes that Richard III rode southwest on his last charge in an attempt to get his hands on the traitor Lord Stanley rather than Henry Tudor. He thus would have encountered the bog at the bottom of the hill in which his horse may have floundered giving rise to Shakespeare's famous: 'A horse a horse my kingdom for a horse'.
A History of Britain 1: 3000BC-AD1603, At the Edge of the World? by Simon Schama, London, BBC Worldwide Ltd, 2003
A History of Britain 2: 1603-1776 The British Wars by Simon Schama, London, BBC Worldwide Ltd, 2003
A History of Britain 3: 1776-2000, The Fate of Empire by Simon Schama, London, BBC Worldwide Ltd, 2003
The Plantagenets by John Harvey, London, Collins Fontana Library, 1967

Sources: By Monarch

Harold: The Last Saxon King by Ian. W. Walker, Stroud, Sutton Publishing, 1997
Hawk of Normandy: The Story of William the Conqueror by George Baker, London, Lutterworth, 1956
Anglo-Norman England 1066-1166 by Marjorie Chibnall, London, Blackwell, 1986
England Under the Norman and Angevin Kings, 1075-1225 by Robert Bartlett, London, Oxford University Press, 2000
William Rufus by Frank Barlow, New Haven and London, Yale University Press, 2000
Henry I by C. Warren Hollister, New Haven and London, Yale University Press, 2001
The Troubled Reign of King Stephen by J. T. Appleby, London, G. Bell and Sons, 1969
The Reign of King Stephen 1135-1154 by David Crouch, London, 2000
Henry II by Judith A. Green and W.L. Warren, New Haven and London, Yale University Press, 2000
Henry II by W.L. Warren, New Haven and London, Yale University Press, 1973
Richard I by John Gillingham, New Haven and London, Yale University Press, 1999
The Life and Times of Richard I by John Gillingham, London, Weidenfeld and Nicolson, 1973
The Life and Times of King John by Maurice Ashley, London, Weidenfeld and Nicolson and Book Club Associates, 1972
King John by W. L. Warren, New Haven and London, Yale University Press, 1998

1215, The Year of Magna Carta by Danny Danziger and John Gillingham, London, Hodder and Stoughton, 2003

The Reign of Henry III by D.A. Carpenter, London, Hambledon Press, 1996

The Three Edwards: War and State in England 1272-1377 by Michael Prestwich, London, Weidenfeld and Nicolson and Book Club Associates, 1980

Edward I by Michael Prestwich, New Haven and London, Yale University Press, 1997

King Edward II, His Life, His Reign, and its Aftermath, 1284-1330 by Roy Martins Haines, Canada, McGill-Queens University Press, 2006

King Edward II by Mary Saaler, London, Rubicon Press, 1997

The Perfect King: The Life of Edward III Father of the English Nation, by Ian Mortimer, London, Jonathan Cape 2006. *A wonderful, monumental and extremely readable work on Edward III.*

The Reign of Edward III by W.M. Ormrod, Stroud, Tempus Publishing, 1999

The Black Prince by Barbara Emerson, London, Weidenfeld and Nicolson, 1976

Richard II by Nigel Saul, New Haven and London, Yale University Press, 1997

Henry IV by Bryan Bevan, London, Rubicon Press, 1994

History of England Under Henry The Fourth, by James Hamilton Wylie, London, Longmans, Green and Co, 1898 Vol IV 1411-1413. *A rare description of Henry IV's funeral with some very detailed notes in Chapter 56pp 111-125.*

Henry V by Christopher Allmand, New Haven and London, Yale University Press, 1993

The Reign of King Henry VI by Ralph A. Griffin, Stroud, Sutton Publishing, 2004

Henry VI and the Politics of Kingship by John Watts, Cambridge, Cambridge University Press, 1996

The Reign of Edward IV by Eric N. Simons, London, Frederic K. Muller Ltd, 1966
Provides an excellent and detailed description of Edward IV's funeral.

This Son of York: A biography of Edward IV by Mary Clive, London, Macmillan, 1973 (paperback by Cardinal 1975).

The Princes in the Tower by Alison Weir, London Bodley Head, 1992, (Folio Society edition, 1999)

Elizabeth Woodville: Mother of the Princes in the Tower by David Baldwin, Stroud, Sutton Publishing, 2004

The Royal Funerals of the House of York at Windsor by Anne F. Sutton and Livia Visser-Fuchs with R. A. Griffiths, London, The Richard III Society, 2005. *One of those glorious books that mines a small piece of history with the enthusiasm that only the dedicated can produce. Invaluable for the funerals of Edward IV and Elizabeth Woodville.*

Richard III by Paul Murray Kendall, London, George Allen and Unwin Ltd, 1955
A very readable and highly detailed biography of the maligned king. A 'revisionist' book very much seeking to put the record straight.

Richard III by Michael Hicks, Stroud, Tempus Publishing, 2000

The Life and Times of Henry VII by Neville Williams, London, Weidenfeld and Nicolson, 1973

The History of the Reign of King Henry the Seventh by Francis Bacon, London, The Folio Society, 1971

Henry VIII by J. J. Scarisbrick, New Haven and London, Yale University Press 1968

Henry VIII, King and Court by Alison Weir, London, Jonathan Cape, 2001

The Reign of Henry VIII Personalities and Politics by David Starkey, London, Vintage, 2002

The Last Days of Henry VIII: Conspiracy, treason and heresy at the court of the dying tyrant by Robert Hutchinson, Weidenfeld and Nicolson, London, 2005.
Includes detailed notes on Cushing's Syndrome and Henry's funeral.

Edward VI by Jennifer Loach, New Haven and London, Yale University Press, 1999

Edward VI: The Lost King of England by Christopher Skidmore, London, Weidenfeld and Nicolson, 2007

The Later Reformation in England, 1547-1603 by D. MacCulloch, London, Palgrave-Macmillan, 2000

Mary Tudor: A Life by David Loads, Oxford, Blackwell Publishers Ltd, 1989

The Lady Mary by Milton Waldman, London, Collins, 1972

The Illness and death of Mary Tudor by V. C. Medival, Journal of the Royal Society of Medicine, Vol 80, December 1987 pp 766-770

Elizabeth I by Anne Somerset, London, Phoenix Press, 1997

Elizabeth I by Alison Plowden, Stroud, Sutton Publishing, 2004

Elizabeth and Leicester by Sarah Gristwood, London, Bantam, 2007

Her Majesties Spymaster: Elizabeth I, Sir Francis Walsingham and the Birth of Modern Espionage by Robert Hutchinson, London, Orion, 2007

The Memoirs of Robert Carey ed. by F.H. Mares, Oxford Clarendon Press, 1972
An important eyewitness account of the last days of Queen Elizabeth I.

Mary Queen of Scots by Antonia Fraser, London, Weidenfeld and Nicolson, 1994

The Diary of John Manningham ed. by R.P. Sorlein, New Hampshire, Hanover Press, 1976

The Cecils of Hatfield House: a portrait of an English ruling family by David Cecil, London, Sphere Books, 1975

King James VI of Scotland and I of England by Bryan Bevan, London, The Rubicon Press, 1996

The Last Illness and Post-mortem Examination of James I translated by William Cock with notes, published in 'The Genealogist' 1884 by the late Wm Munk, London 1933. *From the Latin as printed in the 'History of the Marwood Family (Marvodia)'*

Power and Glory: Jacobean England and the making of the King James Bible, by Adam Nicolson, London, Harper Perennial, 2003

Reformation: Europe's House Divided 1490-1700 by D. MacCulloch, London, Penguin, 2003

King Charles I by Pauline Gregg, London, Dent, 1981

Charles I: The Personal Monarch by Charles Carlton, London, Routledge, 1995

'O Horrible Murder': The trial and execution of King Charles I by Robert B. Partridge, London, Rubicon Press, 1998

God's Englishman: Oliver Cromwell and the English Revolution by Christopher Hill, London, Penguin, 2000

Oliver Cromwell: Our Chief of Men by Antonia Fraser, London, Weidenfeld and Nicolson, 1973, then reprinted in Mandarin Paperbacks, 1993.
Clear, readable, scholarly and evenly balanced this biography is a tour de force particularly detailed on Cromwell's last days and the arrangements made for his funeral.

The Death of Oliver Cromwell by H. F. McMains, Lexington, University Press of Kentucky, 2000.
Claims Cromwell was poisoned by Doctor George Bates and explores various versions of Cromwell's and Ireton's burial and re-burial.

King Charles II by Antonia Fraser, London, Phoenix, 1979

Charles II: Portrait of an Age, by Tony Palmer, London, Book Club Associates, 1979

1660: The Year of Restoration by Patrick Morrah, London, Chatto and Windus, 1960

James II by John Miller, New Haven and London, Yale University Press, 2000

The Age of William and Mary: power, politics and patronage 1688-1702, ed. by R. P. Maccubbin and M. Hamilton-Phillips, Williamsburg, Virginia, College of William and Mary in Virginia, 1989

William's Mary: A Biography of Mary II by Elizabeth Hamilton, London, Hamish Hamilton, 1972

William III and the Godly Revolution by T. Claydon, London, Cambridge University Press, 1996

William of Orange: A Personal Portrait by Nesca A. Robb, Vol 2: 1674-1702, London, Heineman, 1966

England Under Queen Anne by G.M. Trevelyan, 3 vols, London, Longman, 1930-34

Queen Anne by Edward Gregg, London, Routledge and Kegan Paul, 1980

Queen Anne, by Edward Gregg, London, Collins, 1970

George I, Elector and King by Ragnild Hatton, London, Thames and Hudson, 1978

King George II and Queen Caroline by Jhn Van Der Kiste, Stroud, Sutton Publishing, 1997

George III: A Personal History by Christopher Hibbert, London, Viking, 1998

George III and the American Revolution by P.D.G. Thomas, History, new series, 70(1985), pp16-31

George IV: The Grand Entertainment by Steve Parissien, London, John Murray, 2001

George IV by E. A. Smith, New Haven and London, Yale University Press, 1999

The Life and Times of William IV by Anne Somerset, London, Weidenfeld and Nicolson and Book Club Associates, 1980

William IV by Philip Ziegler, London, William Collins, 1971

The Prime Ministers, Vol 1, from Sir Robert Walpole to Sir Robert Peel ed. by Herbert Van Thal, London, George Allen and Unwin, 1974

Queen Victoria: A personal history by Christopher Hibbert, London, Harper Collins, 2000

Victoria R.I. by Elizabeth Longford, London, Weidenfeld and Nicolson, 1990

Queen Victoria: Her Life and Times by Cecil Woodham-Smith, Vol 1, 1819-1861, London, Cardinal, 1975

The Victorians by A. N. Wilson, London, Arrow, 2003

Melbourne by Philip Ziegler, London, William Collins, 1976

The Life and Times of Edward VII by Keith Middlemas, London, Weidenfeld and Nicolson and Book Club Associates, 1972

Edward VII, Prince and King by Giles St Aubyn, London, Collins, 1979

Dreadnought: Britain, Germany, and the Coming of the Great War by Robert K. Massie, New York, Random House, 1991

King George V by Kenneth Rose, London, Phoenix, 2000
Excellent on the death of George V and the subsequent revelation of Dawson's euthanasia.

The Strange Death of Liberal England by George Dangerfield, London, Constable, 1936. *An important source for the constitutional issues involving George V and the passing of the Parliament Act of 1911.*

Battle Royal: Edward VIII and George VI brother against brother by Kirsty McLeod, London, Constable, 1999

The Duchess of Windsor: the uncommon life of Wallis Simpson by Greg King, London, Aurum Press, 1999

George VI by Sarah Bradford, London, Penguin, 1989

The Queen: Elizabeth II and the Monarchy by Ben Pimlott, London, Harper Collins, 2001

Bognor Regis, 258
Brown, John, 241, 243
Bruce, Robert, King of Scots, 63, 66
Bruiser, an old 'war' horse, 261
Brunswick, Caroline of, Queen of George IV, 222
Buckingham House, later Buckingham Palace, 213, 233
Burgh-on Sands, 64
Butler, Lady Eleanor, 109
Caernarfon, castle, 62
Calais, 73, 91, 135
Cambridge, Kings College, 96
Cambridge, Richard, earl of, 90
Canterbury, Cathedral, 42, 75, 88, 105
Cardiff Castle, Robert Curthose held prisoner, 31
Carlton House, 222
Caroline of Anspach, Queen of George II, 201, 205, 207, 208
Caroline of Brunswick, Queen of George IV, 217, 222, 223, 224, 225
Cassel, Sir Ernest, 252
Catherine of Aragon, 1st Queen of Henry VIII, 118, 122, 123, 124, 127, 132, 133
Catherine of Braganza, Queen of Charles II, 170
Catherine Howard, 5th Queen of Henry VIII, 123, 124, 128, 133
Catherine Parr, 6th Queen of Henry VIII, 124, 125, 128, 129, 138
Catherine of Valois, Queen of Henry V, 91, 92, 93, 94, 95, 116
Catholic emancipation, 216, 225, 233
Cavalier Parliament, 169
Caxton, William, printer, 104
Cecil, Robert, 1st (Cecil) Earl of Salisbury, 140, 143
Cecil, Robert, Earl of Salisbury, prime minister, 239, 242
Cecil William, Lord Burghley, 138, 139, 140, 143
Censing, 11
Cerecloth, 11
Chancellor of the Duchy of Lancaster, 88
Chantry Chapels, 11, banning, 130
Charles I, King of England, 127, 149, 151, 152, 153, 154, 155, 156, 160
Charles II, King of England, 155, 160, 167, 168, 169, 170, 171, 172, 173, 174, 175, 176, 183, 184, 185
Charles II, mistresses, 170
Charles IV, King of France, 67, 68, 73
Charles V King of France, 72
Charles VI King of France, 79, 80, 85, 90, 91, 92, 95
Charles VII King of France, 92, 96
Charles V, Holy Roman Emperor, 134
Chalus, 47
Charlotte of Mecklenburg-Strelitz, Queen to George III, 212, 217, 218
Charlotte, Princess, daughter of George IV, 223, death, 224
Chaucer, Geoffrey, 75, 82
'China Dossier', 261

Chinon, castle of, death of Henry II, 42
Churchill, John, 1st Duke of Marlborough, 179, 186, 188, 192, 193, 195, 197, 200
Churchill, Sarah, Duchess of Marlborough, 179, 186, 19, 1921, 193, 195, 197, 200
Churchill, Winston, Prime Minister, 268
Civil War, English (1642-1651), 153
Clarence, George Duke of, 102, 103, 104, 107, 112
Clarence Lodge, later Clarence House, 230
Clifden, Nellie, 240, 246
Clito, William, son of Robert Curthose, 32, 33
Cnut, Danish King of England, 13
Cobbett, William, 228
College of Heralds, 243, 244
Colombiers, (Villandry), 42
Conroy, Sir John, 237, 238,
Conway, castle, 85
Corfe, castle, 70
Covenant, the, 11
Covenanters, 11, 167, 168
Cnut, Danish King of England, 13, 29
Cranmer, Thomas, Archbishop of Canterbury, 125, 132, 135,
Crécy, battle of (1346), 73, 91
Crimean War (1853-1856), 240
Cromwell, Oliver, Lord Protector, 158, 159, 160, 161, 162, 163, 164, 165, 166
Cromwell, Richard, briefly Lord Protector, 163, 164
Cromwell, Sir Oliver, 158
Cromwell, Thomas, 122, 123
Culloden, battle of (1746), 209
Curthose, Robert, Duke of Normandy, 21, 26, 30, 31
Cushing's syndrome, 124
Customs Duties, Edward I, 63
Cyprus, Richard I's conquest of, 46
Darnley, Lord Henry Stuart, husband of Mary Queen of Scots, 143, 146
David II, King of Scots, 74
Dawson, Lord, Doctor to George V, 258, 259
Declaration of Indulgencies, (James II), 178, 179
De la Pole, William, Earl of Suffolk, 97
Despenser, Hugh the Elder and Hugh the Younger, 67, 68, 72
Dettingen, battle of, (1743) 208, 209
Devise for the Succession (Edward VI), 131
Disraeli, Benjamin, 234, Prime Minister, 241, 242, 246
Dissolution of the Monasteries, 11
Domesday Book (1085), 23, 27, 28
Domfront, town in northern France, 30
Dover, Treaty of, 171
Drogheda (1649), 160
Dudley, Guildford, 131
Dudley, John, Earl of Warwick, 1st Duke of Northumberland, 130, 131, 134
Dudley, Robert, Earl of Leicester, 139
Dunbar, battle of (1650), 63, 160
Dutch United Provinces, 183
Dysentery, 92

George IV, Prince Regent, later King of Great Britain, 155,156, 217, 221, 222, 223, 224, 225, 226, 227, 228, 231, Victoria's christening, 237

George V, King of Great Britain, 255, 256, 257, 258, 259, 260, 261, 262

George, Duke of York later King George VI of Great Britain, 263, 267, 268, 269, 270, 271

George VI Chapel in St George's Chapel, Windsor, 270

George, Prince of Denmark, husband of Queen Anne, 191, 192, 194

German Xenophobia, 257

Gillray, James, satirical cartoonist, 221, 222

Gisors, castle of, 27, John loses, 51

Gladstone, William Ewart, prime minister, 241, 242, 248

Gloucester Cathedral, 31, 69, 70

Gloucester, Humphrey, Duke of, youngest son of Henry IV, 95

Gloucester, William, Duke of, son of Queen Anne, 191

Gloucester, prince William Duke of, 274

Glyn Dŵr, Owen, Welsh Prince, 86, 89

Glorious Revolution of 1688, 180

Godwine, earl of Wessex, 13

Godolphin, Sidney, 1st Earl of, 193

Godwine, Harold, King of England

Godwine, Swein, 13, 17

Gordon Riots, 216

Government of Ireland Bill (1912), 257

Great Fire of London (1666), 170, 171

Grenville, George, 214

Grey, Lady Jane, 131, 134, 138, 139, 142

Grey, lord, 233

Gunpowder Plot (1605), 147

Great Exhibition, London, (1851), 239

Gytha of Denmark, mother of King Harold II, 17, 19

Hadradi, Harold, King of Norway, 18, 19

Haley's Comet, (1066) 18 (1910) 252

Halford, Sir Henry, 156

Halifax, Nova Scotia, 230

Hampton Court Palace, 129

Handel, George Frederick, composer, 202

Hanna Lightfoot, 212

Hanover, becomes a kingdom, 218

Hardie, Kier, 262

Harfleur, battle for (1415), 90

Harley, Robert, 1st Earl of Oxford, 193

Harold II, King of England, 17, 18, 19 Tomb of, 19, 20,

Harthacnut, Harold, Danish King of England, 13

Hastings, battle of (1066), 19, 22

Hastings, Lady Flora, 238

Hastings, Lord, 104, 108, 109, 113

Hatfield House, 133, 139, 149

Hearse, 11

Henrietta Maria, Queen of Charles I, 152

Henry I, King of England, 21, 25, 30, 31, 32, death of 33, funeral, 34, 36

Henry II, King of England, 19, 33, 37, 38, 39, 40, system of justice, 41,

Henry III, King of England, 54, 55, 56, death, 57, burial 58, 59

Henry Bolingbroke, later King Henry IV of England, 76, 78, 80, 81, 84, 85, 86, 87, 88, 89, 94

Henry V, King of England, 84, 88, 89, 90, 91, 92, 93, 94, 95, 105

Henry VI, King of England, 95, 96, 97, 98, 99, 100, 116

Henry Tudor, Earl of Richmond, later King VII of England, 99, 100, 114, 116, 117, 118, 119, 120

Henry VII Chapel in Westminster Abbey, 119, 132, 137, 141, 150, 163, 164, 165, 188, 189, 196, 207, 210,

For monarchs buried in St George's Chapel, Windsor see under each monarch and list on pages 9-10

Henry VIII, King of England, 122, 123, 124, 125, 126, 127, 133, 155

Henry Fitzroy, illegitimate son of Henry VIII by Elizabeth Blount, 127

Henry the 'Young King', burial at Rouen, 43, 45

Henry Stuart, Prince of Wales, son of James I, 147, 152, 273

Herbert, Lord William, 116

Herleva, mother of William the Conqueror, 21

Herrenhausen, Palace of, 203, 205

Hitler, Adolph, 264, 267, 268

Holdenby Hall, Northamptonshire, 159

House of Lords, 251, 256

Houses of Parliament, Sir Charles Barry's building, 59

Huddleston, Father, 173, 174

Hursely Church, Hampshire, tomb of Richard Cromwell, 164

Inigo Jones, designer, 151

Ireland Conference (1913), 257

Ireland, John as lord of, 49

Irish Parliament, 216

Isabella of Angoulême, 2nd Queen of King John, 50, 53

Isabella of France, Queen of Edward II, lover of Roger Mortimer, 66, 67, 68, 71, 72, 73

Isabella of Gloucester, 1st Queen of King John, 50, 53

Isabella of Valois, 2nd Queen of Richard II, 80

Jacobites, 11

Jaffa, 46, 47

James I King of England, VI of Scotland, 140, 146, 147, 148,149, 150, 151, 158, 273

James II, Duke of York, later King of England, 15, 144, 170, 172, 173, 176, 177, 178, 179, 180, 181, 182, 184

Jerusalem, 47, 48

Jerusalem Room, Westminster Abbey, 87

Jane Seymour , 3rd Queen of Henry VIII, 123, 127, 129, 133, 155

Jane Shore, 104

Jersey, Island of, 167

Jews, expulsion by Edward I, 63

Joan d' Arc, 95
Joan of Navarre, 2nd Queen of Henry IV, 88
Joan, 'the Fair Maid of Kent', mother of Richard II, 78
Joanna, Queen of Sicily, daughter of Henry II, 44, 46
John, King of England, 45, 49, 50,51, 52, 53, 54, 121
John, King of France, 75
Jonson, Ben, 156, 157
Jordan, Mrs, mistress of William IV, 217, 231, 232
Jumièrges, Robert, Archbishop of Canterbury, 22
Jutland, Battle of (1916), 267
Kenilworth, castle, 68
Kensington Palace, 189
Kent, Earl of, 70
Keppel, Alice Frederica, mistress of Edward VII, 247, 249
Kew Palace and Gardens, 212, 221, 229
Keyser, Sister Agnes, mistress of Edward VII, 247, 249
Kidderminster, 168
King's Langley, Hertfordshire, burial of Richard II, 81, 82
King's Library, British Museum, 212
Kipling, Rudyard, 258
Lampreys, death of Henry I, 33
Lancaster, John, third son of Henry IV, Duke of Bedford, 95
Lanfranc, Abbot of Caen, later Archbishop of Canterbury, 26, 27
Ledger stone, 12
Leicester, 115
Leineschloss Church, Hanover, 203
Lennox, Lady Sarah, 212
Leopold of Austria, at siege of Acre, 46
Leopold of Saxe-Coburg, husband of Princess Charlotte, uncle to Queen Victoria, later King of Belgium, 224 , 238
Levellers, the, 159
Lewes, battle of (1264), 56, 57
Liberal Party, 250, 256
Lloyd George, David, Chancellor of the Exchequer, 250
Lollards, 88
Lords Appellant, 79
Lord Chamberlain, 243
Long Parliament, 12
Louis VI of France, 32 , 33
Louis VII, of France, 40, 45
Louis VIII of France, 52
Louis IX of France, 55, 56, 60, 61
Louis XI of France, 102, 104, 105
Louis XII of France, 122
Louis XIV of France, 167, 171, 180, 183, 184, 185, 188, 192, 199
Lusignans, family, 46, 56, 60
Lusignan, Hugh (the elder), 50
Lusignan, Hugh (the younger), 2nd husband of Isabella of Angoulême, 55
Llywelyn Ap Grufford, Prince of Wales, 56, 62

Lord Protector, creation of, 161
Ludlow, castle, 108, 120
Lyons-la-Floret, castle of, death of Henry I, 34
Lynn, Town of, 52
Macdonald, Ramsey, Prime Minister, 258
Madresfield Court, Worcestershire, 268
Magna Carta (1215), 51
Magnus I, King of Norway, 13
Main, County of, 21
Major Generals, the, 161, 162
Malaria, 162
Maltravers, John, 68
Mante, town of, 24
Manchester, Edward Montague, 2nd Earl of, 158
Margaret, Duchess of Burgundy, sister of Edward IV, 102
Margaret of Anjou, Queen of Henry VI, 97, 98, 103
Margaret de Briouze, 52
Margaret of France, 2nd Queen of Edward I, 65
Margaret Tudor, sister of Henry VIII, wife of James IV of Scotland, 117, 142, 273
Marlborough House, 247
Marston Moor, battle, 159, 167
Mary II, Queen of England wife of William III, 180, 182, 183, 184, 185, 186, 187, 188
Mary of Modena, 2nd Queen of James II, 177, 178, 191, 192
Mary of Guise, mother of Mary Queen of Scots
Mary Queen of Scots, 129, 140, 142 143, 144, 145, 146, 191, 273
Mary, I Queen of England, 15, 132, 133, 134, 135, 136, 137, 138
Mary of Teck, Queen to George V, 253, 255, 259, 261
Mary Tudor, younger sister of Henry VIII, 122
Masham, Abigail, lady, 195
Matilda of Boulogne, Queen of King Stephen, 37
Matilda Fitzempress, daughter of King Henry I, briefly Queen of England, mother of Henry II, 33, 36, 37, 38, 39, 40
Matilda, Queen of Henry I, 31
Matilda of Flanders, Queen of William the Conqueror, 21, 23
Meaux, town in northern France, 91
Melbourne, William Lamb, 2nd Viscount, prime minister, 234, 238
Melusine, daughter of the devil, 49
Melusine, von der Schulenburg, later duchess of Kendal, mistress of George I, 198, 199, 203
Middleham, castle, 102, 104, 108, 112
Milford haven, 116
Monck, General George, 169
Monastery of the Grey Friars in Leicester, once the site of Richard III's tomb, 115
Monmouth, castle, 89
Monmouth, 1st Duke, of, James Scott, illegitimate son of Charles II, 171, 172, 178, 184
Mont San Michel, 30
Morcar, Earl of Northumbria, 17
Mordaunt Affair (1871), 247
More, Thomas, 123